KU-238-332

gorgeous garden boosters

Published by The Reader's Digest Association, Inc.
London • New York • Sydney • Montreal

Contents

Give your garden a superboost

Gorgeous Garden Boosters has been specially created to help you transform your garden, whatever its size, into a stunning showcase. On every page, you'll find 'boosters' that are guaranteed to enhance your garden – tried-and-tested tips, time-saving new tools and products, handy hints and expert know-how that will ensure your plants perform at their peak and help you bring out the true potential of your plot. Clever design ideas, perfect planting solutions and failsafe practical techniques have all been brought together in five chapters filled with inspirational, 'do-it-now' ideas that will prompt you to get out into the garden.

The Top 20 Superboosters

The top 20 'superboosters' featured on the following pages are surefire ways to help your plants grow bigger and better, reduce your gardening workload, and ensure that your plot fulfils your gardening dreams. But they're just a taste of what you'll find as you delve further into this book. In the first chapter, *Making the Most of your Garden*, you'll discover the secrets of professional design translated into helpful, workable advice that you can apply to every area of your garden. *Blooming Beds and Borders* is packed with expertise to help you put together plantings that will delight all year round, while *Fabulous Trees, Shrubs and Lawns* will ensure that you create a beautiful setting for your flowering displays. From asparagus to winter squash, *Prize-winning Produce* gives you the top tips you need to grow the freshest, most flavourful crops, while *Green-fingered Techniques* gives tools, equipment and all the gardening basics the 'booster' treatment with the very best, up-to-date advice.

1 PLANT PERENNIALS IN DRIFTS FOR MAXIMUM IMPACT

Make a bigger splash with gorgeous flowering perennials [see pp.106–15] by planting them in groups of three, five or even seven. It's much easier to make a natural-looking grouping by arranging odd, rather than even, numbers of plants. Follow the recommended planting distances and the plants will soon grow together to create a mass of colour, as in the stunning perennial border shown here.

2 USE ENRICHED COMPOSTS FOR PERFECT PATIO POTS

Take some of the work out of looking after container plants [see pp.135–7] by choosing a premium potting compost that includes plant foods that will last for months, and water-retaining granules to keep the compost moister for longer. It's the easy-care way to achieve the best-ever displays.

3 TURN TROUBLESOME WEEDS INTO NUTRITIOUS PLANT TONICS

Nuisance weeds such as nettles can be made to give something back to the garden – try using them to make infusions or 'teas' that boost the performance of your garden plants [see p.235]. All sorts of troublesome weeds that can't be composted can go into these brews – some gardeners swear by a dilute horsetail tonic to build up their plants' defences against pests and diseases.

4 TAKE THE WORK OUT OF WATERING

Drought-busting irrigation systems [see p.245] make watering no longer a chore, especially when you have lots of containers to care for. Link patio plants with a hose-and-spur system, add an automatic timer to your tap, and you can relax knowing that your plants will thrive.

5 LOOK AT NEW TOOLS THAT MAKE GARDENING EASIER

A long-handled weeding fork could be a new addition to your garden toolkit that your knees and back will thank you for. It's well worth taking a look at other new tool designs that are available [see p.228]. Many have been created with the aim of making garden tasks easier, reducing strain on joints and making handles more comfortable to grip, helping you to garden in comfort for longer.

6 CHOOSE A MOWER THAT MAKES YOUR GRASS GREENER

New 'mulching mowers' [see p.229] chop grass clippings very finely, scatter them over the lawn and then push them into the turf. Invisibly, the clippings decompose to nourish and improve the lawn; they also help retain moisture in the soil, and reduce scorch in hot sun. The result is a fuller, healthier, greener lawn, with no more trips to the bottom of the garden with the grass box. The whirling clippings buffer sound, too, making these machines much quieter than conventional mowers.

7 PLANT NEW VARIETIES THAT FLOWER ALL SUMMER

Look again at some old garden favourites – breeders have produced new varieties that flower for longer [see p.94]. They include heavenly small-flowered lilacs, billowing hydrangeas, voluptuous 'super poppies' (above, 'Medallion'), and the versatile, trouble-free Flower Carpet roses, covered in blooms all summer long.

8 GIVE YOUR PLANTS A LIFT WITH STURDY SUPPORTS

Cane, hoop and ring supports can transform your borders, lifting floppy stems and preventing plants drooping over paths [see p.113]. The secret of using plant supports is to get them in early, before the plant puts on much growth. As the plant grows, its stems and leaves will disguise the support, giving your plantings an effortlessly well-groomed look.

9 WAGE WAR ON APHIDS WITH AN ARMY OF LADYBIRDS

These attractive insects are one of the gardener's best friends – both the juveniles and the adults will devour quantities of greenfly and blackfly as they patrol your garden plants [see p.272]. You can buy a legion of ladybirds by mail from many specialist suppliers, ready to be released into your garden and to get to work.

10 INVEST IN GOOD-QUALITY CUTTING TOOLS

A long-lasting, well-made pair of secateurs makes such a difference to all your everyday pruning tasks [see p.251]. Keep them clean and well-sharpened, and you'll find it easy to deadhead in an instant and make neat, clean pruning cuts that minimise the risk of damage and disease to your shrubs. Add a good pair of loppers or a pruning saw to deal with bigger jobs, and you won't be tempted to blunt or break your secateurs on over-thick stems.

11 HELP TREES AND SHRUBS GROW BETTER WITH MAGICAL MYCORRHIZAE

These beneficial soil-dwelling fungi have a special relationship with plant roots, helping them to take up water and nutrients to enable them to grow better. Products containing these tiny organisms are available to add to the soil when you plant your trees and shrubs [see p.242] and should help them to establish faster and more strongly.

12
POT BULBS UP IN LAYERS FOR A DISPLAY THAT LASTS LONGER

Bulbs are the most self-sufficient of our garden plants, and this means that you can pack them into pots for spring and summer displays. Try layering a selection of bulbs with different planting depths and staggered flowering times in a container [see p.125], and you'll have a continuous, long-lasting spring show.

13
BANISH WEEDS WITH A SMART-LOOKING MULCH

Lock moisture into your soil and smother out weeds by giving your beds, and even your containers, a thick layer of mulch [see p.247]. Use hearty garden compost or smart chipped bark for lusher plantings or, for a Mediterranean or desert look, use gravel and stone – they'll soak up the heat by day and release it at night to keep warm-climate plants cosy.

14
GROW VEGETABLES THE EASY WAY

A raised bed kit takes no time to assemble, and makes a great-looking, neat and productive home for your vegetable plants. And if you dig over the soil just once before you begin, you'll never need to dig it again [see p.239]. Just add a thick layer of garden compost or well-rotted manure whenever the soil is bare, and the worms will take it down into the soil for you.

15

DEADHEAD TO KEEP THE FLOWERS COMING

One of the secrets of spectacular flowering displays of summer bedding [see p.128] is to pick or snip off dead flowerheads regularly. This prevents the plants from setting seed, encouraging them instead to produce flush after flush of beautiful blooms. You can deadhead hardy annuals and even some perennials too, guaranteeing a long season of flowering colour from your garden plants.

16

TRY VERTICAL GARDENING FOR A NEW ANGLE ON PLANTS

Maximise your growing space with pocket wall planters: either fill them with colourful flowering plants to brighten vertical surfaces, or grow salads and leafy herbs such as parsley away from mud-splash and ground pests [see p.182]. You could add some edible flowers, such as nasturtiums or violas, to pep up both your salads and your display.

17

CONSERVE RESOURCES WITH A WATER BUTT

Water is a precious commodity as far as the environment is concerned – and let's not forget that it costs money, too. A water butt fed from guttering on your house, shed or greenhouse will catch gallons of rainwater that would otherwise run down the drain, enabling you to use it to water your plants [see p.245]. There's no doubt that plants prefer rainwater to tap water – so you'll be doing them a favour as well as making savings.

18

MAKE LIGHT WORK OF GARDEN LIGHTING

Inexpensive, convenient solar-powered lighting [see pp.68–9] can transform the way you see your garden after dark. The first solar-powered lights on the market may not have impressed – but technology has developed in leaps and bounds. Now these versatile little lamps are just the job for highlighting paths and steps in the garden, or casting a soft glow onto attractive plants or water features – perfect for introducing a touch of magic to the garden once dusk falls.

19

THWART PESTS WITHOUT USING CHEMICALS

Garden netting is the traditional and foolproof way to prevent birds and other pests feasting on your home-grown produce [see p.274]. Check out the gardening catalogues and you'll see clever new ways to protect your crops with netting, including 'pop-up' netting tents and no-fuss covers especially designed to protect raised vegetable beds.

20

GIVE BED AND BORDER PLANTINGS STATURE

Add height to your borders by growing climbers such as captivating clematis up obelisks and tripods [see p.167]. These structures are attractive features in their own right, but when clad with a beautiful climber in full flower, they'll give real drama to your plantings.

1

MAKING THE MOST OF YOUR GARDEN

The most successful gardens are those that reflect their owners' tastes and lifestyle. Whether you're seeking inspiration for a new garden, or planning improvements to your existing plot, expert tips based on the principles of good design will help you achieve results that will give you lasting pleasure.

Making a garden that suits your needs

HOW DO YOU CREATE A GARDEN that is perfect for you and packed with flourishing plants? Whether you are designing an entirely new outdoor space, or thinking of improving your existing plot, it pays to spend some time organising your ideas.

Getting to grips with design decisions

Be your own designer Everyone wants different things from their garden. The first step in designing, remodelling or improving your outdoor space is to ask yourself the three key questions that any professional garden designer would ask when starting work with a new client. Spend time assessing your requirements in order to work out your design brief, or 'wish list', that will set you off in the right direction – towards a garden that meets your practical needs and solves problems, as well as being a pleasant place in which to spend time.

Who is the garden for? Think of everyone who uses the garden: family, visitors, pets and garden wildlife – and of course yourself. What could you do to make the garden as good as it can be for each of them? The answers could inspire

▼ **This mature, immaculate garden** is perfect for someone who enjoys adding the finishing touches that perfect a display. The topiary and lawn are neat and lush, and hardly a faded flowerhead or flopping stem spoils the look of the border perennials. Views beyond the garden are masked by trees, focusing all attention on the garden itself.

all sorts of garden features, both useful and enjoyable: a treehouse or a wildlife pond, perhaps; a small greenhouse to potter in when the weather is bad, or easily accessible paths and raised beds for a family member with limited mobility. Or maybe it's a secluded, sunny seat in just the right place to unwind with a cup of tea when you get home from work. Think ahead, too: garden features can evolve over the years to serve different purposes: a sandpit, for example, could become a pond when children are older, or a lawned area could become a kitchen garden when you have more time to look after it.

What is the garden to be used for? List as many things as you can think of that you might use the garden for. Include not only fun things like barbecues or trampolines, but also practical elements like drying washing and storing bicycles or a mower. And don't forget about the gardening! Consider how much time and enthusiasm you can dedicate to working in the garden, and choose features and planting styles accordingly. It's essential to create a garden that you can keep up with, otherwise it will become a place in which you'll find it hard to relax.

What's your style? Planning a garden, as when you decorate or furnish a room, will be more successful if it results in a satisfying, coherent space. Taking your cue broadly from the style and proportions of your house will still leave you with plenty of scope for your own tastes and preferences: formal or informal, for instance; enclosed or open, romantic or practical. Have an overall style or theme in mind from the start, and you'll be more likely to produce a garden that you will find attractive and feel comfortable in. If inspiration is elusive, look for ideas that appeal in garden books and magazines and on websites; collect clippings in a folder, or pin them onto a corkboard, perhaps by a window overlooking the garden.

▼ **A garden that will (almost) look after itself** suits a busy household. Paving allows plenty of room for relaxation without the work of maintaining a lawn, and the drought-loving plants thrive with minimal care. A bright-painted wall adds colour, and cascading water contributes movement amid the spiky, architectural plant forms.

▲ **Changes of level** can inspire an exciting garden, especially if steps lead to a new area that cannot be glimpsed from below. This is a striking design, but not an expensive one: sleepers retaining gravel treads are a simple solution for a slope.

Understanding your garden better

Identify what you are working with Once you have worked out broad aims for any new design, the next stage is to assess your existing garden. Even if you are making a new garden from scratch, you won't be working with a blank canvas. You'll need to take your cues from the size and shape of your garden, its aspect and slope, the nature of its surroundings, local climatic conditions and lastly the nature of the soil. Take a camera, notebook and pencil and set about becoming thoroughly acquainted with your site, and start thinking about how you could make the most of positive features and minimize the impact of problem ones. No special skills are needed: just a sharp pair of eyes.

Measure up for size and shape Good design can bring out the best in a garden of any size, but the layout must sit comfortably within its boundaries, without feeling cramped or wasting space. Measure your plot roughly at the start to give you a realistic idea of what you may be able to fit in. Understanding the shape of the plot will also help you to make the most of the space. A long, narrow garden, for example, can easily feel like a corridor, while 'dead space' can be a particular problem with triangular or L-shaped plots. There are all kinds of ways to manipulate space for visual effects in both small and large gardens [see pp.28–39] once you have a good grasp of the shape of the plot.

Work out your garden's aspect The orientation of your garden – the direction it faces – determines its pattern of sun and shade. Map this out (see below) and use this information to guide plant choices and the location of features such as patios, ponds, trees (considering where their shade will fall) or vegetable beds.

Assess slopes and levels A grasp of the contours of your plot will help you to position any steps, terracing and other changes of level for the best effect with the minimum of disruption. Just as with the shape of the plot, slopes can be

HOW DOES IT WORK?
CHANGING SHADE PATTERNS

The parts of your garden that are shaded will change both during the day and throughout the year: the high sun of summer (upper orbit on the diagrams, right) casts less shade than the low sun of winter (lower orbit, right). The smaller or the more enclosed your garden is, the more likely it will be to have corners that are in permanent shade.

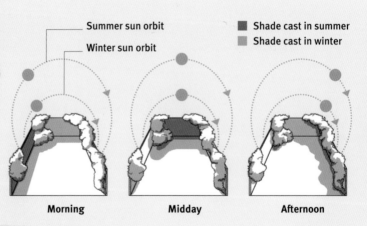

Summer sun orbit
Winter sun orbit
■ Shade cast in summer
■ Shade cast in winter

Morning   **Midday**   **Afternoon**

visually manipulated to reduce or enhance their effect. A dead-flat garden can be made much more interesting by introducing one or two simple changes of level, such as a raised bed or a sunken lawn, or even by using a pergola, an arch or a tree to emphasize the vertical dimension.

Consider your surroundings A garden's setting may be urban or rural; open to wide skies, or enclosed by buildings or trees. The plot will belong to a built landscape – even if that consists only of your own house. The garden is likely to be more successful if its mood, as well as its proportions, materials and plants, give it a connection with its setting. Take photographs to remind you not only of features beyond the boundaries that you'd like to keep in sight, but also of those you'd rather not see. For a professional touch, photograph any architectural detailing that you may be able to echo in hard landscaping.

Assess the climate Maybe you live by the coast with its salt-laden winds; perhaps your house is in a shady, chilly valley, or in an area of low rainfall. Such factors influence what will grow well, and perhaps the way you will want to use the garden. Within the garden itself, there may be trouble spots: the base of a wall may be permanently dry, or a poorly drained area may be permanently damp; one corner may be exposed to strong winds. A sloping garden may have a 'frost hollow' at its lowest point, where cold air sinks and collects. Observing and recording these conditions will help you find solutions with both layout and planting.

Get to know your soil Discover what type of soil you have, and whether it is acid, alkaline or neutral [see p.233], then choose plants to suit it (see overleaf). It's much easier to do this rather than striving to achieve the perfect soil for every plant. Notice whether your soil tends to be damp or dry. Does it drain freely after rain? Is it slow to warm up in spring? And however bad your soil is, there's no need to despair. Improving poor soil even just a little [see pp.234–5] is hugely rewarding because it will increase the range of plants you can grow.

▼ **Dream plantings of billowing rhododendrons** and bright azaleas are only possible on acid soil. Hydrangeas and hardy fuchsias can give a similar effect on alkaline soils, albeit later in the year.

PLANTING TO SUIT THE SOIL

Gardeners often complain about their soil, but remember that in the wild there are few places where nothing will grow: it's just a question of plants and soil being compatible. A quick way to assess what will grow is to look at what is doing well in neighbouring gardens – and in the local landscape, too. Joining a gardening club can also be a good introduction to local conditions.

PLANTS FOR LIGHT, SANDY SOILS

Sandy soil won't retain moisture and has a low nutritional value, so it doesn't please heavy feeders such as roses. The good news is that the plants that grow well in it are naturally drought-tolerant, and ideal for our drier summers.

- Alliums
- Broom *(Cytisus)*
- Centranthus
- *Convolvulus cneorum*
- Eryngiums
- *Euphorbia characias*
- Gypsophila
- Hibiscus
- *Iris unguicularis*
- Lavatera
- Lupins
- Potentillas
- Rock roses *(Cistus)*
- Sempervivums
- Verbascums

PLANTS FOR HEAVY CLAY SOILS

A regular mulch with organic matter [see p.247] will make sticky clay soil so much easier to work, while also retaining its high quota of nutrients. Roses will thrive in it, as will some of the most free-flowering shrubs and perennials.

- Ajuga
- Asters
- Astilbes
- Chaenomeles
- *Cornus alba*
- Forsythia
- Ligularia
- Monardas
- Pulmonarias
- *Salix babylonica* 'Tortuosa'
- Sanguisorba
- Roses
- Weigelas
- Viburnums

PLANTS FOR ACID SOILS

Rhododendrons and heathers growing in neighbouring gardens are sure signs that your soil is acid, and will be loved by woodland plants brought up on soil enriched with fallen leaves that has good water-retaining properties.

- Azaleas and rhododendrons
- Camellias
- Crinodendrons
- Eucryphia
- Fothergilla
- Hamamelis
- Heathers *(Calluna, Daboecia, Erica)*
- *Iris laevigata*
- Japanese maples
- Liquidambar
- Liriope
- Pieris
- Trilliums

PLANTS FOR ALKALINE SOILS

Alkaline soils are also usually dry, light and stony. These soils are perfect for creating beautiful wildflower meadows and Mediterranean *maquis*-style plantings, but there are plenty of traditional border plants that will thrive, too.

- Astrantias
- Buddleia
- Bearded iris
- Campanulas
- Clematis
- Dianthus
- Laburnum
- Lilacs *(Syringa)*
- *Lilium candidum*
- Philadelphus
- Pulmonaria
- Prunus
- Sambucus
- Sedums
- *Verbena bonariensis*

Making changes to your garden

Use a plan as your starting point An outline sketch plan of your existing garden (see below) is such a valuable tool when planning any changes. You will need to take accurate measurements, and then either transfer them on to graph paper, or use one of the software programs designed for garden planning that are available for a home computer. Rectangular plots are easy to measure and depict; irregular shapes can be trickier, but you may have access to house deeds or planning documents that include a site outline. With bigger gardens, large-scale maps or satellite imaging can be an easy way to see the plot in plan view. Photographs taken from upstairs windows are great aids to obtaining a bird's-eye view. If you have made your plan on paper, it's a good idea to make several photocopies of your outline at this stage to give you plenty of scope for experimenting with different layouts.

EXPERT KNOW HOW

MAKING A PLAN OF YOUR EXISTING GARDEN

Draw an outline plan of your garden at the largest possible scale and try to make it as accurate as you can. You will need to establish a suitable scale, using the squares on the graph paper, before you begin.

● Highlight all the permanent features: house, boundaries, mature trees and any features that you want to keep undisturbed, such as paths, sheds and other structures.

● Indicate all access points: doors from the house, garage or shed, and gates from the road or front garden. Planning paths and other routes around the garden will depend on these.

● If you know, or even suspect, that there are underground pipes and cables, do a bit of research and mark their position on your plan. Inspection covers and wires or pipework running into the house wall are good clues as to the whereabouts of drain runs, cables and gas pipes.

● Mark on your plan where there are good views out of the garden and where screening is needed, either for privacy, or to blot out an ugly building or a dominant phone mast or pylon, for instance.

● Note changes of level to help you choose locations for steps and terracing that will minimise earth-moving operations.

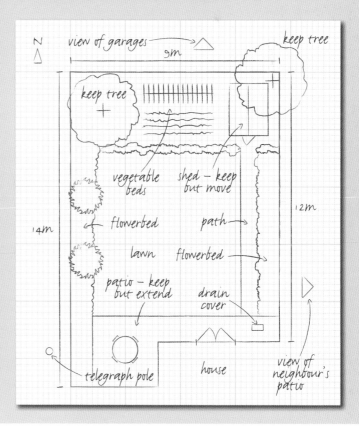

► **This mature apple tree** has earned its place in a new design. It's worth seeking an expert opinion on older fruit trees that are no longer cropping well, to ensure that they will give lasting pleasure.

Spread the cost of a redesign
Few of us start to make a garden from a completely blank canvas, or decide to completely make over an entire garden in one go. Having at least a rough idea of a realistic budget before you start will help prevent the cost of a project running away with you. You may want to take the revamp in stages to spread the work and the cost over a longer period. If so, then make any changes to boundaries and levels your first priority, then lay any new hard surfacing. No matter how much you may love plants, it's likely to prove wasteful and disheartening to start buying and planting until you are happy with the 'bones' of your garden.

● **WORK WITH VALUABLE EXISTING FEATURES** Even if you have inherited someone else's garden, there are likely to be features that are worth keeping – a good-sized shed, for example, or an area of attractive paving. Mark these on your plan, together with other features that will be too impractical or costly to relocate, such as inspection covers and outdoor taps and utility meters.

● **SAVE MONEY BY RECYCLING MATERIALS** Hard landscaping materials are expensive, so don't throw away unwanted paving, bricks, timber or even gravel that you could reuse, even if only in a utility area.

● **RETAIN PLANTS TO GIVE MATURITY TO YOUR NEW GARDEN** If you can work round at least some existing mature trees and shrubs it will not only save you work and money but will also give your new layout an established look. Many overgrown shrubs can be renovated [see p.151], and perennials that are growing well can often be divided and moved or potted up until they can become part of a new planting.

● **GET AHEAD WITH NEW PLANTINGS** One way in which you may be able to gain time with new planting schemes while landscaping work is being carried out is to buy a few favourite shrubs as small container-grown plants, and re-pot them into larger containers. Keep them well fed and watered and you will have bigger, healthy specimens to plant out when the time comes, at a fraction of the cost of buying large specimens from a garden centre.

▼ **Reusing existing materials** can cut down costs: bricks taken from an unwanted raised bed could become a rustic path, for example. Alternatively, salvage yards may be interested in purchasing good-quality garden materials.

Begin to plot your new design
Once you have your existing layout sketched out, including all of the elements you want or need to keep, begin trying out ideas that will help you realise your new 'wish list'. Use copies of your outline plan to sketch out alternative ideas and schemes until you find an arrangement that looks workable, with the features you want and the practical elements you need [see pp.26–7] all fitting in without crowding.

● **ALLOW SPACE FOR YOUR DESIGN TO 'BREATHE'** Beware of cramming in so many ideas that your space becomes cluttered and hard to relax in. An often-quoted rule of thumb in garden design is to aim for two-thirds open space to one-third planting. This shouldn't be applied too strictly because it will vary according to personal taste, but it's important to have a good level of balance and distinct contrasts between these two key elements of the garden landscape.

LET BEAUTIFUL MATURE
FEATURES IN AN EXISTING
GARDEN INSPIRE NEW,
CREATIVE DESIGNS

● **GENERATE MORE VISUAL INTEREST BY DIVIDING THE SPACE** Larger gardens [see pp.34–9] can be made more manageable by creating a series of 'garden rooms', each with a purpose or theme, but even a small garden will seem more interesting if it can't all be seen at once. This can also, surprising as it may seem, make a small space seem larger [see also pp.28–33]. Use planting, screening or hedges to create the impression of separate areas.

GATES, WALKWAYS AND TUNNELS WILL HEIGHTEN EXPECTATIONS OF WHAT LIES BEYOND

● **ENSURE PATHS CREATE A SENSE OF FLOW** Paths around the garden need to be carefully planned [see pp.46–9]. A path that leads around a garden must be practical (or people will take shortcuts) but it should also tell a story, with changes of pace, diversions and perhaps a sense of mystery. Try to avoid cul-de-sacs, and even in a small plot the ideal layout should make it possible to leave the house by one route and return by another.

● **USE STANDARD-SIZED MATERIALS FOR LESS WORK** When planning hard landscaping features, such as paths and steps, bear in mind the dimensions of materials you might use and tailor your plans accordingly. A path will be much easier to lay if you can use whole slabs without cutting, and steps will be more straightforward to build if the depth of the tread corresponds to the width of whole flagstones. If using trellis, find out what size panels are available before you finalize the length of the run, so that you can use whole panels without needing to cut them.

▼ **A series of focal points** give a purposeful feel to paths around the garden. Here, even as the terracotta urn is being admired, a new destination can be glimpsed beyond it – a bench well placed for enjoying an attractive view.

Make your garden work in every dimension
Working from your outline sketch will help you to fill in the basic 'floor plan' of your garden, but unless you have the knack of thinking in three dimensions, you will need to step out into the garden to consider viewpoints, perspective, and changes in height – all crucial aspects that transform a flat plot into a satisfying garden landscape.

● **PLAN FOR STRUCTURES AND PLANTS THAT ADD HEIGHT** Tall features, whether plants or structures, make all the difference – especially in a flat garden. Consider allocating positions to trees, arches and arbours (or, in a large garden, a pergola); obelisks or poles with climbing plants, or shrubs with a narrow, upright shape.

● **USE ENTICING VIEWS TO MAKE THE GARDEN INVITING** Sometimes garden dividers need to be solid – to screen off a utility area, for example. Elsewhere, more open dividers such as airy plantings and open trelliswork can encourage exploration of the garden by offering glimpses of the garden beyond. A pretty archway with a seat or water feature visible beyond it or a sunny area that can be glimpsed from a patch of cool shade provide enticements to move from one area of the garden to another.

● **ADD FOCAL POINTS FOR IMPACT** Striking features that serve as focal points don't need to be purpose-made showpieces such as sculpture; items that have a practical use, such as an attractive seat or a collection of herb pots, can be just as striking and useful, too. A beautifully shaped specimen tree or shrub also makes an eye-catching feature.

● **ALLOW PLENTY OF SPACE FOR WELL-STOCKED BORDERS** Make your beds and borders as generous as you can [see also pp.72–3] to allow space for well-structured planting plans with plenty of variety in height and bold groupings of plants.

Use props to help finalise the design

You can employ all sorts of items to help you visualise how your new design will look on the ground and get shapes, sizes and positions just right. Use pegs and string, or lengths of rope or hosepipe, to define the edges of paths, beds and borders. Dry sand poured from a bottle, or special spray paint manufactured for use on sports turf, also make good, temporary markers. Stick tall canes or bulky prunings in the ground to help you determine the right position for trees and other features; use a beach windbreak to stand in for a garden divider, or move garden furniture to the site of a new patio to see how it would look. Wheelie bins, stepladders and even obliging family members can all be pressed into service to help you to achieve a clearer idea of how your final design will look.

BUILDING A NEW GARDEN PLAN

Because it highlights only those features that you have to or wish to keep, your original plan of the garden [see p.21] can serve as the basis for your new design. Use it in conjunction with your sun-and-shade map [see p.18] so that you can allocate the best positions to your new garden features. Make or print several copies so that you can experiment with different arrangements before settling on a new design.

▶ **In the old garden layout** (right) vegetable beds enjoyed the sun while the patio area was shaded. The redesign (below) sites a new dining area in the sunniest corner, cooled by the formal pool and by dappled shade cast by a planted pergola. A sweeping path makes the garden appear wider. New trees block out unwanted views, while the former patio now houses the relocated shed, with extended paving providing more curves and useful hard standing.

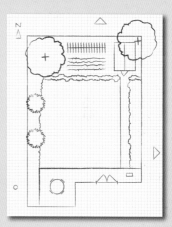

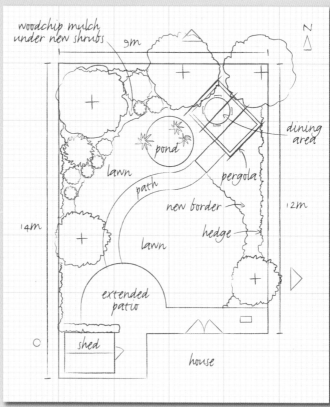

Finding space for the practicalities

Work out what storage you need Most gardens have to incorporate practical features as well as beautiful ones. Storage usually has to be thought of – typically a shed for tools, machinery and materials, garden furniture in winter, and perhaps outdoor toys and bicycles. Composting is on the increase so you need somewhere to put that, and it's important to consider watering and water management: hosepipes, water butts and watering cans.

● **PLAN FOR THE FUTURE WITH AMPLE STORAGE SPACE** If you have the space, buy a shed a size bigger than you think you need. One large shed looks tidier than two or three smaller ones and is easier to organise.

Find the perfect positions It's tempting to site utility features away from the house, but this can be counterproductive. The bottom of the garden, for example, is not necessarily the best place for a shed. It can be inconveniently far from the back door, and unless it's carefully disguised it will tend to draw the eye and be an unwanted focal point. A position to the side of the house may be better, especially if an outdoor tap is then close at hand, making it easier to wash dirt off tools before putting them away and to scrub down used pots and canes for storage.

▼ **A green roof** helps garden buildings blend into their surroundings. The idea is that the plants absorb rainfall, preventing the kind of sudden runoff that can cause flooding in heavy rain, making this a useful as well as an attractive solution.

● **PICK OUT THE BEST SITE FOR GREENHOUSE PLANTS** A greenhouse in a position that gets the morning sun but is shaded by late afternoon is ideal for the plants within: the greenhouse will warm up early in the day, but not bake in the hot afternoon sun. A deciduous tree planted a short distance away on the sunny side will give protection from the hottest summer sun but will let in much-needed light in winter when their branches are bare.

● **FIND THE BEST SPOT FOR COMPOST** You will probably want to hide your compost bin or heap, but avoid a position in deep shade. Good compost needs heat, so locate your compost where it will get sun for at least part of the day to start the process off.

● **MAKE WATERING LESS OF A CHORE** A water butt in a convenient place – near the vegetable patch, for example – can save endless trips with a heavy watering can. You may need to rig up a system of pipework to get rainwater into the butt: a special diverter fitted to a downpipe is the simplest solution.

Leave yourself room to work in Allow for a functional work area outside your shed for 'resting' containers after flowering, potting and cleaning and you will keep mess and clutter well contained. Extending the concrete base for a shed will create a hard surface that can be cleaned thoroughly and easily when required.

● **ALLOW SPACE FOR ACCESS AROUND A GREENHOUSE** on all sides for glass-cleaning and maintenance. Surfaced paths around the greenhouse will help keep your feet dry in winter.

● **RAISE A WATER BUTT ON A STAND** or on bricks or blocks so that you can get a watering can under its tap.

Make utilities less obtrusive Unless you invest in an attractive bespoke shed or a decorative compost bin, the best way to treat practical features is usually to make them as unobtrusive as possible, either by screening (see below) or by blending them in with their surroundings.

● **USE DARK COLOURS TO STAGE A DISAPPEARING ACT** Black mops up light rather than reflecting it, and this gives it almost magical powers as regards making things unobtrusive. Black plastic compost bins are unobtrusive and work well as long as the compost does not dry out, and practical plastic water butts are available in black or in a deep green, too. Painting a weatherboarded timber shed black, or a more subtle charcoal grey, creates a very flattering backdrop to plants.

● **CONSIDER A GREEN ROOF** A roof covering of resilient plants such as sedums and sempervivums works well on garden buildings with flat or gently sloping roofs, though the structure must be strong enough to support the weight of the shallow layer of free-draining growing medium in which the plants take root. There are many landscaping and supply firms and lots of helpful websites that can provide advice on installing and maintaining these attractive and useful features.

▲ **An alternative to screening** garden utilities, such as water butts and compost bins, is to invest in designs that are attractive features in their own right. Beehive compost bins or a traditional banded water barrel can be complemented with colourful planting.

STAR PERFORMERS...

SCREENING SOLUTIONS

Annual or perennial plants can be used to screen an eyesore for the summer months, or for year-round cover, choose a solid structure or evergreen plants.

◄ **A length of trellis fixed between two posts, covered with climbing plants**

● **A rectangular bed of bamboos or tall grasses**

● **Tall plants such as hollyhocks or sunflowers**

● **In a larger garden, a living willow wall [see p.39]**

● **A short length of hedging**

● **Container plants ranged against a willow hurdle or a screen of rush matting**

Great ideas for small gardens

AN EASILY MANAGED SMALL GARDEN suits busy people – but it's hard to relax in a space that feels cramped. There are plenty of ways to make a small garden appear more spacious and interesting while retaining all the advantages of a compact plot.

▶ **A change in level** adds interest to a small plot. The horizontal lines of the steps make the space appear wider, and the pair of charcoal-grey pots anchor the view within the garden, reducing the impact of neighbouring buildings.

▼ **Louvred shutters** and doors in the walls enclosing this terrace can be adjusted either to reduce the sun's glare, or let in cooling evening breezes – perfect climate control for this pretty dining area. The pale paving brightens the space.

Making the most of your space

Create the illusion of a larger garden
The boundaries of a small garden are often only too visible, drawing unwanted attention to the limited space between them. The problem is made worse where narrow, fence-hugging borders surround a central space. Generous planting both up and in front of walls and fences will create the illusion that your garden is not so very small after all.

● **BORROW VIEWS TO BLUR THE BOUNDARIES** Clever planning and planting is the key to making boundaries seem to disappear. If you plant a shrub or two on your side of the fence, in front of a tree or larger shrub belonging to a neighbour, then that tree or shrub will become a visual part of your garden. Position a group of plants to frame a distant view, and a fence in the foreground will become less obvious.

● **USE A LIVING BOUNDARY TO ADD MORE GREENERY** A hedge forms a green barrier that will merge seamlessly with trees and shrubs growing in neighbouring gardens. While it will take time to grow and develop, it will be more attractive to look at and less costly to install and maintain than a fence.

Divide the space for extra interest
Any garden, even a small one, becomes more intriguing if it comprises two or more distinct spaces. There need be no physical barriers between one area and another; it can simply be a question of giving each area a theme or a purpose. A secluded arbour, a tiny vegetable or herb garden with raised beds, or just a simple change of level can make one area feel separate from another, each contributing to make a garden appear more complex and characterful.

● **MAKE A FEATURE OF ATTRACTIVE TRELLIS** Narrow trellis makes a space-saving way to divide a garden. Openwork screening, with or without climbing plants, creates separate areas but keeps the sense of a larger space, which can still be glimpsed through the gaps. Trellis panels can be bought in various heights and widths. Permutations include perpendicular or

FRAME VIEWS LOOKING BACK TOWARDS THE HOUSE, AS WELL AS AWAY FROM IT

GETTING THE MOST OUT OF A NARROW GARDEN

Many urban gardens are longer than they are wide. It's easy for such a garden to become a corridor-like space that feels hemmed-in and lacks any sense of restfulness. Introduce lateral elements that cross the garden from side to side, either horizontally or diagonally – paths, decking or screening, for example – to make the plot look wider. Position a seat facing across the garden towards a focal point or an attractive planting to make the most of the garden's width; keep borders neat and lawns well-maintained so that when you do sit down, views are relaxing rather than a reminder of work to be done. Ample storage space is also invaluable for preventing clutter.

KEY FEATURES

1 **A low retaining wall** and flight of steps set at a strong diagonal visually pushes the boundaries of the garden outwards.

2 **A raised bed** provides an opportunity for a different planting mood: a well-stocked herb garden here is convenient for the kitchen.

3 **An apple tree** obscures views from the raised patio of neighbouring garden buildings; a seat beneath the tree, tucked into this sheltered corner, enjoys views of the borders.

4 **A lawn** bordered by plants is a sensible arrangement for this family home. The curved path maximises the grassed area available for play and introduces another crosswise element.

5 **Fruit is trained** on a sturdy, horizontal post-and-wire structure to about chest height so that the area beyond can be half-seen, creating another 'garden room'.

6 **The raised beds** are used for favourite fresh vegetables such as baby carrots, new potatoes and fresh peas. Cordon tomatoes grown against the shed wall could be supplemented with cherry tomatoes grown in containers on the patio.

7 **A generously sized shed** houses not only tools but garden toys and bicycles so that the garden can be tidied up easily when necessary. Water from the shed roof is collected into a butt for the vegetable beds.

diagonal screen patterns and straight, concave or convex tops. Make sure posts are securely fixed, and exactly perpendicular. Finials fixed to the tops of the posts make a decorative finish.

● **USE PLANTS AS SEASONAL SCREENING** Well-chosen planting is an alternative to built structures as a way of making divisions between one space and another. Some upright herbaceous plants and tall grasses will create a gentle, gauzy veil that doesn't exclude light and is not permanent. *Verbena bonariensis*, with its long late-summer and autumn flowering season, is a good one to try, and for grasses go for upright varieties of molinia, or *Calamagrostis* × *acutiflora* 'Karl Foerster', which will stand well through the winter.

Make the best use of space

'Less is more' is a good maxim to bear in mind when you are designing a small garden – but where do you put all the things you want to include? An easy way both to make better use of space and to cut down on the garden equipment you need to store is to lose your lawn. Lawns can be surprisingly impractical for small spaces. Gravel or paving makes a great easy-care alternative. You'll create a more spacious area for siting garden furniture and container plants, too. There's no mowing to worry about, no mower needing storage space, and no muddy, worn patches of lawn in winter.

● **CONTROL CLUTTER TO HELP YOU RELAX** An overcrowded, muddled garden is not helpful when you need to unwind, so resist the temptation to put in too many plants and other features. Be strict about leaving a good proportion of empty space. It is necessary for good visual balance, to enable you to move around comfortably, and to set off your planting to best advantage. You can reduce container crowding on the ground by using attractive wall planters.

● **GET MORE VALUE FROM DOUBLE-DUTY PLANTS AND FEATURES** Plants that are productive as well as being beautiful, garden furniture that is both practical and attractive, a tool-storage bin that doubles as a low seat – anything that can fulfil more than one function is valuable in a small garden. Conjure up imaginative combinations that will give multiple returns: grow runner beans on cane

▲ **Make patio plantings productive** as well as decorative by growing fruits and vegetables in containers: dwarf apple, peach and even citrus trees, Mediterranean vegetables, herbs and salads will all do well in attractive pots.

DON'T WASTE YOUR WALL SPACE – TREAT ALL VERTICAL SURFACES AS VALUABLE PLANTING AREAS

wigwams or pretty willow obelisks to add height to plantings, enjoy beautiful scarlet, white or pink flowers and harvest fresh produce; or plant a small apple tree and, once it's a good size, train a summer-flowering clematis up it for maximum benefits: a handsome tree, delicate spring blossom, glorious blooms in summer and a basket of fresh fruit to pick in autumn.

Using tricks to deceive the eye

Create special effects to enhance the garden

It's well worth knowing and using some of the clever tricks you can play to manipulate space and perspective. Skilful handling of light and shade, for example, can greatly increase the sense of variety and interest in a small garden, helping it to 'tell a story' and creating a feeling of depth and mystery. A sunny area that can be seen from a shady one lends depth and offers the enticement of warmth and light, in the same way as a glade or clearing in woodland does. You can

emphasise the contrast between light and shade by using a pale plant as a focal point in the sunny place: silver or variegated foliage will reflect maximum light.

● **USE DAPPLED SHADE TO BRING THE COUNTRY INTO TOWN** Overhead foliage – for example, on a pergola or a deciduous tree – suggests woodland, with its seasonal variety. The type of shade it gives is ideal for small gardens. There will be plenty of light and sunshine in winter and spring before the leaves appear, followed by an especially pleasant kind of flickering green shade on hot summer days.

● **ADD SPARKLE WITH A WATER FEATURE** Use the light-reflecting properties of water to add cool, bright highlights. A water feature planned and sited with this in mind makes the best kind of focal point and can transform a small and shady place.

● **OPEN UP MORE SIGHTLINES WITH A MIRROR** A strategically positioned mirror can appear to add space and light to a garden and can make areas of a narrow garden look wider. Experiment with different positions to find the one that works best, and make sure the mirror's edges are concealed by framing or planting.

Make paths and views appear longer In a small garden, paths need to feel leisurely, to give the impression of a larger space. Long, straight paths suggest hurrying to a destination, especially if their components are laid lengthways. Gentle curves tend to slow progress through a small space and make it seem bigger – though you should avoid too many pointless wiggles, or everyone will take short cuts. Another way to 'slow down' a path, visually, is to include wide stripes of bricks, slabs or timber sleepers laid crosswise to the direction of travel.

● **TRY TRICKS OF PERSPECTIVE TO ADD EXTRA DEPTH** A path that narrows slightly as it runs away from you will look longer. This is easier to achieve with paths of loose materials such as gravel or chipped bark than when paving slabs are involved. Another way of exaggerating perspective to create views that appear longer than they really are is to have large plants or objects in the foreground, with smaller but similar ones farther away.

▲ **The view beyond this archway** is an optical illusion created by fixing a full-length mirror to the wall that has the effect of doubling the apparent size of this small courtyard garden.

HOW DOES IT WORK?
CREATING ILLUSIONS WITH COLOUR

Understanding how different colours influence our perception of space can be useful when planning a small garden. In normal light conditions, purples and blues appear to be more distant, so using those colours in planting on the far side of a small space will make it seem bigger. Increase the sense of depth by planting reds, oranges and yellows in the foreground. These hot colours tend to come to the fore and appear larger and closer. Perception differs in low light: blues become more prominent around dawn and dusk, while reds and oranges tend to disappear. As night falls, the shapes and textures of white flowers and silver foliage seem to step forward and become almost luminous.

Add more light to shady gardens Small gardens, especially in towns, are often hemmed in by buildings and tall boundaries that can prevent light reaching the ground, especially in winter when the sun is low. Choosing plants and other features that will bring in some light can make all the difference.

● **PAINT WALLS WHITE TO BOUNCE IN LIGHT** Introducing pale colours is a quick and easy way to dispel the gloom in a shady garden. Give rendered walls a facelift with a fresh coat of whitewash to reflect more light, and paint house doors and window frames too if they need it. Timber structures such as pergolas, gates and arches can also be transformed very quickly using easy-to-apply garden paints for unplaned wood. Here, too, white or cream will add a lightening touch.

● **INTRODUCE WARMTH WITH HARD LANDSCAPING** When choosing surfacing materials, avoid drab grey or khaki pavers or slate chippings, which can look quite depressing, especially when wet. Instead, go for a warm, pale honey-coloured stone effect for paved areas.

● **ADD BRIGHT HIGHLIGHTS WITH PLANTS** Avoid creating a mass of drab, dark foliage in a small, shady garden. Plants with white variegation in their leaves work well if used in moderation among other plants. White flowers also show up beautifully, and a white-themed planting can look cool and sophisticated in low light. Pots of white lilies (*Lilium regale* are the purest white) will add intoxicating fragrance, too. Golden foliage creates the welcome illusion of sunshine on a dull day – but avoid siting golden-leaved plants in very deep shade, because they will turn green if there isn't enough light.

▼ **A restrained colour palette** creates an uncluttered look in a small space, even if it is densely planted. Water flowing down a wall panel of polished concrete into a still pool cools the air, helping the plants to grow lushly.

PLANTS TO BRIGHTEN SMALL, SHADY SPACES

There are plenty of plants with white-variegated leaves or golden foliage, but not all will thrive without sun: these will be suited by full or part-shade.

● *Arum italicum* subsp. *italicum* 'Marmoratum'
▲ *Brunnera macrophylla* 'Jack Frost'
● *Buxus sempervirens* 'Elegantissima'
● *Euonymus fortunei* 'Silver Queen'
● *Hosta* 'Wide Brim'
● *Lamium maculatum* 'White Nancy'
● *Miscanthus sinensis* 'Morning Light'
● *Pulmonaria* 'Mary Mottram'
● *Tolmiea menziesii* 'Taff's Gold'

Getting to grips with larger gardens

A SPACIOUS GARDEN OFFERS SO MUCH SCOPE to realise gardening dreams, whether it's a bold landscaping scheme, a stunning garden feature, a themed planting area, a seasonal spectacle or even a well-stocked traditional kitchen garden. Don't be daunted by a big garden – use clever design and imaginative ideas to realise its potential.

VARY THE HEIGHT OF BOUNDARIES TO BORROW VIEWS OF THE LANDSCAPE BEYOND

Planning a large garden

Create a sense of place

The larger the garden, the more likely it is to develop and evolve in stages: large plots are more of a challenge to design and lay out all in one go. It is especially important to have a clear overall idea of what kind of place you would like the garden to be. Think about using the same features in different areas to give the whole plot a sense of unity, such as repeating landscaping materials, 'signature' plants and perhaps colours, too.

● **PHOTOGRAPH THE GARDEN TO VIEW IT AS A WHOLE** With larger plots, especially in shapes that are more complex to measure, you'll find a series of photos very useful. Photography has a knack of showing up features you may not have noticed. You can also draw on printouts of your photos to give yourself an 'artist's impression' of proposed changes to layout, planting and so on. Trying things out on paper can help to avoid expensive mistakes on the ground.

Draw inspiration from the surroundings

Small city gardens work well as self-contained oases, but a larger plot is more likely to have an out-of-town setting. Plan views out of the garden to give it a feeling of belonging to the wider landscape. Borrow trees, landmarks and wide skies beyond your garden's boundaries and make them part of your scheme.

● **TAKE CUES FROM THE HOUSE** You'll probably want to lay out the area around the house first, as this will always be the most closely scrutinized area of the garden. Make it a flattering setting for the house. Look to the proportions of the house when laying out patios, lawns and beds adjacent to it, and try to echo the style of the house in some of the materials, colours and detailing.

Show off your space

Open up at least one really long view, or vista, that makes a feature of your plot's full size. Ensure there is something to draw the eye at each end: perhaps a striking tree, a sculpture or sundial, or a piece of topiary.

● **PLAN ROUTES TO INVITE EXPLORATION** A large garden needs some sort of narrative to guide you round. Link paths of different types to give plenty of variety as you walk round the garden. Avoid dead ends that make you retrace your steps. Include features that entice you to walk on: a distant view, a collection of unusual pot plants or a glimpse of an inviting seat.

● **MAKE SAFE HAVENS FOR RELAXATION** Large open spaces can feel uncomfortable and even threatening, so avoid making seating areas that are very exposed and lack anything on a human scale around them. Trees, walls and structures, such as arbours, pergolas and gazebos, are some of the features that will help give a context to a seating area and, on a practical level, will give it shelter and perhaps shade, too.

◀ **A meadow planting** is one of those glorious, stop-you-in-your-tracks spectacles that the luxury of space makes possible. A mown path through the meadow flowers invites you to take a stroll.

▼ **Give a human scale** to seating areas in a spacious garden layout to counter any feeling of exposure. Here, small trees anchor a pair of seats with solid sides and backs, providing both shelter and shade.

Features for larger gardens
Create areas with different uses and moods

Gardens are there to be used, and a large one, especially, needs to be made as user-friendly and inviting as possible. Dividing the space into different areas will make the plot more enticing and interesting. Outdoor living becomes more inviting if there are plenty of things to do in the garden too, especially if you have a young family.

● **MAKE AN IMPACT WITH BOLD GARDEN STRUCTURES**

In a spacious garden there is more scope for major garden structures such as a large pergola or a gazebo. If features such as these are chosen and positioned thoughtfully, they are an ideal (and instant) way of defining the space and shaping the garden, but they must work as part of an overall garden plan. A pergola or tunnel should lead somewhere worthwhile, and an ornamental garden building needs a complementary setting. Think about views from a gazebo or summerhouse, as well as the view of it: you may need to consider framing or screening some areas from different angles.

▲ **An avenue of pleached trees** drawing the eye to an arbour dominates this formal, traditional 'garden room'. Be sure to measure out symmetrical set pieces such as this carefully at the planning stage, as mistakes can be hard to correct.

A LARGE GARDEN DIVIDED INTO ROOMS

This house, set back from the road, has a neat, functional front garden and a spacious back garden that has been designed to suit varied gardening interests as well as maximising the possibilities for outdoor relaxation, recreation and entertaining. The back garden has a very gentle slope, and a retaining wall, 90cm (3ft) high at its tallest, has been built to contain the formal, level lawn with its paved surround.

▶ **A summerhouse** is a fun addition to a large garden, and can serve as a den, a sanctuary or even a studio. During the winter months, it provides valuable storage space for bulky cane or rattan garden furniture, which has the perfect look for a decked area but requires a lot of storage space when not in use.

KEY FEATURES

❶ **The terrace** adjoining the house is the central outdoor dining space; the paving is continued around a closely mown grassed area, ideal for lawn games.

❷ **Steps** framing a view of a mature tree lead to the longer, meadow-style grass in the lower part of the garden, which has paths mown through it.

❸ **Sun-loving evergreen shrubs** surround the formal lawn and enjoy the heat from the retaining wall: pittosporum, rosemary, osmanthus and hebes would all look good.

❹ **A shed** houses a small mower for the formal lawn; a larger model or a ride-on mower for the longer grass could be housed in the garage or behind the summerhouse.

❺ **Trained fruit** surrounds the vegetable beds: raspberries trained on posts and wires divide the kitchen garden from the pond area, while pears and cherries benefit from the heat of the house and garage walls.

❻ **An arbour** forms a focal point at the end of two long flower borders, set within a small seating area that catches the morning sun.

❼ **A mixed hedge** of native species, studded with small trees, looks perfectly in keeping dividing the lower meadow-style area of the garden from the neighbouring fields.

❽ **Apple and plum trees** form a mini-orchard within the meadow grass.

❾ **A grouping of small deciduous trees** create a woodland corner, carpeted with shade-loving plants and spring bulbs.

❿ **The informal pond** is in full sun – the best position for healthy water. Planting around and especially behind it provides cover for wildlife to approach.

⓫ **Decking is part-shaded** from the afternoon sun by the summerhouse, ideal for cooling down by the pond. A jetty extends over the water.

● **DESIGN AN OUTDOOR DINING ROOM** A spacious paved area with overhead beams festooned with climbing plants makes an idyllic setting for family meals or entertaining, shaded by greenery from the hottest midday sun and enclosed and protected on chilly evenings. Choose a sheltered spot, and create an access path to the kitchen that is reasonably direct.

Add interest with changes of level A flat, large garden can be given lots of vertical interest with trees and large shrubs, but you can augment this with raised beds. Make them generously sized and boldly planted, perhaps with trailing plants around the edges, to give a sense of changing contours to your garden. Even a decking platform will give a new perspective and a more interesting viewpoint, and perhaps a little extra sunshine, too. Raising up ornamental garden buildings, such as summerhouses, immediately gives them increased presence.

● **GET MORE USE FROM A SLOPING GARDEN** If your garden contains a slope, terracing is a good way to give a plot structure and to increase the amount of usable level space for seating, games areas, a vegetable garden and so on. Retaining walls at the edge of each terrace will add to the cost but will look superb and make a fine setting for planting. Boulder-filled gabions, or metal cages [see p.51], make a more informal retaining structure.

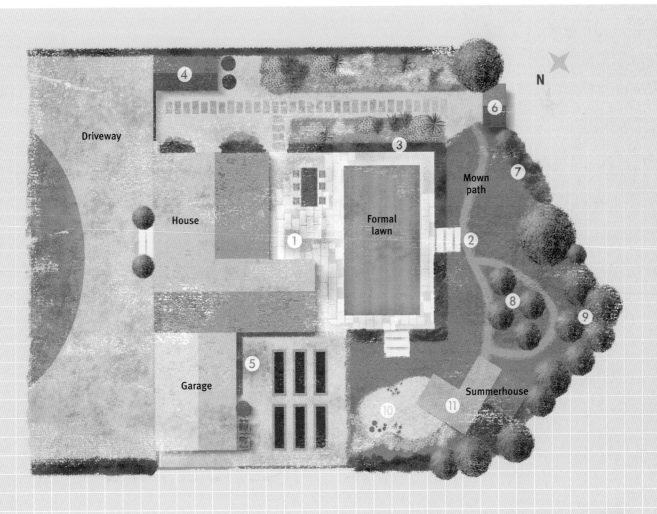

Make the most of growing space One of the best things about larger gardens is the scope they give for growing a wide variety of plants. Try a few new ones every year: there may be failures, but there are sure to be many successes, enabling you to build up a repertoire of stalwarts that will thrive in your garden.

● **ENJOY THE LUXURY OF ONE-SEASON WONDERS** Whatever your planting tastes, larger gardens offer more scope for the dramatic seasonal set-pieces of the plant world. Make the most of the opportunity to enjoy one or more features that make a big splash just once a year, such as a laburnum tunnel, or a spring 'nut walk' – an avenue of hazels [see p.156] densely underplanted with spring woodland flowers.

CREATE SOME BOLD PLANTING FEATURES TO MATCH THE SCALE OF A LARGE GARDEN

● **INDULGE YOURSELF WITH THEMED PLANTINGS** A large garden divided into rooms gives scope to explore different planting moods. One area could contain strictly formal elements such as topiary or a box-edged parterre; a shady area could become a fernery or stumpery, while a sunny one might inspire an exotic garden, where bananas, cannas, dahlias and other fast-growing late summer plants can be grouped in large enough numbers to make a really flamboyant impact.

▼ **Grow your own on a grand scale** with a well-stocked vegetable plot. Here, the decorative obelisks and arches distract the eye from the more functional brassica netting, and provide supports for a fruiting grapevine and, in summer, climbing squash plants and beans.

Grow your own food Home-grown fruit and vegetables have made a huge comeback in recent years, and with a large garden, you can create a really productive space. Your kitchen garden could even increase in size as your success and confidence grow. Choose a sunny place, and consider adding a greenhouse for bumper crops of tomatoes and other Mediterranean crops.

● **CLEAR VIRGIN GROUND WITH A POTATO CROP** Their cultivation keeps the ground disturbed and gives weeds a hard time as the potatoes are planted, earthed up and harvested. Other easy crops for first-time vegetable growers [see also pp.178–209] are salads, squashes, courgettes and beans.

● **PLANT AN ORCHARD** Most fruit trees are beautiful as well as useful, especially if they are looked after and pruned correctly. It's worth spending some time finding out which varieties, grown on which rootstocks, will best suit the space you have available and your soil and climate, as well as your eating habits [see pp.214–19].

● **SET UP A CUTTING GARDEN** Traditional kitchen gardens always included flowers to be cut for the house, and by growing your own, you can include beauties such as poppies and cleomes that are too delicate for the big commercial growers to store and transport. So many wonderful flowers for cutting can be grown from seed, making this an economical way to fill your home with colour and scent, and if you're an organic grower, you can be sure that the flowers that come into your house are free from chemical residues.

Create wild areas that need less maintenance
Leaving or making some wilder areas will cut down on work in a larger garden, and provide valuable resources for wildlife. Consider a mixed hedge of flowering and fruiting native shrubs threaded through with climbers to mark a boundary, perhaps forming the backdrop to a wildflower meadow. Many seed firms provide 'meadow mixes' that produce different effects, and landscaping specialists offer ready-to-lay meadow turf.

● **ADD A WOODLAND CORNER FOR ADVENTURE** A mini-woodland is an ideal low-maintenance option for a family garden, encouraging imaginative play as well as wildlife. If your garden isn't huge, a group of five or six compact trees such as hazels, rowans and apples will make a serviceable woodland area, good for many hours of adventure play or hide-and-seek. If you're lucky enough to have at least one mature tree, it may be suitable for a treehouse – either a basic home-built platform or a luxury model of the kind that a specialist company will build for you. Rope swings and 'flying fox' cableways are fun additions if you have space.

● **MAKE A WILLOW WALL FOR A LIVING SCREEN** Woven willow screens are perfect for dividing wild parts of the garden from the more cultivated areas. Buy rooted willow wands from a specialist supplier and plant them 30cm (12in) apart. As they grow, weave them together and tie in the stems to create a living barrier. Prune regularly to keep it in shape, cutting out new shoots or weaving them in if they fit in with your design. If the idea of creating more elaborate woven structures such as tunnels and dens appeals, look out for courses in your area.

▲ **Bold, themed plantings** can create areas with different moods in a larger garden. Consider, for example, a dedicated rose garden in formal style, a gravel bed studded with architectural, drought-loving plants or a shady walkway through exotic foliage plants such as the palms and bananas above.

Front gardens

A FRONT GARDEN CREATES the all-important first impression of your home. **Give some thought** to its design, the materials you use and how you plant the space, and the result can be a garden that is not only practical – buffering the house from the street, and perhaps also offering car parking – but also looks good all year round.

Combine practicality with good looks

Create an inviting entrance
Use planting that frames the front door to make it the focal point of a front garden: a collection of containers; a pair of clipped bushes such as bay or box; or climbers growing over a porch or on walls to either side. Fragrant plants give a lovely impression as you enter a house, so find a spot for a small winter-flowering shrub such as a sarcococca or a daphne.

● **WELCOME GUESTS WITH SOFT LIGHTING** A warm glow from downlighters feels much more welcoming than a harsh, bright security light that makes you jump when it suddenly comes on as you arrive.

● **MAKE PATHS PRACTICAL** Pathways in a front garden need to take the most straightforward routes from A to B. Otherwise, it can be too tempting for callers or children to take shortcuts across a lawn or flower bed. Lay out practical, direct routes from gate or garage to the front door, and keep roughly to these lines, with no tortuous angles.

Splash out on a stylish fence
It's often unnecessary to divide the front garden from the road, but if you prefer the sense of enclosure that a fence or low wall brings, then it's worth buying something well-made and good-looking. You may need only a short run of low fencing, in which case something custom-made may not be too costly and could make all the difference to the look of your property. Choose something that communicates your style, and add a matching gate to set it off to perfection. Picket fences can't be beaten for rustic charm, or for something more sophisticated consider a craftsman-made fence built with jointed and pegged timber, painted to match the woodwork on the house.

● **AVOID HAVING TO REPAINT IRON RAILINGS** regularly by having them professionally sandblasted and powder-coated – invest in this one-off treatment and the railings will look smart for years, saving you a tedious and fiddly job.

Reduce runoff with porous surfaces
With flooding more widespread in many places, covering front gardens with impermeable materials is becoming less desirable. In heavy rain, if surface water cannot soak into the ground in front gardens, it usually discharges into the road, quickly overloading storm drains. If your front garden includes a parking area, consider alternatives to tarmac and solid paving, such as gravel or interlocking, permeable block paving.

▼ **Symmetrical planting,** whether it's smartly trimmed topiary or a pair of generously planted hanging baskets, draws the eye straight to the front door. These square planters, known as Versailles boxes, are heavy enough to deter casual doorstep thefts.

● **DISGUISE A PARKING SPACE AS A LAWN** Take a look at robust plastic mesh tiles that can be set into the ground, filled with soil and sown with grass seed to create a lawn that will withstand heavy traffic. Choose a grass seed mix suited to shade for when the car is parked there. Or, consider an elevated lawn: a carport with a green roof [see p.27] attracted lots of attention at a recent garden show.

● **BLEND A PARKING AREA INTO THE GARDEN** Consider a planted gravel area [see p.58] that will provide a firm surface for parking that's attractive when empty. The noise gravel makes underfoot is a good security feature, too. Chippings of rough stone are better than pea shingle at bedding down and locking together to make a firm surface. Tough creeping plants like thymes tolerate being driven over occasionally; alternatively, create wheeltracks with two rows of well-laid, solid slabs.

Include plants for all seasons
A front garden is in the spotlight every day of the year so include plenty of out-of-season plant interest. Include shrubs with autumn berries and leaf colour, herbaceous plants that have structural seedheads to make interesting shapes in winter, such as *Sedum* 'Herbstfreude' or *Phlomis russeliana*, and late-winter flowerers such as hellebores and snowdrops.

● **PLANT CLEVERLY FOR LOW MAINTENANCE** Being in the public eye, a front garden needs to be easy to keep neat – especially as you may not want to spend much time looking after it. A simple basic planting scheme using a limited palette of ground-covering, weed-suppressing foliage plants to suit the conditions – whether sunny or shady – is a useful starting point. Add spring bulbs, seasonal bedding in pots, and perhaps a flowering shrub or two to bring highlights of seasonal colour. And don't forget the potential your house's walls offer for climbing plants or wall shrubs.

▲ **This low-maintenance front garden** is designed for functionality as well as good looks. The planting is simple and easy-care, with a weed-suppressing mulch covering any bare ground, and clearing the trunks of the small tree in the foreground has created clear sightlines for security.

Garden boundaries

MOST OF US WANT TO ENCLOSE OUR GARDENS, whether for privacy, safety or shelter. But a boundary can be a positive visual asset as well as doing its job. Walls and fences – even basic ones – are too expensive to be seen as mere utility items when, with a little imagination, they could make a valuable contribution to the look of your plot.

Protect the garden and your privacy

Choose the right boundary for your site
Privacy and security are major factors when considering what form your garden boundaries will take, which is why most of us opt for the solidity of garden walls or panelled fences. If the boundary is needed for shelter in an exposed site, solid walls and fences may not be the best choice. Instead select a boundary that filters and breaks down the strength of the wind while still providing privacy (see facing page).

● **COMPLEMENT YOUR SURROUNDINGS** In small, enclosed urban plots, the garden is often seen as a part of the house: smooth, painted walls can reinforce the link between indoors and out, right down to choice of colour scheme. In rural gardens, take a look at local examples of craftsmanship in the wider landscape that could inspire your choice, such as willow or hazel hurdle fencing, drystone walling, neatly laid hedging, and walls of rendered cob, or brick and flintwork.

▼ **Garden walls** are wonderful assets, and can be given a new lease of life with skilful repointing. Adding a coping of tiles or slate that sheds rain will also protect and prolong the life of the brickwork.

● **CONSIDER NEIGHBOURS TO AVOID DISPUTES** Wherever you live, it's wise to discuss with neighbours any work you plan to do on a boundary, and to consult relevant legislation on maximum permitted heights. If considering a hedge to enclose your garden [see pp.158–61], think about how you will access the far side for trimming: a hedge facing out onto a pavement or open ground will not be a problem, but one that encroaches onto a neighbour's property may cause difficulties. A fence is usually the most practical option between two gardens; you can cover it with climbers on your side to give the appearance of solid greenery.

● **RETAIN ATTRACTIVE VIEWS** With careful planning, you can screen out what you don't want to see while framing other, attractive elements of the landscape. Reduce the height of a fence, for example, in places where screening is not essential, or where there are pleasing views beyond the garden, or add a cleverly positioned gap – perhaps a well-placed gateway or a 'porthole' – in a wall or hedge [see p.160].

● **MAKE A GOOD-LOOKING BUDGET BARRIER** Unattractive chainlink fencing can be transformed into a living evergreen screen by planting variegated ivy or euonymus to scramble up it. Improve the soil at the base of the fence to get the plants off to a good start, and tie the shoots in to begin with. As the plants mature they will cling by themselves. In a mild, sheltered spot you could grow one of the large-leaved variegated ivies such as *Hedera algeriensis* 'Gloire de Marengo', but there are also many prettily variegated cultivars of tough *Hedera helix*: try 'Goldchild' and 'Glacier'. The best euonymus for the job is white-variegated *Euonymus fortunei* 'Silver Queen'.

▲ **Ivy trained over a utilitarian chainlink fence** makes a livestock-proof, inexpensive and attractive 'fedge' – a cross between a fence and a hedge – for a rural garden. These late flowers will be followed by black fruits, a valuable winter food for many garden birds.

Enhance walls and fences

Frame eye-catching features
For a distinctive and individual garden feature that takes up very little space, mount a sculpture or water feature on a wall. The wall needs to be basically sound, especially for a heavy feature such as a stone wall-mounted basin. Many companies and craftsmen make wall sculptures and water features in lightweight materials that are easier to install: from faux lead or fibreglass 'stone' masks, for a traditional garden, to minimalist structures in acrylic or alloy for a contemporary feel.

● **CONCEAL A FEATURE'S WORKINGS FOR AN EFFORTLESS FINISH** A wall fountain may look unfinished if the pipework is showing, so either mortar it into a channel cut into the wall or hide it with planting. You will also need a place in which to conceal a small pump.

● **MAKE THE MOST OF SUPPORTS** It is accepted – and neighbourly – practice to erect walls and fences with their

HOW DOES IT WORK?
FILTERING WIND

Solid boundaries that take the full force of strong winds can cause damaging turbulence in a garden, and solid fencing, especially if it is flimsy, may struggle to stay in place. Instead, choose fencing, such as trellis or picket fencing, that will let the wind blow through it while reducing its force. If you need a visual barrier choose 'hit-and-miss' fencing, which has two staggered layers of slats with gaps between. A robust hedge [see pp.158–61] will also filter the wind, and is very unlikely to be damaged in a windy site.

'best' side outwards, which may mean that their supports can be on your side of a boundary. Try exploiting them by using fence-posts or wall buttresses to frame a feature such as a seat or a sculpture. Site the feature exactly mid-way between two posts or buttresses, and use planting to complete the setting.

Use colour for immediate impact

The simplest and quickest way to smarten a tired fence or dull wall is to paint it. For a really stylish result, make the colour an integral part of your whole scheme, including other materials and the planting. Specialist paints, such as lime paint with added acrylic, can be useful for surfaces of mixed materials, or those where adhesion is a problem. A wide range of fence paints and stains in attractive colours is available, many now water-based and easy to apply even to unplaned timber.

● **ADD LIGHT AND COLOUR FOR A MODERN LOOK** Coloured walls are especially effective in clean-lined contemporary gardens with a simple layout and planting. Use white or pale colours to reflect light in heavily shaded areas or basement gardens.

▲ **Light fencing** may not be sufficiently robust to take the weight of climbing plants. Instead, position tall, narrow plants in front of it. These conifers are ideal; unlike perennials, their sturdy, straight stems will not flop away from the fence.

● **MATCH COLOURS TO MATERIALS** Ashy, Scandinavian-style woodstains and paints in light colours such as cream, grey-green or pale slate blue work best on good-quality surfaces or where a fence is sufficiently well designed to be worth making into a feature. To disguise imperfections in more economical fencing, choose darker colours – even black is certainly worth considering. It will make a fence less obtrusive, allowing planting in front of it to take centre stage.

● **CHOOSE COMPLEMENTARY PLANTING** Choose plants that show up well against their background [see also p.78]. White or cream walls are especially flattering to climbers or wall shrubs with blue flowers, such as clematis or ceanothus. A black fence works particularly well as a backdrop to architectural plants in pale colours, such as silver *Eryngium giganteum* or golden *Stipa gigantea*. The golden hop, *Humulus lupulus* 'Aureus', is an easy climber for a black fence or trellis, with its shapely leaves and vibrant colour and its helpful habit of dying back to the ground in winter so you can repaint the fence.

Give your fence a facelift
Replace part of a solid timber fence with prefabricated trellis panels or with some kind of sturdier openwork fencing, to make the garden feel more open and airy. Trellis panels fitted along the top of a solid fence are attractive, and increase the area on which climbing plants can be trained without creating an oppressive look.

● **TRY A DECORATIVE FACING FOR A NEW LOOK** If you have a serviceable but drab fence, with sound posts, transform its appearance by adding a facing of a different material, supported by the existing posts. Hazel or willow hurdles could be attached for an informal, cottagey effect, or, for a more contemporary look, use prefabricated screening panels of split bamboo or reed, trellis panels, or simple horizontal timber slats, positioned exactly level and painted or stained.

● **PROTECT TIMBER FOR A LONG-LIVED FENCE** Prolong the life of fence posts by bolting them at the base to concrete spurs, and by fitting caps or finials to their tops. Close-boarded fencing can be protected at the top by fitting a bevelled timber capping rail to keep out moisture from the end grain of the wood. Both finials and capping will also give your fence a smarter look. Fences are also prone to rotting at the base where they touch the ground and get splashed. To avoid having to replace a fence when rot sets in, set the fence panels or boards a little higher off the ground and fill the gap with gravel boards – planks fixed on their sides to run along the base of the fence. They will eventually rot, but it's much easier and cheaper to replace them than a whole fence.

Add a finishing touch with plants

Planting can work wonders at disguising or enlivening a boundary. Even if you have a garden wall of beautiful mellow brick or stone that is attractive in its own right, it's a pity not to use it as a backdrop for a specimen plant or two. There is a huge range of climbers [see pp.164–71] and wall shrubs that can be used to add colour and interest.

● **TAKE ADVANTAGE OF THE HEAT OF A WALL** Garden walls can dramatically affect a garden's microclimate, soaking up the sun during the day and releasing it to help keep nearby plants warm on chilly nights. Use that heat to grow more tender, exotic-looking climbers, or to ripen luscious fruits [see p.219].

● **CHOOSE TOUGH PLANTS FOR NARROW BEDS** If you can create a wide border at the base of a wall or fence and plant it generously, it will place attention firmly within the garden rather than on the boundaries that limit it. Sometimes this is not possible – for example, when a wall or fence runs beside a driveway – and plant choice for a narrow bed (see below) is tricky: this will be a dry planting site, and the soil may be impoverished by rubble and difficult for plant roots to penetrate.

▲ **Woven willow panels** can be used to add a fresh facing to walls and fences. Incorporating a narrow raised bed keeps the dampness of the soil within away from brickwork or wooden fence panels.

STAR PERFORMERS...

PLANTS FOR THE DRY BASE OF A SUNNY WALL

Improve the soil with plenty of organic matter, and position plants as far from the wall or fence base as you can to give them a helping hand.

● Abutilon
● Agapanthus
● *Campsis radicans*
● *Convolvulus cneorum*
● Gaillardias
● Gazanias
● Ipomoea
◀ Nasturtiums
● Osteospermums
● Passiflora
● Rosemary
● *Stachys byzantina*
● *Vinca minor*

Paths, steps and changes of level

PATHS ARE THE BONES OF A GARDEN, so think carefully about both their routes and materials. Paths should always lead to where you need or want to go, and the right materials will make the journey both practical and visually satisfying. Add the right steps to cope with any slopes for a garden that will be easy to explore.

Planning your paths

Find the best routes Garden paths may take you directly and practically to a destination, or invite you to explore different areas of a garden, so consider carefully what types of routes you need. A randomly meandering path can look charming, but you'll never use it if you're in a hurry to get to the shed on a wet day. This doesn't mean that paths must always be straight; gentle curves suggest a slower pace and can give a sense of space.

● **BREAK UP A LONG PATH** Long, narrow gardens very often have long, straight paths that only emphasize the garden's tendency to feel like a corridor. Use focal points as reasons to stop or slow down along the path. Make a small paved area to one side, perhaps, with a seat and a collection of pots; plant a tree beside a path so that its branches will eventually frame it; construct an arch or pergola; or distract attention

◄ **A well-laid, attractive path** makes an ornamental feature out of a necessity. Varying the widths of the mortared joints will enable you to make a curved or meandering route using regularly shaped bricks or pavers.

A GENTLY CURVING ROUTE AND RELAXED PLANTING ON EACH SIDE SOFTENS THE HARD LINES OF A PATH

from a path's strong directional pull by embedding crosswise elements into its surface; try rows of bricks, hardwood timbers or tiles on the edges. Creating contrasting areas of light and shade along the path will have a similar effect.

● **TRY OUT ROUTES WITH A TEMPORARY PATH** Chipped bark is ideal for making quick, inexpensive paths, especially useful if you want to try out a new path for a season, or for paths between beds whose layout may change. Disposal is not a problem: over time the bark will degrade and act as a soil conditioner.

▼ **Bricks laid end to end** along a path draw the eye along it and towards yet-unseen destinations in the garden. This technique works well in gardens that are planned as an unfolding journey around different areas of planting.

Choose materials to suit your style Paths should not only be practical; the materials you choose should complement the style of the garden, and match or harmonise with existing stone and brickwork. Where paths lead from a patio or terrace, try to use the same or matching materials to create a sense of coherence and flow.

● **MIX MATERIALS FOR INTEREST** Some of the best garden paths are made from two different materials: bricks and paving slabs, gravel and rounds of timber, stone and grass or concrete and flint. For a harmonious effect, avoid using too many different materials, and choose at least one that takes its cue from the house or another existing feature such as a garden wall.

● **MAKE GRASS PATHS TO INVITE EXPLORATION** In a large garden a neatly mown path leading through a meadow looks calm and inviting. Another option is to create closely mown paths through areas of grass that is trimmed with the mower blades set higher. The contrast immediately gives shape and interest to the space. If you are making a new grass path, work a generous amount of fine grit into the top few inches of soil first to improve drainage and give a firmer surface.

PATH MATERIALS

It's worth visiting a builder's merchant in person to choose materials, rather than ordering from an online catalogue. There should be someone on hand to help with calculating quantities.

▲ **Chipped bark, for an informal woodland effect; consider adding timber rounds as stepping stones**
● **Compacted limestone or slate chippings**
● **Engineering bricks or stable blocks**
● **Frost-resistant bricks set on edge, laid in a basket-weave or herringbone pattern**
● **Stone or concrete paving slabs**
● **Small stone setts, perhaps combined with larger matching slabs**

● **PERSONALISE YOUR PATH FOR A UNIQUE FINISH** Improvised path materials such as broken ceramic tiles, pottery pieces, glass bottle bottoms, pebbles or seashells set in mortar give a stylish, custom-made look, but making a complete path this way over any distance can be laborious. Try, instead, using novel materials as the infill between conventional pavers – the effect will be just as attractive.

● **VISIT THE SHOWS FOR INSPIRATION** Show gardens often contain planting combinations that are difficult to reproduce at home, but all show gardens have paths – where else would the judges stand? The more gardens there are, the wider the range of imaginative and attractive treatments of paths and paving will be, all in one place to compare and contrast. It's in the hard landscaping and practical details that show gardens come into their own with great-looking, workable ideas for the gardener at home, so take a camera with you.

Make paths that protect your garden
Digging up and re-laying paths to follow a different route can be a major upheaval. There are ways to reduce problems caused by the layout of existing paths. Set stepping stones into a lawn, for example, to provide a more resilient surface on well-travelled shortcuts. Cut out rectangles of turf of the right size, and bed each slab on a layer of sharp sand, with the surface a little lower than the grass so that the mower can pass over.

● **LAY A PRACTICAL PATH IN WELL-PLANTED BORDERS** A path of well-spaced paving slabs along the back of a border makes access much easier for hedge-cutting, weeding, planting and pruning, without the risk of compacting the soil or damaging plants.

▼ **Sinuous lines of stone setts** laid end to end emphasise the flow of a path and invite you to follow it to its destination – here a sunlit archway tantalisingily half-hidden beyond lush planting.

Choose fairly thick slabs in a neutral colour, with a non-slip surface, and if the soil is heavy bed each one onto a layer of sand or grit for stability.

● **BUY A TEMPORARY PATH FOR WET-WEATHER GARDENING** A purpose-made plastic or wooden path that rolls up for storage is a worthwhile investment, especially for gardening in cold, damp weather. It enables you to work while standing on a lawn or in a border without damaging the grass or compacting the soil.

Make paths hard-wearing and long-lasting
Provide a firm foundation for your chosen surfacing material to avoid being left with a sunken, wobbly path. Dig down to about 15cm (6in) and lay a good bed of hardcore. Rake it level and then compact it well to give a solid base; hiring a powered compactor, or 'whacker plate', will be worth every penny when you see the finished result. Finish with a layer of builder's sand on which to bed the materials.

● **CHOOSE 'SELF-BINDING' GRAVEL FOR A FIRM SURFACE** Rather than using the washed shingle and stone chippings sold for use as mulches, seek out unwashed gravels from a builder's merchant or online supplier. These include fine fragments and dust that will bind the gravel when compacted, either by feet or a whacker plate, making the surface firmer and preventing the gravel from straying.

● **AVOID SOGGY, PUDDLE-STREWN PAVING IN WINTER** by making one edge of the path slightly higher than the other, so that water runs off the side of the path, not along its length. A slope as shallow as 1 in 100 (1cm fall for every metre of width) will do the job. Paths of compacted gravel, setts or other small units can be laid with a slight rise along the middle so that water is shed to both sides.

● **MAKE TIMBER SAFE IN WET WEATHER** Timber rounds and blocks can become slippery when wet, especially in shade. Ensure a sound footing by stapling galvanized chicken wire to the surface – be sure not to leave any snags or loose edges, and replace the netting when it shows signs of wear.

● **PROTECT OLD BRICK PATHS** Avoid using a pressure washer to clean paths of antique brick: the force of the jet may cause them to split and flake. Use a hose and a stiff brush.

Spruce up a tired path with an edging
A dull path can be given a new lease of life with an edging of a different material such as frost-resistant bricks, stone setts or tiles set on their edges. If the edging is to last well and be weed-free, it should be set on a well-compacted sub-base and properly mortared in. Other ideas include using lengths of trimmed tree branch to edge an informal woodland path of chipped bark or grass, and variations on the familiar log-roll edging – perhaps a line of 30cm (12in) lengths of stout bamboo, driven vertically into the ground at the path's edge.

● **MAKE YOUR OWN EDGING FOR FREE** Use pliable, coppiced hazel or willow stems [see p.167] to make a woven edging, either in the style of a hurdle or as interlocking hoops. They may not last long but they look attractive, give support to plants at the edge of the path and cost nothing.

▲ **Make a customised path** by improvising with novel materials. Here, mosaic-patterned discs have been created by cementing crockery shards onto round pavers, then infilled with more loose pottery fragments.

▼ **Emphasise edging** on geometric paths by adding a row of neat planting. The 'full stop' provided here by the clipped box sphere prevents corner-cutting.

Garden steps and changes of level

Take full advantage of a slope Changes of level can make all the difference to a garden, so focus on them as opportunities to create attractive and interesting features. Planned carefully, steps can be both a clever device for shaping the ground and the space above it, and a focal point that takes the lead in the structure and style of the whole garden. Brick or paved steps suit formal layouts, with materials chosen to convey either a traditional or a contemporary look, while 'donkey steps' (see facing page) are the perfect solution for a sloping, slippery path in an informal part of the garden.

● **MAKE STEPS A FEATURE IN YOUR OVERALL DESIGN** Carefully thought-out steps can lend character to the whole garden and link it to the house. Experiment on paper by sketching different layouts and shapes. A change in direction on the steps, a terrace half-way up, or a 'wedding-cake' arrangement of semicircular steps can turn a practical feature into a really handsome, important piece of landscaping.

● **FLATTER AND SOFTEN STEPS WITH PLANTING** Sloping ground to each side of a series of steps allows you to create naturally tiered arrangements of the same plant, or for plants of a similar height. On the steps themselves, allow space for a container or two, or allow plants to spill over from the sides, or put seed into cracks in informal steps: this will quickly give new hard landscaping an established, settled look. Creeping plants such as ivy or dwarf cotoneaster can be trained along the risers of the steps.

▼ **A sloping site** can inspire the entire design of a garden. This Mediterranean-style creation uses symmetrical planting to emphasise the geometrical shapes of the steps and terracing.

Make steps easy to see and negotiate

Find a way to draw attention to steps, especially single ones, so that they are not a hazard. Try a pair of matching container plants on either side. Make sure that the edges of the treads are easily visible as you walk both up and down, so that one step doesn't blend into the next. Consider downlighters to make steps safer in the dark, and perhaps add a decorative handrail.

● **KEEP GARDEN STEPS SHALLOW** Outdoor steps look better and feel more relaxed if their proportions suggest that they are less like hard work than an indoor staircase. Each step should be a comfortable stride: usually, a tread depth of 30–50cm (12–20in) will feel right, with a riser height of 7.5–15cm (3–6in).

● **CONSIDER A RAMP FOR PRACTICALITY** A ramp can be surprisingly useful in a garden, giving easy access for mowers, wheelbarrows, prams and wheelchairs. Keep the slope gentle (no more than 1 in 12, ideally), and make certain that the surface is not slippery. A slight cross-fall on the ramp, with drainage to the side, will ensure that water does not simply run down the path.

CREATING RUSTIC DONKEY STEPS

For each step you will need two sawn logs, 10cm (4in) in diameter and 75cm (30in) long, two 25 x 25mm wooden stakes, 60cm (2ft) long, and some hardcore. Deciding how to make the first step is the only tricky part; you can either make it very shallow, or use shuttering boards (as below) to hold in the infill.

1 To form the first step cut into the base of the slope to about the height of one log. Hammer in the two stakes 15cm (6in) from each end of the step. Slot the two logs, one on top of the other, behind the stakes. Trim the stakes.

2 You will probably need two side boards, nailed to the ends of the logs, to hold the first step together. Once these are in place add a layer of hardcore to the tread area and compact it using a rammer (for example, an uncut post).

3 Make the next log riser and trim the stakes. Dig out the soil from the tread to make room for the hardcore layer; you can use this soil to cover the hardcore on the step below. Repeat until the flight is completed.

Terrace a slope to create level planting areas The methods used to terrace a slope are equally suitable for creating raised beds that could complement the terracing in another part of the garden. Well-built retaining walls are the most permanent solution, perhaps in brick or flint for a traditional garden or rendered and painted in a more urban setting. Building walls such as these will entail a major garden upheaval, and possibly earth-moving equipment, so may only be practicable if you plan it as part of a major redesign.

● **MAKE A SPEEDY RETAINING WALL** Timber sleepers can be stacked on top of each and secured with sturdy vertical steel supports (using the same principle, on a larger scale, as donkey steps), or sunk vertically into the ground, to create a robust earth-retaining wall. Beware of old railway sleepers, which may have been treated with toxic preservatives that can leach into the soil and even ooze out of the timber in hot weather as a black, sticky tar. New sleepers made from untreated hardwood are just as useful; they will soon weather attractively.

● **USE GABIONS FOR A MODERN LOOK** The strong rectangular wire cages known as gabions both look very contemporary and are a low-cost alternative to permanent walls. Filled with heavy materials such as stones, flints or bricks, gabions make instant, bulky walling modules that are heavy and strong enough to hold back earth. Pieces of geotextile worked in between the stones as the gabion is filled can be used to form pockets of soil for planting. The plants will dry out very quickly, so they need to be drought-tolerant.

▼ **The wire cages** known as gabions can be filled with rubble, broken terracotta land drains or tiles or even empty bottles to create low retaining walls. Lay pavers or planks across the tops to serve as extra garden seating.

Patios and terraces

WELL-SITED SEATING AND DINING AREAS make outdoor living easy.
A well-laid patio or terrace may form the perfect outdoor extension to your home, or a garden hideaway in which to relax and unwind. From smooth pavers to reclaimed terracotta tiles or breezy, nautical-style decking, the choice of materials has never been greater.

Creating beautiful, practical spaces

Choose the perfect position
Most patios and terraces form the interface between house and garden, and proximity to the kitchen is certainly a help when entertaining. If the back of your house is shaded in the morning or early evening, consider adding a second paved or decked area – perhaps not so large or elaborate – in a part of the garden that will allow you to enjoy breakfast coffee or an evening drink in the sunshine.

● **FIND THE MOST PEACEFUL SPOT** Noise may be one reason for siting your main seating or dining area some distance from the house, especially if you live on a busy road. Any other built feature such as a wall, a fence or a shed will buffer noise to some degree, so see if you can pinpoint the quietest spot that is practicable to use. Try planting to soften the soundscape, too: a hedge, or rustling bamboo, or wind-blown grasses such as miscanthus. A water feature can distract attention from unwanted noise with the sound of splashing or falling water.

● **CREATE YOUR OWN SECRET SANCTUARY** Find room for a small paved space in a sunny border where you can sit undisturbed among your favourite plants. Level the soil, add a raked layer of sand or grit, and lay out a double row of four standard paving slabs close together. Add a couple of stepping stones through the planting to make it easy to reach from the nearest lawn or path.

Use matching materials to link house and garden
Where rooms in the house open onto a patio, continuing the same flooring material will unify the indoor and outdoor spaces, making the garden seem inviting from the house, and vice versa. Floorboards can be echoed in decking, and many other materials can be used both inside and out, such as flagstones, brick paving, slate and tiles.

● **PLAN GENEROUS STEPS FOR SAFETY** Ease any changes of level from house to patio to garden with broad, shallow steps, perhaps with room for a planted container or two. Where a drop between patio and garden is unavoidable,

▼ **A level space** large enough for a small table and a chair or two could be all you need for breakfast or a break from looking after the garden.

make a visual barrier with planters or an actual barrier with rails to help prevent that unsettling feeling of being on the edge of a precipice.

● **KEEP HOUSE WALLS FREE FROM DAMP** Where a patio or other paved area adjoins a building, ensure that the surface slopes away from it so that water does not accumulate at the base of the walls. The surface of the patio should also be at least 15cm (6in) below a damp course in a house wall to prevent any moisture getting into the walls. A narrow void filled with shingle between the patio and the wall will also help keep a building dry.

Make the space feel comfortable
Patios that are too small for comfort will become infuriating. Allow enough space for the size of table you want and the number of chairs (with the chairs pulled out), plus room to enable you to move easily around the table – essential for refreshing glasses!

● **ENCLOSE A PATIO FOR SHELTER** A large, breezy expanse is not a comfortable place to relax in. Use trellis, hedges or planters to the sides to give some sense of enclosure – or consider building a wall. A low wall of gabions [see p.51] can be a handy solution at the edge of a terrace; with a timber top, they can serve as seating, too.

● **SELECT SMOOTH BUT NON-SLIP SURFACES** To prevent furniture wobbling, avoid gravel, cobbles, setts and deeply riven slabs. Choose flat paving or timber decking, but beware of using very smooth surfaces in shady areas where the surface is slow to dry out and algae can build up. Rough-surfaced slabs or grooved timber are a better choice in these situations. Before you buy, try to find out how your chosen surfacing looks and behaves when wet. Some suppliers create small show gardens where customers can see materials in place.

▲ **A permanent barbecue** is a fuss-free option that will make outdoor eating more spontaneous. It could be a simple brick-built feature or a custom-made treat.

▼ **Rectangular pavers** laid lengthways accentuate the feeling of being beckoned out of the house to enjoy this stylish outdoor dining area. Painted brickwork in the garden reinforces the illusion of an 'outdoor room'.

● **CREATE SOME SHADE FOR SUN PROTECTION** A patio that receives full sun can become unpleasantly hot for summer lunches. A parasol, awning or sail is a practical solution, but for something more permanent that provides pleasant, dappled shade, overhead foliage is the answer. A tree with an airy, light canopy (such as a rowan or gleditsia) may help; or consider constructing a pergola with overhead beams to support deciduous climbers. The leaves of wisteria or jasmine provide a pretty, green roof in summer when the shade is needed, but the bare stems won't keep out the light in winter. Flowers and fragrance are a bonus.

Choosing and laying surfaces

Easy steps to perfect paving
The natural choice for a patio area is paving: weatherproof, permanent and easy to keep clean. A huge choice of suitable materials is now on offer. Uniform slab sizes that mimic interior flooring work well for a patio that is closely associated with the house, or in a minimalist, modern garden, but for a more informal look in a garden setting, mix slab sizes.

● **GIVE PAVING A FIRM FOUNDATION** As with paths, a solid sub-base of compacted hardcore overlaid with builder's sand is essential to ensure firm and level paving. For a perfectly smooth, unbroken surface, close-set the slabs on a bed of mortar and mortar between the joints, or for a more informal look – and better drainage – bed the slabs onto the sand farther apart, leaving wider gaps that can be infilled with grit, and perhaps planted with tough creeping plants (see facing page).

▼ **Paving reflects heat,** which you can temper by siting a seating area next to water. Be sure to use paving materials with a non-slip surface. Here, a sail-like awning in natural canvas and a screen of bamboo adds to the atmosphere of a welcome oasis.

STAR PERFORMERS...

PLANTS FOR PAVING

Grow plants in cracks between paving, or even omit or lift a paver or two to form planting pockets, topping them up well with gravel to maintain a level surface.

- *Alchemilla mollis*
- *Asplenium trichomanes*
- *Erigeron karvinskianus*
- *Geranium robertianum* **'Album'**
- *Origanum vulgare*
- **Sempervivums**
- **Sisyrinchiums**
- **Thymes**
- *Viola riviniana* **Purpurea Group**

● **RE-USE MATERIALS FOR A WELL-WEATHERED EFFECT** Paving does not need to be, or even look, new. If you have an older house, recycled materials may actually suit it better. There is a thriving market in reclaimed landscaping materials. These will not always be cheaper than new materials, but they have a character and a patina that is hard to find in their modern mass-produced counterparts, and they can help give your garden an established look much more quickly.

● **CONSIDER CONCRETE FOR EASY-TO-LAY PAVING** Natural stone paving in random sizes looks beautiful but it is expensive and difficult to lay, because the slabs vary not only in size but in thickness. It is now possible to buy concrete paving in a range of slab sizes which makes a passable imitation of real stone. The uniform thickness of the slabs makes them easier to lay than stone, and some makers offer helpful diagrams of laying patterns so you know how many of each size to order, and exactly where to place each one.

● **VARY MATERIALS TO FIT IRREGULAR SHAPES** Laying paving is much easier if no cutting is involved. Combining two materials of different sizes, such as paving and bricks or setts, may offer a practical and attractive solution in an awkward space. Use the smaller-sized units such as setts to negotiate awkward corners, curves and odd shapes.

▼ **Precut slabs** that can be laid to create circular or rectangular patios of set dimensions are readily available in kit form, saving on waste and cutting.

Plant in paving joints for an established look

Small plants growing in paving cracks soften the look of new paving and work wonders at breaking up large expanses of hard surface. Plants will often seed themselves into old paving where the mortar is starting to break up, but with new paving that has been efficiently laid you may need to scrape out some of the mortar, replacing it with a mixture of compost and grit. Into this you can sow seeds or plant small rooted cuttings (best done in damp weather). It may take several attempts before the plants take hold, so be patient.

● **HELP PLANTS TO SPREAD FOR A NATURALISTIC EFFECT** Once you have established a few plants in paving, they may well spread by themselves, but you can give them a helping hand by gathering fresh seed and sowing it where you would like more plants.

Custom-built decking can be designed with voids allowing it to be fitted around mature trees and shrubs. Make sure the space is large enough to allow trunks to expand with age without chafing against the edges of the timber.

▶ **A raised decking platform,** with plants springing up to either side and climbers casting welcome shade, makes a leafy urban retreat. Make sure decking receives some sun each day to dry out any moisture.

Use stylish decking for design impact Choose a sheltered, sunny aspect for decking if you can: that way, your deck will not only seem more inviting and be used more often, but will also wear better and last longer because it will be able to dry out thoroughly in the sun. Use a partial overhead canopy or awning or a lightly climber-clad pergola if protection from the sun is needed, rather than something that will cast permanent shade over the surface.

● **TRY DECKING NEAR WATER FOR A PERFECT PARTNERSHIP** Decking looks fabulous at the edge of a pond, or even overhanging it. In these situations the understructure for the decking needs to be really well constructed: it may need to be designed to resolve varying levels and must also be strong enough to support every board adequately. Be sure to use good-quality rust-proof fixings, too.

● **ADD RAILINGS FOR A FINISHED LOOK** Even if a barrier is not necessary for safety reasons, custom-made railings can add a touch of style to your deck. Natural materials such as matching wooden posts and hemp rope work well, especially beside water. The barrier will be sturdier if the posts are part of the deck's structure, but they can be bolted on later if necessary. Try to match the wood of the deck, or stain everything to match.

● **ENSURE SAFETY WITH A NON-SLIP SURFACE** Decking isn't always the ideal material for damp climates, but using grooved boards will help prevent slippery surfaces. By using decking tiles (see below) you can create a pattern of alternating checkerboard or diagonal grooving.

● **AVOID ROT AT THE BASE OF POTS** Stand container plants on pot feet on decking, or sit them in saucers, so that the boards under the pots are not constantly damp.

● **CARE FOR TIMBER FOR A LONG-LASTING DECK** Oiling or resealing your decking from time to time will not only improve its appearance but will also make it more weather-resistant and prolong its life. Repair any damaged areas and make sure the wood is clean and dry before you start.

DECKING MATERIALS

Decking is available as grooved planks for self assembly, in a similar manner to laminate flooring, or in preformed panels or tiles. Always check that the timber used has FSC (Forest Stewardship Council) or equivalent accreditation to avoid using wood from non-sustainable sources, especially when considering tropical hardwoods.

☐ SOFTWOOD

● Widely available, softwood decking timber is obtained from commercial conifer plantations and thus is relatively inexpensive. It is not as long-lasting as hardwood decking, and must be pretreated or sealed to withstand damp. It lends itself to being painted with special decking paints and stains in a range of colours.

☐ HARDWOOD

● Durable and attractive hardwood decking may be made from ash, oak or tropical trees such as ipe and iroko. Made from woods that are naturally resistant to decay, it can be left to weather to darker or more silvery colours, or stained; for the richest finish, oil it regularly to bring out the beauty of the wood.

☐ DECKING TILES

● These preformed squares are useful for roof gardens, balconies and other places where weight is an issue, or for courtyard gardens and other small spaces where major constructon work is impractical. They are usually made from short-lived softwood, but are easily replaced individually when they show signs of age.

**PLANT LUSHLY WITH
COOLING FOLIAGE TO MAKE
A SANCTUARY FROM THE
HEAT OF THE CITY**

Rock, stone and gravel

NATURAL STONE IS THE KEY ELEMENT in some of the most attractive and distinctive garden styles. Use it to create the naturalistic look of a coastal, Mediterranean or desert planting, or the studied formality of a Japanese garden – or update the traditional garden rockery with an alpine bed studded with jewel-like plants.

▲ **Stone absorbs and reflects heat,** making it a natural partner for desert plants such as yuccas and agaves. The thick, smooth, greyish (or 'glaucous') leaves of such plants are perfectly adapted for spells of drought.

▶ **A looser style of planting** is possible in a gravel garden than in a traditional border: the thick layer of gravel mulch allows plants to be set further apart without a serious weed problem developing.

Gardening with gravel

Create a practical but plant-friendly surface

More affordable and easier to lay than paving, and requiring a fraction of the work of a lawn, gravels and shingle make attractive, practical garden surfacing. To make a stylish gravel garden, extend the gravel layer to cover not only paths but planting areas such as beds and borders, too. It will act as a mulch that helps to retain soil moisture in dry soils, and will eventually work into the ground to lighten heavy soils.

● **EXTEND THE THEME TO INSPIRE NEW PLANTINGS** Using the same material over an entire garden, or perhaps just part of a larger garden, has a wonderfully unifying effect that will suggest and inspire new schemes using plants that will flourish in this setting.

Adapt your planting to enhance the style

Gravel gardens look at their best when plants are not tightly packed, as in a traditional border. Space the plants more widely to create a sparser, more naturalistic look, almost as if the plants have seeded themselves in their positions. Think about the arrangement of coastal plants on a shingle beach, or in a dry river bed, to achieve the look.

● **CHOOSE PLANTS THAT WILL THRIVE AND LOOK GOOD TOO** Plants that like hot, dry conditions grow well in a gravel garden, benefiting from the heat-reflecting properties of the stone and from the free drainage around the base of their stems. Be sure to include some bold specimens of statuesque, architectural plants such as yuccas or the furry grey spires of *Verbascum bombyciferum*. Highly cultivated, showy flowering plants often look out of place: instead, opt for tougher-looking, silvery plants such as sea-hollies, thrifts, wiry Mediterranean herbs and grasses.

● **EDIT YOUR PLANTINGS FOR BEST EFFECT** Plants that self-seed [see p.114] do a great job of enhancing the scattered, random effect that is key to this style. Look out for self-sown seedlings: if they are well-placed, let them grow; if not, hoe them off or carefully lift and pot them up. Grow them on over the summer and plant out in autumn.

● **PLANT SMALL SPRING BULBS FOR EARLY COLOUR** Crocuses, scillas, chionodoxas, muscari, small alliums and many less well-known but delightful species tulips are all worth trying in a gravel area. Gravel is the ideal medium for a dwarf bulbs: many plants of this type begin their growth cycle in winter, when the ground is damp, then flower in spring and become dormant in summer so that drought has no effect on them. Some, such as tulips, positively enjoy a summer baking so free-draining gravel is perfect for them.

Consider the practicalities
A covering of geotextile fabric under a shingle or gravel layer is sometimes recommended as a weed suppressant, but think carefully about the pros and cons before taking this route. It will make it harder for the loose stones to bed down and make a firm surface where you walk through the garden, and patches of the fabric often become visible at the edges or where the gravel has become thin.

● **FIND THE BEST WEED CONTROL SOLUTION FOR YOU** Geotextile fabric will help suppress perennial weeds, but they can make their way through openings cut for plants, and annuals will still seed into the stones. A thick layer of gravel, especially when compacted by foot traffic, should keep weed problems sufficiently light on a small area of gravel; just hand-weed or hoe from time to time, raking the gravel even where necessary, or for larger areas an excellent solution is a propane-powered wand (or 'flame-weeder') to burn off weed seedlings.

● **DON'T LET GRAVEL TRAVEL** Avoid bringing a surface of loose gravel right up to doors leading into the house. If you do, little pieces of stone will inevitably be picked up on shoes and be trodden indoors, so install a buffer area of paving between gravel and the doorstep.

STAR PERFORMERS...

PLANTS FOR GRAVEL GARDENS

Choose plants that tolerate dry spells, and your gravel garden will be easy to maintain. Include grasses to create an atmospheric, wind-blown look.

● *Aeonium* 'Schwarzkopf'
● Alliums
● Armeria (thrift)
● *Astelia chathamica*
● *Crambe maritima* (seakale)
● *Eremurus* (foxtail lilies)
● *Eryngiums* (sea-hollies)
● *Onopordum acanthium*
● Pennisetum
● Phormiums
● Poppies
● Rock roses *(Cistus)*
● Scabious
● Sedums
● *Stipa tenuissima*
● Verbascums
● *Verbena bonariensis*
● Yuccas

Using rock and stone in the garden

Be inspired by styles old and new Stone looks beautiful paired with plants, and you can use it in both naturalistic and highly stylised ways to enhance the garden. There are so many sources from which to take inspiration, from classical grottoes and Oriental courtyard gardens through 19th-century imitations of alpine landscapes to contemporary slate obelisks or faux millstones.

USE BEAUTIFUL WEATHERED STONE TO CREATE NATURAL, HARMONIOUS GARDEN SCULPTURES

● **PROTECT NATURAL RESOURCES TO GARDEN MORE SUSTAINABLY** Natural stone is a precious and expensive material these days, and may have been transported many miles. Choose local stone if you can, and consider flint and slate as well as the more widely available sandstone and limestone. Try to establish the environmental and ethical credentials of any stone that you buy. It's a good idea to seek out recycled rockery or building stones from an architectural salvage company; look online for possible suppliers. Another option is to make imitation stones from tufa, a mixture of cement, sand and leafmould.

▼ **Reminiscent of Buddhist stupas,** these little piles of graduated stones form a tiny vignette beside a path. Individualistic touches such as this are the secret of some of the most distinctive gardens.

Create your own garden art You don't need to have serious artistic aspirations, or spend a small fortune, to create your own eye-catching garden focal point. You can make your own original contemporary garden sculptures. They could be as simple as a carefully crafted stack of slates or 'still-life' arrangement of boulders, washed cobbles or flints. Choosing the right position for a feature such as this is the key to its success. Use natural materials, site them for effect and keep things simple, and you can't go far wrong.

● **COLLECT INTERESTING MATERIALS TO PRODUCE ORIGINAL EFFECTS** Keep a lookout for suitable oddments such as slates and pieces of building stone and think of intriguing ways to display them. You should not take stones from beaches, but beach-combing for driftwood and other interesting pieces of flotsam can be productive.

● **CHANGE YOUR EXHIBITS FOR VARIETY** Improvised sculptures don't have to be permanent: you can take them apart and create something different whenever you have a new idea.

Make a Japanese feature Stone and gravel are key elements in the Japanese garden tradition. Materials and plants are meticulously selected and positioned in a careful composition designed to inspire a contemplative state of mind and reflect the

natural world, even in a tiny space. A proper understanding of the Japanese
tradition and its symbolism deserves committed study, but borrowing ideas from
the Japanese style can work well even if you know little about it, especially in
small urban gardens and other confined spaces.

● **CAPTURE THE MOOD** Important features in Japanese design include a minimalist
absence of clutter, and carefully considered siting of a small number of plants
and features. Focus on sculptural and textural qualities in both plants and
materials: favourite set-pieces include contrasting partnerships such as large,
weathered natural stones with immaculate gravel, or foliage with still water.

● **USE PLANTS APPROPRIATE TO THE STYLE** Typical planting in a small, enclosed
garden might include clump-forming types of mosses, dwarf evergreen shrubs
(perhaps clipped) and Japanese maples. Add a clump of coloured-stemmed
bamboos as a backdrop [see p.111], or a screen made from split-bamboo panels.

Display the beauty of alpine plants
An expertly built rock garden
in the right place can be a wonderful feature, but a traditional rockery is hard
work to create, and can very easily look incongruous and old-fashioned in an
ordinary garden. If you are interested in rock plants – and many are exceptionally
beautiful – a raised alpine bed can be a much better way to grow a number of
small treasures in a limited space. On an even smaller scale, you can easily create
a miniature alpine garden in a large container such as a trough or sink.

● **CREATE IDEAL CONDITIONS FOR ALPINES** Many alpines are very drought-tolerant,
and the base of a south-facing wall or the edge of a sunny patio can be a good
location. They thrive on sunshine and good drainage but like to have access to
cool soil beneath rocks or gravel where their root systems can expand. Their chief
enemy is waterlogging in winter, but using a free-draining medium in the bed or
container, such as soil mixed with horticultural grit, will help prevent this.

▲ **Raked gravel** surrounds
craggy boulders in this striking
interpretation of a Japanese garden,
in which beautiful plant forms take
precedence over colourful flowers.

▼ **A tumbling rock fall on a slope,**
carefully staged for a naturalistic
look, is an ideal home for small
alpine plants in glowing colours.

Ponds and water features

WATER WILL ENLIVEN ANY GARDEN by introducing reflected light, movement and sound. Whether you have a small courtyard or a large garden with expanses of lawn, there is a water feature to suit your space as well as your budget, and there's a huge variety of beautiful aquatic plants with which to stock it.

WATER ADDS A TOUCH OF MAGIC AND A SENSE OF RELAXATION TO ANY OUTDOOR SPACE

Designing ponds and water features

Plan water schemes for success

A large pond or water feature is a major project that will have a considerable impact on your garden, so it's important to think your scheme through very carefully before you start. Take time to consider what you want from your water feature. This could be a comfortable place for sitting and relaxing with an area of decking or paving, or a more natural-looking feature to attract birds and other wildlife into your garden.

- **CREATE FORMAL ELEGANCE WITH A LARGE POOL** A good position will be crucial to success, both visually and practically: an open, sunny site is far better than one overhung by trees. Construction – usually of concrete blockwork walls and a concrete base – is probably a job for the professionals, but if you have the space the effect of a large expanse of still, reflecting water can be breathtaking.
- **BUILD A RAISED POND FOR EASY MAINTENANCE** A rectangular, square or circular pond raised up from ground level with an overhanging edge that is wide enough to sit on makes a lovely garden feature that is eye-catching as well as practical. With no plants around the edges to care for, maintenance is straightforward.
- **ENJOY A SENSE OF TRANQUILLITY WITH A RILL** These slow-moving 'streams' contained within narrow channels are a traditional feature of formal gardens. They can work well in smaller spaces when combined with restrained planting and introduce gentle soothing movement to a garden.
- **TRANSFORM A SMALL SPACE WITH WATER** A wall-mounted spout and basin or letterbox-style waterfall will add soothing sounds of water to a town or city courtyard garden and muffle traffic noise. Position a small water feature close to a window if possible, so that you can appreciate it from indoors.

Enhance your water feature

Plan adequate access to new ponds and water features, and include space for seating so you can make the most of the opportunities for relaxation that water offers, and the effects you can achieve by understanding and exploiting its visual properties to best effect in your space.

- **CREATE ILLUSIONS WITH WATER** Still water brings reflected light and an impression of space into a small garden. A pool with a black liner reflects light best and you can also add a special non-toxic black dye (in powder form) to the water for an even more reflective mirror-like surface – although you will need to be scrupulous about scooping out any floating debris to maintain the effect.
- **CHOOSE THE RIGHT SURROUND TO MAXIMISE LIGHT** Use light-coloured materials, such as pale paving, for the surround of a pool to enhance the illusion of light and space. Reflective surfaces such as stainless steel also work very well in contemporary spaces or you can paint the faces and edges of a raised concrete pool in white or another light colour for a cool, relaxing effect.

◄ **Cascading water** adds movement without losing as much water through evaporation and drift as a fountain. It will still add some moisture to the air, keeping poolside plants lush and green. A pump recirculates the water from the lower to the upper reservoir.

▼ **The architectural or sculptural qualities of a water feature** can be as important as the water; this sphere has inspired the bed and path that surrounds it. A moving-water feature that looks as good when switched off as when switched on is doubly valuable.

● **ADD IMMEDIATE INTEREST WITH A CROSSING** Adding a crossing to even a small body of water brings interest and excitement to a garden. A bridge made of a simple, stout hardwood plank securely fixed at both ends is a straightforward option – or consider stepping-stones if the water is shallow. For a larger pond you could incorporate a bridge of timber boards, complete with a decorative handrail.

● **SAVE MONEY BY USING FREE ENERGY** Solar-powered pumps are improving all the time, and using one to power your water feature saves on the expense and upheaval involved in laying mains electricity as well as being more environmentally sustainable. Many pump and fountain kits now come with a solar-charged battery so that your fountain won't stop as soon as the sun goes in.

Make a family-friendly water feature
Water fascinates children, but toddlers can drown in a very small amount of it. If you have very young children or grandchildren, a bubble-jet feature is a safe choice and makes a fantastic focal point. Features of this type have a jet of water spilling over a millstone or other large stone, or a pile of pebbles, with a safely concealed reservoir beneath from where the water is recycled. The water reservoir may be covered by pebbles (see below), or take the form of a heavy-duty plastic tub sunk into the ground.

● **PROVIDE A MINI-POND FOR YOUNGSTERS** Even though it is wise to wait until children are older before building any kind of large pond, a mini-pond in a

EXPERT KNOW HOW

MAKING A PEBBLE FOUNTAIN

Small pump kits allow you to create your own, individualistic recirculating water feature or bubble fountain. The pump may be powered by a safe, low-voltage current that runs via a transformer from an indoor socket [see p.69], or with a lead running to a small solar panel placed in a nearby but hidden sunny spot.

1 Place the pump in your chosen vessel (here a glazed ceramic bowl). Run the lead out to the side then use bricks to make a support for the grille: a round kettle barbecue grille will be ideal here.

2 Feed the hose through the grille, cut it so that 1–2in (2.5–5cm) protrudes, then fit a 15cm (6in) rigid pipe to it. Stack pebbles to hold the pipe upright, then add more to cover the grille.

large container, such as a half-barrel, is a great idea for youngsters, especially if it attracts frogs or other aquatic creatures to watch. Consider fitting it with a detachable metal grille across the surface for extra safety.

Making a garden pond

Get the shape right Ponds may take any shape but unless you garden on a particular kind of clay soil, all will require a waterproof lining. Rigid liners are available in geometric as well as standard pool designs such as a kidney shape, but can be tricky to install because you must contour the hole precisely to their shape. A flexible sheet liner allows you to be much more imaginative with your pond and its planting possibilities. Before building a pond, have all the materials and tools to hand and make arrangements to deal with the spoil that is dug out of the hole.

● **CREATE A NATURAL POND** A haven for wildlife, a natural pond needs only occasional maintenance once it is established. Provided that you achieve a good balance of planting and other pondlife (see overleaf) to keep the water oxygenated and pure, there is no need to install and maintain a pump and filter, so the whole operation is more straightforward than a built water feature.

● **MAKE YOUR POND LINER LAST** Good-quality butyl liner is the best choice of flexible liner if you don't want a standard-shaped pool. Cheaper materials may deteriorate more quickly and are easily punctured. But even butyl can be torn, so protect your liner right from the start and it will last much longer. Once you have dug the hole for the pond, remove any visible stones, and line the hole with an even layer of soft sand and then cover with purpose-made pond underlay. To

▲ **This large, contemporary pond** has a sharply defined raised edge that makes an impromptu seat. The circular shape is echoed by the domed fountain spray, the arched seating area and the mound-forming plants set in light-reflecting gravel.

▼ **Stepping stones** that appear to float on the water's surface are a striking feature. They must be set on sturdily constructed blockwork plinths with an overhang on each side to create the illusion.

calculate how much liner you need to buy, measure the length of the hole and add twice the depth plus a 50cm (20in) overlap, then measure the width, again adding twice the depth plus a 50cm (20in) overlap.

● **KEEP LINERS OUT OF SIGHT** Use a spirit level to ensure edges are level when you dig the hole, to ensure that uneven areas of pond liner are not visible above the water level. Conceal the edges of the liner with turf, paving or large flat stones bedded on waterproof mortar, or with a 'beach' of loose pebbles or slate paddles.

● **VARY THE DEPTH TO BENEFIT POND-DWELLERS AND PLANTS** Dig your pond with at least one deep area, down to 60cm (2ft) or so, to protect water-dwelling creatures from extremes of temperature. Ensure that at least some of the edges slope very gently so that birds, and mammals such as hedgehogs, can easily reach the water to have a drink. For added planting interest, create shelves at different depths so you can grow a range of beautiful aquatic plants of different types.

Set up your planting scheme For a pond to attract wildlife and

establish its own, well-balanced ecosystem you need to furnish it with a range of plants: some that like to root in deep water, some for shallow water, and some more functional oxygenating pondweeds to live in the water itself. Always check the depth range for each plant (see facing page, and plant labels) before you decide where to sink it in the pond: most waterlilies thrive in the deepest part, but plant arum lilies on a shelf up to 30cm (12in) deep.

● **PLANT IN SPRING FOR BEST RESULTS** Late spring onwards, when water temperatures have started to rise, is the best time to put in acquatic and marginal plants. They will establish and grow away rapidly at this time of year.

● **GET WEEDS WORKING FIRST TO CLEAN THE WATER** Oxygenating weed is best added at an early stage (you simply drop in weighted bunches) so that it can establish and start doing its valuable work. Choose a native variety: in many countries

▼ **Plentiful planting** soon makes a pond look established and will attract a variety of wildlife. Create 'corridors' of planting that link the pond to other, densely planted areas so creatures can use these routes to approach the water.

foreign species of pondweed bought unwittingly by gardeners have escaped from garden ponds into the wild, choking waterways.

● **MAKE DEEP-WATER PLANTS EASY TO MANAGE** Use purpose-made aquatic baskets to anchor the roots of deep-water plants on the bottom of the pond: these can then simply be lifted when you need to divide the plants. Fill the baskets with special aquatic compost – potting mixes are too rich and will promote weed growth and algae – and hold it down with a top covering of grit.

● **INCLUDE NATIVE PLANTS TO ATTRACT WILDLIFE** Some native aquatic plants are just as beautiful as foreign exotics and will attract bees and butterflies. Choose varieties to suit your locality and the conditions you can offer: damp-loving plants are the obvious ones to grow close to the edges of a pond. Native wildflowers also look stunning planted around natural ponds.

Stay on top of pond maintenance If

your pond does become clogged with weeds, such as blanket weed, remove it from the surface by using a long stick and twirling the weed around it. Duckweed is easily scooped out with a rake or a child's fishing net. To prevent algae developing in your pond and turning the water murky, fish out fallen leaves and other plant debris promptly.

● **KEEP WATER LEVELS AND PLANTS UNDER CONTROL** A natural pond requires only occasional but nevertheless essential maintenance. Make sure the water level does not drop too much in dry weather and top up with rainwater from a water butt if possible, rather than with tap water. Overgrown planting may need to be thinned out in late summer or early autumn but leave any plant debris beside the pond for a day or two to give pondlife a chance to return to the water.

● **PREPARE FOR WINTER** A deep natural pond will seldom freeze completely and oxygenating plants can still work beneath a layer of ice, provided they are receiving light. Natural ponds can, on the whole, be left alone. Fountains and pumps, on the other hand, need attention well before winter frosts are likely, so lift and drain the equipment and clean and store any removable components.

DEEP-WATER PLANTS

This group of plants thrives at a depth of 30–90cm (12–36in). It includes most waterlilies, which have exquisite flowers in a range of colours from white to shades of pink and lemon-yellow.

- ◀ *Nymphaea* 'Froebelii' (pink waterlily)
- ● *Nymphaea* 'Marliacea Chromatella' (lemon-yellow waterlily)
- ● *Nymphaea* 'Walter Pagels' (white waterlily)
- ● *Zantedeschia aethiopica* (white arum lily)

MARGINAL PLANTS

With their roots and the lower part of their stems submerged, these plants grow best in water that is 7–15cm (3–6in) deep.

- ● *Butomus umbellatus* (flowering rush)
- ◀ *Caltha palustris* (kingcup or marsh marigold)
- ● *Iris laevigata* (Japanese water iris)
- ● *Iris versicolor* (blue flag)
- ● *Mentha aquatica* (water mint)

BOG PLANTS

These damp-loving plants flourish in wet soil and are good for boggy patches in the garden as well as for pond margins.

- ● *Filipendula rubra* (queen of the prairies)
- ● *Geum rivale* (water avens)
- ● *Iris sibirica* (Siberian iris)
- ◀ *Primula denticulata* (drumstick primula)
- ● *Valeriana officinalis* (common valerian)

Garden lighting

WELL-DESIGNED LIGHTING CAN DO MUCH MORE than simply enable you to use your garden after dark. It can lend a whole new dimension to the garden, creating changes of mood and emphasis that make it feel like a completely different space. Whether hi-tech or low-tech, use lighting creatively to discover a new side to your garden.

Transform your outdoor evenings

Choose the right lighting system
Outdoor lighting ranges from simple, cable-free solar-powered lamps dotted around the garden to fully integrated systems wired directly into your mains supply (see facing page). To choose the one that is best for you, you need to consider not only the effect you want to achieve, but also the budget you have available and how much – or little – disruption you are prepared to tolerate in order to put the system in place.

▼ **Uplight the foliage** of airy-branched trees and shrubs and the plant itself will appear to glow. White light is the best source for a contemporary, clean effect.

● **INSTALL MAINS-POWERED LIGHTING FOR A DESIGNER LOOK** If you use your outdoor lighting regularly and want to create the most stunning effects, it may be worth calling in the professionals to install – and even design – a mains-powered system. It's far easier to design and install a major lighting system as part of the garden construction process, so make this a key consideration in any plans for building a new garden, or remodelling your existing one.

● **CREATE A PARTY MOOD WITH LOW-VOLTAGE LIGHTS** Simple and safe plug-in low-voltage lighting is widely available from DIY and homeware centres in a variety of forms, from single spotlights to a series of softly glowing lamps or strings of pretty fairy lights. They are not powerful, but can be used to produce a soft, ambient light ideal for outdoor entertaining, with single spots used to illuminate garden features or to make life easier for the barbecue cook.

● **TAKE THE LOW-TECH ROUTE FOR SIMPLICITY** Solar-powered lighting needs no outside power source and solar units are improving all the time in terms of design, durability and output. It produces a gentle glow that makes it perfect for waymarking paths and steps around the garden, or perhaps lighting a small water feature or patio plant. Candlelight, of course, is as magical as ever and is a simple but effective form of garden lighting that needs no power at all.

WHAT TYPE OF GARDEN LIGHTING?

The simpler the system, the easier and cheaper it will be to set in place. If installing permanent, mains-powered lighting, consider the effect of your planned scheme on neighbouring properties. Ensure that any motion-sensor-triggered security lighting you have won't clash with, and spoil, gentler lighting schemes.

☐ **MAINS VOLTAGE**

A lighting system wired directly into your mains supply must only be fitted by a qualified electrician. It gives the most effective and professional-looking results, will be reliable and durable, and can be fitted with sensors and timers, but it is expensive both to install and to modify, should you decide to redesign your garden.

☐ **LOW-VOLTAGE**

Easy-to-install low-voltage systems run through a transformer plugged into the mains indoors, and are manufactured to be safe for garden use, but they must still be carefully and correctly wired to ensure that nothing can go wrong. Never try to bolt on extra lights to ready-made kits; you risk overloading the transformer to hazardous levels.

☐ **SOLAR-POWERED**

Solar-powered lights are not powerful, but are inexpensive and versatile: you can position and reposition one anywhere where the solar panel will receive sufficient sunlight to charge it. Keep them clean for maximum light input and output. Units fitted with brighter, long-lasting LED bulbs are more efficient.

Use lighting to create atmosphere Garden lighting needs to be much subtler than the flat, bright wash of light created by security lighting. Creatively planned illumination to highlight chosen plant shapes, hard landscaping textures or water features is what makes an inspirational scene.

● **ANGLE LIGHTS FOR IMPACT AND INTEREST** Think of the dramatic effect of low, late-afternoon sunlight on plants such as grasses or bamboos in autumn, and it's easy to see that the angle from which light falls can make a huge difference to its effect. The flat overhead light of the midday sun is not flattering to plants and garden features; slanting light is immediately more interesting as its bright highlights and long shadows create a sense of mystery and reveal textures.

● **EXPERIMENT WITH FLASHLIGHTS TO PLACE LIGHTS EFFECTIVELY** Save time and, possibly, costly mistakes by deciding where your lights should be before any installation begins. Experiment by holding powerful torches in different places in the garden and at different angles. Light a tree or sculpture from beneath, or flood a wall with light from the base or the side. Study the effects from different parts of the garden, and from the house windows, until you have a plan that works for you.

● **BE CAREFUL WITH COLOUR** Sometimes coloured lights may be what is needed for particular theatrical effects, but they can very easily look garish and spoil the magic. 'Less is more' applies to lighting just as much as to many other design decisions.

● **CONCEAL LIGHT FITTINGS TO CREATE MYSTERY** Garden lighting is usually more effective and attractive if the light source is concealed or at least inconspicuous: a bright light source in the field of vision tends to make eyes less sensitive to detail in shadowy areas, and visible hardware can easily destroy the magic of a sensitively lit garden.

▼ **Solar-powered lamps** that automatically illuminate at dusk are a great choice for safety lighting, indicating the routes of paths and, especially, the position of steps around the garden.

BLOOMING BEDS AND BORDERS

2

Combine plants and colours with confidence and you'll have flower-packed plantings that will be the envy of all. Discover how to boost your beds and borders with a wealth of advice and handy hints that will help you to grow the most perfect perennials, beautiful bulbs, brilliant bedding and much, much more.

Setting out borders

FLOURISHING BED AND BORDER PLANTINGS packed with colour and interest make a garden special. Personal taste and your garden conditions will govern your plant choice, but there is a wealth of tips and techniques that will help you arrange your plants in pleasing and successful ways, and keep maintenance to a minimum.

Plan your plantings for success

Map out your ideas A really attention-grabbing border needs a properly thought out planting scheme. For a successful arrangement, you need to know the heights, colours and flowering times of the plants you have in mind, and this is where a scale drawing is useful – preferably coloured and with flowering times

AIM TO CREATE PLEASING VIEWS OF PLANTINGS FROM ALL ANGLES, NOT JUST FROM THE FRONT

▼ **Tiered narrow borders** flank a path here that leads to the wider garden. The effect is of curtains being drawn to reveal the vista beyond, inviting exploration.

marked on it. Garden design programs for your computer can be useful if you are unsure of your draughtsmanship, but even a sketched plan will help you create new borders and remodel existing ones, and organise your planting ideas.

● **THINK ABOUT SIZE** Big as you can is the rule for really breathtaking border designs, so grab as much space as you dare without making paths uncomfortably narrow. Try to avoid creating shallow, straight borders around a central lawn, as this gives a rather mean, ungenerous impression. If your children have outgrown the lawn as a play area, commandeer some of that space for plantings; pave or lay gravel over what remains, and you'll never need to mow and edge again.

● **THINK ABOUT SCALE** The dimensions of your bed or border will determine the types of plants you need to stock it. Most successful plantings rely on a framework of structural plants, or focal points, around which plants of lesser stature are arranged. A really large border can accommodate small trees as its structural plants, and a small bed could be built around tall perennials, but in most gardens, shrubs fulfil that function. Choose 'double-duty' shrubs that have not only a flowering period, but also interesting foliage [see p.91] to act as colourful,

MAKING A PLANTING PLAN

Creating a planting plan for a new bed or border will enable you to realise your ideas in a more successful way and calculate how many plants of each type you will need to buy, especially if planting a border with drifts of perennials, as here.

1 Note the planting area's aspect (sun or shade), what the soil type is and whether it is sheltered or not; then make a 'wish list' of plants you want to grow – tall, medium-height and small – that will thrive in the border's conditions.

2 Measure your planting area and transfer its dimensions to squared paper.

3 Start by adding any big, structural single plants (top right, **A** and **C**). Fill out the back row with blocks of your other tall plants (**B** and **D**).

4 Start to add drifts of medium-height plants (**E–I**), perhaps bringing a couple towards the front (**E** and **H**) for more interesting contours.

5 Fill in the front row with groups of your low-growing plants (**J**, **K** and **L**).

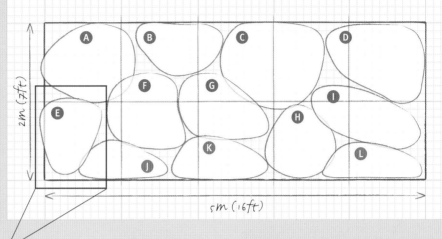

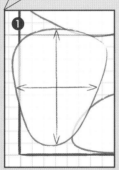

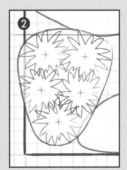

6 Work out how many plants you need to buy (left). Calculate the rough area of each block or drift (**1**). Check the mature spread of the plant you want in that spot, and work out how many will fit in once fully grown (**2**). Choose young perennials for economy, and fill gaps with annuals, or buy well-grown plants for quick impact – but be prepared to divide them sooner.

leafy foils for flowering perennials and annuals. Small conifers with a strongly vertical growth habit, such as *Juniperus scopulorum* 'Skyrocket', make striking statements without shading out plants around them.

● **THINK ABOUT ACCESS** Unless you have very small planting areas, you will need to get in among your plants to maintain them. At the back of a large border, remember to leave space for access between the hedge, wall or other background and the first groups of plants. Try setting a few paving slabs into beds and borders as stepping stones, or create mini-paths through a large planting with wide ribbons of chipped bark.

Make it work for you To enjoy your borders, you must not make yourself a slave to them. Consider how much time you have to spend in the garden, and, more importantly, how much of that time you want to give over to gardening. If you love rearranging your schemes and find a plant sale irresistible, then pack your border with perennials and annual plants. Close planting will smother out weeds, so you'll be able to spend more time tending the plants you love and less

time hoeing and hand-weeding. For plantings that take less time to maintain, use more shrubs and evergreen foliage plants. These require less cutting back, deadheading and general tidying up than flowering perennials and bedding.

Inject your own personality
Beware of overstyling your border plans to suit whatever is the fashion of the moment. Just as 'trendy' interior design schemes can pall over the years, you may lose interest in heavily stylised plantings. Choices that reflect your own tastes and personality are much more likely to remain pleasing. Extend this not only to plants but to features in your borders. Choose ornamental supports – arches, obelisks and trellises – that suit your style: plain and simple for a modern look, or more ornate for traditional plantings. Select garden ornaments and sculptures to set among your plants that will give you lasting pleasure, just as you would choose a piece of art for the home.

▲ **A tracing-paper overlay** reveals the structure of this border. Placing the tall plants at the back and layering the planting in tiers down to ground level allows each plant to be appreciated, and creates a lovely, well-stocked vista looking along the border.

● **SEEK INSPIRATION, NOT DETAIL, AT THE BIG FLOWER SHOWS** Many of the plants will have been grown in artificial conditions to be at their peak at just the right time, and you will find it hard to reproduce some planting combinations. To find perfect plant pairings and groupings for your borders, visit open gardens in your area, and be sure to ask the owners or guides for the names of plants that catch your eye. They will probably volunteer some useful cultivation tips, too.

Arrange plants by height
A border needs structure – its tall plants at the back, gradually coming down in height to low-growing ones at the front. In a bed that can be seen from all sides, the tall plants need to go in the centre. In a long border, you could create a series of pyramid-shaped forms or bays, rising and falling along the length of the planting.

● **ADD NATURALISTIC TOUCHES** Don't be too regimented in graduating your plants by height, or your border will take on a 'stadium' effect. Here and there, bring a tall plant forward among those of medium height, and a medium-sized plant further towards the front to give interesting contours to the planting. If you bring forward light, airy plants such as gaura and gypsophila they will not obscure the plants behind.

● **USE PLANT SUPPORTS TO INCREASE HEIGHT** Climbing plants trained over free-standing supports such as pillars, rustic wigwams and obelisks [see Roses, p.119] will add height and add variety to your planted 'landscape'.

● **BE PREPARED TO ADJUST YOUR BORDER** for a year or two after planting to get the effect absolutely right. Expected heights may be different in your garden conditions, and colours can vary slightly according to the acidity or alkalinity of the soil, so what seemed exactly right at the garden centre may need moving elsewhere when it flowers in your border. Wait until autumn to move plants around and they will establish well over winter and spring to grow away the next season.

▲ **Traditional herbaceous plants** contrast with ultra-modern hard landscaping, colour blocking and formally pruned shapes. Some of the most dazzling plantings, like this one, play with our style expectations.

Make stunning plant groupings
However tempting displays at garden centres, shows and nurseries may be, resist the urge to pick up one of everything you like, or your borders will look fussy. Your planting will look much more coherent and confident if you buy more plants of fewer varieties, and arrange them in groups or larger drifts. Buy in odd numbers if you want to create a naturalistic effect; it's much easier to make a natural-looking group with three, five or seven plants rather than with two, four or six.

● **CREATE RECURRING PATTERNS THAT ARE EASY ON THE EYE** Try repeating the same plant, or the same combination of two or three varieties, along the length of a border; this adds a restful air of continuity and rhythm.

● **REMEMBER TEXTURE AND FORM** is as much a part of visual appeal as flowers. Varying leaf shapes and sizes creates a tapestry of interest, so consider bold-leaved plants like hostas, crambe, *Viburnum rhytidophyllum*, *Cotinus* 'Grace', ferns, phormium and yucca. Where space is no problem, groups of grasses contrast well with shrubs that have variegated foliage and the larger-leaved forms of hosta.

Build in seasonal interest
Timing adds another dimension to a planting design [see also pp.90–99]. Spread plants with varying flowering times evenly throughout your bed or border so that you don't have all the early-flowerers in one part, and all the later ones grouped together elsewhere. Position plants flowering later in the season next to those with an early flush and no repeat; to continue a splash of yellow, for example, place heleniums near doronicums; when the latter have finished and been cut back, the heleniums will fill out and hide the gaps.

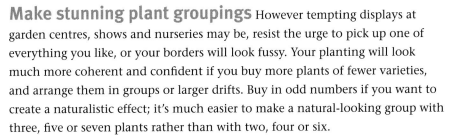

◄ **Repeat planting** creates rhythm in this contemporary border. Clumps of feathery deschampsia grass alternate with the pompon heads of the tall biennial *Angelica gigas*, and a wide band of oregano contains the planting at the front.

Backgrounds and foregrounds

Set the stage with a great background A good backdrop will perfect an already stunning border. It will not only create shelter and screening, but may also give you an opportunity to add climbing plants. A sunny wall will reflect heat back into a border, enabling you to grow plants that thrive in warm conditions. A well-maintained fence also provides a good backdrop; there are many styles to choose from to complement your planting style. Curved or trellis tops are especially attractive when fronted by a border in full growth. If you're dividing a garden with a bed, make a support of trellis panels – it looks less solid and allows the flowers of climbers trained on it to be seen from both sides.

● **GREEN-UP VERTICAL SURFACES WITH CLIMBERS** Climbing plants [see pp.164–9] will transform a drab fence or wall while adding extra height to a border. Most blend in well with shrubs, perennials and even bedding plants; those with good foliage and unfussy flowers, such as parthenocissus, lonicera (honeysuckle), akebia, actinidia and trachelospermum, set off brightly coloured perennial borders most effectively, while climbing roses, clematis and other long-flowering climbers will fill in the gaps between taller shrub plantings from spring to the end of autumn.

● **KEEP HEDGES PLAIN AND FORMAL** A neat, well-maintained hedge makes a superb backcloth to any planting. Choose species that don't detract from the border itself with, for example, variegation or splashes of colour on their leaves. Yew, green beech, green privet, Lawson cypress and holly all work well.

EXPERT KNOW HOW

CUTTING OUT A CURVED BORDER EDGE

Although laying a trail of sand is a good method for marking out bed edges, a hosepipe is more convenient and quick to reposition if changes are required. Ideally, choose a warm, sunny day for setting out curves with a hose; the heat will make it more pliable and easily manipulated into the desired outline.

Lay the hose flat on the ground and adjust it until you are satisfied with the shape, then peg it down (**1**). In a lawn, cut out the edge against the hose with a sharp spade or edging iron (**2**), then slice off the turf with a sharp-edged spade. Stack the slabs of unwanted turf face-down in an out-of-the-way corner – they will rot down to make a good soil improver.

Create front-of-house appeal The shapes used to define the edges of your beds contribute greatly to the overall look. Neat edging suggests control and formality, but also really brings out the elegance of a sweeping curve or precisely cut corner. Alternatively, choose plants that will spill over the edges of a bed to emphasise a romantic, billowing look.

● **USE STRAIGHT LINES AND GEOMETRIC SHAPES FOR A FORMAL LOOK** Symmetry between bed shapes and plantings can also look effortlessly stylish. Two parallel, straight-edged borders in which the plants mirror each other, separated by a wide grass or gravel path, is a classic but still beautiful way of leading you from one part of a garden to an area beyond.

● **SHAPE INFORMAL BORDERS WITH VOLUPTUOUS CURVES** to flatter a naturalistic planting style. Make the curves of your border generous and undulating to add interest as its depth graduates from narrow to deep.

● **AVOID FIDDLY SHAPES** because they will be tricky to plant up and maintain. Sharp angles protruding into a lawn are also difficult to mow around, and will soon become annoying to walk around too. Wiggly edges are also to be avoided: once plants at the front of the border start to grow, it will be hard to tell if the border edge is supposed to be curving, or just straight but badly cared-for.

● **SPEND LESS TIME ON EDGING** Formal borders edged with box or lavender look fantastic, but need work to keep the effect immaculate. Instead, use plants that are naturally low and neat in habit (see right) – or edge with paving or bricks to keep beds and borders well defined.

STAR PERFORMERS...

PLANTS FOR EDGING BORDERS

Form a low hedge of neat, densely growing plants if you want to give borders a clean, defined look. To enhance an informal style, choose plants with a spreading habit to soften and blur the distinction between plantings and paths or paving.

NEAT EDGING PLANTS

- ● Bergenia
- ● *Euonymus fortunei* 'Silver Pillar'
- ◀ French marigolds *(Tagetes)*
- ● Liriope
- ● Miniature rose 'Baby Masquerade'
- ● *Potentilla fruticosa* 'Manchu'
- ● *Salvia officinalis* 'Icterina'
- ● Santolina

SPREADING EDGING PLANTS

- ● Aubretia
- ● Arabis
- ● *Campanula portenschlagiana*
- ● Helianthemums
- ● *Lysimachia nummularia* 'Aurea'
- ● *Persicaria vacciniifolia*
- ● *Phlox subulata*
- ◀ Thymes
- ● Stachys (lamb's ears)

Using colour in design

Combine colours with confidence The colours you use in your borders or beds are entirely a matter of personal choice, so go ahead and indulge your own tastes. Most colours in nature work well together, and in fact it is surprisingly difficult to put plants together in a way that isn't pleasing to the eye. The only combinations many professional designers avoid, simply because they have a less than restful effect, are blue-reds with vermilion-reds and some oranges with purples. You can still use plants with flowers in these colours if they bloom at

▶ **Sometimes the simplest** colour schemes are the most effective. These bands of blue cornflowers and orange marigolds are annual plants, easily grown from seed. The strength of the combination lies in the contrasting of two opposite or 'complementary' colours from the colour wheel (see below).

different times, of course. If in doubt about colour, study the colour wheel (below) so that you can work out colour themes and combinations you might enjoy.

● **CREATE MOODS WITH COLOUR** Think about how you use your garden, or different parts of your garden – a cheerful place for the family, a vibrant space for entertaining, or a relaxing sanctuary after a busy week. Colour greatly affects atmosphere and can be used to create specific ambiences – hot reds, oranges and yellows are lively, vibrant shades that make you feel energetic and sparkling, while blues, greens, mauves and whites are tranquil, restful shades.

● **USE SHADE FOR COOL PLANTINGS** A shady border can never be as bright as one in full sun, as shade-loving plants tend to produce less colourful flowers. Turn this to your advantage by planning a border that exudes serenity and peace. Use lush foliage plants [see p.109] that will enjoy being out of the sun.

● **ADD COLOUR WHEN THE GARDEN NEEDS IT MOST** Don't forget autumn and winter. Colours may be different at these times, but can be just as striking. Bright berries and leaves that change colour add zest to an autumn planting.

Work with your hard landscaping
The exterior walls of your house, the materials that outbuildings are made of and the hard surfaces of your garden – paths, terraces, driveways and edging material – have colours and textures too. Keep in mind the colours of brick or stonework near your border, and make sure that flower and foliage colours are shown to best advantage when seen against them. Red brickwork, for example, is an ideal foil for yellow plants, but can be a disaster with some shades of red, purple and orange; cream flowers and cream-splashed leaves can look dirty against bright white masonry or woodwork.

HOW DOES IT WORK?
THE COLOUR WHEEL

Colour themes and pairings can be considered as you select your plants by using the colour wheel. Harmonising colours are those between two of the primary colours (red, yellow and blue) on the wheel. Complementary colours are opposite each other on the wheel: for example, red and green, or blue and orange. They are in contrast to one another, and when paired, are visually stimulating.

◀ **Use the colour wheel** to combine, complement and contrast colours. A hot colour, for example, from its right side adds punch to a scheme composed of the cool colours on the left.

▲ **Harmonising colours** sit close together on the wheel; if they include a bright primary colour (here red) they convey a strong but controlled mood, especially when tempered with coordinating green leaves.

▲ **Colour triads,** made by forming triangles within the wheel, give an opportunity for variety and bright contrasts. They often work well if one flower colour predominates, with the second providing accents.

USE STRONGLY
CONTRASTING
COLOURS FOR
MAXIMUM IMPACT

BEST TRUE BLUES

Blue flowers without a hint of mauve are few and far between, but these should give you rich, true colours, from aquamarine through cobalt to navy, to make your borders really vibrant.

- Agapanthus
- *Brunnera macrophylla*
- *Camassia leichtlinii*
- *Campanula lactiflora* 'Pouffe'
- *Corydalis flexuosa*
- *Delphinium* 'Lord Butler'
- *Eryngium x oliverianum*
- *Iris sibirica* 'Perry's Blue'
- ◀ *Meconopsis grandis*
- *Platycodon grandiflorus* 'Mariesii'
- *Polemonium caeruleum*

Bring out your inner designer Beds and borders containing plants with themed colours, either complementary or harmonising, will add a 'designer' look to your plantings. Even small borders may be set out in this way, but there may have to be a narrower selection of species. Start your scheme off as early in the year as possible: begin the season for a red or 'hot' border, for example, with suitably coloured tulips, primulas and wallflowers; or launch a white or cream theme with Christmas roses, white narcissi and the shrubby honeysuckle *Lonicera fragrantissima*. Keeping to a particular theme can be difficult from late autumn to early spring, when the choice of colours is more limited. If so, take the opportunity to fit in another seasonal theme – for example, a yellow spring border.

● **CHOOSE BLUES THAT HOLD THEIR COLOUR** Blue is the perfect colour to bring peace and calm into the garden. Select your plants carefully: many blues change colour with age, either fading or taking on reddish or purple tints. The most successful blue-themed border should contain only true blue flowers (see above), although really blue-leaved foliage plants may be added for effect.

● **COOL OFF WITH A WHITE THEME** to temper hot summer days. White borders may contain foliage plants as well as flowers, with leaves in shades of grey and creamy-white. To be absolutely true to the theme, make sure that any flowers they produce are also white; otherwise, remove any buds before they start to show colour.

● **GET MAXIMUM IMPACT FOR MINIMUM MAINTENANCE** If you're short of time for gardening, go for shrubs and ground-cover perennials with colour-themed, unusual foliage – gold and gold-variegated; silver, cream and white-variegated; or purple and red.

● **MAKE A WARM WINTER BARK BED** Many shrubs are just as attractive in winter as in summer – often more so – with their fiery-coloured bark (see facing page). Group several together for a stirring winter display; in summer, they make good foliage plants for a mixed border.

● **BE RUTHLESS WITH GIFTS** Many people will offer you plants to start off a new border; be absolutely sure that they will fit into your scheme before you plant them. Pot them up until they flower, then work out if and where they could fit in.

▼ **Complement the colours** of hard landscaping with your plants. Soft grey foliage echoes the paving and coping here, while red callistemon flowers and a spiky chocolate cordyline tone with the sand-coloured walls and teak lounger.

Pile on the style with sophisticated schemes Unusual colour themes might not be to everyone's taste, but really striking combinations can lift a tired-looking garden and give it a modern atmosphere. You will need to spend a little time researching suitable species.

● **GO MONOCHROME FOR A BORDER THAT'S BANG UP-TO-DATE** A black and white theme can look great in, say, an urban courtyard. White flowers and foliage are easy to come by, but 'black' flowers take rather more finding. Among the best are the tulips 'Black Parrot' and 'Queen of Night'; petunia 'Black Velvet'; *Viola cornuta* 'Bowles Black'; *Iris chrysographes*; and the black hollyhock (*Alcea rosea* 'Nigra'). As an alternative, use red instead of white for a totally different effect.

● **CREATE DRAMA WITH PALE PINK AND DEEP PURPLE** There is a wealth of these colours among flowering perennials. Add white flowers or white-variegated foliage to freshen up the scheme, or for real sultry sophistication, omit white entirely and use lots of dark, dusky foliage with burgundy or coppery hues.

● **USE SILVER AS A SOLUTION FOR A HOT, DRY SPOT** Most grey and silvery-leaved plants thrive in this situation. Many, such as lavender, artemisia and santolina, have the bonus of aromatic leaves.

EXPERT KNOW HOW

ADD A BURST OF COLOUR IN WINTER

Some varieties of dogwood (*Cornus*) and willow put on a spectacular show of coloured bark once the leaves have fallen. The colour is most intense on young stems; if you prune the shrub every other year you can keep it to a manageable size while also enjoying a brilliant splash of colour during the winter months.

1 Every other spring, cut down shrubs grown for their decorative bark to a few centimetres above ground level to encourage new stems, which always have the best colour.

2 By the summer, the shrub will form a neat, leafy bush, providing a plain background to your flowering plants. Many dogwoods, like this one, have foliage that colours well in autumn.

3 In winter, after leaf fall, the beauty of the bark will be revealed. This is *Cornus sanguinea* 'Midwinter Fire'; other good dogwoods are 'Sibirica' and 'Winter Beauty', or try *Salix alba* 'Britzensis'.

Planting for rapid results

THE 'INSTANT GARDENS' seen at the big flower shows require a big budget and a lot of corner-cutting – but with clever plant choice, you can have a well-filled bed or border within a single growing season without breaking the bank. It's the perfect way to fill a new planting space if you want results as soon as possible.

INVEST IN A BIG PLANT FOR IMPACT, THEN SURROUND IT WITH FAST-GROWING BEDDING PLANTS

Fine displays in half the time

Start with some statements Large architectural plants such as yuccas, phormiums, tree ferns and bamboos give instant impact. They are generally pricey, but they will last for years, and you can balance out the investment by surrounding them with low-cost bedding plants for the first season.

● **SEEK OUT PLANTS WITH 'READY-MADE' GOOD LOOKS** In summer, you will be able to find well-grown fuchsias, coleus and other attention-grabbing plants at most nurseries and garden centres. Buy containerised roses in flower, and you can have a rose bed in full bloom at the end of a day's planting. Roses and fuchsias grown as standards (on a tall stem) add height in a flash. Mature perennials in big pot sizes are also increasingly available, as are climbers that are developed enough to clad an obelisk in no time. Take a look at heathers and conifers, too. Most growers produce plants in a range of pot sizes; the bigger the pot, the quicker the plant will settle and fill out, with proper care.

● **CONSIDER MATURE PLANTS** Mature trees and shrubs can be found on the internet if your local garden centre cannot help you. With a generous budget, you can have a newly planted shrubbery that looks as though it has been growing for years. It will need more watering than if you'd started with young plants, but on the plus side, you can see the effect immediately, and there is no danger of overplanting to fill up the bed. Ready-made topiary and even pre-grown box hedging sold 'by the yard' are other expensive but immediately satisfying options.

Choose vigorous shrubs

Shrubs that make rapid growth (see right) will soon give your plantings substance, if you prepare the ground really well. Look out, too, for smaller shrubs that are cut back hard in spring and flower late in the season, such as hardy fuchsias, perovskia and *Spiraea japonica*; in a year, just one of these can bush out to fill as much space as several small perennials. A framework of strategically positioned, fast-maturing shrubs gives a border an established feel while other plants grow to realise their potential.

● **GROW A 'LAVENDER HEDGE' IN HALF THE TIME** Use a row of fast-growing nepeta (catmint) for much faster results; or choose *Perovskia* 'Little Spire' or *Caryopteris* 'Ferndown'. All three can be cut back hard in spring.

Add quick-growing perennials

Fill gaps between larger plants with fast-growing, spreading perennials (see right). Plant closely so that the leaves are almost touching and they will soon knit together.

◀ **A large sculptural plant** such as this spiky yucca will not be cheap, but the impact it creates is invaluable in a new garden. Red pelargoniums and yellow coreopsis make cheerful and inexpensive companions, while the emerging red-leaved canna bulbs will soon put on a fantastic show.

STAR PERFORMERS...

BEST FOR QUICK RESULTS

When you don't want to wait years for results, fast-growing plants will give you the desired effect quickly. Make sure those that you choose are just speedy growers, not rampant invaders.

FAST-GROWING SHRUBS

- ● *Ceanothus* 'Gloire de Versailles'
- ● Cytisus (broom)
- ● Hydrangeas
- ● *Hypericum* 'Hidcote'
- ● *Lavatera* 'Barnsley'
- ◀ *Phlomis fruticosa*
- ● *Sambucus* 'Black Lace'
- ● Spartium

FAST-SPREADING PERENNIALS

- ● *Alchemilla mollis*
- ● *Artemisia schmidtiana*
- ● *Ceratostigma plumbaginoides*
- ● *Epimediums* (some)
- ● *Euphorbia robbiae*
- ● *Geranium sanguineum*
- ● *Houttuynia cordata*
- ◀ Nepeta

Annuals – one-season wonders

Fill beds with fast-growing flowers Everyone wants to see a border full of permanent colour as soon as possible, yet there are times when you might need or prefer a temporary solution for part of your garden. Let annuals and bedding plants come to your rescue: in a matter of weeks they can make a dazzling display, while you can concentrate on designing a long-term planting scheme.

● **MAKE A CHEAP AND CHEERFUL BED WITH HARDY ANNUALS** You will find a good choice of seed varieties at garden centres, and an even wider one if you order from a seed company's catalogue. Sow a seed mixture for a meadow effect, or sow different varieties in patches or drifts (see below) for a more structured look, placing the tallest annuals – cleomes, for example, and sunflowers – at the back.

● **CREATE THE LOOK OF A MATURE BORDER** Hardy and half-hardy annuals aren't just for creating a small-scale, cottagey look. There are annual species of classic border perennials such as lupins, rudbeckias and delphiniums (larkspur). *Papaver somniferum* varieties can be every bit as blowsy and showy as perennial oriental poppies. *Hordeum jubatum* and *Lagurus ovatus* are lovely annual grasses, while *Euphorbia marginata*, with white-splashed leaves, is a fantastic foliage plant – or for the lime green of perennial euphorbias, try *Bupleurum rotundifolium*.

● **MAKE A SPLASH WITH BRILLIANT BEDDING** Ready-grown in individual cells or pots, bedding plants take no time at all to fill out. The best time to buy bedding

EXPERT KNOW HOW

SOWING DRIFTS OF ANNUALS

Hardy annuals are best sown where they are to flower; some don't like the root disturbance caused by planting out and most make much stronger plants when sown direct. Sowing in drills rather than scattering the seed over the soil will help you to distinguish and remove young weeds from among your seedling annuals.

1 Mark out a plan on the soil, using fine sand, to indicate where each variety is to grow. Draw thin grooves or drills at a different angle in each patch, spaced at the final distances of each plant type.

2 Sow each type of seed in its patch, cover and water. Add a pinch of seed to neighbouring patches for a naturalistic effect. Plunge in some twiggy sticks to keep off birds and support the plants.

3 Pull out weeds and thin the seedling annuals to the spacing recommended on the packet in order to make strong, bushy plants. This display took just 10 weeks from sowing to flowering.

that will grow away quickly is just as it is reaching the flowering stage. Plants in full bloom are tempting, but these may well be stressed from being too long in their pots and will take much longer to re-establish. Space the plants slightly closer than recommended and water regularly to see bare earth covered quickly.

Don't overlook edible plants

Most vegetable plants grow to maturity in a single season and many look great in a border. You could opt for an entirely edible planting, or add in traditional kitchen garden flowers such as dahlias, marigolds and zinnias. Mix the coloured foliage of beetroot and red lettuce with bright bedding, or liven up a border edge with ferny carrots and bright nasturtiums (which have edible flowers) for a productive and attractive display.

● **KEEP THE FOLIAGE COMING WITH LEAFY CROPS** Choose 'cut-and-come-again' varieties, so that you can pick just enough for a meal without leaving gaps in your plantings. Look for pretty looseleaf lettuces that you can harvest over time, or the chard 'Bright Lights', with its bold leaves and brilliantly coloured stems.

● **GIVE HEIGHT TO THE PLANTING** with wigwams of runner and climbing french beans, many of which have beautiful flowers. Sow or plant sweetpeas between the beans and they will scramble up the supports too. You could complete the display with an edible edging of 'Hestia' dwarf runner beans.

● **VISIT A HERB NURSERY FOR MORE INSPIRATION** Some of the more unusual leafy herbs make really substantial and quick-growing plants. Look for lovage and borage, hyssop (agastache), fennel, valerian and lemon verbena, and edge beds with fast-growing, fragrant sweet woodruff (*Galium odoratum*).

▲ **Mix edible plants** with young perennials and summer bulbs for a fast-growing, good-looking and productive display. Here, cabbages, kales, chard and yellow-flowered courgette plants share space with creeping houttuynia, pink poppies and the frondlike stems of lilies.

Reinvigorating displays

ALL PLANTINGS NEED SOME REFURBISHMENT after a while, but you don't have to rip everything out and start again. Whether you need everything to look at its best in double-quick time, or want ideas to improve your displays for next year, there are plenty of ways to bring the sparkle back to your garden.

A fast garden makeover

Top tips for a rapid tidy-up Every gardener has times when the garden needs to look great in a hurry – an upcoming garden party, for example. If you get your priorities right, you can transform your garden (or at least, the most visible parts of it) with just half a day's work. Make a good tidy-up top of your list – it makes everything look fresher and healthier. Gather up debris such as dead heads and prunings and consign it to the compost heap or recycling bin. Move empty pots to the garden shed and rearrange containers so that the ones looking at their best are to the fore, and any tired ones are tucked away.

● **REMOVE DEAD HEADS AND WEEDS** If you've been a little neglectful of late, take a pair of secateurs or a garden knife and remove as many dead flowerheads and brown stems as you can. Weed around your plants, then rake everything up and you'll restore that well-groomed look.

EXPERT KNOW HOW

NEATENING EDGES

Crisp lawn edges can make beds and borders look really well cared for. A well-sharpened half-moon edging iron allows you to recut and define your planting areas.

Always define the edge you want to neaten with a garden line (or hose for a curve) then, wearing stout shoes, cut against it with the iron. Trim off as little turf as possible, otherwise your borders will gradually get larger and your lawn smaller. Remove the trimmings to the compost heap immediately so they don't start to regrow.

- **MOW AND EDGE THE LAWN** if it needs it. Nothing makes borders look instantly smarter than a smooth, green foreground and razor-sharp edges.
- **GIVE FLOPPING PLANTS AN INSTANT LIFT** with canes and ties, hoops or twiggy sticks [see p.113] and tie in straying stems of climbers. They may look a little awkward at first, but the stems will re-orient themselves in a day or two. Look at shrubs from different angles and cut back badly placed branches that make paths hard to negotiate or spoil views of other plants.
- **CLEAN PATHS AND PAVED AREAS** with a pressure-washer for a sparkling finish. These handy machines can be used on most types of garden furniture too. Weed between paving slabs; an old kitchen knife makes an ideal tool.

Fill gaps in a flash A container plant from your patio could be just the thing to fill an empty spot in the border – drop in pots of bold summer bulbs, like lilies and cannas, for an exotic uplift. Raid the garden centre, too, for good-looking plants and decorative items to liven up dull or bare areas. Look out for large pots of spring bulbs or summer perennials in flower, or pick up bold-leaved evergreens such as *Fatsia japonica* to introduce sumptuous foliage.

- **POSTPONE PLANTING TO SAVE TIME** You do not need to plant any new border gap-fillers immediately. Keep the plants in their pots and either position them among neighbouring plants, or drop them into holes quickly dug in the soil, and they will look fine. Just remember to plant them properly later.
- **ADD A FOCAL POINT TO A PLANTING** with a large pot or urn (no need even to plant it up), or look among garden sculpture and ornaments for a striking piece – the range has never been wider. Try to avoid trampling plants as you set the object in place, and take a little time artfully arranging stems and foliage around it so it looks at home.

▼ **Revitalise a tired planting** scheme (see inset) with finds from the garden centre: two smart conifers, a pair of mirrored ornaments and some late-flowering perennials and crimson-leaved heucheras add instant lift.

MATCHING MULCHES

Mulching, as well as being good for the garden, ties your plantings together and sets off the plants well. Using the same mulch in your containers looks stylish and coordinates the overall display.

◀ **Chipped bark** suits woodland plants in a shady setting.

● **Coir fibre,** cocoa shells and dark, well-rotted compost or manure give general, well-tended good looks.

● **Composted pine needles** look great around conifers.

● **Dark slate** flatters minimalist designs.

● **Gravel or stone chippings** perfect a hot, sunny bed.

● **Seashells** are a pretty look for a coastal garden.

Improve your borders year on year

Make plans for new plants Summer is often the time when we notice disappointing gaps and dull areas in plantings, but this is not the best time to be choosing and planting young plants. Make notes on a garden plan so you'll remember where you want to introduce new plants in autumn or spring – or use permanent marker on garden labels to pinpoint exactly where new plants are needed. Add a few words, such as 'tall, yellow' or 'silver-leaved' to remind you what you had in mind and help you to choose the right plants when the time comes.

Prepare your plants to give their best Hungry plants will not perform well. Make sure all your existing plants fulfil their potential in the next growing season by feeding in autumn with a slow-release fertiliser, such as bone meal, and then again in the spring with a fast-acting multipurpose garden feed.
● ADD A SMART FLOOR COVERING FOR A FRESH, TIDY LOOK A mulch [see also p.247] applied generously to your beds will flatter your plants and is also good for weed control. Choose materials that coordinate with your planting style (see above).

▼ **Transform your garden** by painting a wall in a striking colour. New paint mixing systems mean that masonry paint is no longer restricted to 'safe', neutral colours.

Revitalise your planting schemes

● RATIONALISE AND RESHUFFLE TO IMPROVE PLANTING SCHEMES Move or remove plants that upset your colour combinations and substitute better varieties. Swap the positions of tall plants that are hiding shorter ones.
● REPLACE POOR PERFORMERS Dig out plants that just aren't earning their keep and replace them with more exciting varieties, such as the new forms of oriental poppies that flower repeatedly throughout the summer.
● PERK UP OLDER PLANTS Divide perennials, renovate shrubs and roses, and take cuttings of untidy short-lived plants that are overgrown or straggly. Clump-forming perennials can be divided easily at the beginning and the end of the year; the replanted sections will regrow

strongly the following summer. Many old shrubs, roses and other woody plants (but not all conifers) can be rejuvenated by hard pruning [see also p.151].

● **PLANT BULBS TO ADD COLOUR** Ensure you get your first choice of colours and varieties by ordering from growers in good time, or watch your local garden centre for the autumn and spring arrivals. Plant up some bulbs in containers, too.

● **USE CLIMBERS TO ADD INTEREST TO EXISTING PLANTS** Plant flowering climbers such as clematis to grow in more unusual places – into established small trees, through bushes, or as ground cover in shrub borders. Climbers scrambling through other plants add more interest and give a garden a mature, established look.

Freshen up your landscaping
Early spring is an excellent time for garden DIY, leaving the coming season free for relaxation. Repair broken fenceboards, replace damaged trellis, renew pavers and edging and repoint walls. Take the opportunity to fit supports for climbers if necessary. Make sure hedges start the season neatly trimmed, and fill in any gaps with young hedging plants.

● **EXPERIMENT WITH COLOUR ON BORDER BACKGROUNDS** Once the weather is fine enough, try a bold new shade of paint or stain on a wall or fence to make an inspired new backdrop for your planting's colour scheme.

● **ADD A NEW EFFECT** Consider adding a new feature in your garden for the coming year. A clump of rustling bamboo, some subtle lighting [see p.68], or the sparkle and sound of a small water feature [see p.65] will all enhance your plantings.

EXPERT KNOW HOW

REINVIGORATING BEARDED IRISES

Bearded irises, in their huge range of colours, are superb early plants for the flower border. As plants get older, flowering performance tends to deteriorate as the fleshy roots (rhizomes) grow woody and sprawling, leaving an ugly bare centre in the clump. Divide and replant them every few years, after flowering.

1 Use a garden fork to spike around the clump, far enough away to avoid damage to the young leaf spikes on the outer edges, then lift it carefully.

2 Gently pull off the youngest parts of the rhizomes with strong, healthy roots attached, then trim back the foliage to a few inches from the base.

3 Replant the young sections firmly, leaving the top of the rhizome exposed to ripen in the sun. Discard all the old, non-productive parts.

Planting for year-round interest

MAKE YOUR GARDEN MORE INVITING by planning your beds **and borders** so that there is something to catch the eye all year round. Careful plant choice and a few simple design tips can ensure that whatever its size, your garden offers delights through every season.

PLUMED GRASSES TOUCHED BY THE FIRST FROSTS ADD MAGIC TO AUTUMNAL PLANTINGS

Plantings with lasting appeal

Give structure to beds and borders

Well-shaped shrubs and evergreens will give your borders a framework that will last throughout the year while flowering plants come and go around them. Take photographs of your plantings through the seasons, then compare them to see where a well-placed structural plant – a columnar conifer, perhaps, or a rounded evergreen shrub – could add presence and improve the year-round appearance of your garden.

● **USE EVERGREENS FOR STRONG OUTLINES** Look for evergreen shrubs that have a naturally well-defined shape, like many conifers and hollies, or those that can be clipped or trained easily into interesting shapes [see pp.162–3]: for example, a box spiral, pyramid-shaped bay, or lollipop *Euonymus fortunei* 'Emerald n' Gold'.

● **CHOOSE HARD-WORKING DECIDUOUS SHRUBS FOR MIXED BORDERS** to give the best value throughout the year. Select shrubs not only for their flowers but for interesting foliage colour and leaf shape and good autumn colour, perhaps accompanied by berries, to prolong their season of interest (see below).

Enjoy wildlife through the seasons

Wild creatures visiting the garden provide interest and entertainment even when plants are dormant. Provide plants and features that wildlife finds attractive [see pp.272–3], and you may also see a reduction in garden pest problems.

● **INCLUDE EARLY-FLOWERING PLANTS** to provide nectar for early-waking bees. In return they will pollinate your plants, improving fruit crops and autumn displays of ornamental berries. Flowering currant *(Ribes sanguineum)* can come into flower very early in the spring, and on a warm day is often covered with bees.

● **MAKE FENCES AND WALLS WILDLIFE-FRIENDLY** as well as more attractive by training ivy or pyracantha on them. Both provide nesting and roosting sites for birds, ample shelter for insects, and a plentiful food supply for the birds if allowed to flower and berry freely. If you need to trim them, wait until late summer when nests will be empty.

◀ **Late autumn is a time** when plantings can take on a sparer, more ethereal beauty. Don't be too hasty to tidy up for winter – seedheads and flowerheads left in place can provide protection for plants and resources for wildlife.

STAR PERFORMERS...

SHRUBS FOR MIXED BORDERS

Use shrubs with good shapes, colourful foliage and fruits in autumn to extend interest beyond their flowering period.

● *Amelanchier* x *grandiflora* 'Autumn Brilliance'
● *Cornus alba* 'Spaethii'
● *Corylus avellana* 'Contorta'
● *Cotinus coggygria* 'Pink Champagne'
● *Cryptomeria japonica* 'Elegans'
● *Ilex* x *meserveae* 'Blue Angel'
◀ *Philadelphus coronarius* 'Aureus'
● *Rosa rugosa* 'Schneezwerg'
● *Viburnum opulus* 'Notcutt's Variety'
● *Weigela florida* 'Foliis Purpureis'

1m (40in)

USING STRUCTURE AND SYMMETRY FOR YEAR-ROUND INTEREST

This bed, at the end of a small town garden, is on view year-round from the house and has been planned for strong structural interest, provided by both the design and the use of evergreens with neat outlines. Symmetry and a pronounced use of repeat planting emphasise formality and strength, softened by drifts of grasses and by the flowering climbers, bright fuchsias and winter-flowering hellebores that contribute long periods of seasonal interest. The ornamental obelisks (7) are attractive features in their own right during winter. The bed is shown here in early summer, just as the flowers of the hebes are fading.

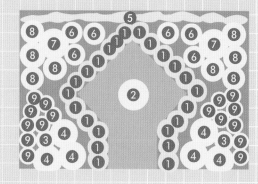

KEY TO PLANTS (H = mature height, S = mature spread)

STRUCTURAL PLANTS

Bought as two-year-old plants, the box, bay and yew will take 5–8 years to reach maturity.

1. **24 x *Buxus sempervirens* 'Suffruticosa'** Small box variety trained and trimmed as a low hedge. H 30cm (12in), S 30cm (12in).

2. **1 x *Laurus nobilis*** Bay tree trained as a pyramid. H 1.2m (4ft), S 50cm (20in).

3. **2 x *Taxus baccata* 'Standishii'** Columnar golden yew. H 1.2m (4ft), S 80cm (32in).

4. **6 x *Hebe pinguifolia* 'Pagei'** Mound-forming evergreen shrub. H 30cm (12in), S 80cm (32in).

FLOWERING PLANTS AND GRASSES

5. **1 x *Rosa* 'New Dawn'** Wall-trained, repeat-flowering climbing rose. H 1.8m (6ft), S 4m (12ft).

6. **6 x *Fuchsia* 'Tom Thumb'** Hardy fuchsia. H 35cm (14in), S 30cm (12in).

7. **2 x *Clematis* 'Celebration'** Summer-flowering clematis [see p.171] trained up matching wrought-iron obelisks. H 1.8m (6ft).

8. **8 x *Helleborus argutifolius*** Evergreen perennial. H 90cm–1.2m (3–4ft), S 90cm (3ft).

9. **16 x *Molinia caerulea* 'Variegata'** Perennial grass. H 30cm (12in), S 20cm (8in).

Use plants that stimulate all your senses The pleasure of a garden does not solely rest in colour and visual appeal. Include plants that offer more elusive attractions such as scent, sound and texture and your borders will have extra interest, especially at times of the year when there is little to look at.

● **ENHANCE WINTER WALKS WITH GORGEOUS SCENTS** Winter-flowering *Daphne odora* and sarcococca may not have the most spectacular blooms, but their knockout perfume will stop you in your tracks. Position plants with aromatic foliage, such as rosemary, by paths where you will brush against them; take sprigs of rosemary into the house and add them to open fires or wood-burning stoves for the scent of summer. Fill cracks in paving with creeping thymes that will release their pungent fragrance as the leaves are stepped on.

● **BE TEMPTED BY TEXTURES** Grow feathery fennel and dill, furry-leaved stachys and the magnificent *Verbascum bombyciferum*, tasseled amaranthus and velvety cockscomb celosias for their irresistibly tactile qualities. Plant willows and hazels for their velvety catkins in spring.

● **ENJOY THE BEAUTY OF BARK** Plant trees such as *Prunus serrula*, snakebark maples and silver birches with striking bark that demands to be seen – and touched. Grow willow and dogwood varieties that can be pruned hard for young, bright-barked stems in winter, and shrubs with unusual growth habits, such as the corkscrew hazel (*Corylus avellana* 'Contorta') with its twisted stems.

● **ENHANCE THE ATMOSPHERE WITH RESTFUL SOUNDS** Together with birdsong and the buzzing of bees, whispering grasses and leaves and the gentle splashing of water are sounds that add to the tranquillity of a garden. Install a small water feature with a fountain or cascade [see p.64], and plant tall ornamental grasses such as miscanthus, or trees such as *Populus tremula* 'Pendula', which has leaves that rustle and tremble in the slightest breeze.

▼ **Perfect for a hot border,** amaranthus are annual plants that can be grown for upright flower plumes (*Amarathus cruentus*, or prince's feather, below) or for hanging tassels (*A. caudatus*, or love-lies-bleeding).

Prolonging your flowering displays

Include some long-flowering stalwarts Some plants naturally bloom for a long period (see below): use these plants to provide continuity in the border, bridging the gaps between other plants, such as peonies, that you cannot live without but which flower only too briefly. Remember, too, that if you love the look of a particular plant, there may be related species that have the same look but flower at different times: if you have the space, you could have a ceanothus in bloom somewhere in the garden from spring through to autumn.

● **EXTEND THE SHOW WITH REGULAR WATERING** Border and container plants usually flower for longer if they never get too dry, especially in hot weather. A good soaking at the roots, once or twice a week in the evening, will work wonders; keep the water off the flowers as it can spoil them.

● **LOOK AT NEW VARIETIES WITH MORE FLOWER POWER** 'Stella d'Oro' was the first of several repeat-flowering hemerocallis (daylily) to be offered to the gardening public, and since then breeders have produced more longer-flowering perennials, such as the new 'super poppies' – repeat-flowering oriental poppies such as 'Medallion' and 'Snow White' – and new repeat-flowering versions of classic shrubs such as 'Endless Summer' hydrangeas, 'Red Prince' and 'Carnaval' weigelas, and 'Bloomerang' and 'Josee' lilacs.

● **SELECT PERFECT PLANTS FOR GAP-FILLING** by visiting your local garden centre. Plants in flower always sell better, so you'll always be able to see a good selection in bloom. Look for those just coming into bud to see what will follow on.

● **INCORPORATE SOME QUICK-FIX COLOUR** Don't forget how useful bedding plants can be to tide plantings over between flushes of flowers. They have been bred to flower for months on end, often until quite late in the season.

Develop an eye for deadheading

Many perennials and some shrubs will flower for longer, or produce a second flush of flowers, if dead flowerheads are pinched, snipped or sheared off. The key to successful deadheading is to do it in a way that takes into account the growth habit of the plant (see below), and to feed the plant with a high-potash fertiliser to boost its strength for renewed flower production.

● **PICK OFF INDIVIDUAL FLOWERS TO ENCOURAGE MORE TO FORM** The classic plants that reward deadheading are the modern, repeat-flowering roses [see also pp.116–21], but it also brings out the best in annuals and summer bedding [see p.128]. It's well worth deadheading perennials, too, except for those that you are keeping for their seedheads – many will form new flowers, and they will all look fresher.

STAR PERFORMERS...

LONG-FLOWERING PLANTS

Many perennials and some shrubs flower for many weeks without help from the gardener, and others will flower for a second time if cut back to a point lower down the stem. Choose any of these for extra value in a bed or border.

NATURALLY LONG-FLOWERING

- *Campanula* 'Elizabeth'
- *Coreopsis grandiflora* 'Mayfield Giant'
- *Geranium endressii*
- *Hemerocallis*
- *Hibiscus syriacus*
- ◀ *Hydrangea macrophylla*
- *Scabiosa caucasica*
- *Veronica teucrium*

DEADHEAD FOR A SECOND FLUSH

- *Aconitum* 'Bressingham Spire'
- *Ceanothus x pallidus* 'Marie Simon'
- ◀ *Centaurea dealbata*
- **Delphiniums**
- **Hardy geraniums**
- **Leucanthemums**
- *Lychnis chalcedonica*
- **Russell hybrid lupins**

PLANTING A TRADITIONAL BORDER WITH LONG-FLOWERING PLANTS

This rectangular border, shown in summer, has been stocked with plants that flower over a long period, or that can be deadheaded for a second flush of blooms (see facing page). Deep enough to accommodate tiers of plants that graduate in height from front to back, it includes some repeated plants (not always in the same flower colour) to give continuity along its length. Vertical accents provided by tall flowering spires and spiky iris leaves are complemented by plenty of softly rounded, billowing forms.

KEY TO PLANTS (H = mature height, S = mature spread)

TALL PLANTS

① **1 x *Syringa meyeri* 'Palibin'**
Small-flowered lilac; shrub. H 1.2m (4ft), S 1m (40in).

② **1 x *Rosa* 'Felicia'**
Hybrid musk shrub rose. H 1.8m (6ft), S 1.2m (4ft).

③ **3 x *Delphinium* 'Galahad'**
Perennial. H 1.8m (6ft), S 45cm (18in).

④ **1 x *Lavatera* 'Barnsley'**
Shrub. H & S 1.8m (6ft).

⑤ **3 x *Delphinium* 'Blue Jay'**
Pacific Giant hybrid; perennial. H 1.8m (6ft), S 45cm (18in).

⑥ **1 x *Echinops bannaticus* 'Taplow Blue'** Globe thistle; perennial. H 1.2m (4ft), S 75cm (30in).

MID-HEIGHT PLANTS

⑦ **3 x *Lupinus* 'The Governor'**
Russell hybrid; perennial. H 60–80cm (24–32in), S 40cm (16in).

⑧ **3 x *Papaver* 'Shasta'**
Repeat-flowering; perennial. H 75cm (30in), S 30cm (12in).

⑨ **3 x *Geranium* 'Johnson's Blue'**
Perennial. H 50cm (20in), S 60cm (24in).

⑩ **3 x *Iris* 'Rosalie Figge'**
Repeat-flowering; perennial. H 80cm (32in) (in flower), S 30cm (12in).

⑪ **3 x *Euphorbia characias* subsp. *wulfenii*** Perennial. H 80cm (32in), S 40cm (16in).

⑫ **3 x *Lupinus* 'Noble Maiden'**
Russell hybrid; perennial. H 60–80cm (24–32in), S 40cm (16in).

LOW-GROWING PLANTS

⑬ **12 x *Dianthus barbatus*** Sweet williams; biennial. H 30–40cm (12–16in).

⑭ **6 x *Achillea argentea***
Two groups of three plants; perennial. H 15cm (6in), S 20cm (8in).

⑮ **2 x *Hosta* 'Halcyon'**
Perennial. H & S 45cm (18in).

⑯ **3 x *Geranium endressii* 'Wargrave Pink'** Perennial. H 45cm (18in), S 30cm (12in).

⑰ **3 x *Veronica teucrium* 'Crater Lake Blue'** Perennial. H 35cm (14in), S 30cm (12in).

⑱ **5 x *Dianthus* 'Doris'**
Scented garden pink; perennial. H 20–30cm (8–12in), S 20cm (8in).

⑲ **3 x *Eryngium variifolium***
Perennial. H 45cm (18in), S 35cm (14in).

⑳ **10 x Brompton stocks**
Biennial. H 45cm (18in).

1m (40in)

USING RICH, WARM COLOURS FOR A LATE SUMMER BLAZE

Hot, vibrant, even clashing colours can give a border a modern feel – and a terrific lift on an overcast day. A dark, formally clipped hedge in the background, warm brick paving at the edge of the bed, a mulch of tobacco-coloured coir or cocoa shells and the two large shrubs with deep wine-red foliage give strong, long-lasting structure. The planting is designed to build in intensity: the bed is shown in late summer when, just as the last of the roses are fading, a host of perennials hit their stride for a glorious late-season display. Many of the plants have good-looking seedheads that will stand through autumn and winter, providing interest and attracting wildlife.

KEY TO PLANTS (H = mature height, S = mature spread)

TALL PLANTS

① **3 x *Heliopsis* 'Golden Plume'** Perennial. H 1.2m (4ft), S 35cm (14in).

② **1 x *Physocarpus opulifolius* 'Diabolo'** Shrub. H 1.8m (6ft), S 1.2m (4ft).

③ **1 x *Rosa* 'William Lobb'** Old-fashioned moss rose. H 1.8m (6ft), S 1.5m (5ft).

④ **1 x *Miscanthus* 'Malepartus'** Perennial grass. H 1.5m (5ft), S 1.2m (4ft).

⑤ **3 x *Kniphofia* 'Fiery Fred'** Red-hot poker; perennial. H 1.2m (4ft), S 35cm (14in).

⑥ **1 x *Cotinus* 'Royal Purple'** Shrub. H 1.8m (6ft), S 1.5m (5ft).

MID-HEIGHT PLANTS

⑦ **3 x *Dahlia* 'Arabian Nights'** Perennial with frost protection. H 80cm (32in), S 40cm (16in).

⑧ **6 x *Crocosmia* 'Lucifer'** Montbretia; perennial. H 60cm (24in), S 30cm (12in).

⑨ **3 x *Hemerocallis* 'Glowing Gold'** Daylily; perennial. H & S 60–80cm (24–32in).

⑩ **3 x *Rodgersia pinnata* 'Elegans'** Perennial. H 1m (40in), S 45cm (18in).

LOW-GROWING PLANTS

⑪ **6 x *Antirrhinum* 'Black Prince'** Snapdragons; annual. H 40cm (16in).

⑫ **3 x *Salvia* 'Mainacht'** Perennial. H 45cm (18in), S 30cm (12in).

⑬ **5 x *Imperata cylindrica* 'Red Baron'** Perennial grass. H 40cm (16in), S 20cm (8in).

⑭ **5 x *Gazania* 'Daybreak'** Annual. H 15–18cm (6–8in).

⑮ **3 x *Sedum* 'Ruby Glow'** Perennial. H & S 20cm (8in).

⑯ **3 x *Lychnis x arkwrightii* 'Vesuvius'** Perennial. H & S 30cm (12in).

⑰ **3 x *Helenium* 'Sahin's Early Flowerer'** Perennial. H 90cm (3ft), S 40cm (16in).

⑱ **3 x *Uncinia rubra*** Perennial grass. H 45cm (18in), S 40cm (16in).

⑲ **12 x *Tagetes* 'Red Cherry'** French marigold; annual. H 18–20cm (7–8in).

1m (40in)

● **CUT BACK TALL STEMS FOR NEW FLOWER SPIRES** Once the main flower spire of delphiniums and aconites has faded, cut the whole stem back to a sideshoot (or, if you cannot find one, to a healthy leaf about halfway down) and the plant should produce several new, smaller flower spires later in the season. You can use the same technique on penstemons, solidago, lupins and *Phlox paniculata*.

● **SHEAR BUSHY PLANTS FOR A SECOND FLUSH OF GROWTH** Plants such as hardy geraniums that are covered in small flowers are impractical to deadhead; instead, use shears to give the whole plant a 'haircut' – this will remove a lot of fading, tatty foliage, too. The plants will produce a new, much fresher flush of growth and, often, a second flush of flowers. Shear lavender and *Spiraea japonica* immediately the flowers start to fade and they will flower again in the autumn.

Cut plants back to flower later If you're going on holiday in summer, there's no need to miss the show. You can postpone the flowering of dahlias and put many bedding plants, such as *Bellis perennis*, pansies and antirrhinums, 'on hold' by stripping off all buds and flowers before you leave. By the time you return, new flowers will just be opening.

● **STAGGER FLOWERING TIMES WITH CLEVER PRUNING** You can delay the flowering time of many plants, especially small shrubs like hebes and herbs, by cutting them back fairly hard in spring or early summer, just as they are starting to produce new shoots. Alternatively, cut back half the shoots so that the plant as a whole flowers over a longer period. The shoots that were cut back will regrow and come into flower as the first flush of blooms is fading.

Keep the flowering momentum going So many plantings start to fade at the end of summer that it's easy to forget that there are several weeks of good flowering weather left once the popular plants have finished for the year. Make sure you have plenty of plants with striking seedheads (see below), such as sputnik-like alliums and pepperpot poppies, but don't give up on colour yet: the

STAR PERFORMERS...

FOR SEEDS AND FRUITS

Some plants give you an extra treat which can all too easily be forgotten – their flowers mature to stunning seedheads or berries. Always leave plenty of seedheads standing for seed-eating birds, such as finches, in the winter.

- *Allium giganteum*
- **Callicarpa (beauty bush)**
- *Clematis tangutica*
- *Eryngiums (sea holly)*
- *Humulus lupulus*
- **Iberis (candytuft)**
- *Nectaroscordum bulgaricum*
- *Papaver somniferum*
◄ *Physalis franchetii*
- **Pyracantha**
- *Rosa glauca*
- *Rosa moyesii* 'Geranium'
- **Symphoricarpos (snowberry)**

► **Birch bark** comes into its own over winter, here surrounded by bright heathers and, in the background, colourful dogwood stems. As the spring bulbs begin their show, the old bark will flake away to reveal a pristine new layer beneath.

daisy-flowered prairie-style perennials, such as echinaceas, rudbeckias and heleniums, are great for late colour, but asters and chrysanthemums reign supreme at this time of year. Don't forget bulbs, too: nerines, gladioli, dahlias and schizostylis will flower until the first really severe frost.

● **THINK PINK FOR A CHEERFUL WINTER SIGHT** Find a spot visible from a window, and plant varieties of *Erica carnea* (winter heath) or underplant a tree with pink and white winter-flowering cyclamen for a burst of colour to lift the spirits.

● **USE BULBS TO MARK THE END OF WINTER** Plant snowdrops, aconites and the earliest crocuses among scented winter treats, such as daphne, shrubby honeysuckle *(Lonicera fragrantissima)* and sarcococca, and you'll be able to spot the very first signs of spring as their leaf-tips emerge from the soil.

PLANTING FOR LATE WINTER CHEER

If you have a small corner in a large garden to spare, make a winter and early spring bed of plants to enjoy before the rest of the garden comes back to life. Combine winter-flowering shrubs, spring bulbs and bright bark to inspire you with colour and fragrance at the beginning of the gardening year. Apart from the dogwood, which requires pruning every 1–2 years [see p.81], all of the shrubs and perennials here are evergreen and easy-care, making this an attractive, low-maintenance bed for the rest of the year.

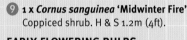

KEY TO PLANTS (H = mature height, S = mature spread)

SHRUBS AND EVERGREEN PERENNIALS

① **3 x *Sarcococca ruscifolia*** Christmas box, scented flowers; shrub. H 80cm (32in), S 45cm (18in).

② **6 x *Erica carnea* 'Vivellii'** Winter heath; shrub. H 15cm (6in), S 30cm (12in).

③ **5 x *Helleborus niger*** Perennial. H 30cm (12in), S 45cm (18in).

④ **1 x *Skimmia japonica* 'Highgrove Redbud'** Dome-shaped shrub. H 60cm (2ft), S 1.2m (4ft).

⑤ **1 x *Daphne mezereum*** Very fragrant; shrub. H 80cm (32in), S 60cm (24in).

⑥ **6 x *Erica carnea* 'R.B. Cooke'** Winter heath; shrub. H 15cm (6in), S 30cm (12in).

⑦ **1 x *Skimmia japonica* 'Rubella'** Shrub. H & S 75cm (30in).

⑧ **1 x *Ilex* x *attenuata* 'Sunny Foster'** Yellow-variegated holly; shrub. H 1.2m (4ft), S 1m (40in).

⑨ **1 x *Cornus sanguinea* 'Midwinter Fire'** Coppiced shrub. H & S 1.2m (4ft).

EARLY-FLOWERING BULBS

⑩ **Snowdrops and species (early-flowering) crocus (100 of each)** H 15cm (6in).

⑪ **50 x *Narcissus* 'February Gold'** H 30cm (12in).

1m (40in)

Matching plants to places

ALL PLANTS HAVE LIKES AND DISLIKES, some preferring open, sunny sites at one extreme, others moist, shady ground. That's good news for gardeners because no matter what conditions your garden has to offer, from boggy soil or drying winds to roadside traffic, there will be plenty of amazing plants that will thrive there.

Transform problem areas with clever planting

Highlight shady beds with cool, elegant schemes Most gardens have some shade, so unless it really is a problem don't fight it. Instead, turn such an area into a calm, relaxing part of the garden. There are dozens of lovely plants for shade (see facing page for some examples), including many with variegated foliage that will help to brighten a shady spot [see also p.33].

● **CREATE SUBTLE COLOUR SCHEMES** Plants that thrive in shade often have more discreet colours than the brighter sun-lovers, allowing you to create a gentler effect. Good colour themes to try include an all-white display, or one with various shades of pink, especially when set against lush green leaves.

● **CHECK SOIL CONDITIONS TO PICK THE BEST PLANTS** Don't assume that shaded soil is damp – dig a hole, and look at and feel the soil to assess its moisture levels. Many shade-loving plants tolerate a wide range of soil conditions, but if your shady site is very dry – or indeed particularly wet – check that the plants you want to grow will flourish there before buying.

▼ **This naturalistic scheme,** with pink-flowered candelabra primulas, paddle-leaved hostas and moisture-loving ferns, takes full advantage of a damp, shady patch. It's much easier to go with 'problem' conditions than to try to change them, and the results can be both unexpected and appealing.

BRIGHTENING A SHADY CORNER

This planting (shown in early summer) breaks up a shaded area by alternating bright-leaved, airy plants and pale flowers with darker accents. In a sheltered corner many of the perennials will be evergreen, contributing to the winter structure provided by the shrubs **(5, 8)** and the miscanthus **(2)**. In spring the epimedium, skimmia and tiarella will be covered in flowers, with bright, lime-green new growth on the alchemilla and euphorbia.

KEY TO PLANTS
(H = mature height, S = mature spread)

CLIMBERS AND TALL PLANTS

1 1 x *Hydrangea petiolaris* Self-clinging climber. H 3m (10ft), S 4m (14ft).

2 1 x *Miscanthus sinensis* 'Variegatus' Perennial white-striped grass. H 1.5m (5ft), S 1m (40in.)

3 1 x *Aruncus dioicus* Goat's beard; perennial. H 1.5m (5ft), S 1.2m (4ft).

4 3 x *Polygonatum x hybridum* Solomon's seal; perennial. H 1.2m (4ft), S 30cm (12in).

MEDIUM-HEIGHT PLANTS

5 1 x *Skimmia x confusa* 'Kew Green' Evergreen shrub. H 60cm (24in), S 1m (40in).

6 3 x *Geranium phaeum* Perennial. H & S 60cm (24in).

7 3 x *Euphorbia amygdaloides* 'Rubra' Perennial. H 50cm (20in), S 30cm (12in).

8 1 x *Euonymus fortunei* 'Emerald Gaiety' Variegated evergreen shrub. H 90cm (3ft), S 1.5m (5ft).

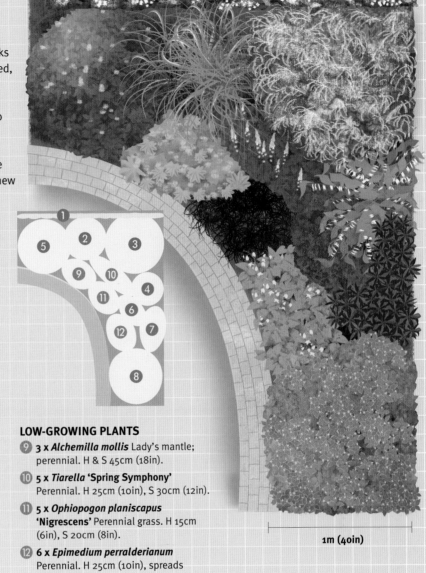

LOW-GROWING PLANTS

9 3 x *Alchemilla mollis* Lady's mantle; perennial. H & S 45cm (18in).

10 5 x *Tiarella* 'Spring Symphony' Perennial. H 25cm (10in), S 30cm (12in).

11 5 x *Ophiopogon planiscapus* 'Nigrescens' Perennial grass. H 15cm (6in), S 20cm (8in).

12 6 x *Epimedium perralderianum* Perennial. H 25cm (10in), spreads indefinitely.

1m (40in)

● **MAKE A WOODLAND WONDERLAND** The deepest shade in a garden can be cast by mature deciduous trees, but it's not so hard to plant these areas – simply follow the patterns seen in deciduous woodland. Choose spring-flowering bulbs – perhaps snowdrops and bluebells – and early-flowering perennials such as brunnera and pulmonaria: these will put on their show before the leaf canopy closes over. Add tall, shade-loving foxgloves, ferns and Solomon's seal *(Polygonatum × hybridum)* for summer interest, and pop in plenty of autumn-flowering crocuses and colchicum for a carpet of flowers to accompany the autumn leaf tints.

● **IMPROVE DRY SOIL TO HELP PLANTS GROW** Overhanging trees keep rain off the soil, and mature trees with a large root system also leave the ground dry and impoverished. Help plants to grow by forking in bonemeal in autumn and adding a thick organic mulch after heavy rain to help lock moisture in the soil.

Choose wetland plants for a boggy spot

An entire garden on badly draining soil really needs to be addressed as a whole with a long-term plan to improve the soil [see p.234] or perhaps with the installation of a system of land drains, but just one boggy patch in a garden can be turned into a wonderful planting feature. Anything recommended for the margins of a pond [see p.67] will thrive here, and these include some really eye-catching plants such as *Rheum palmatum*, with its enormous leaves, and the firework-like yellow spires of *Ligularia przewalskii*.

● **FIND THE MOST TOLERANT PLANTS FOR A WET/DRY SPOT** Some boggy areas are actually prone to drying out during a long spell without rain, making plant choice for such a spot very tricky. Try easy-going perennials that tolerate short-term flooding, such as eupatoriums, loosestrifes (*Lythrum*) and *Iris sibirica*.

Exploit the warmth of a hot, dry spot

A border that is backed by a sunny wall or high fence will often have dry soil, as will parts of gardens with porous, quick-draining, sandy soil that get the sun for most of the day. It's possible to make such growing conditions suit a wider range of plants – but you can save a lot of time, effort and watering by growing plants that thrive in dry, sunny soil. Plants with fleshy roots, such as bearded iris, will appreciate having 'dry feet' as well as plenty of sun, and so will summer bulbs (see below) and shrubby Mediterranean herbs, such as sages.

● **INCLUDE SOUTH AFRICAN PLANTS FOR COLOUR AND GLAMOUR** Lots of brilliantly coloured plants native to the Cape are perfect for hot spots and many can withstand winters that aren't too severe. Choose crocosmias, kniphofias, phygelius and osteospermums, and don't forget South African bulbs – nerines, agapanthus, schizostylis and acidanthera will flower prolifically year after year, and you probably won't even have to lift the slightly tender ones at the end of summer.

● **ADD SUCCULENTS FOR STYLE** Fleshy and spiky plants such as agaves, kalanchoes, aeoniums and aloes will contribute stylish architectural shapes, but remember to keep them frost-free in winter [see pp.254–5]. You could even use some succulent summer bedding as edging – dry ground is ideal for colourful mesembryanthemums.

● **HARDEN PLANTS WITH GRAVEL** Covering the soil with gravel after planting [see pp.58–9] looks attractive and reflects heat up onto the plants. This helps ripen their growth before winter and prevents damage during cold, wet spells.

▲ **African plants** thrive on the summer baking they receive in a sunny bed with free-draining soil. Their flower colours are often particularly clear and vivid, and can be used to create striking contrasts, as with these mauve agapanthus and orange crocosmias.

Create shelter in windswept gardens

Windy gardens are a special challenge. Many exposed new plots experience damaging winds until boundary fences, walls or hedges are in place. A hedge or a slatted fence that filters the wind is a much more effective solution than a solid surface [see p.43]. If planting behind a solid wall or fence that takes the full force of strong winds, leave a generous gap between the wall and the first line of planting to protect plants

PLANTING A HOT, DRY BORDER

This sunny, sheltered summer border, shown at the height of the season, has light, sandy, free-draining soil, calling for plants that are capable of conserving moisture – grey, furry leaves are one way they achieve this. The 'statement' plant here – and one that will draw the eye in winter among the seedheads of the other plants – is the yucca. It may take many years to bloom, but there are plenty of other fast-growing shrubs that will be covered with flowers in the meantime.

KEY TO PLANTS
(H = mature height, S = mature spread)

CLIMBERS AND TALL PLANTS

1. **1 x** *Yucca gloriosa* **'Variegata'** Shrub. H 1.2m (4ft) (flower spikes to 2m (6ft), S 1m (40in).

2. **1 x** *Hibiscus syriacus* **'Blue Bird'** Shrub. H 1.5m (5ft), S 1.2m (4ft).

3. **2 x** *Jasminum officinale* **'Argenteovariegatum'** Twining climber trained horizontally on trellis. H & S to 3m (10ft).

4. **1 x** *Hebe* **'Midsummer Beauty'** Evergreen shrub. H 1.2m (4ft), S 1m (40in).

5. *Acanthus* **'Tasmanian Angel'** Perennial. H 1.2m (4ft), S 80cm (32in).

MID-HEIGHT PLANTS

6. **1 x** *Phygelius* x *rectus* **'African Queen'** Shrub. H 90cm (3ft), S 45cm (18in).

7. **1 x** *Phlomis fruticosa* Shrub. H 80cm (32in), S 1.2m (4ft).

8. **6 x** *Papaver* **'Heartbeat'** Two groups of 3 plants; perennial. H 80cm (32in), S 60cm (24in).

9. **1 x** *Caryopteris clandonensis* **'Worcester Gold'** Shrub. H 90cm (3ft), S 45cm (18in).

10. **1 x** *Spiraea japonica* **'Goldflame'** Shrub. H & S 80cm (32in).

LOW-GROWING PLANTS

11. **3 x** *Ruta graveolens* Evergreen shrub. H 60cm (24in), S 80cm (32in).

12. **3 x** *Nepeta* **'Six Hills Giant'** Perennial. H & S 60cm (24in).

13. **1 x** *Salvia officinalis* **'Purpurascens'** Shrubby perennial. H 60cm (24in), S 80cm (32in).

14. **1 x** *Artemisia* **'Powis Castle'** Evergreen shrub. H 60cm (24in), S 90cm (3ft).

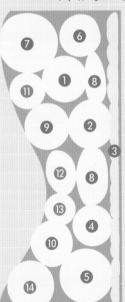

1m (40in)

from taking a battering from backdrafts. If you must plant right where the wind blasts over the wall and back down, choose very sturdy, resilient shrubs.

● **BUY HEDGING PLANTS YOUNG FOR STABILITY** When selecting hedging, do not be tempted by large, mature plants, thinking that they will provide a quick solution. Their roots will take a long time to anchor in the ground while the bulky top growth will catch the wind like a kite, and the whole plant could go flying in the first gale. Buy young plants instead and erect a temporary windbreak in the form of screening or fine-mesh netting to protect them in their first two or three years.

● **GIVE CONTAINER PLANTS HEAVY, STABLE POTS** Plants growing in containers are doubly vulnerable in windy gardens. Winds will suck moisture from their foliage and the compost, and also from porous terracotta pots, necessitating more frequent watering, and the containers themselves may blow over, damaging the plant. Choose squat containers made from heavy, non-porous materials – glazed pottery or lead, for example – or weight down lighter containers by putting bricks in the base. Make sure that container plants do not become top-heavy by repotting larger plants into larger pots when necessary.

● **SELECT COASTAL PLANTS FOR SEASIDE GARDENS** A garden that experiences incoming blasts of salty winds and spray requires plants that like to be beside the sea. Shrubs at the top of your list for shelter should include *Elaeagnus × ebbingei*, *Euonymus japonicus*, *Griselinia littoralis*, *Pittosporum tobira*, *Tamarix tetrandra* and brooms *(Cytisus)*. In mild areas, *Olearia macrodonta*, a hollylike shrub covered in white flowers in midsummer, makes a tough but attractive windbreak. Look also for plants with 'sea' in their common name – sea buckthorn *(Hippophae rhamnoides)*, sea thrift *(Armeria)* and sea holly *(Eryngium maritimum)*, for example.

▼ **Coastal conditions** can be challenging for plants, but these sturdy phormiums and the blue-flowered, whippy-stemmed perovskias are coping well. The shingle path, duck-egg blue woodwork and wave-shaped fence reinforce the seaside theme.

Choose tough plants for the urban jungle

Plants were never meant to grow beside busy roads and although air quality is considerably better than it was many years ago, traffic pollution is still a problem for many plants. Airborne soot and other particles can clog leaf pores and adversely affect transpiration (essential moisture evaporation from the leaves) and respiration (breathing); and salt or other chemicals can damage the waxy cuticle on the leaves of plants. Fortunately, there are plenty of attractive plants (see facing page) that will thrive in these conditions, but even these will benefit from a helping hand from time to time. After a hot, dry spell, spray-wash the foliage to rinse off the layers of dust and pollutants that have built up on the leaves. This will improve the plants' looks and unblock any clogged pores. But don't do this when the sun is shining, or you may scorch the foliage.

PROBLEM-SOLVING PLANTS

Whether your borders are flattened regularly by strong winds or take a thumping during family play with pets or footballs, whether your plot turns into a swamp in heavy rain or your frontage is salt-sprayed every time the roads ice over, there are plants that will not only cope well with these conditions but positively thrive in them – and look great, too.

PLANTS FOR BOGGY SOIL

Some of the most attractive and interesting garden plants need moist or even wet soil to survive. Rather than attempt to drain a soggy part of the garden, turn it to your advantage and create a planting to delight.

- ◀ *Astilbe arendsii*
- ● *Caltha palustris*
- ● *Eupatorium cannabinum*
- ● *Filipendula ulmaria*
- ● *Gunnera manicata*
- ● *Iris pseudacorus* 'Variegatus'
- ● *Ligularia* 'Desdemona'
- ● *Lobelia siphilitica*
- ● *Osmunda regalis*
- ● *Primula florindae*
- ● *Trollius* x *chinensis* 'Golden Queen'
- ● *Zantedeschia aethiopica*

PLANTS FOR WINDY GARDENS

It can be frustrating when strong winds flatten carefully tended treasures. Erecting windbreaks will help, but often it's better to go with the conditions as they stand and grow the right plants in the first place.

- ● *Anemone* x *hybrida* 'Bressingham Glow'
- ● *Aster* 'Lady in Blue'
- ● *Cryptomeria japonica* 'Vilmoriniana'
- ● *Helleborus orientalis*
- ● *Hippophae rhamnoides*
- ● *Juniperus squamata* 'Meyeri'
- ● *Miscanthus sinensis*
- ● *Philadelphus* 'Belle Etoile'
- ◀ *Pinus mugo* 'Carsten's Wintergold'

POLLUTION-TOLERANT PLANTS

Roadside pollution may be on the decrease, but gardens on busy roads can still suffer unless the right plants are chosen. Tough shrubs such as privet (*Ligustrum*) and laurel (*Aucuba*) and glossy-leaved perennials will do well here.

- ● *Aucuba japonica* 'Crotonifolia'
- ● *Berberis julianae*
- ● *Bergenia cordifolia* 'Purpurea'
- ● *Buddleja davidii*
- ● *Cotoneaster franchetii*
- ● *Forsythia* x *intermedia* 'Spectabilis'
- ● *Ligustrum ovalifolium*
- ● *Rosa rugosa*
- ● *Symphoricarpos alba*
- ◀ *Viburnum opulus*

CHILD-PROOF PLANTS

Gardens are meant for children to play in. Don't worry if plants get in their way; choose tough shrubs that recover quickly from an assault. You can always replace some of them with more special plants once your nest is empty.

- ● *Amelanchier lamarckii*
- ● *Berberis stenophylla*
- ● *Corylus avellana* 'Aurea'
- ● *Escallonia* 'Iveyi'
- ● *Lonicera nitida* 'Baggesen's Gold'
- ◀ *Pyracantha* 'Soleil d'Or'
- ● *Ribes sanguineum* 'Pulborough Scarlet'
- ● *Sambucus nigra* 'Guincho Purple'
- ● *Senecio* 'Sunshine'
- ● *Spiraea japonica* 'Anthony Waterer'

Perennials

THE MAINSTAYS OF A BORDER, versatile perennials add variety and style to plantings. With their flowers and foliage in a myriad colours, textures and forms, these are the plants with which to create eye-catching combinations. And while most die back in winter, there are plenty that will provide lasting interest until spring comes round again.

STAR PERFORMERS...

PERENNIALS FOR IMPACT

You cannot fail to notice some perennials as soon as you enter a garden. Plant these to give your borders that 'wow' factor.

- Acanthus
- *Crambe cordifolia*
- ◄ *Eryngium bourgatii*
- *Euphorbia characias*
- Kniphofias (red-hot pokers)
- Macleaya (plume poppy)
- Pacific Hybrid delphiniums
- Rodgersia

Designing with perennials

Add lasting style and variety to your borders

Perennial plants – strictly, 'herbaceous perennials' – provide colour and interest year after year. Unlike shrubs, their stems die back in winter, and then the plants renew themselves with fresh growth the next spring. Some retain their foliage over winter, but it will eventually fade, to be replaced with the new season's growth. Use perennials to fill the spaces between structural plants such as trees and shrubs with beautiful groupings of colours and textures, combining plants with different flowering times to create displays that change as the seasons unfold. Not all perennials last for ever, but by getting into the habit of lifting and dividing plants [see p.115] you can reinvigorate your perennials so they perform well for years.

◀ **Eye-catching kniphofias** (red-hot pokers) give a border planting instant impact. Best of all, their robust, upright flower stems need no staking.

USE PERENNIALS THAT FLOWER AT DIFFERENT TIMES TO GIVE PLANTINGS LONG-LASTING INTEREST

Get the heights right

It is essential to check the eventual height of perennial plants before you buy: there is huge variety in size and shape within this group of plants, and sometimes even within a single species. Buy the wrong phlox, for example, and you could find yourself with a shy, mound-forming plant buried within your border, instead of the 1m (3ft) spires you had in mind.

● **CREATE IMPACT WITH BIG PERENNIALS** Choose bold-leaved and tall perennials for the back of a border, or in the centre of a bed that can be viewed from all sides. Many perennials are statuesque enough to take the place of shrubs, and can give a lighter effect. *Crambe cordifolia*, which grows up to 2.5m (8ft) tall, with huge, airy clouds of tiny white flowers above greyish leaves, adds height without bulk. Tall spires such as verbascums and delphiniums add stature without looming over and shading other plants. Many perennials with big leaves, such as gunnera, rheum and ligularia, prefer moist soil: these are star performers for a bold, lush look near an ornamental pond.

● **ADD SUBSTANCE AT MID-HEIGHT** Medium-sized perennials can be used to create dense blocks and drifts of colour. For a meadow-like effect, use plenty of daisy-flowered plants; or arrange ascending tiers of flower spires with plants such as veronicas and astilbes.

● **PLANT LONG-LASTING EDGING** At the front of a border, where plants are always on show, use small perennials with a long flowering period, such as geum or potentilla, or those with foliage as attractive as the flowers – *Sedum* 'Purple Emperor', for example. Low-growing perennials like epimediums and pulmonarias also make ideal ground cover around shrubs, and attractive underplanting for shrubs in containers. Choose varieties with striking or variegated foliage to maintain interest once flowering is over.

▼ **Mid-height perennials** can be used to create broad swathes of colour. The open, flat flowers of these asters and rudbeckias will also attract beneficial insects, helping keep down garden pests.

MAKING FLOWER FORMS WORK FOR YOU

Perennial flowers can do much more in a border than just captivate with their exquisite colours. Their very varied forms can be used as design elements in your beds and borders, making a huge contribution to the style and overall impression of a planting and even creating illusions of perspective.

DELICATE FLOWER SHAPES

Gentle, dainty flowers give a graceful, light and airy feel to a border. Look for dierama, filipendula (meadowsweet), thalictrum (above) and gypsophila, or where height is needed, *Aruncus dioicus* (goat's beard).

BOLD VERTICALS

Upright 'punctuation points' draw the eye and seem to bring a planting closer. Eremurus (foxtail lily, above), kniphofia (red-hot poker), *Ligularia* 'The Rocket' and lythrum (loosestrife) will fit the bill, or for a low border, try *Veronica spicata*.

FLAT-TOPPED FLOWERHEADS

Achilleas (above), sedums and plants with daisylike flowers such as heleniums and rudbeckias smile up at you from the border. Planted in drifts, they have a floating, dreamy quality that can give the illusion of distance.

Arrange plants to best effect To maximise impact, plant in drifts, groups or clumps, rather than isolated plants of single varieties. Vary the size of individual groups of plants for a naturalistic look. Where space is no problem, broad swathes of substantial perennials such as aruncus, *Acanthus mollis* (bear's breeches), astilbes, lupins and euphorbias can look truly breathtaking. In a more restricted space, planting in groups of three, five or more of the same variety makes more of a show than growing one plant each of many different kinds. See pages 72–81 for more tips on grouping plants within beds and borders.

● **CHECK THE SPREAD OF PLANTS** Don't be tempted to plant too closely when starting a new perennial border, or you will soon have to lift and move plants. If the bed looks sparse in its first year, pack it out with bedding plants, planting these in good-sized groups to reflect your intended effect.

● **GIVE BIG PLANTS PLENTY OF SPACE** The shade cast by large plants and the spread of their leaves can adversely affect the plants around them. Big plants will make the most impact when they are allowed to grow naturally, without the need to control them for the sake of other plants in the border.

● **CREATE A VISTA ALONG THE BORDER** Setting swathes of grouped plants at an oblique angle to the front of a border creates a generous impression of distance as you look along the planting.

● **ADD A TOUCH OF PERFUME** Drifts of scented perennials will add a whole new experience to a garden. For sheer heaven, plant a patch of ethereal-looking, white *Hesperis matronalis* var. *albiflora* and drink in the fragrance on a warm summer's evening.

The value of foliage

Balance flowering and leafy plants
A traditional border planting contains one type of plant grown for the beauty of its foliage for every two or three grown for their flowers, to carry over the display between flowering times. How you allocate space in your garden is a matter of personal taste; you could, for example, weight your planting towards flowering perennials that have especially interesting, attractive foliage even when not in flower, such as *Phlox paniculata* 'Norah Leigh' and *Polemonium caeruleum* 'Brise d'Anjou'.

● **POP IN A HOSTA WHERE YOU NEED FOLIAGE IMPACT** These amazingly varied, broad-leaved plants tolerate a wide range of positions and all but hot, dry soil, and establish rapidly to give a good show.

● **CREATE A FOLIAGE TAPESTRY** Make a stunning arrangement of several coloured-leaved cultivars of heuchera. Their dainty flower spikes are produced throughout the summer, while the astounding range of leaf colours in these evergreen plants, from deep purple through amber to bright yellow, will keep up the show throughout winter.

▼ **A bed with moist soil,** especially near water, is the perfect spot to create a Lost World-style planting with big-leaved plants like gunneras (to the rear) and hostas.

STAR PERFORMERS...

TOP FOLIAGE PERENNIALS

Foliage perennials add texture and form to planting schemes in beds and borders, but they are also really useful for covering large areas of ground. They smother weeds efficiently while providing something interesting to look at, and require little in the way of care.

● **Bergenias**
● *Brunnera macrophylla* **'Aluminium Spot' and 'Hadspen Cream'**
● *Euphorbia characias*; *Euphorbia* x *martinii* **'Ascot Rainbow'**
● **Ferns**
● *Geranium phaeum* **'Variegatum'**
● **Heucheras**
● **Hostas**
● *Lamium galeobdolon* **'Hermann's Pride'**
● *Polygonatum odoratum* **'Variegatum'**
● **Pulmonarias**
● *Symphytum uplandicum* **'Grandiflorum'**
● **Tiarellas**

● **ADD INTEREST IN WINTER** Perennials with evergreen foliage, such as spiky kniphofias or glossy bergenias, will make a bed more interesting to look at in winter. If they are looking scruffy when spring arrives, cut back the old outer leaves, being careful not to damage any new emerging growth.

● **CREATE STRIKING LEAF CONTRASTS** Groupings of just two or three plants with contrasting leaf shapes, colours and textures can be very exciting – combine paddle-leaved hostas with serrated, spiny acanthus foliage, for example, or with strap-leaved liriope and dusky *Anthriscus sylvestris* 'Ravenswing' (purple-leaved cow parsley). For a lighter, blue-grey-silver combination, underplant spiky eryngiums with furry-leaved *Stachys byzantina* (lamb's ears).

Don't forget ferns
The ultimate in easy-grow perennials, ferns are not just for areas of damp shade. Provided that you water them well when young, *Asplenium*

▲ **Fern fronds unfurling** into fresh, green growth are a beautiful sight early in the year. Spring bulbs like these bluebells are perfect companions; after flowering, their leaves will die back to allow the ferns to fill the space.

scolopendrium, *Dryopteris affinis* and *Polystichum aculeatum* will grow quite happily in dry shade once established, making them valuable foliage plants for these difficult conditions. Most common hardy ferns can tolerate sun, too, provided that the soil is damp: athyriums are especially adaptable.

● **PUT SPENT FERN FRONDS TO GOOD USE** The dead leaves of deciduous ferns make excellent insulation for slightly tender plants such as penstemons in winter; cover the crowns with a layer in the autumn [see also p.255].

ORNAMENTAL GRASSES PLANTED IN GROUPS GIVE A BORDER A MODERN SCULPTURAL LOOK

Add gorgeous grasses to bring a border to life One of the most popular trends in gardening has been the increased use of ornamental grasses – a huge and varied group that also includes sedges, rushes and bamboos. Choose grasses to add lightness, movement and sound to your borders. Their neutral, natural tones and airy forms make a perfect framework for contemporary planting schemes, from the fresh clumps of fine leaves early in the season to the waving, plume-like flowerheads in fawn and gold later in the summer. A border totally comprised of grasses of different forms and colours is a spectacular feature, but they combine happily with flowering perennials. Liven up both summer and winter containers and baskets by including at least one colourful grass with evergreen foliage – blue *Festuca glauca* works well in just about every instance.

STAR
PERFORMERS...

TOP GRASSES FOR COLOUR

Ornamental grasses in groups give planting schemes a modern, sculptural look. Combine different colours, heights and habits for really up-to-date impact.

- *Carex morrowii* 'Evergold'
- ◀ *Festuca glauca*
- *Glyceria maxima* var. *variegata*
- *Helictotrichon sempervirens*
- *Imperata cylindrica* 'Rubra'
- *Luzula sylvatica* 'Hohe Tatra'
- *Milium effusum* 'Aureum'
- *Miscanthus sinensis* 'Morning Light'
- *Pennisetum setaceum* 'Rubrum'
- *Uncinia rubra*

● **TRIM GRASSES IN SPRING** Grasses are easy to care for: simply cut down the dead growth with shears or, if evergreen, comb through with a garden rake to neaten them up. Leave this until spring so that over winter, the seedheads can feed seed-eating birds while the leaves and stems shelter hibernating insects. Untrimmed grasses look striking when frosted, transformed into marvels of silvery-white.

● **CHECK THE GROWTH HABIT** Some grasses grow in neat clumps, while others spread rapidly by means of running roots through the soil. Check labels for the words 'clump-forming' and choose these grasses for the border: you will save yourself a great deal of work controlling unruly, invasive plants. Panicum and pennisetum varieties are among the most well-behaved grasses. Rampant, spreading types like phalaris make good ground cover for difficult sites. If you like their looks, they can also be grown in containers to confine their spread.

● **PLANT GRASSES BY WATER FEATURES** For damp places, plant sedges and rushes, which thrive in moist soil and cool areas. Used around a garden pond, they give a natural, informal feel and make excellent shelter for frogs and toads.

▼ **Bamboos are ideal** plants for narrow beds, which will contain their tendency to spread. Thin out the canes if you want them to show up well against an attractive background.

Be bold with bamboos
Bamboos make fantastic architectural plants, whether you want to create a garden with an oriental feel, or are just looking for something with a different form and look to add to a border. Some bamboos can be rampant growers, but there are plenty that are suitable for small to medium-sized gardens; check labels carefully and ask for advice from the nursery or garden centre. Bamboos with beautifully coloured canes, or stems, are particularly good value for the smaller garden: those of *Phyllostachys nigra* 'Boryana' are dark green, turning yellow and purple, while *Sasa veitchii* forms dense thickets of purple canes with broad leaves.

● **HARVEST THE CANES** Bamboos need thinning from time to time, for which you will need a good pair of loppers and stout gloves. For a supply of ready-made plant supports to use elsewhere in the garden, cut the canes as near to the base as you can; keep your gloves on to strip the leaves, which can be sharp.

▲ **A prairie planting** composed of drifts and ribbons of grasses and flowering perennials needs little more than cutting down each spring to stay looking good year after year.

Make an easy-care prairie planting The prairie planting style originated as a way to create almost maintenance-free landscaping. It mixes medium-to-tall grasses planted in broad swathes or ribbons with drifts of easy-care flowering perennials, many hailing from North America, such as echinaceas, heleniums, monardas ('Prairie Night' is a beautiful variety), *Eupatorium maculatum* and the prairie gayfeather, *Liatris spicata*. The heights of plants should vary unevenly, rather than graduating from the tallest down, making this an ideal solution for a large island bed or a deep border.

● **RESTRICT YOUR PLANT CHOICE TO GET THE LOOK** A limited number of different plants and a restrained colour scheme are key to the prairie style. The grasses will provide the neutral tones; two ranges of colour that work well are pale pink through raspberry to bronze-purple, or primrose-yellow through orange into rust.

● **BE GUIDED BY PLANT NAMES** Flowering plants with 'meadow' as part of their common name will also have exactly the right look for this style of planting. Look for meadowsweet (filipendula), meadow rue (thalictrum), meadow clary (*Salvia pratensis*) and meadow cranesbill (*Geranium pratense*).

● **REVIVE AN OLD FAVOURITE** Pampas grass, or *Cortaderia selloana,* so popular in the 1970s, has made a comeback as a perfect structural plant for the prairie look, so if you have never lost your affection for it, this is the perfect way to use pampas grass in your garden in a really contemporary style.

Caring for perennials

Anticipate the needs of your plants The secret of happy, healthy perennials is to give them what they want before they start to need it. Good soil preparation before planting is vital. Be sure to dig the ground thoroughly and remove every perennial weed root; this will save you no end of maintenance work in the long run. Add plenty of organic material such as well-rotted manure, and then leave the bed for a few weeks before planting so that you can hoe off the first crop of annual weeds just before you introduce the new plants.

● **USE SLOW-RELEASE FERTILISERS** A spring feed of a balanced fertiliser like fish, blood and bone scattered in perennial borders will give the plants access to a slow, steady supply of nutrients from the moment they start into growth. Plants fed in this way grow much more strongly than those 'dosed' with quick-fix, fast-acting feeds only when they start to look starved.

● **ADD SUPPORTS EARLY ON** It's much more difficult to give support to plants that need it once they have grown and are flopping over. By getting your supports in at the start of the season (see below), you are much less likely to damage plants.

PLANT SUPPORTS

To keep taller perennials looking good throughout the summer, give them support. Keep the supports unobtrusive to maintain the impression that the plants are growing naturally. Never bunch stems together and tie them to a single cane; this always looks inelegant and will spoil the whole planting.

HOOPS AND RINGS
Circular supports are ideal for holding up wide, heavy plants such as peonies (above) and lupins. Some can be linked together to create larger enclosures.

CANES AND TIES
Support heavy flowering stems such as those of delphiniums individually with canes. Tie them in loosely, or clamp with small purpose-made rings.

TWIGGY STICKS
Use prunings from trees and shrubs to make wigwam supports for medium-height, clumping plants such as phlox; they will disappear as the plant grows.

When to cut back plants

Flowering perennials that die down in winter will look neater at the end of the season if they are cut back almost to ground level, but as with grasses, the dead and dormant growth is a valuable resource for wildlife over the cold months, and the seedheads of some flowering plants – sedums and asclepias, for example – will remain attractive for some time. Leave evergreen perennials until the spring before tidying them up.

● **LEAVE PLANT MARKERS IN THE GROUND** If you are cutting back in autumn, leave short stumps of old stem on the clumps, so that in spring you can see where the plant is growing. It is very easy to forget, then attempt to plant something else in the same place if the soil is completely bare.

● **ENCOURAGE A SECOND FLOWER FLUSH** Many perennials will flower again if they are cut back after flowering [see also p.94]. Some, like *Achillea millefolium*, should be cut back to ground level; with others – delphiniums, for instance – look for side shoots bearing buds lower down the stems, and cut cleanly across the stem just above them.

Minimise plant problems

Mildew is the most common problem affecting perennials; it is more unsightly than harmful, although if allowed to continue year after year, plants will weaken. Some perennials are naturally healthier than others: the rudbeckia 'Goldsturm', for example, rarely suffers. You can also choose disease-resistant cultivars of plants especially prone to mildew; among phlox, look for 'David' and 'Miss Pepper', for example – and among asters, seek out 'Mönch', 'Bluebird' and 'Lady in Black'.

● **WATER IN DRY SPELLS** Established perennials do not need regular watering as a matter of course, but in hot, dry weather they will need a good soaking from time to time, before they start wilting. To give a boost to plants that have been struggling with drought, add a soluble, phosphate-rich flower feed after watering.

● **RESCUE PLANTS FROM WEEDS** If plants have become weed-infested, the solution is to lift them in autumn to clean them up, then replant; it is much easier to disentangle the weeds from the roots of the perennials when out of the ground.

▲ **Ground-hugging perennials,** such as these hardy geraniums, benefit from clipping over with shears after flowering or when they start to look untidy. They will send up neat, fresh new growth, and many varieties will also produce a further flush of flowers later in the season.

STAR PERFORMERS...

TOP SELF-SEEDERS

Perennials that self-seed readily are so convenient – they take all the work out of raising plants yourself, and, in the right spots, can quickly produce dense plantings ideal for keeping weeds at bay.

● *Alchemilla mollis*
◀ **Aquilegias**
● *Arum italicum* **'Marmoratum'**
● **Brunnera**
● **Cirsium**
● *Euphorbia dulcis* **'Chameleon'**
● **Foxgloves**
● **Hardy geraniums**
● **Symphytum**
● *Viola labradorica* **var.** *purpurea* **(dog violet)**

DIVIDING PERENNIALS

Autumn is the best time for dividing perennials; the soil will still be warm enough to promote new root growth before the winter. If that's not possible, then wait until spring. Choose a day when you have time both to dig up and divide the parent and replant or pot up the new pieces straight away, so they do not dry out.

BY HAND
Perennials with light, fibrous root systems such as this hepatica may be pulled apart easily by hand to make several smaller new plants.

FORK TO FORK
Old, congested clumps (for example, of hardy geraniums) can be split by inserting two digging forks, back to back, into the clump and levering it apart.

CUT OR CHOP
Grasses and plants with straplike leaves (excluding bearded iris; see p.89) can be divided without lifting; simply dig out a section of the clump and replant.

Plants for free

Make more of your plants The vast majority of perennials can be both reinvigorated and multiplied by division. This involves digging up an entire clump and splitting it into smaller pieces, which can then either be replanted or potted up. Divide the plant into small pieces; these will re-establish much quicker. When replanting divided perennials, only use the young growths around the edge of the clump – discard old, woody non-productive material. Keep the new plants well-watered the following year until well-grown.

● **CHOOSE PLANTS THAT PROPAGATE THEMSELVES** Some perennials, like *Fragaria* 'Pink Panda' (ornamental strawberry) and sempervivums (house leeks) form complete baby plants, often with well-formed roots, at the side of the parent or along creeping stems called runners. These plantlets can be detached and potted up. Unlike many perennials raised from home-collected seed, the new plants will be exactly the same as the ones they were taken from.

Plant super self-seeders Lots of perennials will propagate themselves by seed all around your garden (see facing page). When weeding around these perennials in spring, watch out for young plants with the same leaf shapes. These offspring may differ from their parents, especially in flower colour, but may be no less attractive for that. Either leave them to grow where they are, carefully lift them and replant elsewhere, or pot them up and grow them on.

Roses

COMBINE THE TRADITIONAL CHARM of roses with the skills of specialist growers and the result is a wealth of new and exciting ways to grow roses in the garden. Use them not only in the border but also in patio pots, as ground cover, and even to plant up problem areas. It's not hard to grow roses well and enjoy their beauty year after year.

Know your roses

Get in with the growers Order rose catalogues from specialist growers – they open up an astonishing world of choice (there are, literally, thousands of rose varieties) and will demystify all those baffling rose terms such as 'hybrid tea' and 'floribunda'. All the old boundaries between rose categories are breaking down as breeders work to offer more growing options and as gardeners find more imaginative ways of growing roses. All you need to do is to find a rose of the right height and growth habit – whether stocky and bushy, tall and statuesque, spreading, climbing or even miniature – with flowers in a colour you love.

● **BUY ROSES BARE-ROOTED FOR THE BEST START** By all means admire roses you see in display gardens and shows in full bloom in the summer – but try to resist buying them. Order instead from the growers, who will deliver sturdy bare-rooted plants lifted fresh from their growing beds between late autumn and early spring, when the plants are dormant and the time for planting is right.

EXPERT KNOW HOW

PLANTING BARE-ROOTED ROSES

When you buy bare-rooted roses you can see how growers insert buds of the chosen variety onto the rootstock of a wild rose; these grafted buds then grow into the named rose. The join between shoots and roots is called the bud union.

1 In frost-free weather, dig a generous hole and add organic matter at the base. Unwrap the rose and trim any thick roots to about 25cm (10in). Look for the bud union and use a cane to check that the hole is deep enough for this to sit just below the soil level.

2 Hold the rose in the hole with one hand while you scoop and firm soil in around the roots with the other, keeping the bud union at about 2.5cm (1in) below the finished soil level. Firm in with your knuckles, then finally with your foot. Cut any holding twine, and water in well.

● **GET THE BEST VALUE FOR SMALL GARDENS** by looking for the words 'repeat-flowering'. These are the roses that, especially if deadheaded regularly [see p.120], will keep producing new flowers for months – vital where space is at a premium.

● **CHOOSE CLIMBERS FOR HEIGHT** Leave rambler roses for planting spots where you need a vigorous climbing plant. Beautiful though they are, they are too big to be accommodated in beds and borders in any but the largest gardens. Instead, choose climbers to train up arches across paths, arbours and obelisks (see overleaf).

● **ENJOY THE BEST OF OLD AND NEW** Look for growers that specialise in producing roses with lovely, old-fashioned flower shapes and scents but also desirable modern qualities: better resistance to disease, sturdier growth, and flowers that go on all summer rather than opening all at once in one short, splendid flush.

Great ways to grow roses

Bring colour to your borders
Most modern gardens are not large enough to give over a whole area to a rose garden, but roses are perfect for mixed or shrub borders. They will give extra appeal to the planting, especially at times when other plants are out of flower, and fragrant roses will perfume the air for a longer period than most other plants. Bush roses are best planted in groups of three or five of the same variety, while larger shrub roses may be planted singly.

● **SHOW FLOWERS OFF TO PERFECTION** A dark yew hedge makes a superb backdrop to roses grown in a border, the sober, plain foliage showcasing the beauty of the blooms as they unfold. A dark-painted fence is also an effective backdrop to roses.

● **CREATE AN OLD-WORLD LOOK** Include old-fashioned shrub roses in a herb garden – try fragrant varieties with deep red petals suitable for pot pourri. Or, find space near a sunny sitting area for a classic pairing: old-fashioned roses with lavender.

● **TRANSFORM A DIFFICULT SITE** such as a dry bed or sloping bank with easy, low-maintenance ground-cover or 'carpet' roses – fast-growing varieties with a prostrate or spreading habit, such as 'Suffolk', 'Grouse' and 'Scented Carpet'. Pruning is confined to clipping back when necessary, and modern varieties will flower right through the summer and autumn with no deadheading needed.

▲ **Roses with vivid,** strong colours, such as this unusual variety, 'Rhapsody in Blue', will not fade and lose their colour so quickly if planted in part-shade (shade for half the day, or dappled shade).

▼ **Let clematis scramble** through modern shrub roses such as 'Raymond Carver' (foreground) for a beautiful combination. Use named varieties of later-flowering clematis (not species) such as 'Etoile Violette' and 'Perle d'Azur' that can be cut back hard in spring, allowing you to prune the roses.

STAR PERFORMERS...

FRAGRANT ROSES

Wonderfully scented roses enhance any garden – plant them near paths and patios, and drink in the fragrance.

◄ 'Double Delight' (bush)
● 'Elizabeth Harkness' (bush)
● 'Etoile de Hollande' (climbing)
● 'Fragrant Delight' (bush)
● 'Fritz Nobis' (shrub)
● 'Lilac Rose' (shrub)
● 'Mme Alfred Carrière' (climbing)
● 'Pink Prosperity' (shrub)
● 'Souvenir du Dr Jamain' (shrub)
● 'Velvet Fragrance' (bush)

Add height with roses If your border looks rather two-dimensional, train a shrub rose, climbing rose or strong-growing bush rose on an obelisk. Another great way of introducing height is with standard and half-standard roses, with their lollipop heads on tall, clear stems.

● **USE STANDARD ROSES TO ADD FORMALITY** Edge a path with standard roses underplanted with lavender, box or potentilla; or plant a single standard as a centrepiece to a paved area. Look out for ground-cover roses grown as standards. They make naturally weeping specimens: in a small garden they are a lovely alternative to trees such as weeping cherries and willows, and will never outgrow their space.

● **CREATE A THORNY BARRIER** Make a stunning hedge with shrub roses. Plant slightly closer than in the border and choose repeat or long-flowering varieties: hybrid musks such as 'Prosperity', 'Buff Beauty' and 'Ballerina' are ideal. If you need extra security, or want to keep neighbours' pets off your garden, a screen of dense, prickly species (wild) roses, such as *Rosa rugosa*, *R. glauca*, *R. canina* (dog rose) and *R. moyesii* will do just that. Many have attractive hips after flowering, which will attract birds to the garden.

Make a big impact with small roses

'Patio roses' are generally smaller than bush roses, with neat, bushy growth. Seldom out of flower during summer, their modern breeding means that they are robust and disease-resistant. They and their even smaller relatives, the miniature roses, are perfect for beds and borders near the house, or as a diminutive hedge around a patio. They also thrive if planted in large pots or – better still – in long, deep troughs or boxes, enabling you to create the effect of a small bed with several roses in one container.

● **PLANT CONTAINERS WITH TRAILING ROSES** Make a hanging basket or window box with a difference by using a carpet rose instead of bedding plants. A large, solid-sided basket is best; plant in soil-based compost and feed regularly with tomato feed; the rose will give years of pleasure with hardly any maintenance.

● **CREATE A PEACHY COCKTAIL** 'Sweet Dream' is a lovely little rose, upright and bushy, with masses of apricot-peach flowers standing above attractive, glossy foliage. Try a combination of this and deep apricot 'Cider Cup' in a trough or a miniature bed made by omitting or lifting a few paving stones on the patio.

● **USE SMALL CLIMBERS IN POTS AND PLANTERS** Patio climbing roses, such as 'Good as Gold' and 'Ginger Syllabub', are delightful new additions, generally shorter than normal climbing roses and flowering all summer from top to bottom. They are naturally healthy and ideal for small spaces and containers.

EXPERT KNOW HOW

TRAINING ROSES ON AN OBELISK

A rose on an obelisk adds grace and height to a planting. In summer, the rose will be the main source of interest; in winter, the obelisk itself will be a welcome focal point while plants are dormant.

Roses that grow straight upwards tend to flower only at the tips of their stems, right at the top of the structure. To produce flowers from top to bottom, bring the stems closer to horizontal, spiralling them diagonally around the obelisk and tying them in. This encourages short flowering shoots to grow from the leaf joints at all levels. Snip off spent flowers and new flowers will form on short new sideshoots.

◀ **Link borders** across paths with a glorious archway of fragrant roses. 'Kathleen Harrop' is ideal, as it is thornless; 'Zéphirine Drouhin' is also thorn-free, with fuller flowers in a deeper pink.

THE MOST DISEASE-RESISTANT ROSES

For trouble-free roses less likely to be disfigured by disease, choose varieties that are known to be naturally resistant.

- 'Champagne Moment' (bush)
- 'Chinatown' (bush)
- 'Flower Power' (patio)
- 'Fred Loads' (shrub)
- 'Graham Thomas' (shrub)
- 'Loving Memory' (bush)
◀ 'Raubritter' (ground-cover)
- 'Silver Jubilee' (bush)
- 'The Fairy' (ground-cover)
- 'The Generous Gardener' (shrub)

Grow roses like a pro

Keep plants growing strongly Roses need moisture to produce strong new growth and to absorb the nutrients that encourage plentiful flower production. Choose specific rose fertilisers tailor-made to provide the balance of elements necessary for a healthy bush with an abundance of flowers through the season. Apply one feed in early spring and another after the first flush of blooms, and water thoroughly during hot, dry weather so that the plants are able to take up the nutrients, and your roses will look good enough for a show garden.

HOW DOES IT WORK?
SUCKERS

Suckers – strong shoots from the rootstock of a grafted rose – are often stimulated to grow when roots are damaged by hoeing too deeply or digging too close to the rose. They can take over from the named variety, so remove them quickly. Scrape away the earth and pull (not cut) them off at the point where they spring from the root **(1)**, to prevent regrowth.

Top growth of the rose is the named, or desired, variety

Bud union is where the named rose has been grafted onto rootstock

Wild rose rootstock may throw up its own shoots, or suckers

● **GIVE ROSES A LATE MEAL** An autumn feed pays dividends. Bone meal will release nutrients slowly throughout the winter, building up strong roots and shoots. For a real boost to future performance, use an autumn lawn fertiliser – this contains all the right ingredients for a breathtaking show the next summer. Bone meal is completely safe, but wear gloves to handle it.

● **DEAL WITH SUCKERS FAST** Remove any rogue, strong shoots that spring from the wild rose roots onto which your variety has been budded, or grafted (see left). If you leave suckers, they will sap all the energy out of your rose. They don't always have the tell-tale sign of seven leaflets instead of five, but they do tend to look vigorous, and possibly a fresher green than the rest of the plant.

● **DEADHEAD TO KEEP THE FLOWERS COMING** With repeat-flowering roses, deadheading – removing the spent flowers – hastens and increases the production of new flowers, so keep on top of it and your roses will reward you. Cut off the dead head or cluster down to the first leaf with five leaflets for quick repeat flowering – or prune lower down if the bush is getting straggly.

Don't be a slave to pruning Regardless of what you might hear, all roses can be pruned similarly, following a few simple rules. In autumn or early spring, remove any damaged and dead wood first, then take out stems crossing each other or the centre of the plant so that air can circulate freely – this reduces the risk of disease. Then if it is a mature plant, take out one or two really old branches at ground level, to encourage young shoots to form low down. Finally, shorten all other stems by about two-thirds for a bush rose, and one-third to half for shrub roses, cutting to an outward-pointing bud or sideshoot [see Pruning Made Easy, p.250].

ENCOURAGE BENEFICIAL INSECTS SUCH AS LADYBIRDS TO HELP CONTROL GREENFLY ON ROSES

Protect your roses Roses can be more prone to problems than some other plant groups, but preventative measures go a long way to keeping them healthy. If you spray early in the season with rose fungicide you will greatly reduce the risk of the main rose diseases – black spot and white, powdery mildew. Encourage birds, ladybirds and lacewings into the garden [see pp.272–3] and they will help control greenfly, the main rose pest. Good garden hygiene around roses also really helps. Remove fallen and spotted leaves regularly and do not leave debris lying around that may harbour disease spores. It is best not to compost rose prunings, as diseases can then be carried over from one year to the next – take them to the recycling centre.

EXPERT KNOW HOW

DISBUDDING ROSES

Removing spent flowers or flower clusters from repeat-flowering roses boosts flowering, but you can also borrow a tip from show-growers – selective removal of buds, or disbudding – to create perfect blooms.

Floribunda, or cluster-flowered roses have an annoying habit – the central bloom opens and dies before the others, spoiling the look. While buds are still green, nip out the central or 'king' bud (see right) for perfect, even flower clusters. For the most elegant single blooms on hybrid tea (large-flowered) roses, pinch off any small single buds that develop around the main one.

Bulbs

FROM THE FIRST SNOWDROPS in late winter to autumn's brilliant colchicums, bulbs provide colour and interest almost year-round. These self-sufficient plants with their conspicuous flowers are so easy to grow that there's no excuse not to pack your beds, borders and containers with bulbs for spring cheer and summer splendour.

STAR PERFORMERS...

THE LOVELIEST TULIPS

If you only have room for a few tulips, these are some absolute beauties to take you right through the spring.

- ◄ 'Angelique' (late spring)
- 'Apricot Beauty' (mid-spring)
- 'Ballerina' (mid-spring)
- 'Blushing Bride' (late spring–early summer)
- 'Early Harvest' (early spring)
- 'Golden Artist' (late spring–early summer)
- 'Sweetheart' (mid-spring)

A bulb for all seasons

Be bolder with bulbs Make a resolution to plant more bulbs this autumn and spring: they'll appear year after year to delight you through the seasons. The earliest spring bulbs, such as snowdrops and winter aconites, can be seen peeking through the snow in some years while winter still holds its grip, to be followed by all the spring favourites, from early crocuses to the last of the tulips. Be bolder with summer-flowering bulbs, too – the choice is so much wider than lilies and gladioli. Choose lesser-seen bulbs such as fragrant freesias, radiant white chincherinchees, red-hot tigridias, spiky eucomis (the pineapple lily), flag-like cannas and stately crinums. The last flowering bulbs of the season – dahlias, *Cyclamen hederifolium*, nerines, colchicums, *Crocus speciosus* and sternbergia – will take you through the autumn until the first frosts.

Be sure to buy the best Bulbs will last for years, if properly looked after. For the best flowering performance and long-lived bulbs, it pays to select really choice examples when buying. Look for plump, firm, disease-free specimens; avoid those which are soft or showing signs of mould or rot, or those which have been kept too warm at point of sale and have started to shoot or look dehydrated.

◄ **Late tulips and early alliums** bridge the gap between the seasons for spring and summer bulbs. Both the bulbs and the forget-me-nots planted between them were planted in autumn.

SELF-SUFFICIENT PLANTS

The term 'bulbs' is used to cover plants with one thing in common – they grow from an underground storage organ that may take the form of an onion-like bulb, a knobbly corm or a fleshy tuber. These organs contain all the food the plant needs to tide it over its dormant period during winter cold or hot, dry summers.

☐ BULBS

A bulb consists of layers of juicy stem base tissue, usually protected by a brown, papery 'tunic'. Make sure that the tunic is intact when buying daffodils, tulips and hyacinths for the strongest plants. The loose layers of tissue forming lily bulbs are modified leaves, and the flower stem develops from the centre of these.

☐ CORMS

Corms, like bulbs, are made up of stem base tissue but are far more solid than bulbs. Tiny cormlets develop around the parent and replace it every year, so the plants progressively spread outwards – which is why cormous crocuses and colchicums spread out when naturalised in grass.

☐ TUBERS

Tubers are swollen, fleshy underground stems or roots with dormant eyes (buds) from which both roots and shoots grow. The starchy tissue they contain enables the plant to survive a dormant period, allowing gardeners to lift and store dahlia tubers, for example, over the winter months.

BEAT THAT!

● **How much is one of your snowdrops worth?**
In early 2011, a single bulb was sold on an internet auction site for £357. It was a rare, pure-white variety with six equal-sized petals, named 'E. A. Bowles' after the famous horticulturist and plantsman. It was discovered in 2004 at Myddelton House, north of London, Bowles's garden and home. In recent years snowdrop collecting has become increasingly fashionable and prices have soared – although they're still nowhere near as high as those paid for prized tulips during the 17th-century Dutch 'Tulipomania' craze.

A very few bulbs, such as aconites, snowdrops and bluebells, establish well if planted just after flowering, with leaves still attached; look out for these bulbs sold 'in the green'.
● **BUY EARLY FOR THE BEST CHOICE** Select your spring-flowering bulbs as soon as they appear in shops and garden centres in late summer and early autumn. Most are best planted straight away, but tulips can flower better if planted later – up to early winter if the weather is mild and dry.
● **ORDER QUALITY BULBS FROM THE GROWERS** Bulbs obtained from specialist bulb-growers and sellers are likely to have been stored in optimum conditions and will be dispatched to you at just the right time for planting.
● **PLANT AT THE CORRECT DEPTH** Two or three times the depth of the actual bulb is the rule of thumb – a useful one when buying bulbs loose from garden centres.

Spring bulbs

Add early colour to beds and borders
In most gardens, there is always room for a group of daffodils or tulips, or something more unusual, such as the majestic crown imperial fritillaries. Don't forget the small, dainty bulbs, like anemones, *Iris reticulata*, chionodoxa and snakeshead fritillaries. Place these at the front of beds and borders among low-growing perennials; the bulbs will have time to flower while the shoots of the perennials are still emerging. Or, bring their delicate flowers closer to the eye by planting them in a raised bed.
● **FIND NEW PLACES FOR BULBS** Pop in markers in spring where you see gaps in the border that could be brightened with bulbs; that way, when the spring bulbs go on sale in autumn, you'll know just where to put them.

Produce the best displays
For great results from your spring bulbs, good ground preparation before planting in the autumn pays dividends. Dig over the area thoroughly; bulbs need good drainage, so improve wet soil by digging deeply and incorporating plenty of fine grit or sharp sand. Add bone meal a week or two before planting; this releases its nutrients slowly to boost the bulbs once they start to grow.
● **PLANT CLOSELY FOR THE BEST EFFECT** Plant your bulbs in tight groups – make the spaces between them just two to three times the width of the bulbs.
● **GROUP BULBS FOR A NATURALISTIC LOOK** Unless you want a formal effect, spring bulbs look better planted in drifts, rather than orderly rows. Groups of the same variety are more effective than dotted mixtures of species and colours, although colour-contrasting mixes of just two varieties can be stunning. Try low-growing blue muscari (grape hyacinths) with taller tulips in a warm orange.

Ensure next year's flowers
After flowering, pinch off the dead flower heads. Allow the leaves to remain for at least six weeks after flowering, watering in dry spells and feeding with a general purpose fertiliser to build the bulbs up

▼ **Pots of snowdrops** are often offered for sale 'in the green' in spring, after flowering but before the leaves have died down. Either plant them together or tease them apart carefully to minimise damage to the roots. This is also a good time to lift and divide established clumps in the garden.

well for the following year. Don't knot the leaves; this will interfere with the plant's natural processes.

● **PROTECT PRECIOUS TULIPS** The small species tulips can be left in the ground year after year, but the showy hybrid types give a better display in subsequent years if dug up after flowering. Clean the bulbs and store in a cool, dry, dark place until October, then plant out again. Hyacinths always flower best the spring after planting; in following seasons the flower heads will be much smaller. Replant them somewhere out of the way if you cannot bear to discard them, and replace with new stock.

Plant up pots of spring cheer Container-grown bulbs give a lift to any garden, large or small. The one essential is to make sure that the containers

have drainage holes, as bulbs will rot in waterlogged compost. To be doubly safe, put a layer of gravel, pebbles or fragments of broken pots in the base of the container before adding the compost. Keep containers well-watered – the bulbs can easily dry out on warm or windy days. When flowering is over, you can either plant the bulbs out in the garden, or lift, clean, dry and store them in a cool, dry place until autumn planting time.

● **ADD COLOURFUL UNDERPLANTING** When making up containers planted with shrubs, conifers, foliage perennials and other permanent plants, leave gaps for bulbs to provide extra seasonal colour. They can be set straight into the compost, or grown in pots for dropping in, still in the pots, when the buds show. They are then easy to remove and replace with summer bedding.

● **PLANT A WHOLE BULB GARDEN** in a large container. Buy a selection of bulbs to take you through the season – starting with species crocus and 'January Gold' daffodils, then narcissi, tulips, scillas, hyacinths and on to Dutch iris and the first of the alliums. Plant each type at its recommended depth, in layers, in a large tub or trough on the patio. This will never be out of flower from late winter until midsummer, and will last for at least three years without replanting.

▲ **Group several containers** planted with different spring bulbs for a really bright show. Punch drainage holes in the bottom of improvised containers such as buckets to prevent the compost becoming sodden after spring rain, which will rot the bulbs.

▼ **Snakeshead fritillaries** are one of the most exquisite small spring bulbs. As the flowers finish, the dark-leaved *Anthriscus sylvestris* 'Ravenswing' around them will grow up to hide the dying foliage.

Summer and autumn bulbs

Cut down maintenance with hardy bulbs Colourful half-hardy bulbs such as dahlias, gladioli, cannas, ixias, sparaxis, chincherinchees and triteleia are hard to resist, but they do need lifting and storing over winter to ensure their survival year after year. For summer bulbs that you can leave in the ground, choose hardy border favourites such as alliums, crocosmias, Asiatic lilies and schizostylis. If you don't experience very hard winters regularly, you may find that dahlias, alstroemerias, agapanthus and even gladioli will come through the winter if you protect them with a generous layer of garden compost, straw or bracken [see p.255].

DAHLIAS IN RED-HOT SHADES GIVE A CARNIVAL ATMOSPHERE TO ANY SUMMER PLANTING

- **MAKE A COOL START TO SUMMER** Among the bulbs that bridge the gap between the classic spring and summer varieties are alliums, camassias and brodaeia, in the most intense shades of purple and blue. If your spring garden is dominated by yellows and pinks, use these bulbs to create a refreshing change of mood.
- **GROW STURDIER LILIES** Lilies are among a number of plants that grow roots from their stems, so plant them deeply and these roots, once grown, will give the tall stems extra anchorage. Watch out for lily beetle [see p.274].
- **EDGE A BORDER WITH DWARF LILIES** Look out for these new introductions. Very low-growing, they make a real splash of colour at the front of beds or in pots.

EXPERT KNOW HOW

GROW FABULOUS DAHLIAS

Exuberant and brilliant, the dahlia has surged back into fashion to become the top summer-flowering bulb. Dahlias are enormously popular with show growers, who compete fiercely to produce the biggest and most exquisite blooms, but with a few simple tips, you too can grow show-stopping dahlias.

- Provide a well-drained, sheltered site in sun. Give taller varieties stout stakes at planting time so that you can tie the stems in to support them as they grow.
- Space tall varieties 90cm (3ft) apart, and medium-sized varieties 60cm (2ft) apart; dwarf dahlias can be planted more closely.
- For bushy plants with more flowering stems, pinch out the shoot tips of young plants back to the first pair of leaves.
- For larger single flowers atop individual stems, remove the sidebuds.
- Water thoroughly in dry weather, particularly when the buds are forming, and feed with a soluble high-potash fertiliser throughout the season according to the manufacturer's instructions.

● **ENJOY A SPRING SHOW IN AUTUMN** For the most extraordinary late-autumn show of pale pink blooms on slender stems, plant *Nerine bowdenii*. Despite its springlike appearance, it associates beautifully with shrubs that colour up in autumn in shades of dark red and purple; pair nerines with the spindle bushes *Euonymus europaeus* or *E. alatus* for a stunning late-season combination.

Add stature to container plantings

Lilies and cannas, which bear their leaves on their flower stems, will provide strong, vertical accents in container arrangements, underplanted with summer annuals or bedding for colour at the base. Choose bulbs in which the flower stems stand up amid a clump of arching leaves, such as agapanthus and *Gladiolus callianthus*, to fill a container by themselves, packing the bulbs in for the greatest impact. Many gardeners find that agapanthus flower better and more quickly if pot-grown, and require only occasional repotting.

▲ **Not all gladioli** are frost-tender: the elegant, shocking pink *Gladiolus communis* subsp. *byzantinus* at the front of this border, teaming gracefully with the feathery grasses and pompon-headed alliums, can safely be left in the ground over winter.

Avoid winter losses Some summer bulbs, like the stunning cannas, can be expensive. You can avoid having to buy replacements each year by lifting and storing your half-hardy bulbs. Once the top growth dies back, cut it down to a few inches, and shake as much soil as you can from the bulbs (do not try to clean them thoroughly at this stage). Lay them out in a dry place for a couple of weeks so that the remaining soil dries out, then brush this off along with any other flaking debris. Store the bulbs in trays in a cool, dark, frost-free place over winter (a garage is ideal), preferably in just-damp sand to prevent drying and shrinkage, but leafmould [see p.142] and spent, dry compost from containers will also suffice.

● **MAKE LIFTING BULBS EASIER** by planting them in large pots or mesh baskets (look in the aquatic section of the garden centre for these), then sink the baskets into the soil. In autumn you can simply lift the whole container. There is no need even to 'plant' the baskets if placed among tall plants that will hide them from view, but be sure to keep them well-watered.

▼ **Shallow trays** are best for storing bulbs over winter; like kitchen onions, they can be prone to rots. Check bulbs in storage from time to time and discard any that are soft.

Make more of your bulbs

Reinvigorate your displays Most bulbs will reappear for many years without lifting or dividing, but some become shyer to flower when the clumps get congested. The simple remedy is to dig up clumps after flowering but while still in leaf, separate out the best of the individual bulbs and replant them singly at their original spacings. In a couple of years they will be back to full strength.

● **GROW ON YOUR OWN BULBS** When you lift clumps of bulbs or corms, you will find smaller bulblets, or cormlets, have developed around the parents. Plant these in pots and grow them on for a year, and they'll be ready to plant out in the garden. You can do the same when you lift clumps of summer bulbs in autumn.

Annuals and biennials

NO GARDEN PLANTS GIVE a more brilliant display faster than annuals and biennials. Though short-lived, they are so easy to grow and quick to flower, filling beds and containers with colour for months on end. Whether you grow from seed or buy ready-grown plants, make space in your garden for dazzling new varieties each year.

Fast-growing and fabulous

Introduce masses of colour You can add colour almost year-round with annuals and biennials – all ideal as gap-fillers between perennial plants, in containers or massed together in their own bed. You can be either bold or subtle, livening up a seating area, for example, with vibrant patches of red, orange and yellow to give a feeling of warmth or toning down a hotspot with cool colours.

● **CHOOSE SEED FOR THE BEST VALUE** For the price of one choice perennial or container-grown shrub you could buy half-a-dozen packets of annual seeds – enough to fill a small bed. So-called 'hardy annuals' can be sown straight into the ground, but the 'half-hardy annuals' will need to be sown somewhere warm – a propagator on a windowsill, perhaps [see p.266] – then grown on until any danger of frost is past, when they can be planted out in borders or containers.

▼ **Pack in the colour** by combining biennials such as foxgloves with annual phlox and cosmos and tender summer plants such as penstemons and diascias.

EXPERT KNOW HOW

MAXIMISE FLOWERING PERFORMANCE

Most annuals flower prolifically, to maximise their seed production over their short lives, but you can turbocharge their flowering performance with a few expert tricks.

● Don't improve the soil too much. Rich soil often encourages leafy growth at the expense of flowers.

● Thin out seedlings of annuals sown directly into the soil so the rest grow bushy and strong.

◄ Pinch out shoot tips early on to encourage branching stems and greater flower density.

● Water in dry spells, and use a 'flower feed' – a high-potash fertiliser – every 2–3 weeks.

● Deadhead regularly, nipping out spent flowerheads with finger and thumb or snipping off with scissors. Unable to set seed, the plants will produce more flowers, prolonging the flowering season.

- **SPEND A LITTLE MORE FOR SPEEDIER RESULTS** Skip seed-sowing and buy well grown plants to fill gaps or boost summer colour.
- **NURTURE PLUG PLANTS IN A GREENHOUSE** Midway in cost between seeds and garden-ready plants, plugs can be potted up individually and grown on in a sheltered environment until ready to plant out. This is a useful option for plants that are tricky to raise from seed, such as antirrhinums (snapdragons), pelargoniums, nicotiana (night-scented stocks), impatiens (busy lizzies) and petunias.
- **FOR THE EARLIEST FLOWERS GET A YEAR AHEAD** Sow biennials such as foxgloves, forget-me-nots and honesty in early summer, to flower the next year, and sow hardy annuals and plant more biennials in autumn (see overleaf) for a spring display.
- **PLANT IN BLOCKS OR GROUPS FOR IMPACT** Large patches of one variety are more effective than odd plants of several types, so sow in drifts [see p.84] or plant in groups for maximum impact. To be able to recognise seedling annuals from young weeds, sow in rows or concentric circles rather than scattering the seed over the soil.

Create a casual look Annuals and biennials are ideal plants for an informal, country style. To enhance the naturalistic effect, sow or plant in patches of different sizes and shapes. Stagger sowing times so that plants of the same variety start and finish flowering at different times. Sow a pinch of hardy annual seed wherever there is a gap between perennial plants for a random, 'self-sown' look.

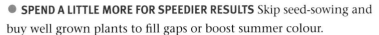

STAR PERFORMERS...

SUPER-FLOWERERS

Growers vie with each other to produce varieties that will outflower their competitors; these are some of the best.

- *Bellis* (daisy) 'Tasso Mixed'
- *Campanula medium* (Canterbury bells) 'Calycanthema'
- *Chrysanthemum carinatum* 'Sunset'
- *Dianthus barbatus* (sweet william) 'Fragrant Fever'
- *Erysimum* (wallflower) 'Heaven Scent'
- ▲ *Eschscholzia* (California poppy) 'Fruit Crush'
- *Godetia* 'Thoroughly Modern Millie'
- *Pelargonium* Pac 'Peach Kiss'
- *Petunia* 'Easy Wave'
- *Tagetes* (French marigold) 'F1 Durango Series'

SECRETS OF SUPER SWEET PEAS

Pretty, deliciously fragrant sweet peas are a must for any summer garden, and they're so easy to grow. If you don't have space to let them climb, choose dwarf, bushy varieties, which are ideal for hanging baskets, tubs and window boxes.

● For the strongest plants and earliest flowers, sow in early to mid autumn and overwinter the plants in a coldframe or unheated greenhouse. You can also sow at the end of winter, raising the seedlings on a windowsill.

◀ Sweet peas have long roots that don't like to be disturbed, so sow seed in long 'tube' pots filled with multipurpose compost. Make your own pots from cardboard tubes or corrugated card, and you can then plant the whole pot out rather than disturbing the young plant roots. The card will rot down in the soil.

● Plant in a sunny spot, and keep the plants well watered but not overfed.

● Provide netting or trellis for climbers to scramble up before or as you plant.

● Sweet peas will stop flowering if they set seed, so pick flowers regularly to enjoy in the house and remove any spent flowers before they form pods.

● Snap tendrils that reach out to twine around flower stems; they will kink the stems and make them less useful as cut flowers.

● **CREATE A VARIETY OF HEIGHTS** Use some taller annuals and biennials, such as tall varieties of stocks, sunflowers, larkspur, Canterbury bells and spider-flowered cleomes. Use rustic twiggy sticks or canes and twine where plants need support.

● **ATTRACT SUMMER WILDLIFE** Draw bees and butterflies into your garden with pollen and nectar-rich flowers with a traditional, old-fashioned look, such as cosmos, single-flowered French marigolds, agastache, calendula and sweet alyssum.

● **INCLUDE FRAGRANT PLANTS** Add scented annuals to pots or beds by windows and doors that you open in summer. Favourites include nicotiana, sweet rocket (*Hesperis*), sweet peas and Virginia stocks (*Malcolmia maritima*).

Make a lush, tropical display Annuals and biennials can transform an area of the garden into a sumptuous, luxuriant spectacle, transporting you to a place altogether more exotic without leaving your deckchair. To create an exciting scheme for a patio area, for example, choose bedding plants that come from warmer climates than ours, and use plenty of those that have lush, lavish leaves. Heat-loving lantanas, *Hibiscus* 'Luna' and *Impatiens* New Guinea Hybrids have flowers that are ideal for creating the feel of the tropics. Bold foliage plants such as coleus, alternanthera, ricinus, ipomoea and ornamental millet are fast-growing choices for a leafy, jungle effect.

● **ADD SULTRY TONES TO A BORDER** Make a planting altogether more arresting by popping in pots of annuals in steamy red, deep orange and purple shades. Look out for zinnias, heliotrope, verbenas and torenia in the garden centre.

● **PILE ON THE PERFUME** Exotic-looking annuals with heady scents that intensify at dusk, such as mignonette (*Reseda odorata*), night-scented phlox (*Zaluzianskya*) and tall, pale *Nicotiana sylvestris* are perfect for summer evenings. Mix in scented summer bulbs, like lilies and the stunningly perfumed polianthes (tuberose).

BEAT THAT!

● **The record for the tallest sunflower** in the world, according to the 2004 Guinness Book of World Records, is held by one grown in the Netherlands, which reached a staggering 7.75m (25ft 5in) tall. Try the variety 'Giant Russian' or Kong Hybrids to grow your own super-sunflowers.

Grow biennials for spring cheer

Biennials are plants that grow from seed in one year, and flower the next, so you need to sow them in early summer, or set out young plants in autumn, perhaps to replace summer bedding that is past its best. Some biennials flower very early, from late winter onwards. Plant wallflowers and forget-me-nots around your tulips, and continue spring interest into summer with foxgloves and sweet williams.

● **CHOOSE CHAMPION FLOWERERS** Cheerful pansies and their shyer cousins, violas, are available as young plants almost year-round, and are hard to beat for flowering stamina. You can find them in colour-themed collections – sunset shades, pink and blue, red and yellow – that suit all kinds of planting schemes. Deadhead regularly, and they will flower for months; remove the stalks too, otherwise they will keep growing and make the plants look untidy.

▲ **Flamboyant foliage plants** with large leaves in unusual colours add heat to displays. This bronze-purple ricinus (castor-oil plant) will only last the summer, but is worth it for its dark good looks.

Keep your plants going

Try overwintering some plants
If you have ever grown a pelargonium on a windowsill over winter, you'll have realised that many of the tender plants we treat as annuals, including osteospermums, diascias and gazanias, are actually perennial in their native climates. We use them as 'disposable' bedding because they cannot survive our winters outdoors – but in a greenhouse heated just sufficiently to keep the frost off [see p.257], they should make it through to spring and will grow even bigger in the garden the next summer.

● **DON'T DISCARD PRIMROSES** and polyanthus after flowering; although sold as colourful bedding they are perennial, and will keep growing in the garden to make bigger plants, which after the first year can be divided to increase your stock.

STAR PERFORMERS...

SOW AND PLANT IN AUTUMN

Market stalls are a great source for pots and bundles of spring bedding and biennials. Supplement them with autumn sowings of tough hardy annuals.

● Annual lupins
● Bellis
● Brompton stocks
● Candytuft *(Iberis)*
● Forget-me-nots *(Myosotis)*
● Larkspur
◀ Pansies and violas
● Pot marigolds *(Calendula)*
● Sweet williams
● Wallflowers

Container gardening

BRING YOUR GARDEN RIGHT UP to your doorstep with wonderful displays of container plants. Think outside the box with imaginative choices of plants and pots, and use every trick in the book to keep the plants vigorous and healthy. Given the prominent positions containers often take, they need to look at their very best.

GROUP PLANTS IN POTS CLOSELY TOGETHER TO MIMIC A WELL-STOCKED BORDER DISPLAY

Amazing plants in pots

Make displays that stand out from the crowd

Every year, growers and garden centres present selected plants recommended as ideal for container growing. The truth is that there are very few plants that cannot be grown in pots, for annual display or even longer periods. To inject real style and originality into your container displays, don't restrict your plant choice to the suggested 'patio selections', but try more unusual plants – grasses, for example. Be imaginative with your choice of containers, too. If an object is capable of holding compost and will drain, it can be planted. Visit reclamation yards, hardware stores and builders' merchants for inspiration.

Use long-lasting plants for less work

Containers filled with bedding plants need quite a lot of maintenance – deadheading to keep the plants looking good, conscientious watering, feeding and, of course, replanting or shifting around with the seasons. For much less work and years of pleasure, use more permanent plants such as small trees, shrubs, perennials, bulbs and conifers in pots and evergreen baskets of ivy or periwinkle *(Vinca)*.

- **USE PLANTS THAT CREATE IMPACT** Small, shapely trees (see below) will thrive in big containers and add height and form to a patio. Fill the space around the stems with low-growing plants or cover with an attractive mulch to complete the effect.
- **ADD A LIVING PATIO DIVIDER** Grow a length of box hedging in a large, rectangular planter fitted with castors or small wheels to create a soft, green backdrop that you can reposition as you rearrange container displays.
- **COPY YOUR BORDER PLANTINGS** Plant up pots with flowering and foliage plants that grow in your beds and borders to tie together your garden planting scheme.

Broaden plant choice by growing in pots

Use containers to increase the scope of what you can grow in your garden. Pots allow you to add plants with exacting soil needs and to cultivate tender treasures that can be

▲ **For a modern, formal look** plant a row of matching foliage plants such as these dwarf box balls in prominent, stylish containers.

◄ **Emulate the planting scheme** of a traditional border with containers, making tiers of pots and plants of different heights rising up from front to back.

STAR PERFORMERS...

TOP TREES AND SHRUBS FOR CONTAINERS

Plants with beautiful shapes and handsome foliage give the best value in small spaces. If you have more room, you can add really special flowering trees and shrubs.

◄ *Acer palmatum*
- **Box**
- **Callistemons**
- **Camellias**
- *Cordyline australis*
- *Fatsia japonica*
- *Magnolia stellata*
- *Malus sargentii*
- *Prunus pendula* **'Rosea'**
- **Rhododendrons and azaleas**
- *Salix exigua*

moved under cover at the end of summer. If you have alkaline soil, you can grow acid-loving plants, such as camellias, rhododendrons, heathers and Japanese maples (*Acer palmatum*), in pots filled with acid or 'ericaceous' compost. If you have heavy soil but love Mediterranean plants such as sea thrifts (*Armeria*) and rock roses (*Cistus*), they will thrive for you in containers filled with compost mixed with grit.

● **PROTECT TENDER PLANTS FROM WINTER COLD** by growing them in pots of a manageable size so that they can be taken into the greenhouse or conservatory for the winter. Choose containers with wheels or invest in a garden trolley (sometimes called a sackbarrow) for larger plants such as citrus, daturas and olive trees.

FOR A STYLISH FEATURE, USE THE SAME PLANT IN A GROUP OF DIFFERENT POTS OF VARYING HEIGHTS

Creating great displays

Use height to add impact Clusters of small plants in small pots around the edges of a patio tend to look fussy; to add stature, make some bold groupings with plenty of height. Include pots of taller plants or some tall chimney-style pots to give presence towards the back of an arrangement. In a single large container, put some taller plants either in the middle or at the back, depending on whether the display is seen from every angle or is positioned against a wall.

● **SHOWCASE SMALLER PLANTS** Group pots on garden shelving or staging, or stand a pot on top of another, upturned, to give more height to a small display.

● **MAXIMISE YOUR PLANTING SPACE** by gardening vertically: use all available walls and fences to support hanging baskets, window boxes, racks and other types of wall planter.

▼ **A ribbed wooden panel** or length of trellis on a wall makes a canvas that you can decorate with planters. Choose containers with hooks, or rimmed pots that you can support with heavy-duty wire looped around and under the rims.

Hang the most beautiful baskets Nothing adds cheer to a garden like a healthy, flower-covered hanging basket. For really superb results, it pays to spend a little more on an enriched compost specifically recommended for pots and baskets, containing slow-release fertiliser granules and a water-retaining compound.

● **SAVE MONEY ON PLANTS WITH NEW SOLID-SIDED DESIGNS** Nowadays there is a huge range of attractive baskets with solid sides, as opposed to wire mesh. They look good even when not covered with growth, so require far fewer plants to make a brilliant show.

● **LIVEN UP BASKET LININGS** Many materials other than pre-formed shells and moss make excellent basket liners. Try dead grasses, hay and reeds, fern fronds and even fabric or colourful old jumpers that are past their best for different effects. Add an inner lining of well-perforated polythene to help retain the water.

● **INCLUDE SOME EDIBLE TREATS** Lots of vegetables and fruits thrive in containers [see p.183]; try strawberries and cherry tomatoes tumbling from a basket.

PLANTING A TRADITIONAL WIRE BASKET

A traditional hanging basket in full growth should have both the top and the sides completely covered with plants, so neither the wire nor the liner shows through. Don't be afraid to cram plants in, as this is the best way to create a really stunning effect – a large basket can take as many as 30 plants.

1 Support the basket on a large plant pot or bucket. Line the sides with enough moss or moss substitute to hold the compost, and place a saucer in the base as a water reservoir.

2 As you fill the basket with compost, plant up the sides. Wrap the rootballs in rolls or cones of thin card and post them through the mesh to minimise root damage. The card will rot away.

3 Put tall plants near the centre and spreading ones at the outside to cover the edges once established. Leave the basket in a shady, sheltered place for a few days to settle before hanging.

Caring for container plants

Pick the right pots for success Glazed and plastic pots dry out less often than terracotta pots; because clay is porous, water evaporates from the sides of the pot as well as from the compost at the top. Plastic pots are light and easy to move – good-quality ones can be virtually indistinguishable from terracotta.

● **PROTECT PLANTS FROM WATERLOGGING** Improvised containers such as wooden crates, water troughs and old preserving pans add interest to displays – but for healthy plant growth, they must be drilled with drainage holes at the base.

● **AVOID 'COOKING' PLANTS IN METAL CONTAINERS** Containers made from aluminium and other metals look great in a modern or urban setting, but be wary of placing them where they will receive full sun in summer. The temperature of the compost can be raised to levels that are harmful to plants.

Use composts that will make plants thrive For successful displays, match container composts to the needs of your plants. Annuals, bedding and short-lived perennial plants will thrive in good-quality multipurpose compost, but trees and shrubs need a soil-based compost, which is more substantial and also heavier, reducing the risk of plants blowing over.

● **GROW ACID-LOVING PLANTS SUSTAINABLY** There is now no need to use quantities of peat in order to grow lime-hating plants such as heathers – look for newer reduced-peat and peat-free formulations. Composted bracken and pine needles are additives that reduce soil and compost pH.

Balconies and terraces exposed to winds need plants with tough or grey leaves that are less likely to dry out. Choose lightweight containers but use a substantial, soil-based compost mix that will not be blown away and will hold water more effectively.

● **SAVE ON COMPOST COSTS** and reduce the weight of a big container by placing an upturned plastic pot in the base before filling it with compost. When using a deep container, plant your display in a shallower one of the same diameter; this can be set on top of the big one to reduce the volume of compost you need. A basket planting need not hang from a hook – it will look just as good perched on top of a large urn, with the plants trailing down the sides.

Position plants where they will grow well
Plants in containers need the same care and attention paid to their siting requirements as they do in the border. Many, but not all, container plants need good light, so remember this when choosing them. Shade need not be a problem if you pick the right plants (see below).

● **BRIGHTEN A BALCONY OR ROOF TERRACE WITH CONTAINER PLANTS** – but remember that plants in these situations are very exposed to drying winds. Choose drought-tolerant plants [see also pp.102–3] with grey, spiky or waxy leaves and succulent plants that hold water in fleshy tissue, such as sedums and sempervivums, to stand up to high-rise conditions.

● **USE CONTAINER PLANTS TO CONCEAL UTILITY FEATURES** in the garden such as unsightly manhole covers, but avoid using pots so large that they are hard to move if maintenance work on drains, for example, is needed. Use a spreading plant in a smaller, lighter pot instead.

Feed and water regularly for strong growth
Regular feeding and watering is vital to keep your containers looking good. Many proprietary container fertilisers are available: for flowering plants, choose one containing plenty of potash (potassium), or to enhance foliage effect, use a feed rich in nitrates (nitrogen). Slow-release pelleted fertilisers added to the compost will keep plants well fed if you are short of time for weekly liquid feeding.

STAR PERFORMERS...

CONTAINER PLANTS FOR SHADE

Begonias and impatiens (busy lizzies) will flower beautifully in shade, but any plant recommended for a shady border will do just as well in a pot. Include plenty of foliage plants for a cool, lush effect.

- ● Ajuga (bugle)
- ● Begonias
- ● Ferns
- ◄ Fuchsias
- ● Heucheras
- ● Impatiens (busy lizzies)
- ● Ivies
- ● Lysimachia
- ● Mimulus (monkey flower)
- ● Plectranthus
- ● Torenia
- ● Vinca (periwinkle)
- ● Violas

PEST-PROOFING YOUR POTS

Keep a close eye on your container plants and pick off or deal with pests as soon as you see them. Keep a lookout for disease too – mildew (a white, powdery coating on the leaves) is the most likely, especially in hot, dry weather. Spray with a garden fungicide as soon as you see signs of this fungal infection.

◀ Ring pots with copper tape, which deters slugs and snails. Choose pots with solid rims – snails will gather and overwinter in turned-over rims.

● Check pansies and violas regularly for aphids, which congregate on the stem bases to feed and weaken the plants. They can be controlled with any garden insecticide.

● Root-feeding vine weevil grubs can be fatal to fuchsias, begonias, primulas, heucheras and impatiens. Mulch the pots with sharp grit or pea gravel, so the adult weevil lays its eggs elsewhere, or smear petroleum jelly around pot rims to trap the flightless adults before they reach the compost. Otherwise use a biological control [see pp.275–6]; if you keep losing plants, use a proprietary vine weevil killer before you see signs of wilting.

● **GIVE PLANTS THE BENEFIT OF A GOOD SOAKING** Unless you are growing succulents such as sempervivums, water thoroughly and never let pots dry out. This may mean watering daily, or more, in hot, dry or windy weather. If you have lots of pots, an automatic watering system [see p.245] cuts down on the work.

● **GET A LITTLE HELP FROM WATER-RETAINING GRANULES** Added to compost, these considerably reduce the need for watering. Never use more than the recommended amount or the compost will become slimy, and the plant roots will suffer.

● **RESCUE DRY PLANTS SUCCESSFULLY** Plants may be overlooked when watering – and some composts become very difficult to re-wet once they have dried out. Water applied from above will just run out where the compost has shrunk away from the pot sides. Rescue the plant by sitting the pot in a large bowl, sink or even bath half-full of water and let it absorb the water slowly from below.

● **MIMIC SEASONAL RAIN PATTERNS** In autumn, ease up on the watering as growth slows. In winter, check pots periodically to make sure plants are neither too wet nor too dry. Stand containers on pot feet or bricks to allow free drainage. In spring, gradually increase watering and exchange the pot feet for saucers and dishes slipped under the containers to aid water retention in summer.

Protect plants and pots in winter
If you intend to leave your pots outdoors in winter, make sure that ceramic ones are frost-proof, or opt for wooden containers; wood is also a good thermal insulator, so it will protect plant roots better. Plants in pots are more exposed than those in the ground; if really cold winter spells threaten plants, wrap pots well in bubblewrap to protect rootballs from freezing, but choose a porous material such as horticultural fleece to wrap the plants themselves, to allow the foliage to breathe.

BEAT THAT!

● **The oldest known container plant** in the world is an ancient cycad, collected on one of Captain Cook's voyages of exploration, that has resided at London's Kew Gardens since 1775. In 2009, it took nine gardeners and a crane to repot the now-massive plant into a new, bespoke mahogany planter containing a tonne of soil.

3
FABULOUS TREES, SHRUBS AND LAWNS

Great structural planting makes a garden look good whatever the season. Discover how to create a beautiful framework for your garden with graceful trees and striking shrubs; dress walls and fences with gorgeous climbing plants, then carpet the ground beneath with the lushest of lawns.

The building blocks of the garden

TREES AND SHRUBS GIVE A GARDEN STRUCTURE. With a fantastic range of shapes and forms, these plants offer both a permanent framework and seasonal highlights to enjoy all through the year. They hold the key to a successful planting scheme so choose wisely and they'll give you pleasure for many years to come.

▲ **Bright-barked trees and shrubs** such as dogwoods *(Cornus)* and willows give structure to borders and a lift to the garden in winter. Plant them where you can see them from indoors so you can enjoy their cheerful colour on the dullest days.

Make the most of trees and shrubs

Choose plants to suit your garden plan

Trees and shrubs with strong shapes and bold foliage will add impact to your scheme. Clipped and trained evergreens will provide formality and year-round focal points, but if you prefer a more informal look, others look their best when allowed to grow naturally. Use trees and, especially, shrubs to make great backdrops for more showy plants, too.

● **WORK OUT SIZES RIGHT FROM THE START** Moving trees and large shrubs is not easy so spend time researching the best plants for your site and soil before you buy. Size and vigour are critical so it pays to find out a plant's ultimate size at maturity, or at least after 10 years, as well as how fast it will grow. If you want a large, fast-growing tree or shrub, then give it sufficient space to grow and expand and avoid siting it too closely to a slower-growing variety that it might swamp or shade out.

● **GET THE MOST VALUE FOR SMALL SPACES** The smaller your garden, the more each plant has to earn its keep, so choose trees and shrubs that have more than one season or feature of interest: both attractive flowers and autumn berries, for example, or a strong shape, good-looking bark and colourful foliage.

● **CREATE FOCAL POINTS WITH STRIKING 'SPECIMEN PLANTS'** Showcase trees and shrubs that have extra-special qualities such as a beautiful branch structure, bold foliage or spectacular flowers, by giving them plenty of space and a position where they can shine – ideally against a neutral background, perhaps in front of a dark hedge or in a small bed of their own in a lawn.

● **BALANCE PERMANENT AND SEASONAL INTEREST** While evergreens provide year-round structure, they may lack the seasonal interest that flowering deciduous trees and shrubs provide. Too many deciduous, woody plants may make a garden appear empty in winter, or open up unwelcome views. Useful gap-fillers to add interest are shrubs with dense, twiggy growth such as berberis or those with evergreen stems, such as *Kerria japonica* and the Himalayan honeysuckle *(Leycesteria formosa)*.

● **REPEAT PLANTS TO UNIFY YOUR DESIGN** Plant identical trees or shrubs to give a sense of cohesion to your planting scheme. Repeating one particular plant or a grouping of plants also leads the eye through the garden and adds a sense of rhythm. If space allows for a more formal effect, plant rows of single species or varieties, especially along main pathways, or use groups of trees to frame a view or a piece of sculpture.

Transform plants by shaping and training

Grow trees and shrubs in exciting new ways by employing basic training and pruning skills. Some bushy trees and shrubs can be grown on one or more tall, clear stems to lift them from ground level and allow colourful underplanting, while shrubs such as the smoke bush *(Cotinus coggyria)* can be pruned hard to encourage bigger leaves or flower heads [see p.149]. Species of both trees and shrubs can be trained and trimmed into blocky, solid shapes to create formal hedges and elegant topiary shapes [see pp.158–63].

▼ **A spectacular shrub** such as the glorious *Viburnum plicatum* (far right) needs to be given an uncluttered planting position, with enough room for its graceful branches to spread and flower freely.

STAR PERFORMERS...

SPECIMEN TREES AND SHRUBS

Plant these in a prominent position to create a dramatic, stand-alone feature.

TREES
● *Acer japonicum* 'Vitifolium'
● *Betula utilis* var. *jacquemontii*
● *Cornus kousa* var. *chinensis*
● *Pyrus salicifolia* 'Pendula'
● *Sorbus aucuparia* 'Fastigiata'
● *Styrax japonicus*

SHRUBS
● *Cornus alternifolia* 'Argentea'
● *Fatsia japonica*
● *Magnolia* x *soulangeana*
● *Viburnum plicatum* f. *tomentosum* 'Mariesii'
● *Yucca gloriosa*

Attract wildlife with food and shelter The cover afforded by trees and shrubs will encourage more birds to visit, roost and nest in your garden as well as attracting other beneficial creatures. A mix of dense evergreens and trees and shrubs with more open canopies, particularly native varieties, will provide a range of opportunities for them to exploit. Growing a range of woody plants that have autumnal displays of fruit and berries will also provide food for hungry birds and other creatures during the colder months.

Create different effects with foliage When choosing trees and shrubs, consider what the overall effect will be when their shapes and foliage are combined, as this will dramatically affect the style, mood and atmosphere of the garden. Plants that have to compete with shrubs or trees that have showy flowers, strongly coloured foliage or leaves with bold markings will struggle to stand out. Site plain-leaved foliage shrubs behind your favourite flowering plants to provide a complementary backdrop. Grey-leaved plants such as artemisias make lovely foils for flowering perennials and annuals.

● **MATCH LEAF COLOURS TO ADD STYLE** Using foliage from the same palette, rather than mixing too many different colours together, will give your garden a recognisable theme. Try combining a range of trees and shrubs with silver and grey foliage, or group golden- and yellow-leaved plants together. Eye-catching reds and purples also work well in combination, but take care not to overdo it or the effect will become heavy-handed and over-dominant.

● **KEEP IT GREEN FOR A RESTFUL LOOK** A really beautiful, subtle but interesting effect can be created by combining leaves in toning greens but with dramatically different shapes and textures: bold-leaved fatsia with a spiky yucca, for example.

● **USE CONTRASTS TO ENERGISE THE MOOD** For a lively effect, pair plants that have contrasting foliage: silver santolina with a red-leaved berberis, for example, or cream-variegated *Buxus sempervirens* 'Elegantissima' with purple *Prunus × cistena*.

▲ **Make a bold statement** with dramatic contrasts of leaf shape, texture and colour – here a silver-leaved santolina, red berberis and variegated phormium.

▶ **An autumn blaze** of Japanese maples combined with the strong shapes and varied greens of conifers creates an oriental look. Bright sorbus berries (far right) add a textural contrast.

HOW DOES IT WORK?
WHY DO LEAVES CHANGE COLOUR?

When plants prepare to shed their leaves for winter, the green, food-producing pigment chlorophyll breaks down and other pigments present in the leaf but masked by the green, such as orange and yellow carotenes and xanthophylls, start to show through. Other pigments react with sugars in the leaf to create red and purple tones. Weather plays an important part in determining the intensity of autumn colour in any particular year. Expect the most stunning displays when the weather during autumn is cold, dry and bright.

● **MAKE ROOM FOR AUTUMN COLOUR** Use just one dazzling tree, such as an acer, or create a tapestry of shrubs in fiery shades (see facing page) to end the season with a breathtaking display.

Put fallen leaves to good use Fallen leaves will rot down into border soil and improve it, but leaves you rake up from lawns and paths can also be transformed into a valuable soil conditioner. Pile the leaves into a chicken-wire cage or fill plastic sacks, making a few holes in them with a garden fork. Wait a year or two and the leaves will have rotted down into dark, crumbly leafmould, a free garden resource that is perfect for mulching.

STAR PERFORMERS...

AUTUMN COLOUR

These shrubs and trees will put on a fantastic show, so plant them where they can be seen from the house.

- *Acer palmatum 'Sango-kaku'*
- *Acer japonicum*
- *Amelanchier lamarckii*
- *Berberis thunbergii*
- *Crataegus persimilis 'Prunifolia'*
- *Callicarpa japonica*
- *Euonymus alatus*
- *Hamamelis mollis*
- *Liquidambar styraciflua*
- *Malus tschonoskii*
- *Prunus sargentii*
- *Sorbus 'Embley'*

Success with shrubs

USE SHRUBS TO CREATE A FRAMEWORK for your plantings and to provide long-term interest in the garden. An immensely varied group of plants, they offer a huge range of sizes, shapes and ornamental features. Let them grow naturally for easy-care garden choices, or try some selective pruning to create striking new effects.

Choosing shrubs for the garden

Match shrubs to your garden conditions for healthy growth Shrubs have been collected from every corner of the world, then nurtured and bred to create a huge range of varieties ideal for gardens. Despite this wealth of choice, some shrubs require particular conditions to grow well, so it pays to check these out before buying to avoid costly mistakes. Reliable garden favourites such as cotoneaster and weigela are relatively unfussy, but others such as rhododendrons need acid soil [see p.20] to thrive.

● **GROW PLANTS THAT FIT YOUR STYLE** When choosing shrubs for their shape and decorative qualities, decide what effect you want to achieve. For an exotic look try palms, or for a cottage-garden feel choose free-flowering and berrying shrubs.

▼ **Colourful hydrangeas** in shades of pink, purple and blue provide an array of late-summer colour in a woodland garden. Leave the flower heads on over winter for frost protection.

- **MIX LARGE-LEAVED GIANTS IN DAMP SHADE** Plants that prefer damp or even wet positions often come from moist woodland margins and so are also shade-tolerant. Shrubs such as hydrangeas, viburnums and mahonia are ideal for such conditions, as are many Japanese maples, which often suffer from leaf scorch in dry soil and strong sun.
- **MAKE A DROUGHT-RESISTANT PLANTING** Beat the increasing tendency to hot, dry summers by planting shrubs that flourish in these conditions. Many hail from the Mediterranean region, and have deliciously aromatic foliage. Look for plants with small leaves covered in grey or white down, powdery dust, or a waxy coating. Choose from buddleias, California lilac *(Ceanothus)*, cotton lavender *(Santolina)*, lavender, Mexican orange blossom *(Choisya)* and rock roses *(Cistus)* for drought-busting combinations. Plants with tiny leaves and evergreen stems such as brooms *(Cytisus)* and tamarix also work well and cope with windy sites, including coastal locations, too.

Create interest throughout the year
In planning your scheme try to achieve a balance between evergreen and deciduous flowering shrubs. In a larger garden, you can group shrubs that flower at the same time for impact – or, especially in smaller spaces, choose shrubs with flowering seasons that follow on from one another to provide a succession of bright centres of interest around the garden. For maximum value in small spaces,

STAR PERFORMERS...

EARLY SPRING-FLOWERING SHRUBS

The first shrubs to flower often use bright flower colour or powerful fragrance to act as beacons for early-flying pollinating insects.

- *Camellia japonica*
- *Chaenomeles x superba*
- *Corylopsis pauciflora*
- *Daphne mezereum*
- *Daphne odora* 'Aureomarginata'
- *Forsythia x intermedia*
- *Kerria japonica*
- *Mahonia japonica*
- *Osmanthus delavayi*
- *Ribes sanguineum*
- *Viburnum x burkwoodii, V. tinus*

choose varieties that earn their keep with both flowers and, in autumn, fiery autumn leaf colour or brightly coloured berries, such as the spindle bush *(Euonymus europaeus)* or *Cotoneaster franchetii.*

● **DON'T SWAMP SMALL SHRUBS** Site slow-growing and small shrubs with care, bringing them close to the front of plantings where their qualities can be readily appreciated. If space allows, plant them in small groups so they make an immediate impact, thinning them out as they grow over time.

● **GROW ON SMALL SHRUBS TO SAVE MONEY** If you can't afford a good-sized specimen of a shrub, such as a camellia or a Japanese maple, to create drama in a border immediately, buy a younger plant and grow it on for a couple of years in a large pot on the patio, so you can enjoy it at close quarters before planting out.

Discover more ways to grow shrubs

Make the most of low-maintenance plantings
Select shrubs that require little care and attention, except for occasional pruning, if you are short of time for gardening. Plants such as berberis, broom, cotoneaster, mahonia and viburnum are just a few of the wide selection of easy-going plants available.

● **PLANT A WEED-SUPPRESSING CARPET** Drifts of low, hummock-forming evergreen shrubs such as hebe, *Euonymus japonicus* varieties and dwarf conifers mixed with evergreen grasses such as blue *Festuca glauca* will create a low-maintenance tapestry of shape, texture, colour and flower. Planting through geotextile fabric [see p.150] will help stop weeds growing up while the shrubs establish.

▼ **A low-maintenance planting** doesn't need to be uninspiring. These beautiful bronze grasses with fountain-like foliage combine well with low-growing evergreens to keep weeds down and maintain structure and interest over winter.

● **USE SHRUBS ON UNEVEN OR AWKWARD SLOPES** A low covering of shrubs on sloping ground will preserve the contours of the garden but save on maintenance, which can be difficult on steep slopes without terraces. Prostrate varieties of juniper are perfect: drought-tolerant and evergreen, they will soon cover the ground in a mat of colourful foliage. For large areas, use varieties of *Juniperus × pfitzeriana* or *Juniperus sabina* 'Tamariscifolia'; for smaller areas and edging, try varieties of *Juniperus rigida* and blue-leaved *Juniperus squamata.*

Grow acid-lovers in raised beds, pots and troughs
If you have neutral to alkaline soil, you will need to grow azaleas and rhododendrons in containers, but there are other small, acid-loving plants that make a lovely evergreen display in a raised bed or trough. Winter or summer-flowering heathers and dwarf hebes combine well with small tussocky grasses or sedges, such as *Carex comans* 'Bronze Perfection', or with low-growers like the dwarf pink, *Dianthus deltoides.*

BUILDING UP A SHRUB BORDER

Give shrubs enough space to enable them to reach their mature sizes without crowding. The bed will be gappy at first: spread a bark mulch to keep down weeds and/or plant fast-spreading perennials. Annuals sown from seed also make great gap-fillers in a new border [see Planting for rapid results, pp.82–5].

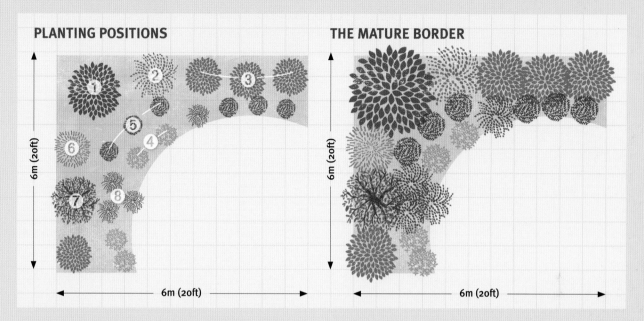

PLANTING POSITIONS

THE MATURE BORDER

6m (20ft)

6m (20ft)

6m (20ft)

6m (20ft)

● A large, bushy shrub **(1)** in a corner, such as a holly or cotoneaster, blurs sharp edges where boundaries meet more effectively than a bare-trunked tree.

● Vase-shaped shrubs (wider at the top than at the bottom) such as forsythias or *Spiraea* 'Arguta' (bridal wreath) are good for spaces between two bushier shrubs **(2)**.

● A row of background shrubs **(3)** could be mixed for seasonal variety, or made up of different varieties of the same species: *Hydrangea macrophylla*, for example, or shrub roses. Or, to introduce movement, consider tall grasses or bamboos.

● Small shrubs with golden or white-variegated leaves **(4)** brighten the base of darker, bulkier shrubs.

● Foreground groupings of small shrubs **(5)** often work better if the shrubs are the same, or similar in form or style: choisyas, skimmias and hebes for solid green, for example, or cistus, potentillas and artemisias for a lighter look in a sunny site.

● Use a conical or columnar conifer **(6)** as a vertical accent.

● Offset a small feature tree **(7)** with good autumn colour, such as a Japanese maple or amelanchier, so that it shows up well against a background of evergreen foliage.

● Good, easy-care ground-cover shrubs for below a small deciduous tree **(8)** include *Cotoneaster horizontalis* and *Berberis thunbergii* f. *atropurpurea*, their bright berries complementing the tree's autumn leaf colour.

● **CHOOSE PATIO RHODODENDRONS WITH THE BONUS OF FRAGRANCE** *Rhododendron* 'Daviesii', a scented, deciduous white azalea, is a great choice for a pot or tub, but if you have a cool greenhouse or conservatory for protection over winter, the exquisite *Rhododendron fragrantissimum* is an absolute must. Many deciduous azaleas and rhododendrons put on a good show of autumn colour, but if year-round structure is important, select evergreen varieties for your pots.
● **SELECT THE RIGHT CONTAINER TO ENSURE STABILITY** Rhododendrons have shallow roots, so when choosing larger specimens, match them with a substantial, squat container. A half-barrel filled with ericaceous compost is perfect for a large plant and will prevent it from toppling over in windy weather, while providing enough space for the plant to establish well.

SHAPELY CONIFERS

You can trim upright conifers lightly with shears to neaten their shape; if a spreading conifer gets out of hand, remove lower branches close to the trunk so that upper ones hide the cut.

- *Cedrus atlantica* 'Glauca Pendula' (softly weeping, blue-grey foliage)
- *Juniperus scopulorum* 'Skyrocket' (upright, very narrow, grey-green)
- *Picea glauca* var. *albertiana* 'Conica' (conical, sugarloaf shape)
- *Pinus sylvestris* 'Fastigiata' (upright, very narrow, dark green)
- *Taxus baccata* 'Semperaurea' (columnar shape, gold-leaved)
- *Tsuga canadensis* 'Pendula' (multilayered, weeping form)

Train shrubs on walls to maximise growing space

In small gardens, train shrubs to grow against a house or garage wall, keeping their growth restricted by pruning. When buying a shrub for this purpose, choose a plant that is as 'flat' and two-dimensional as possible, and fix a sturdy support system to the wall, such as stout trellis or strong wires, before planting.

● **MAKE A WELL-BALANCED FRAMEWORK FOR THE BEST DISPLAY** Train a framework of sideways-spreading branches against the wall, and cut back to two or three leaves any stems that grow outwards; do this 'spur-pruning' yearly after flowering, or, if you choose pyracantha or another berrying shrub, wait until spring. This spur-pruning technique is also used in winter on climbing roses, wisteria [see p.170], and also apple and pear trees grown as espaliers, fans and cordons to keep them flat against their supports and encourage flowering and fruiting.

● **EXPLOIT WARM WALLS TO GROW TENDER SHRUBS** In cool temperate regions, slightly tender shrubs such as flannel bush (*Fremontodendron*), abutilons and bottle-brush (*Callistemon*) will flourish on sunny walls that are sheltered from cold winds. These shrubs benefit not only from the aspect and shelter but also from the heat retained by the masonry during sunny days, which then radiates out at night.

Use conifers to make striking focal points

Carefully sited conifers draw the eye as well as providing year-round structure. Select the best position by viewing it from all angles and ensure that the plant has enough space and light to grow well. For impact, plant blue and golden-leaved varieties or those with strong outlines (see left).

▼**Punctuate a planting scheme** with boldly shaped conifers: these upright cypresses give a Mediterranean air, paired with brick, terracotta and a honey-coloured gravel on paths.

● **INJECT DRAMA INTO BORDERS WITH CLEVER PLACEMENT** Instead of placing an upright conifer in the middle of a planting scheme, offset it to one side about a third of the way along for a more dramatic composition. Low-growing or mound-forming plants in the bed will emphasise the vertical impact.

Grow shrubs as standards

Standard shrubs, trained as heads of leafy growth on top of a tall, clear trunk, increase planting opportunities in the garden. The ground beneath them isn't shaded out by the compact heads of the shrubs, so you can make the most of the space by underplanting with bulbs or other flowering plants. Standards can be grown in the ground or in unfussy containers that complement their strong shape to make stylish focal points.

● **LOOK AT UNUSUAL SPECIES** Dense-leaved evergreens such as *Euonymus japonicus*, box, bay and holly are the most widely available standards, but deciduous shrubs such as small-leaved lilac and weigela are increasingly seen and make beautiful garden features. Standard roses also make long-flowering focal points, especially in a formal setting.

● **SAVE MONEY BY TRAINING YOUR OWN STANDARD** You can get good results in as little as two years by training a fairly fast-growing shrub, such as a fuchsia, yourself. Pinch out the tip of a strong, single stem at the desired height, then allow the sideshoots that form below it to grow, but keep pinching them out so that a bushy head forms and thickens. Allow leaves but not sideshoots to grow on the length of stem below the head. Stop pinching the shoots in the head when it has filled out, and remove the leaves on the stem to clear it.

Create different effects with hard pruning

Some shrubs can be pruned almost down to the base each year, or every other year, to produce a crop of young stems with brilliantly or unusually coloured bark [see Making a winter splash of colour, p.81]. The most popular choices are dogwoods (*Cornus*) and willows (*Salix*), with bark colours ranging from acid-yellow to almost black.

● **STIMULATE MUCH LARGER LEAVES AND FLOWERS** Use the pruning technique above on smoke bushes, especially *Cotinus coggyria* 'Royal Purple' and 'Grace', and on ornamental elders such as *Sambucus racemosa* 'Plumosa Aurea', and the result will be a more flamboyant display of enlarged, purple or golden foliage respectively. *Hydrangea paniculata* can also be pruned in this way for strikingly large flowerheads borne slightly later than on unpruned plants.

EXPERT KNOW HOW

CHOOSING A STANDARD

Shrubs trained as standards are increasingly offered at garden centres as well as at specialist tree and shrub nurseries; to ensure that you get the most attractive, evenly shaped specimen, take some time inspecting what's on offer.

● If you can, lift the shrub from its pot and check that it is not root-bound [see p.242]. With high-value items, turnover can be slow, and a plant that has been in its pot for too long will struggle to establish.

● Rotate the plant or walk around it to check that the stem is vertical from every angle.

● If buying a rose or deciduous standard when it is leafless, consider the placement of the branches in the head: will it form a balanced crown?

● Ask if the plant has been 'top-grafted' – if so, peer into the crown at the graft points at the top of the stem to check there are no cracks or signs of disease.

▼ **A small-flowered lilac** needs careful and lengthy training to attain the proportions of a large tree. Deciduous shrubs trained as standards will shed their leaves in winter to open up the garden.

▲ **Planting shrubs through geotextile** landscape fabric (here a row of dwarf box) retains water in the soil to help them get going. Cutting back some top-growth will reduce water loss from the leaves of evergreens and help the plants grow bushy.

▼ **Clearing the lower branches** of an overgrown shrub can transform the planting space: these viburnums, normally clothed to the ground in growth, have been pruned to allow a contrasting, billowing underplanting.

Planting and aftercare

Help shrubs to establish quickly Both deciduous and evergreen shrubs should be planted when the soil is warm, and neither waterlogged nor frozen. Container-grown shrubs are available to purchase year-round and can be planted [see pp.242–3] at any time, provided that you are prepared to care for the young plants well. Early autumn is the best season, particularly for any bare-rooted and root-balled plants, since the soil is still warm enough for plants to settle in and roots to grow and develop before growth starts in spring.

● **STOP YOUNG EVERGREEN FOLIAGE FROM DRYING OUT** Plants naturally lose water from their leaves as they grow – a process known as 'transpiration'. Young evergreen shrubs, in particular, can lose a lot of moisture, especially in hot weather or during cold, windy spells, which makes it difficult for them to establish well. Protect newly planted evergreens with a windbreak of hessian or polypropylene fabric. Alternatively, ask your garden centre for an anti-transpirant spray to use on the foliage. In sunny or windy weather ensure plants remain moist to prevent wilting and stop leaves getting scorched.

● **FEED IN SPRING FOR HEALTHY GROWTH** All shrubs will benefit from being fed in spring to help boost new growth and encourage flowers. Work in a general balanced granular fertiliser around the base of each shrub. A mulch of garden compost carefully forked in around the roots will also help to keep moisture in.

● **BE TOUGH WITH DROUGHT-TOLERANT SHRUBS** Plants that you have chosen because they grow well in dry conditions, such as Mediterranean species, must not be overfed or overwatered, especially while they are establishing. If the soil is heavy, dig in grit to improve drainage, but do not add fertiliser. Water in once, but do not keep constantly wet: this will encourage soft, sappy growth which will rot or be susceptible to frost damage. Mulch beneath these shrubs, with gravel or chippings rather than organic matter: the stone will reflect heat, provide good drainage around the stem bases and encourage strong growth.

Prune to enhance the display As a rule of thumb shrubs that bloom from early spring to early summer flower on growth made the year before and so are best pruned after flowering. Those that flower from midsummer onwards usually do so on growth made in the current year and so are best pruned before growth starts in spring [see Pruning, pp.252–3].

● **CLEAR STEMS TO ALLOW UNDERPLANTING** To let in light and air below a shrub and make more space beneath it for plants, cut its lower branches back to the main trunk. Improve the ground by removing weeds and debris and lightly forking in some organic matter before adding shade-loving plants below the shrub, perhaps interplanted with some spring bulbs.

● **KEEP VARIEGATED SHRUBS FROM TURNING PLAIN** Shrubs with leaves that have paler markings often produce shoots with plain green leaves, a process known as reversion. These plain shoots are very vigorous and can soon overwhelm the plant so remove them as soon as you spot them, cutting right back to their point of origin. Pull (not cut) off shoots that grow on the clear stems of standards, too.

Dealing with overgrown shrubs

Renovate or replace for a fresh start Shrubs are often not taken in hand until the increasing size and unkempt growth of the plant has become a problem. Many species and varieties can be rehabilitated by hard pruning, or even transplanted (see below), but some plants will not regenerate if cut back hard or moved and are better replaced – these include many grey-leaved plants such as cistus and halimiums, and also daphnes. With any overgrown or poorly performing shrub, consider first whether you really do like the plant – this could be an opportunity to replace it with something more exciting.

● **GIVE SHRUBS A NEW LEASE OF LIFE** Badly misshapen or overgrown plants may require heavy pruning. Use secateurs for pencil-thick stems, loppers for thicker material and a saw for thick branches. Cut back sprawling stems, removing crossing branches and congested or thin twiggy growth. This enables more air and light to penetrate, encouraging healthy growth. Work in a fertiliser around the base and apply a thick mulch of organic matter.

EXPERT KNOW HOW

MOVING A SHRUB TO A NEW POSITION

Most shrubs can be moved in autumn or spring if they've outgrown their site or are just in the wrong place. The secret is to cut around the rootball well ahead of time (for larger shrubs this might be a year or so in advance), take as large a rootball as you can, ensure that the new planting hole is large enough, and water regularly until the plant is settled in.

1 As far in advance as you can, slice down with a sharp spade all around the shrub, ideally at the outer edge of the leaf canopy. When you are ready to move the plant, tie up the top growth to keep it out of the way, and dig out a circular trench. This will give you room to undercut the rootball cleanly.

2 Once the rootball is fully detached, rock it to and fro to allow you to manoeuvre a sheet of heavy-duty plastic, hessian or polypropylene beneath it so it can be carried to its new planting hole. If you have a fair distance to travel, it is worth securing the fabric with rope to ensure the rootball does not crumble.

Garden trees

TREES ARE USUALLY THE MOST DOMINANT and longest-lived elements in a garden and no other group of plants requires such careful choice. The smaller the space available, the more carefully you should consider which particular tree will bring the most beauty and interest to your garden.

PLANT SILVER BIRCHES WHERE THEIR GLEAMING WHITE BARK WILL BRING LIGHT TO THE GARDEN

Trees for presence and structure

Choose the right tree for the right space

Trees make strong statements and can influence both the environment and appearance of your garden, so choose ones that precisely meet your needs, will suit the space available and will thrive in your garden's conditions. An evergreen tree will provide screening all year-round but may cast too much shade in winter, so a deciduous tree with spring blossom and attractive bark might be more suitable.

● **BEWARE OF FAST-GROWERS IN SMALL SPACES** Avoid large trees that are over-vigorous as they will eventually become too big for your site. Whatever steps you take to control the top-growth, the roots will still spread freely: willows and poplars, for example, have vigorous, questing roots which can invade water courses and pipes or even house foundations. They can also ruin lawns when the knobbly 'knees' of the roots emerge at ground level.

● **CHOOSE COMPACT TREES TO AVOID DISPUTES** Full-grown, spreading trees overhanging boundaries or shading neighbouring gardens and buildings can be the cause of major conflicts. For smaller gardens, there are many beautiful trees that are naturally compact or slow-growing (see below) and will create the effect you want without causing unnecessary trouble.

● **AVOID CREATING TOO MUCH SHADE** Check the shape and width of the mature canopy of a tree, as well as its height, before you buy: the wider the tree and the denser the growth, the more shade it will cast. Slender, graceful trees, such as birches, cast a dappled shade that is perfect for a seating or eating area.

● **BUY YOUNG TREES TO SAVE TIME IN THE LONG RUN** Trees are on sale in a variety of sizes, from small single stems, known as whips, through to large, semi-mature plants that offer instant impact – but at a price. Young trees require patience but they are the more reliable and certainly the cheapest option. Carefully chosen, sited and planted they establish quickly, often attaining the same height and girth in just a few years as those bought as semi-mature specimens.

◀ **Repetition of one type of tree** adds impact to a garden scheme. Here, the verticals of the silver-barked birches are echoed by the white foxglove spires and the grey-painted walkway uprights. The light, airy canopy of the birches prevents too much shade being cast.

STAR PERFORMERS...

TREES FOR SMALLER GARDENS

These attractive all-rounders will not dominate a garden large enough for a small lawn. In tiny spaces, consider growing trees in good-sized containers [see p.133].

● *Acer davidii, A. pensylvanicum*
● *Betula pendula* 'Youngii'
● *Cornus kousa* 'Chinensis'
◀ *Laburnum* x *watereri* 'Vossii'
● *Magnolia* 'Leonard Messel'
● *Malus* 'Red Sentinel', *M. transitoria*
● *Morus alba* 'Pendula'
● *Prunus* 'Kiku-shidare-zakura'
● *Pyrus nivalis*
● *Robinia pseudoacacia* 'Frisia'
● *Sorbus cashmeriana, S. hupehensis, S.* 'Joseph Rock'

SPRING BLOSSOM

There are trees that are beautiful in flower for gardens large and small [see also p.153]; with a little research, you can choose the ideal candidate for your planting position.

- *Aesculus hippocastanum* 'Baumannii'
- *Amelanchier* x *grandiflora* 'Ballerina'
- *Arbutus menziesii*
- *Cercis siliquastrum, C. canadensis* 'Forest Pansy'
- *Cornus florida* 'Cherokee Chief'
- *Crataegus* 'Rosea Flore Pleno', *C.* x *lavallei* 'Carrierii' (hawthorns)
- *Cydonia oblongata* (quince)
- *Davidia involucrata*
- *Mespilus germanica* (medlar)
- *Magnolia stellata, M. salicifolia* 'Wada's Memory'
- *Malus* 'Golden Hornet', *M.* 'Evereste' (crab apples)
- *Prunus avium, P.* x *yedoensis, P.* 'Okame', *P. sargentii, P.* 'Shirotae' (below), *P.* 'Ukon' (flowering cherries)
- *Pyrus calleryana* 'Chanticleer' (ornamental pear), *P. salicifolia* 'Pendula' (weeping pear)
- *Sorbus aria* 'Lutescens', *S.* 'Embley'

● **CHECK OUT GARDEN-SIZED VARIETIES OF NATIVE TREES** Few gardens have the space for the magnificent trees that grace our landscapes, but most of the trees that grow wild in your area will have forms or cultivated varieties that are more suitable for a garden setting. Native trees grown in gardens are a real boon for wildlife, but even a non-native tree can be a valuable resource for a host of wild creatures.

● **ENJOY A FEAST OF SPRING BLOSSOM** Ornamental cherries *(Prunus)*, crab apples *(Malus)* and *Sorbus* are among the most reliable, power-packed spring-flowering trees, offering plenty of choice for small and medium-sized gardens, too. Trees that bear spring flowers on bare branches or just as their leaves unfold are especially striking. These include some of the magnolias – the star magnolia *(Magnolia stellata)* is particularly attractive – or try the multi-stemmed Judas tree or redbud *(Cercis)*, lovely trees with shocking-pink to magenta flowers that look fantastic against their bare, grey-brown branches.

● **DON'T MISS OUT ON FLOWERS** If you live in a cool temperate region be aware that some of the more exotic flowering trees such as acacias and the foxglove tree *(Paulownia)* may grow well in your garden, but will never – or only in very occasional years – bear flowers. See if you can discover a flowering specimen that grows locally and try to replicate the conditions it grows in to increase your chances of success.

● **CONSIDER A PRODUCTIVE TREE** Apple and pear trees [see also pp.216–17] are not only fruitful but beautiful trees in their own right, with exquisite blossom in spring and silvery bark that becomes attractively gnarled with age. Grafted trees are available in a range of

▼ **The beautiful Mount Fuji cherry,** *Prunus* 'Shirotae', makes a wide-spreading tree with a low canopy. Mowing beneath it can be tricky, so take the opportunity to create a 'mini-meadow' below the canopy, studded with spring bulbs.

heights to suit every garden and even container-growing. Take a look at more unusual fruits (both quince and mulberry trees are very attractive) and also nut trees such as almonds or, in a large garden, a walnut tree.

● **BRING LIGHT INTO SMALL SPACES WITH FRESH, GREEN FOLIAGE** In a large garden, trees with dark leaves can act as wonderful focal points. In an enclosed space, on the other hand, a mass of dark green and especially dark purple foliage can appear to suck the light out of the garden, especially if the leaves have a matt, non-reflective surface. Choose small trees instead with silvery or very fresh green foliage, such as an ornamental pear *(Pyrus)* or laburnum.

● **CHOOSE A TREE THAT'S A FANFARE OF COLOUR** *Robinia pseudoacacia* 'Frisia' and *Gleditsia triacanthos* 'Sunburst', a variety of honey locust, have golden-yellow foliage that creates a cheerful, sunny impression all through the season. The leaves take on warmer, richer tones in autumn before they fall.

Managing trees

Get young trees off to the best start

Before planting a newly purchased tree, whether it is a container-grown specimen or a small, single-stemmed whip, make sure that you prepare the ground well by clearing the area of weeds, digging over the soil and, if drainage is poor, adding plenty of organic matter [see Planting out, p. 243]. Don't plant in ground that is frozen or waterlogged.

● **HELP YOUNG TREES TO GET ESTABLISHED AND GROW FASTER** Wait until young trees are growing well before you underplant with shade-loving plants or spring and autumn bulbs. Trees planted in lawns will also grow more slowly if the grass is allowed to grow right up to the trunk and compete with the tree for water and nutrients. Keep an area at least 90cm (3ft) in diameter clear of turf and weeds, for example by covering it with a porous landscape fabric and then mulching the surface. Make sure you use a fertiliser that can be diluted in water, not granules, so that the nutrients will soak through the fabric into the soil.

Keep pruning to a minimum Kept
healthy, appropriately sited and given enough room to grow, trees should require little pruning, although dead and diseased branches should be promptly removed to prevent disease taking hold.

EXPERT KNOW HOW

CREATING A CLEAR TRUNK

With gradual pruning, you can increase the length of clear trunk on a young tree to raise the canopy and better display attractive bark. Cutting away the low growth in stages enables the tree to continue developing strongly.

1 In the first autumn following planting, use a pair of clean, sharp secateurs to cut off the sideshoots from the lowest third of the trunk to leave it clear of growth. The young sideshoots are called 'feathers' so this process is sometimes known as 'feathering'.

2 Next, concentrate on the second third of the trunk and shorten the sideshoots in this section by half, leaving the top third of the tree unpruned. Repeat this process every autumn until you have a good length of clear trunk, then allow the tree to branch out naturally.

Most deciduous trees are pruned in late autumn and winter, except for cherries and maples, which 'bleed' sap and so are pruned in late summer. Evergreens are generally pruned in spring.

● **REMOVE WAYWARD GROWTH BUT KEEP THE NATURAL FORM** Take time to think through what you are doing before pruning young trees because cutting out branches will affect both the shape and form of the tree. As it grows cut out crossing and diseased branches and remove ill-positioned branches at the trunk, rather than continually snipping back new growth.

● **CUT OUT UNWANTED GROWTH PROMPTLY** If your tree has variegated foliage, remove any shoots that have plain green leaves at their base.

▲ **These parasol-shaped crowns** on a pair of catalpas have been created by pollarding, which entails cutting the new growth back to a stubby framework either each year or every 2–3 years, depending on how large you want the crown to be.

These indicate that the tree is reverting to its natural form, which needs to be discouraged. Some trees, such as limes, poplars, willows and hawthorns, are prone to producing suckering shoots at the base of the trunk, which weaken the plant. Wearing gloves, pull off these suckers by hand, rather than by cutting them, as dormant buds in stubs left behind will produce new sucker growth.

Grow trees in smaller spaces using traditional techniques

Large trees can be grown as smaller plants to great ornamental effect by employing age-old woodland management techniques in the garden. Coppicing and pollarding involve regularly pruning a tree's stems, either to ground level (coppicing) or to a stubby framework at the top of the trunk (pollarding). In gardens, you can put these techniques to good use and achieve a flush of

PLANT A GROVE OR 'NUT WALK' OF HAZELS FOR PRETTY CATKINS AND TASTY COBNUTS

vigorous young growth with colourful bark on winter stems [see p.81], or to produce abnormally large and, often, more intensely coloured leaves. Trees commonly coppiced or pollarded in gardens are willows, poplars, hazels, Indian bean tree *(Catalpa)*, eucalyptus and bright-leaved *Acer negundo* 'Flamingo'.

● **GROW HAZELS FOR NUTS AND POLES** Harvest your own nuts by planting hazels *(Corylus avellana* for cobnuts, *C. maxima* for filberts). Prune them every three years, cutting out only the oldest stems at ground level each time. The best nut crops are borne on one and two-year-old stems. Wait until the plants are at least three years old before you start coppicing, then prune either in late autumn or at the end of winter and use the cut stems for supporting climbing beans or tall perennials.

● **ENJOY COLOURFUL WILLOW STEMS IN WINTER** A pollarded willow tree will form a lollipop-shaped crown that loses its leaves to reveal a firework-like display of bright stems. Allow the tree to develop a clear trunk about 2m (6ft) tall before starting to pollard, cutting the branches to within 2.5–5cm (1–2in) of the trunk. To develop and maintain a head of growth in proportion to the height of the trunk, prune only one in three stems each year, choosing the oldest to cut back.

Dealing with overgrown trees

Consider calling in the professionals
Some overgrown trees can be reduced in size as an alternative to felling, but in nine out of ten cases this is a job better undertaken by a professional tree surgeon. Amateur branch cutting is not only dangerous for the gardener but can also endanger the tree; cuts made incorrectly can be fatal to it, and a tree can also become unstable through unconsidered removal of large limbs. Remember, too, that whatever technique is used, it may need to be repeated every few years to keep the tree in shape.

● **REDUCE THE CANOPY TO LET IN LIGHT**
Removing or trimming back branches within a tree's crown or canopy can reduce its impact on the garden surroundings. These techniques can be attempted on a small tree by an experienced gardener, but on large trees they must be left to the professionals (see right). Done sensitively, crown reduction will retain the natural shape of the tree.

● **'TOPPING' CONIFERS** It is possible for a tree specialist to reduce the height of conifers that are too tall by cutting across the main trunk at the required height. This will produce an unnatural-looking and often misshapen tree but may be the only way to stop a large conifer going skywards. If you are pruning smaller conifers yourself, don't cut into old wood, as many, including the Leyland cypress used for hedging, will not regrow. One new technique to control the spread of a pine tree that is of a manageable size is to cut back its new shoots by half each year. Do this as the shoots unfurl in late spring but before they start to extend to maximum length.

HOW DOES IT WORK?
CROWN REDUCTION

Tree surgeons may be able to offer solutions that will reduce the impact of a large mature tree in your garden if you are unable to remove it, either owing to local planning laws or because it would destabilise surrounding features, such as walls or banks. Crown thinning is a good option for trees with dense canopies, as it will allow more light to pass through, while lifting the crown by removing lower branches will open up the ground beneath. Never employ a tree surgeon without checking their credentials; personal recommendation is valuable, too.

▲ **Crown thinning** involves removing specific branches (shown in blue) from the entire canopy of the tree to reduce the density and create a lighter effect.

▲ **Raising the crown** is easier than crown thinning: lower branches are removed to open up the area beneath the canopy for access and more light.

Hedges and topiary

A WELL-KEPT HEDGE WILL ENHANCE any garden and there is a style to suit every taste, whether you prefer your hedges uniformly leafy or covered with flowers in spring and berries in autumn. And if you enjoy clipping and shaping, you can create eye-catching topiary for a fraction of the cost of ready-pruned specimens.

KEEP HEDGES AND TOPIARY AT A MANAGEABLE HEIGHT TO MAKE CLIPPING AND PRUNING EASIER

Make living boundaries and dividers

Choose a hedge to suit your garden
Hedges can do much more than simply mark a boundary. They can be used as screens, to provide shelter, divide up space in the garden and offer a refuge for wildlife. Formal hedges are usually evergreen and made up of one type of plant, such as yew or privet. They need to be kept tightly clipped for a crisp, solid effect. Semi-formal and informal hedges usually comprise a row of shrubs grown and pruned in a more relaxed way, and can include flowering and berrying plants for seasonal interest.

● **USE EVERGREENS FOR PRIVACY YEAR-ROUND** but make sure your conifer hedges don't grow excessively high to avoid disputes with neighbours. In many countries legislation restricts the height of garden boundary hedges, so check beforehand whether rules apply to both front and back gardens.

● **DETER INTRUDERS WITH A PROTECTIVE HEDGE** made up of thorny and spiny plants such as berberis, pyracantha, hawthorns and hollies. The hedge can be composed of one species or of different plants, but if you are using a mixture ensure you match them for size and vigour so the plants knit together evenly.

◄ **If you enjoy precision clipping** this garden, filled with immaculately shaped plants, is for you. To ensure that box hedging is perfectly uniform, use plants grown from cuttings from the same parent stock, so that there will be no variation in growth habit and leaf colour.

EXPERT KNOW HOW

PLANTING A DOUBLE BEECH HEDGE

Two rows of beech saplings will form a thick, dense hedge more quickly than a single row. Alternating green and copper or purple beech creates a striking effect. Order inexpensive bare-rooted young trees and plant in autumn when the soil is still warm. Installing a seep hose [see p.245] will get them off to a good start.

1 Unbundle and soak bare-rooted beech plants in a bucket of water for about an hour before planting. Trim off any damaged roots and shorten very long thick ones with sharp secateurs.

2 Using a marked-off cane, set up two strings 45cm (18in) apart as planting lines, and lay the plants out 45cm (18in) apart along them. Stagger the rows to maximise the density of the hedge.

3 Make a hole and set each plant at the depth it was growing at (below the original soil mark the stem is a darker colour). Firm in and water well, then prune back the top growth by a third.

PLANTS FOR FLOWERING HEDGES

A semi-formal hedge can be made with shrubs that will reward you with a mass of flower in spring or summer and require a more relaxed pruning regime than a formal hedge. Prune it after flowering, or to enjoy rosehips or berries, wait until spring.

- Escallonias (white or pink-tinged white flowers, summer)
- Forsythia (yellow, very early spring)
- *Garrya elliptica* (long, tassel-like catkins, spring)
- Hardy fuchsias (red, purple and pink, summer)
- Pyracantha (white, spring, plus red or yellow berries in autumn)
- *Ribes speciosum* (flowering currant, deep pink flowers, spring)
- *Rosa pimpinellifolia* (creamy-white), *R. rugosa* (fuchsia-pink), *R. canina* (pale pink), *R. xanthina* (yellow)

● **CREATE A SHELTERED 'GARDEN ROOM'** Hedges can be used to divide your garden and create a sheltered, enclosed area that offers a degree of shade in summer, perhaps around a seat. For a lighter yet structured effect grow fruit trees as cordons or espaliers [see pp.214–19], training them on a stout wooden or metal framework strung with wires.

● **DESIGN INTRIGUING GARDEN VIEWS** Make a window or portal in a hedge to give views through to other parts of the garden. While the hedge is growing create a shaped wire frame and secure it into the hedge at the required height, then train and prune new growth around the frame to create your living window.

● **MAKE A GARDEN LOOK LONGER** by gradually reducing the height of boundary hedges as they recede from the house, which will create the illusion that the end of the garden is farther away.

● **CHOOSE THE BEST LAVENDERS FOR LOW HEDGES** Large species such as the classic English lavender *(Lavandula angustifolia)* can make a very bulky, spreading hedge, especially when in flower. If space is tight use compact varieties such as *Lavandula spica* 'Hidcote', or try French lavender *(Lavandula stoechas),* which has unusual flower heads with ear-like tufts and is lower-growing than English lavender.

Make an easy-care, wildlife-friendly hedge

In rural gardens an informal hedge made up of local plants will look in keeping with its surroundings, require less work, and be a fantastic resource for wildlife, so get out and about and note what grows well in and among hedgerows in your part of the country: perhaps hawthorn, blackthorn,

▼ **Lavender hedges** are glorious in flower, but the larger species make a very wide low hedge, so be sure to allow it a generous amount of space. If choosing hedging species for a family garden, bear in mind that lavender will attract quantities of bees.

field maple and guelder rose (*Viburnum opulus*), with wild honeysuckle (*Lonicera*) or old man's beard (*Clematis vitalba*) clambering through them. You could add edible fruiting plants, such as cherry plum (*Prunus cerasifera*), crab apple and a thornless blackberry. Include wild or species roses: they have single flowers that insects find more valuable than the many-petalled blooms of named varieties. *Rosa glauca* and *Rosa moyesii* give a superb display of hips, too.

Keep formal hedges in trim

Clip little and often for great results
The best-looking formal and semi-formal hedges are those which are well grown and properly cared for. Even informal hedges will require some pruning, but formal hedges need regular trimming to keep their lines crisp and clean. Frequent clipping also encourages flushes of new growth, helping to maintain the density of the hedge.

● **TRIM AT THE RIGHT TIME** Most hedges need trimming at least twice a year. The best time to trim is midsummer, when growth starts to slow and there is no longer any danger of disturbing nesting birds. A second trim in autumn may be necessary to neaten up the hedge before winter.

● **PRUNE TO MAKE A PRACTICAL SHAPE** Formal hedges should be slightly narrower at the top than at the base. This allows light to fall on all parts of the hedge to keep it healthy and will also offer some protection from wind and falling snow. To create an even top and sides on a large, formal hedge, use lengths of twine held taut between canes or posts as a guide. If you are aiming for a very precise angled finish, lash a batten between the posts or canes at the desired height and move this frame along the hedge as you cut.

● **AVOID UNSIGHTLY CUTS** Take care when cutting hedges composed of large-leaved evergreens such as cherry laurel, laurel or hollies. If possible cut individual shoots back using secateurs rather than using a hedge-trimmer, which will cut leaves in half; when these brown and die, the effect is unsightly.

● **BE GENTLE WITH CONIFERS FOR HEALTHY GROWTH** Prune conifer hedges with care, even Leyland cypress. Trim back but do not prune off all green growth. Hardly any conifers will regenerate from bare brown stems.

Renovate to bring a hedge back into line
Tackle a seriously neglected hedge over two years to reduce the stress on the plants. Either cut back one side one year, the other the next, or cut back all the major outgrowths in the first year and then trim to the final shape in the second. It's best to cut to 15–30cm (6–12in) below the desired height, to allow new growth to form the hedge top. This makes trimming easier, as you won't be cutting back to thick knotted stumps. Remove any brown growth from the bottom, and if any plants have died, replace with new, young plants as space allows, planting them in fresh soil, watering well and adding a balanced slow-release fertiliser. Weave the new growth into gaps in the face of the existing hedge.

● **REJUVENATE BOX HEDGING** by hard-pruning thin or straggly plants to 15–30cm (6–12in) of the ground: this often results in thicker growth.

BEAT THAT!
● **The world's biggest hedge** is the Meikleour Beeches in Perthshire in Scotland – some 530m (580 yards) long and a staggering 30m (100ft) tall. Planted in 1745, it takes four people six weeks to clip, working with the aid of cranes. The hedge lines a stretch of the A93 Perth–Blairgowrie road, so is worth a detour to admire during a driving tour.

▼ **Maintain an even shape** when shearing the side of a formal hedge by stretching string or garden twine along it to act as a guide. Making the hedge slightly A-shaped will allow snow to be shed more easily and lessen the risk of damage.

Water and feed the plants well in advance, especially if they appear dry and starved (bronzed foliage is a sure sign that box is deficient in nutrients, particularly nitrogen). Balding, patchy brown box may have box blight, an untreatable fungal disease that causes defoliation and eventual death, especially in dwarf hedging varieties. If your box is affected, remove the diseased plants and consider evergreen alternatives, such as shrubby honeysuckle *(Lonicera nitida)*.

Craft your own topiary

Choose the best species for clipping
Box is the classic plant choice for creating neat, clipped forms, but certain evergreen trees, particularly those such as yew that have dense, small-leaved foliage, are also well suited to topiary. Holly is another evergreen shrub that responds well to clipping and shaping. You may also be successful with deciduous plants that have dense, twiggy growth and retain some dead leaves in winter, such as beech or hornbeam.
- **REFRESH YOUR GARDEN SCHEME** by using topiary to inject drama, to create focal points, or simply to add structure and interest to a border. If you are short of time, you'll find it easier to keep topiary plants neat if you grow them in pots rather than directly in the soil, where they can become vigorous, particularly some conifers, and will need clipping and shaping much more frequently.

EXPERT KNOW HOW

CREATING A TOPIARY SHAPE USING A FRAME

Topiary frames and templates are widely available and will help you achieve a balanced effect. Try simple shapes such as spheres or cones (as below) until you feel ready to move on to more complex forms such as a spiral. You may even be inspired to try some freehand clipping on your tired old conifers!

1 Choose a well-grown, bushy plant (here box) that ideally has a shape that suggests the form you are aiming for. Select a frame in a size slightly smaller than the plant, and secure it in place.

2 Hooks supplied to fix the frame into the soil make a perfect tool for teasing long shoots through the holes in the framework – or fashion your own from coathanger wire using pliers.

3 Trim off all growth that protrudes beyond the wire. Remove the frame – if any overlooked shoots spring out, trim these by eye using the broad outlines of the shape already created.

- **DOUBLE UP FOR ADDED STYLE** Use pairs of topiary shapes to mark the end of a path or grow them in pots on either side of a door to create a stylish entrance. Turn topiary in containers occasionally so sunlight can reach all sides and ensure even growth – important for a matched pair. Frequent watering and a weekly feed with a balanced liquid fertiliser during the growing season will also keep plants in pots growing well.
- **INVEST IN THE RIGHT TOOLS** Consider buying a pair of special, one-handed topiary shears: the blades are very sharp and will give a precise cut. Long-handled shears are also useful for crisp, clean lines on cones and pyramids.
- **CLIP LITTLE AND OFTEN** to encourage a dense network of side shoots. Trim from early to late summer every fortnight or so when the plants are in active growth, with a final clip in autumn to neaten them up for winter.
- **CREATE MAGICAL EFFECTS BY LIGHTING YOUR TOPIARY** with draped strings of low-voltage and solar-powered outdoor lighting [see pp.68–9]. This will add another dimension to your garden at night and during the winter months.

Make a striking silhouette with cloud pruning

The rounded forms of trees and hedges pruned to resemble clouds – a practice that originated in Japan – make really eye-catching garden features (see above). Ready-pruned shrubs are expensive, so why not make your own? Pine, yew, juniper and the false cypress *(Chamaecyparis)* are all suitable plants – or you can achieve the same effect with evergreens such as box, privet and euonymus. Choose a multi-stemmed or multi-branched specimen and decide where to retain growth to form the 'clouds' – you must make several to retain enough foliage to sustain the plant. Remove all the other leafy stems to bare wood. Do not over-manicure the clouds in the first year; just pinch off the tips of stems, then you can trim to shape in the second and successive years.

Train ivy to form instant topiary

For fast results train ivy over frames, which can be bought ready-made in traditional geometric forms or as novelty shapes, such as birds. For a really large globe, wire together two hanging baskets so that they create a sphere, or make your own customised forms from galvanised chicken wire or plastic mesh, moulded and secured into shape. These ivy sculptures work well in the garden but look even more effective in a pot or tub.
- **USE DENSE, SMALL-LEAVED IVIES FOR BEST EFFECT** – avoid the large ground-cover types such as *Hedera helix* 'Hibernica'. Go for green-leaved varieties, which tend to grow more vigorously than those with coloured or variegated leaves.

▲ **A perfect, cloud-pruned** hornbeam like this mature specimen seen in a show garden can be just the inspiration you need to get started on topiary. You may have to start small, unless an existing shrub in your garden looks as if it would be suitable.

Climbing plants

ATTRACTIVE AND HIGHLY VERSATILE, climbers will cover both vertical surfaces and structures with colourful foliage, flowers and sometimes even fruits, as well as dividing or enclosing space or highlighting a focal point. They are particularly useful for clothing dull walls or fences and for adding height to plantings.

Cladding walls and fences

Create beautiful living boundaries Vertical surfaces can double your planting space, so don't let them go to waste. There are climbers for every aspect and situation, even the shadiest walls and fences, so take advantage of what climbers have to offer and use them to cloak house walls and boundary walls and fences with soft foliage and colourful flowers.

● **CHOOSE EVERGREEN CLIMBERS FOR YEAR-ROUND COVERAGE** There are plenty of flowering climbers with foliage that remains green all year, such as certain clematis (see facing page) as well as foliage favourites such as ivies.

● **GROW RAPID-IMPACT ANNUALS** that will flower in their first year of growth, such as sweet peas (*Lathyrus odoratus*), canary creeper (*Tropaeolum peregrinum*) or black-eyed susan (*Thunbergia alata*). Annual climbers are great plants in their own right but can also be used to cover surfaces and structures for a season while you are waiting for a permanent climber, such as a rose, to get established.

● **BRIGHTEN A GLOOMY WALL** with an evergreen climber with variegated or coloured foliage, or one that has a long-lasting display of white or pale-coloured flowers, such as a climbing hydrangea.

▼ **Beautifully scented star jasmine** (*Trachelospermum jasminoides*) thrives in a sheltered spot and in an enclosed garden its perfume will be even more prominent. Its lush green foliage softens a brick wall, and the pale flowers add light.

● **USE SELF-CLINGING CREEPERS TO CLIMB HIGH** without the need for supports, such as Virginia creeper or Boston ivy (both *Parthenocissus*). They are suitable for concrete or brick walls, but not rendered surfaces or those that need regular painting.

● **ENJOY THE FRAGRANCE OF SCENTED CLIMBERS** by training them on patio walls or around doorways or windows where you can really enjoy their perfume. Jasmines and fragrant varieties of climbing and rambling roses look and smell wonderful. Check honeysuckle (*Lonicera*) labels carefully: several, including some of the more exotic-looking varieties, are not scented. The old-fashioned types, such as *Lonicera periclymenum* 'Graham Thomas', are often the most fragrant.

● **SOFTEN A RETAINING WALL** by training a cascading climber along the top: its sideshoots will hang down to form trailing curtains of foliage and flowers. Virginia creeper with its fiery autumn colour and early-flowering *Clematis montana* with its masses of blooms make ideal choices.

CHOOSING THE RIGHT CLIMBER

Selecting climbers is just like choosing any other plant. Different species are suited by different sites and conditions and some will be hardier than others in your garden. As a rule of thumb, climbers prefer their roots to be in moist shade and their tops in sunshine, which reflects how they grow in their natural woodland habitat – rooted in the forest floor and growing towards the light.

FOR HOT SUNNY WALLS

If you're fortunate enough to have a warm, sheltered wall in full sun, you can enjoy climbers with colourful and exotic-looking flowers that originate in Mediterranean climates, which are often drought-tolerant.

- *Actinidia kolomikta*
- *Ampelopsis brevipedunculata* 'Elegans'
- ‹ *Campsis x tagliabuana* 'Madame Galen'
- *Clematis florida* 'Sieboldiana'
- *Clematis rehderiana*
- *Jasminum officinale*
- *Passiflora* 'Incense'
- *Schisandra grandiflora*
- *Solanum jasminoides*
- *Trachelospermum asiaticum*

FOR SHADE

Climbers grow towards the light, so careful choice is needed on shady walls, otherwise the plant is likely to grow up and over a boundary into your neighbour's garden as fast as it can – giving them, not you, the benefit of its flowers.

- *Celastrus orbiculatus*
- *Clematis montana* var. *grandiflora*
- ‹ *Clematis* 'Nelly Moser'
- *Hedera colchica* 'Variegata'
- *Hydrangea petiolaris*
- *Jasminum nudiflorum*
- *Lonicera henryi*
- *Lonicera x tellmanniana*
- *Parthenocissus tricuspidata*
- *Schizophragma integrifolium*

FAST-GROWING CLIMBERS

Fast-growing annual climbers are ideal for a quick display. The more permanent, perennial varieties are perfect choices for covering a garden eyesore such as an ugly shed or garage, but beware – some can be very rampant.

ANNUALS
- *Cobaea scandens*
- *Eccremocarpus scaber*
- *Ipomoea lobata*
- *Tropaeolum peregrinum*
- *Thunbergia alata*

PERENNIALS
- *Clematis orientalis, C. montana*
- *Humulus lupulus* 'Aureus'
- *Fallopia baldschuanica*
- *Lonicera x americana*
- ‹ *Solanum crispum*

EVERGREEN CLIMBERS

If you want a clothing or screening effect to last all year round, there is an evergreen climber to suit most gardens. Some have the additional bonus of beautifully scented flowers to complement their foliage.

- *Akebia quinata*
- *Berberidopsis corallina*
- ‹ *Clematis armandii* 'Apple Blossom'
- *Clematis cirrhosa*
- *Hedera helix* 'Buttercup' and 'Goldchild'
- *Holboellia coriacea*
- *Lonicera sempervirens* 'Superba'
- *Passiflora caerulea*
- *Pileostegia viburnoides*
- *Trachelospermum jasminoides*

CHOOSE PALER-FLOWERED
WISTERIAS FOR THE
STRONGEST VANILLA PERFUME

Climbers on free-standing structures

Add stature to a garden with climbers
Trained over pergolas, arches, arbours and other structures, climbers take flowering displays to new heights, and also contribute dappled shade without casting the dense shadow of a tree's canopy – a perfect middle way for a seating area.

● **COMBINE CLIMBERS FOR A LONG SEASON OF INTEREST** Planting different climbers on either side of a structure such as a garden arch that flower at different times is a clever way to keep the show going, as long as the plants are equally matched in vigour so one doesn't dominate the other. Try combining large-flowered clematis with long-flowering climbing roses, such as 'Zéphirine Drouhin', or choose two varieties of honeysuckle, one early and one late-flowering.

● **ADD INSTANT HEIGHT TO BEDS AND BORDERS** by growing annual climbers such as sweet peas up tripods or metal obelisks, or for a more natural effect use structures woven from hazel or willow (see below). Perennial climbers, such as large-flowered clematis or honeysuckle, can also be trained up a stout post.

◄ **A mature wisteria** in full flower is a wonderful sight, but you don't need a large supporting structure such as this tunnel to grow these exquisite climbers. Train one up a sturdy post and you can keep it pruned [see p.170] to form a graceful, weeping feature.

EXPERT KNOW HOW

MAKING A RUSTIC WIGWAM

In gardens with an informal planting scheme, structures made from cut lengths of willow or hazel create a very natural effect and make good supports, either in borders or in containers, for pretty, twining or tendril climbers such as sweet peas and clematis.

1 Hazel or willow poles are easy to source, or you can grow your own [see p.156]. Choose six matching poles of the desired height and drive them into the compost or soil to form a circle about 60cm (24in) in diameter.

2 Bind the tops together to create the wigwam shape. Wire or plastic-coated twine make the most durable bindings, but you may prefer jute for its natural look. Trim the tops of the poles to the same height, if desired.

3 To give strength to the structure, make two circlets around it, at around one-third and two-thirds of the way up, by weaving thinner wands of whippy willow or other garden prunings in and out of the poles.

4 Trim and if necessary bind in any stray ends of stems, and your wigwam is ready to be planted. Two wigwams in matching pots, covered with flowers or even climbing beans, would look attractive flanking a kitchen door.

A HINGED TRELLIS FOR EASY MAINTENANCE

Adding hinges and hooks to trellis will enable you to lower the panel, with the plant attached, to repair or repaint the wall or fence behind. Use this method only for plants with flexible, twining stems such as honeysuckles: lowering the trellis may damage woody, stiff-stemmed plants such as climbing roses and wisteria.

1 Cut two lengths of 5cm (2in) batten to the width of the trellis panel, then screw them to the garden wall or fence at the levels where the top and bottom of the panel will be. Use two or three hinges to secure the base of the panel to the lower batten.

2 Lift the panel up and lightly hammer in a nail through the trellis into the top batten to hold it in place. Add hook-and-eye fixings at either end of the batten and panel. Secure them, then remove the holding nail.

Providing sturdy supports

Match the support to the climber Climbing plants have developed a number of ways to scramble up and over their supports, so establishing how your climber attaches itself and then selecting the right way to help it climb is the key to success. Ivy and climbing hydrangeas, for example, cling to bare surfaces with fine roots, so after initial guidance to get them started, both can manage to climb unaided. Twining climbers, such as clematis, honeysuckles and summer jasmines, must have something to twine around, such as a sturdy trellis or wires, while climbing roses and winter jasmine need tying in.

● **INSTALL SUPPORTS WELL BEFORE PLANTING** This may sound like obvious advice but if you put up supporting structures, such as trellis or an arch, after plants are in the ground, you can easily damage the plants and set back their growth.

● **USE THE RIGHT FIXINGS FOR STABILITY** When fixing heavy-gauge wires or trellis to walls always use masonry bolts and screws. If the wall is old or the mortar is not very hard, then drill holes directly into the brick or concrete with a masonry bit. Mortar may disintegrate over time causing fixings to become loose: this will make the support unstable and will also lead to damage to the masonry.

● **CHECK PANELS AND POSTS FOR WEAR** before planting climbers, and make sure that the structure can carry the weight of the plant when mature. Posts should be securely concreted in the ground, and panels should show no signs of decay.

● **LET AIR CIRCULATE TO ENSURE HEALTHY PLANTS** When attaching wires, netting or trellis to walls or fences ensure there is space to allow air to circulate behind the climber. Use vine eyes to hold wires away from a wall or fence, and fix trellis to battens screwed firmly in place to create some air space behind the support. This makes training and pruning much easier, and also reduces the risk of fungal disease.

● **SELECT THE RIGHT TIE FOR THE CLIMBER** When fixing climbers in position, bear in mind that annual climbers can be secured with twine or raffia, but stout climbers, such as roses and wisteria, need stronger, more durable ties made of galvanised metal, wire or UV-stabilised plastic. There are many custom-designed products and kits for securing climbers on the market and it is often better in the long term to use these than to make your own.

● **MAINTAIN FIXINGS AND TIES TO KEEP CLIMBERS IN PLACE** Always check for wear and tear, replacing damaged or worn fixings and attaching new ties to make sure any new growth is properly secured. Autumn and winter winds can loosen the roots of a climber that is not securely supported or tied in, and it will then spend time re-establishing itself in the next season rather than making new growth.

Growing climbers up other plants

Choose compatible partners for success Some climbers are
rampant plants, so when choosing one to grow through a tree or shrub, make sure your host plant is up to the job and that its canopy won't disappear under a heavy mass of stems and flowers. Vigorous rambling roses such as 'Bobby James' look fantastic grown through large, mature trees, as do certain vines with bold leaves which colour strongly in autumn, such as *Vitis coignetiae*. Sweet peas are a good choice for smaller trees. Another decision to make when choosing your climber is whether you want the season of interest for both plants to be at the same time, for maximum impact, or at a different time, to extend the display.

● **LIVEN UP EVERGREENS WITH A CLIMBING PARTNER** Evergreen shrubs are ideal hosts for less vigorous clematis varieties such as *Clematis × durandii*, which has purple flowers in late summer and can be cut back in early spring. The perennial sweet pea *Lathyrus latifolius* will give a summer boost of bright pink flowers to dark-leaved hedges, such as yew, and can also simply be cut down to the ground each year.

● **PLANT CLIMBERS AWAY FROM HOST PLANTS** to reduce the competition for water and nutrients. When growing a climber through a tree, plant it at least 60cm (2ft) from the trunk, guiding it to the trunk with an angled bamboo cane or up a rope staked into the ground, so that rainwater can drip from the tree's leaves on to the climber's root area.

● **GET THE FLOWERS ON YOUR SIDE** Climbers will grow towards the sun, so if you want your garden, rather than your neighbour's, to get the benefit of the flowers, choose host trees and shrubs that are on the sunny side of your garden, not the shady side.

▼ **An old apple tree** that is nearing the end of its productive life can be reborn as a robust, handsome support for a rambling rose. Most ramblers only flower once, but their summer show is quite spectacular.

Established wisterias need to be pruned in two stages at two different times during the year to keep them flowering well. This pruning keeps their strong, leafy growth in check and helps to ensure that you get flowers rather than just abundant foliage.

SUMMER PRUNING

Once flowering is over, tie in any long, sturdy outer shoots that are needed to create a framework that will fill the allotted space. Prune all the other shoots back to five or six leaves. Take care to cut well clear of the last leaf so as not to damage the new bud in the joint between leaf and stem.

WINTER PRUNING

In late winter, cut back the summer-pruned stems to 8–10cm (3–4in), leaving only two or three buds. If you failed to prune in summer, cut back all of the shoots to two buds now. Missing an occasional year of summer pruning will not make too much difference to performance.

Planting, training and pruning

Get climbers off to a good start for rapid growth Soak the rootball of a newly purchased climber in water before planting and mix plenty of organic matter and a slow-release fertiliser into the hole before planting and filling in with soil. Water the plant in thoroughly and remember to keep it moist in dry weather. A mulch of organic material such as garden compost or leafmould [see p.142], or a decorative mulch of pebbles or slate, will also help to keep the roots of climbers cool.

● **AVOID DRY SPOTS AT THE BASE OF WALLS** The soil at the base of a wall can often be dry and impoverished and overhanging eaves can also prevent rain from reaching a climber's roots. Plant climbers about 30cm (12in) away from house or garden walls, tying them to a bamboo cane and leaning this in to the wall to guide the stems. Planting away from walls also encourages climbers to root into soil further afield, helping to prevent roots penetrating foundations.

● **PLANT CLEMATIS DEEPLY TO COMBAT DISEASE** The fungal disease clematis wilt can cause the entire plant to collapse and die. Plant clematis deeper than the planting level of their original pot, so that the stem bases are covered with about 8cm (3in) of soil. This can help healthy growth to shoot from buds below the soil even when the original top growth has died.

Easy ways to encourage fantastic flowers The vast majority of climbing plants are grown for their glorious flower displays. Regular feeding, pruning and deadheading will keep your climber in the best possible shape, encourage new flowering shoots to form and promote bigger and better displays.

● **FEED CLIMBERS FOR BUMPER DISPLAYS** As climbers start making new growth, encourage more flowers to form by feeding them with a high-potash fertiliser. You can either mix granules into the soil or use a liquid feed, which is particularly beneficial for annual climbers.

● **PINCH OUT AND KEEP PICKING FOR MORE FLOWERS** To encourage side shoots to form, which will then produce more flowering stems, pinch out the tips of annual climbers. You can do the same with passion flowers *(Passiflora)*, pinching out stem tips when plants have filled their allotted space. When flowers form on sweet peas, harvest them continually to keep more flowers coming, and remove faded blooms from repeat-flowering roses as soon as you can, either by snapping or snipping off the head just below the swelling at the base of the flower.

● **PRUNE AT THE RIGHT TIME FOR HEALTHY GROWTH** Generally speaking, if your climber flowers in winter or spring, prune it straight after flowering, removing the flowered stems and any other weak or damaged growth. If it flowers in summer, prune in winter or early spring before growth starts, again removing spent shoots and any untidy growth that is spoiling the shape.

● **REINVIGORATE OLD HONEYSUCKLES** These plants often become straggly with age, flowering in a tangle of growth high up where both flowers and scent cannot be appreciated. Hard-prune down to within 45cm (18in) of the ground in autumn or winter to encourage a flush of new shoots to form low down in spring.

PRUNING CLEMATIS

Clematis species and varieties fall into three basic groups, based on the time that they flower, and each of these groups has different pruning requirements. If you don't know what group your clematis belongs to and don't want to take the risk of pruning it incorrectly, leave it for a year and note when it flowers.

☐ EARLY-FLOWERING

Clematis that flower from late winter to late spring do not need regular pruning once established, although they can be thinned and any untidy growth removed. If you need to prune, cut out spent flowering shoots immediately after flowering to encourage new growth to form and ripen for next year's display. Don't cut these clematis back hard, as some, such as *Clematis montana*, may take a long time to recover.

Early-flowering clematis include: *Clematis montana*; *C. macropetala* (left, 'Lagoon'); *C. alpina* and hybrids; *C. cirrhosa* and *C. armandii*.

☐ SUMMER-FLOWERING

This group contains the majority of large-flowered clematis that bloom from early summer onwards and also includes some of the double-flowered varieties. All flower on growth made in the current season, so lightly trim the previous year's growth in late winter or early spring. Prune back to large buds and thin out weak growth to encourage vigorous shoots that will produce larger flowers.

Summer-flowering clematis include: *Clematis tangutica*; *C.* 'Nellie Moser'; *C.* 'Henryi' (left); *C.* 'Mrs Cholmondeley' and *C.* 'Marie Boisselot'.

☐ LATE-FLOWERING

In this group are clematis that flower from mid to late summer on growth made in the current season. Remove all the previous season's growth by hard pruning each stem back to a pair of strong buds about 6–12in (15–30cm) from the ground in early spring.

Late-flowering clematis include: *Clematis jackmanii* and hybrids; *C.* 'Ville de Lyon; *C.* 'Ernest Markham' (left); *C. texensis* and *C. viticella*.

Lawns and lawn care

SOFT UNDERFOOT AND GREEN ALL YEAR ROUND, a well-kept lawn enhances any garden and sets off plants to perfection. Spend a little time on maintaining your lawn, whether it is a green expanse or the size of a pocket-handkerchief, and your garden will look at its very best in every season.

The secrets of lush lawns

Feed, weed and mow for a splendid sward
A good lawn maintenance regime – feeding and weeding, nipping problems in the bud and mowing like a pro (see facing page) – really is the sure-fire way to a lush green lawn. The quality of your lawn also depends on the type of grasses that grow in it. Many lawns are made up of tough, utilitarian grass mixes, whereas the highly manicured surfaces found on golf greens are created using very fine-growing grass species. Take a sample of your lawn to a turf supply specialist to learn what your grass type is, and to find out what you can expect from it.

● **TOP UP NUTRIENTS TO KEEP LAWNS GREEN** Rain and mowing deplete food supplies in the soil, so for a healthy lawn feed regularly (except in prolonged dry spells). Always follow the instructions when applying powdered or granular feed and be sure to scatter it evenly. For large areas, consider hiring a wheeled spreader from a tool-hire centre. Liquid lawn feeds are also available and are very easy to use.

● **SAVE TIME BY COMBINING WEEDING AND FEEDING** If there are lots of weeds in your lawn that need eliminating then consider using a 'weed and feed' product – a proprietary mix of herbicide and fertiliser. To allow the weedkiller to act, do not mow for at least three days after application.

▼ **Neat brick lawn edging** set just below the level of the grass makes mowing easier and keeps the lawn well-defined. Here, it also helps prevent gravel from the paths migrating onto the lawn.

EXPERT KNOW HOW

TOP MOWING TIPS FOR A PERFECT LAWN

All grass plants grow from the base, not from the shoot tips, and this is why they can be mown short without killing them. Mowing also stimulates grass plants to produce sideshoots which root into surrounding soil, thickening the lawn and filling gaps that would otherwise be colonised by weed species.

● At the start of each year, ensure mower blades are clean and sharp and moving parts well-oiled so that your grass gets a precision cut, not a battering.

● Mow twice weekly in summer and once a week in spring and autumn.

◀ For a truly professional effect, use a cylinder mower [see p.228] and mow in absolutely straight lines. Site pegs or canes at each end of the lawn to use as sightlines. Ensure the next pass back just butts up to the edge of the previous strip. Practice will make perfect.

● To achieve an even cut, always push the mower forward rather than manoeuvring it to and fro like a vacuum cleaner.

● In prolonged dry conditions, raise the blades for a slightly higher cut, and leave the clippings on the grass. Letting the grass grow a little longer also helps to smother weeds.

● After rain, wait until the grass is dry before you mow for a better cut.

● **GET TO THE ROOTS TO BANISH TROUBLESOME WEEDS** If you have only a few persistent weeds such as dandelions or plantains, dig them out, root and all, before they flower using a narrow trowel, old kitchen knife or daisy grubber tool. Fill the space with compost and sow a pinch of grass seed or fill with a plug of turf and water in. Lawn weedkillers in convenient spot applicators are also available.

● **MOW IN STAGES TO GET ON TOP OF LONG GRASS** If the grass has become overlong by the time you're ready to make the first cut of the year, or because you've been away, set the blades high at first and only cut the tips. Lower the blade a little at the second cut, then resume normal cutting height at the third mowing.

● **BE SMART IN PERIODS OF DROUGHT** If your lawn withers in prolonged hot, dry weather try to live with it: lawn grasses are selected to be highly durable and will flush with new growth when rains return. If absolutely necessary, and if there are no watering restrictions in force, use sprinklers sparingly and only where really needed, once a week on normal soils or twice on well-drained soils.

CUT AN OVERLONG LAWN IN STAGES TO AVOID SHOCKING AND WEAKENING THE GRASS

● **DEFINE EDGES FOR A CLEAN LOOK** If your lawn butts up to your borders, invest in long-handled, L-shaped edging shears to keep the edges crisp and neat. To prevent turf growing into border soil and to make edging easier, use an edging iron [see p.76] or a sharp spade to create a 10cm (4in) deep channel at the edge of the lawn, sloping up into the border. Use a hoe to keep the channel clear of fallen soil.

● **ADD FIXED EDGING FOR EASIER MOWING** Flexible edging strips made from weatherproof plastic or galvanised or painted metal are widely available. Some have spikes along the bottom edge to fix them in place.

LAWN CARE CALENDAR

You'll get the most out of your lawn if you carry out routine maintenance at the right time. Frequent summer mowing is a fact of life, but give your lawn a little attention in spring and autumn and you'll be rewarded with beautiful, healthy grass.

☐ SPRING

Start the new season by giving your lawn a spring boost. Winter rains will have depleted the soil of nutrients, so apply a granulated, nitrogen-rich lawn fertiliser now to stimulate growth. Make sure, too, that your mower is clean and the working parts are well oiled, then choose a dry day to make your first cut, with the blades set at about 3cm (1½in).

☐ SUMMER

Mow once or twice weekly with the blades set at a height of 2.5cm (1in); regular mowing will help to maintain a balanced mixture of grasses and thicken your lawn. High-quality lawns can be mown to half this height, but no shorter or you will weaken the grass. During very dry spells or with a new lawn, water in the early morning or evening to reduce evaporation.

☐ AUTUMN

Apply a second feed in early to mid-autumn using an autumn lawn fertiliser mix. Scarifying and aerating (see right) are other important tasks best done now, and it's also a good idea to top-dress your lawn every two or three years in autumn: make a mixture of 4 parts loam to 2 parts sand and 2 parts peat-free compost, and scatter this evenly over the grass.

Rescue a neglected lawn

Take renovation one step at a time An overgrown, neglected or damaged lawn can be daunting, but there are easy techniques to restore it. Make a list of all the procedures that will help restore your neglected lawn and when they should be best carried out (see left). It's a good idea to review the shape and style of your lawn at the same time to suit any new garden plans. If making a border deeper releases turf, for example, you can save money by using the sections you remove to repair edges or fill gaps elsewhere.

● **SCARIFY THE GRASS TO REMOVE MOSS AND THATCH** If your lawn is soft and spongy it is likely to be full of moss or 'thatch', a layer of old grass leaves and stems that reduces the air supply to grass roots and encourages disease. Take a spring-tined rake and comb a patch of grass vigorously. If the material you rake out is mostly moss, proprietary moss-killers can help, including traditional lawn sand (which despite its innocuous name is not organic). If the debris is dry and plentiful, this indicates thatch. Remove it by pulling the rake through the lower level of the turf, a process known as scarifying.

● **AERATE THE LAWN FOR LUSHER GROWTH** If areas of your lawn or pathways across it are compacted (look for where surface water accumulates after rain), grass roots will be deprived of air, growth will be poor and moss may flourish. To relieve compaction and let in air, use a garden fork to make holes in the lawn surface. Push the tines in to a depth of 10cm (4in), rocking the fork gently before removal. You can also use a special hollow-tined aerator or, for large areas of lawn, consider hiring a mechanical aerator.

● **RE-SEED TO COVER UP BARE PATCHES** in spring or early autumn. There are now lawn repair kits available that contain seed that has been impregnated with mycorrhizae: beneficial fungi [see p.242] that help grass plants to root well. Cover re-seeded areas with mesh or criss-cross with thread to deter birds from eating the seed.

● **MAKE QUICK-FIX REPAIRS TO DAMAGED TURF** by removing the dead or bare patch, leaving a rectangular shape for a new turf patch. If you need a matching patch for a damaged area in a prominent position, take one from another, less important area of the lawn, lightly fork over the surface of the soil, water well and fit the replacement patch in position. You can then reseed or add new turf to the less prominent hole. Always cut replacement patches of turf to fit snugly.

● **SMARTEN UP EDGES BY REPAIRING BREAKS** Simply remove the square of turf with the broken edge, turn it round so this edge is now within the lawn and re-seed the gap.

● **FILL IN HOLLOWS FOR AN EVEN SURFACE** Shallow dips in the lawn are easy to correct by top-dressing them (see Autumn, left), spreading the soil mix thinly over the area with the back of a rake. The grass plants will soon root into the mixture and new growth will begin to show.

Alternatives to a traditional lawn

Relax your mowing regime for less work If you have a large area of lawn and are daunted by the amount of mowing necessary to keep it in tip-top condition, consider changing the way you manage your grass. You could keep only one or two areas adjacent to the house closely mown and maintained, for example, and let grassed areas further away grow longer.

● **LET YOUR LAWN FLOWER** Some plants considered as 'lawn weeds', such as daisies, speedwells and clovers, are attractive when in flower. They also attract helpful insects, such as bees. Mow straight after flowering to stop the plants setting seed.

● **REAP THE BENEFITS OF CLOVERS** These useful plants will fertilise your lawn naturally and they are also drought-tolerant, remaining green when grass has turned brown. Clovers fix nitrogen from the air in their roots, which is then released into the soil, helping to fertilise the surrounding grass.

● **CREATE A MINI-MEADOW** Set aside an area of lawn and mow it less frequently, then plant a range of small spring bulbs and low-growing wildflowers to grow there. The best way to get wildflowers established is to buy them as small plugs from mail-order nurseries and plant them straight into the lawn.

EXPERT KNOW HOW

NATURALISING BULBS IN GRASS

Spring bulbs look charming naturalised in lawns. The best to plant are snowdrops, crocuses, narcissi, snakeshead fritillaries (below) and muscari (grape hyacinths). Don't mow until about six weeks after flowering, when the foliage has died down.

PLANTING SMALL BULBS

Cut three sides of a square in the turf, peel it back, place a handful of small bulbs on the soil beneath, and pat the turf down again.

PLANTING LARGE BULBS

A bulb planter, which takes out a core of soil, is ideal for planting large bulbs and also small wildflower plants such as cowslips.

PRIZE-WINNING PRODUCE

4

Whether you're inspired to grow crops that will be 'best in show', or simply want to feed your family with healthy, home-grown produce, there's a host of handy hints and expert techniques that will help guarantee bumper harvests of the freshest and most flavoursome vegetables, salads, herbs and fruits.

Growing vegetables

'GROW WHAT YOU LIKE TO EAT' sounds like obvious advice, but home-grown produce is all about enjoying your favourite vegetables and salads, bursting with new-found flavour and freshness. Go for what tastes best when picked straight from the garden – even the smallest plot can be productive and put to good use.

Deciding what to grow

Make the most of varieties Different vegetable varieties have very different characteristics – size, shape, colour, flavour and harvest times all vary widely. Experiment with as many varieties as possible to discover which of them do best on your plot and in its growing conditions.

● **CHOOSE MODERN VARIETIES FOR HIGH PERFORMANCE** Seed companies are continually breeding new varieties, including premium F1 hybrids (see below), that they claim taste better, crop more heavily, store for longer and are more resistant to pests and diseases. Why not take advantage of all their hard work?

● **TRY 'HEIRLOOM' VARIETIES FOR NOVELTY AND FLAVOUR** The forgotten varieties that your grandparents may have grown are being rediscovered and offered for sale once again. Old-fashioned yellow carrots, black tomatoes and blue potatoes are certainly a talking point. What's more, they often have a wonderful flavour.

● **GROW WHAT'S NOT IN THE SHOPS** Oriental leaves such as pak choi and mizuna, unusual varieties such as yellow courgettes and purple brussels sprouts, and lesser-known herbs such as chervil are often hard to buy but easy to grow yourself.

▶ **Raised beds** with wooden sides provide easy fixing points for netting to protect crops from birds. The closely spaced rows shown here reduce the need for weeding.

HOW DOES IT WORK?

F1 HYBRIDS

F1 hybrids like these 'San Marzano Lungo' tomatoes are the thoroughbreds of modern crop breeding. The seeds come from the careful cross-breeding of two 'pure' parent varieties. The plants they produce are strong, healthy and true to type, with no risk of any random or unpredictable genetic strains. Although more expensive, they are completely dependable.

It's all about timing

Avoid gluts and shortages Guarantee a steady supply of fresh produce by growing both early and late-cropping varieties, by staggered sowing, by starting off your first seeds of the year indoors or under cover, and by using cloches in autumn so your crops continue to ripen.

● **KEEP SUPPLIES FLOWING** through the second half of spring – traditionally the leanest period of the year for harvesting. Cabbages and lettuces planted the previous autumn and protected over winter will be ready for picking in mid-spring, as will oriental salad leaves and baby turnips sown under cover early in the year.

● **SOW LITTLE AND OFTEN** is a mantra worth remembering. Many crops, such as carrots, have a sowing season that spans several months, so if you sow a few seeds every few weeks you will be able to harvest until autumn.

● **SKIP THE SOWING STAGE** and buy module-grown starter plants if it is too late in the season to grow from seed, or if your own sowings have failed to germinate. They are available from garden centres or via mail-order.

● **RAISE WINTER-HARDY CROPS** that can withstand low temperatures [see also p.254] for supplies of fresh produce in the colder months.

[see also p.254]

STAR PERFORMERS...

CROPS FOR QUICK RETURNS

The fastest-growing crops are the oriental salad leaves. Given the right conditions, they may take just eight weeks from sowing to harvest. Hard on their heels are baby roots that you can pick and eat as tender mini-veg. Choose varieties listed as 'early' as these are often the fastest-growing.

● **Baby turnips**
● **Beetroot**
● **Carrots**
● **Chinese cabbage**
● **Courgettes**
● **Dwarf french beans**
● **Mizuna**
● **Pak choi**
◀ **Radishes**
● **Rocket**
● **Spinach**
● **Summer lettuces**

Make a traditional kitchen garden

Choose the right spot Most vegetables grow best somewhere light and sunny but sheltered from strong winds. Avoid frost traps, dark corners and shady spots overhung by trees, and steer clear of damp, waterlogged soil.

● **DIVIDE YOUR VEGETABLE PLOT** into beds and separate these with permanent paths. That way, when you add compost, manure and other soil improvers, it goes only on the beds, where the nutrients are really needed. You also restrict foot traffic to the paths, where it belongs.

● **ADD STEPPING STONES** Slabs of paving stone or old bricks laid into the soil make useful stepping stones for wider beds. They give you somewhere to stand, preventing you from tramping down and compacting the soil when working. Alternatively, lay scaffolding planks to walk on.

EXPERT KNOW HOW

A FOUR-BED VEGETABLE PLOT

Divide your plot into quarters and make four raised beds, separated by access paths (see facing page). A tried-and-tested four-year rotation plan for the beds will keep your soil healthy and your vegetables growing and cropping successfully.

Starting in year one with the main crop groups listed below, move them one bed clockwise every year. Salad crops can be fitted in anywhere, wherever there is space. Top up the beds regularly with organic matter as different crops come to an end.

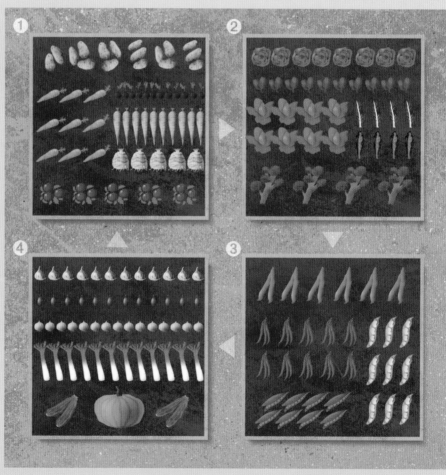

❶ Potatoes and other root crops – carrots, beetroot, parsnips, celeriac; outdoor varieties of tomatoes.

❷ Brassicas and leafy crops: lettuces, spinach, cabbages, kale, purple sprouting broccoli.

❸ Climbing runner beans, dwarf french beans, peas and broad beans, which can be followed by sweetcorn.

❹ Garlic, shallots, onions and leeks together with courgettes and squashes or pumpkins.

● **NO NEED TO DIG** Once you've dug your plot the first time, just spread a 10cm (4in) layer of compost or manure over the surface of the beds each autumn or winter and let worms do the job of taking it down into the soil. As long as you weed regularly, digging is unnecessary; in fact, it can disturb the natural structure of the soil.

Rotate your crops each year Note down what you grow where and don't grow the same crops in the same place the next year. This crop rotation prevents the soil from becoming exhausted and helps to avoid the build-up of pests and diseases. Never follow potatoes with tomatoes, for example, or vice versa. They are from the same family and attract some of the same diseases.

● **PLANT SALAD CROPS ANYWHERE** Lettuces, spinach, rocket and other salad leaves are not too fussy about crop rotation. Use them to fill in gaps – in flower beds and borders as well as on the vegetable plot.

DIVIDING A PLOT INTO FOUR RAISED BEDS

1 Prepare the site by carefully digging over the soil to remove all traces of perennial weeds. Rake the surface level.

2 Use pegs and string to mark out four squares for the beds. Make paths between and around the beds that are at least 50cm (20in) wide.

3 Hammer in 30cm (12in) stakes at each corner. Screw or nail treated wooden battens (10cm x 2.5cm/4in x 1in) of the required length to join them.

4 Cover the paths with a thick layer of shredded bark or grit. To help suppress weeds, you could first cover the soil with geotextile mulching fabric.

5 Add generous quantities of well-rotted organic matter, such as farmyard manure, to each bed. Either leave it on the surface or rake it in.

6 As soon as you begin planting, keep the beds well watered. Weed regularly but avoid treading on the soil, especially when it is wet.

Out with one crop, in with the next Do not let ground stand empty. As soon as one crop has finished, sow or plant something else. In space that is temporarily vacant between one main crop and the next, grow 'catch crops' – fast-growers that are soon ready for picking. In summer, after harvesting early broad beans or new potatoes, you can easily squeeze in a crop of salad leaves before planting out autumn garlic, Japanese onions or spring cabbages.

● **PLAN FOR MAXIMUM PRODUCTION** In mid-spring, be ready to follow winter cauliflowers and cabbages with lettuces, tomatoes and sweetcorn. Then in midsummer, once you've harvested early potatoes, sow carrots or plant out leeks; and when broad beans and peas are over, plant beetroot, sprouting broccoli and autumn cauliflowers. In late summer, after harvesting second early potatoes, peas and french beans, follow with lettuces, kale and spring cabbages.

▲ **Grow fast-growing lettuces** between and among rows of crops that are slower to mature to get the most use from your growing space. These lettuces will be picked to allow the brassicas room to expand.

Vegetables in small spaces

Maximise your growing space With good planning, even the smallest of gardens can be very productive. Many vegetables are decorative enough to be grown in beds and borders, and growing produce in pots is the solution for a patio, a roof terrace or a balcony. And because containers are movable, you can also place them in the very best growing position. Even potatoes can be grown successfully in containers [see p.185].

● **MIX FAST AND SLOW-GROWERS** in the same growing space. Sow fast-growing oriental salad leaves, small lettuces, spinach and shallots in among slower-growing sweetcorn, tomatoes, leeks, parsnips and winter brassicas. The fast-track crops will be harvested and gone by the time the late developers need the space.

● **GET THE MOST FROM GROWING BAGS** by plumping them up before planting and standing them on end to make deep planters for potatoes. You can also set up a drip-feed watering system [see p.245] to keep the compost moist.

● **BOOST SLOWER-GROWING CONTAINER CROPS** such as tomatoes, peppers, aubergines, beans, cucumbers and squashes with a weekly dose of high-potash fertilizer. Fast-growing leafy vegetables are unlikely to need feeding.

Try 'vertical' gardening When space is so tight that the only way is up, vertical gardening is the solution. Climbing beans produce a bumper harvest without taking up much room at ground level, and wall-mounted planters can keep you in fresh cut-and-come-again salad leaves for much of the summer.

● **GROW CLIMBING COURGETTES AND SQUASHES** Trailing varieties can be trained upwards if you tie them into the same sort of wigwams, frames and trellises you would use for climbing beans and cucumbers. Try 'Black Hawk' or 'Tromboncino' courgettes, 'Red Kuri' squash or the mini-pumpkin 'Munchkin'.

● **PLANT HANGING BASKETS WITH CROPS** Cherry tomatoes, herbs and young salad leaves grow well in hanging baskets and are easy to harvest, as well as looking pretty. You can also use windowboxes or wall-mounted lengths of guttering for a micro-vegetable plot of spring onions, lettuces, radishes and baby vegetables.

▶ **Ladder allotments** are racking systems for supporting containers, growing bags or trays of plants such as the salad leaves, pak choi and edible marigolds shown here. When the ladder is inclined against a wall or fence, the tiered shelves allow sunlight and rainfall to reach crops on each level.

STAR PERFORMERS...

BEST VEGETABLES FOR CONTAINERS

Choose crops for pots that are compact and grow quickly. Look out for those sold as special 'patio' varieties.

- Aubergines
- Baby sweetcorn
- Chantenay carrots
- Chard
- Cherry tomatoes
- Dwarf french beans
- Mixed salad leaves
- Peppers and chillies

Root vegetables

GET THE LONGEST SEASON OF EATING by growing both 'early' and 'maincrop' varieties of potatoes and carrots. Early varieties have a fairly short growing season. Eat them straight after picking when they taste at their very best. Maincrops are usually larger, have a longer growing season and are better for storing.

Smart ways to grow potatoes

Keep potatoes on the menu To maintain supplies over a long period, grow a few of each type – first earlies, second earlies and maincrops. Plant first early potatoes when the soil warms up in early spring; they produce a smallish crop but are ready for lifting in early summer. Two or three weeks later plant second earlies for cropping in midsummer, and after another fortnight or so plant maincrops for the autumn.

● **BUY TOP-QUALITY SEED POTATOES** Don't plant supermarket potatoes or tubers you've saved from last year: it's a false economy because they are likely to be diseased. Certified seed potatoes may be more expensive but they are guaranteed to be virus-free.

▲ **Chit seed potatoes** by arranging them in single layers on seed trays or in egg cartons. Make sure you have the growing end with its small buds, or eyes, facing upwards. The eyes will soon produce tiny shoots.

● **START SEED POTATOES INTO GROWTH EARLY** and reduce the time between planting and harvest by 'chitting' them before planting (see left). Keep the seed potatoes in a light, cool room until they develop healthy young shoots, or chits, that are about 2.5cm (1in) long. Plant them rose-end upwards – that is, with the end that has the most buds at the top. Be careful; they are easily broken off.

● **CUT SEED POTATOES IN HALF** to double the number of plants for half the cost. Cut in such a way that each portion has a number of strong shoots or 'eyes'.

STAR PERFORMERS...

BLIGHT-RESISTANT POTATOES

To minimise the risk of potato blight (see facing page), choose from these varieties, which are naturally less susceptible.

- ● 'Cara' (maincrop, baking)
- ◀ 'Charlotte' (early, good for salads)
- ● 'Cosmos' (early, waxy)
- ● 'Lady Balfour' (early, for boiling and roasting)
- ● 'Orla' (early, for baking and mashing)
- ● 'Santé' (maincrop, for chips and mashing)
- ● 'Sarpo Axona' (maincrop, creamy)
- ● 'Sarpo Mira' (maincrop, floury)

- **HARVEST POTATOES FOR CHRISTMAS** by buying and planting specially prepared, cold-stored seed potatoes in late summer or early autumn for a crop on Christmas Day. Plant them in containers (see right) so that you can move them to a sheltered spot or greenhouse if severe frosts are forecast.

- **TAKE MEASURES AGAINST BLIGHT** This serious fungal disease can destroy your whole crop. Tell-tale signs are dark patches on the leaves, sometimes with a white, powdery mould beneath. Cut off and destroy infected foliage immediately to prevent spores washing into the soil and causing the tubers to rot. Blight is at its worst from midsummer on, especially when the weather is warm and humid. If there are two consecutive nights warmer than 10°C (50°F) with still, damp air, consider spraying with a fungicide. Grow resistant varieties (see facing page), or early varieties, which you should be able to harvest before blight takes hold.

- **EARTH UP REGULARLY FOR BIGGER CROPS** When young potato plants are about 20cm (8in) tall, use a rake or a draw hoe to pull the soil up around the stems so that just 10cm (4in) of the foliage is visible. When the shoots have doubled in height repeat the process, drawing up more soil to cover the lower half of the plants.

HOW DOES IT WORK?
EARTHING UP POTATOES

Potatoes can be 'earthed up' to as much as 60cm (24in) above where the original seed potato was set in the soil. The reason why the seed potato cannot simply be planted 60cm below the ground is that the shoots from the seed potato would not have enough energy to grow that far up and out of the soil. Earthing up must be done in stages, with leafy growth always above soil level to manufacture energy for the plant.

Add compost until just a tuft of leaves shows

Original seed potato

1 Once the potato plant is about 20cm (8in) tall, bury the shoots to about half their height by drawing up the soil or, if growing in a container (as here), by adding another layer of compost. More tuber-producing roots then grow from the stems beneath the soil.

2 Repeat the process either once or twice until the plants develop their flowers, when growth slows. The deep covering of soil that earthing up creates also prevents the tubers being exposed to sunlight, which will turn them green and poisonous.

Other root crops

Maximise harvests of carrots, parsnips and radishes
For a long-running supply of home-grown carrots, select both early and maincrop varieties and sow successively, starting under cover in early spring. Sow parsnips directly in outdoor beds in mid- or late spring: they need a long time in the ground to mature fully and develop their flavour. Radishes, on the other hand, mature very quickly so sow them little and often.

- **PREVENT ROOTS FORKING** by growing carrots and parsnips in raised beds or containers filled with sieved, free-draining soil mixed with sand. Don't grow in freshly manured ground and don't add extra fertiliser. On soil that is heavy or shallow, grow short, stumpy carrot varieties such as 'Rondo' or 'Parmex'.

- **KEEP TRACK OF PARSNIPS** It can be tricky to locate parsnips for harvesting because the leaves die down completely over winter. Always mark the position of your crops with canes at the ends of the rows before the foliage disappears.

CREATE A CARROT 'NO-FLY' ZONE

To keep carrot fly away from your crop, the best method is to erect a barrier around the plants, 45–60cm (18in–2ft) in height. This will deter the females: they tend not to fly any higher than this when they're looking for somewhere to lay their eggs. These eggs hatch into white grubs that eat the plants' roots.

◀ This professional-looking enclosure is made from horticultural fleece stretched onto a wooden frame. The sides are high enough to deter the flies and the material allows light and air to reach the plants.

● Planting rows of onions or spring onions between your carrots is said to confuse carrot flies, which locate the plants using their highly developed sense of smell. The scent of the onions helps to mask the scent of the carrots.

● Thin your carrots very carefully so that you don't attract any female flies: bruising the seedlings' leaves when uprooting them releases the scent. It's best to choose an overcast, still evening for thinning. Water the crop as soon as you've finished to damp down the soil.

● **SOW CARROTS LIKE A PRO** Reduce the need for thinning seedlings later by sowing just the right amount of carrot seeds. These seeds are so tiny that they are hard to sow evenly; they stick to your fingers then fall suddenly in clumps. Before you begin, measure them out accurately (about 3–4g for 10 sq m/30 sq ft). Dampen the soil in shallow drills so that the seeds don't blow about in the wind before you have time to cover them. If you still find the seeds too fiddly, try using a sowing aid or mixing the seeds with sand or used coffee grounds [see p.265].

FOR THE BEST-TASTING PARSNIPS, WAIT TO HARVEST THEM UNTIL AFTER THE FIRST FROSTS

● **MULTI-SOW PARSNIPS FOR RELIABLE GERMINATION** These seeds germinate slowly so sow them where they are to grow rather than raising plants under cover and transplanting; alternatively, pre-germinating seeds on damp kitchen paper will increase your chance of success. Sow in clumps of three or four seeds at a depth of 10cm (4in) and when the strongest reaches 2.5cm (1in), thin out the rest.

● **SOW RADISHES AS ROW MARKERS** Radishes are much faster to germinate and crop than carrots or parsnips. Mix the seeds and sow them together so that when your radishes come up they mark the row, making hoeing more accurate. Harvest the radishes as you thin the carrots or parsnips.

Branch out with eye-catching beetroot and turnips

Try unusual varieties of beetroot with different colours and shapes as well as the traditional type. Look out, too, for tapering white 'Blanc de Croissy' turnips.

● **FAST-TRACK YOUR TURNIPS FOR TASTY BABY ROOTS** Modern varieties such as 'Snowball' and 'Tokyo Cross' are very fast-growing. Sow them in module trays,

▶ **Purple, red and white carrots** have been around for a long time. The first orange carrot did not appear until the 1500s, when it was bred in honour of the House of Orange, the Dutch royal family.

three or four seeds to each cell, then pot on the clumps into containers or plant them out in the garden. Harvest them when they're golfball-sized – just five or six weeks after sowing. And because they mature so quickly, you can grow them between slower cabbages and cauliflowers.

● **DON'T THROW AWAY THINNINGS** – they're far too tasty for the compost heap. Tiny seedlings of beetroots and turnips are nutritious and make a great addition to salads.

● **SAVE TIME ON THINNING** by growing special 'monogerm' types of beetroot; these will produce only one plant per seed. Soak the seeds in water before sowing to soften them and help speed up germination. Sow them sparingly and there should be no unwanted seedlings to thin out at all.

Grow versatile celeriac
The earthy root of this knobbly vegetable has a distinctive celery-like taste; it's much easier to grow than celery, and will stand in the ground for longer. Celeriac can't always be found in the supermarket and it can be expensive, but it's so versatile: use the grated root raw in salads, oven-bake it in a gratin, mash it with butter or turn it into hearty soups.

● **FATTEN UP CELERIAC** during mid- and late summer by watering and weeding regularly and giving a weekly feed of liquid fertiliser. Pull off any low-growing leaves or shoots to leave the top of the root exposed.

● **PROTECT FROM FROST** by spreading a layer of straw around the plants if cold weather is forecast. Celeriac can be stored but it tastes much better if you leave it in the ground until you need it.

STAR PERFORMERS...

UNUSUAL BEETROOT

Not all beetroots are purple. Nor are they always round. It's worth tracking down the uncommon yellow or white varieties as they don't stain in the way that regular purple ones do.

● **'Albina Vereduna' and 'Blankoma'** (white skin and flesh)
● **'Alto' and 'Cylindra'** (long, cylindrical shape, ideal for slicing)
● **'Burpees Golden' and 'Golden Detroit'** (yellow-fleshed)
● **'Cheltenham Green Top'** (heirloom variety, long tapering roots)
▲ **'Chioggia'** (red skin, target-like striping when sliced across)

The onion family

ONIONS, SHALLOTS, GARLIC AND LEEKS are all members of this family, and among the easiest vegetables to grow. The bulbs – onions, shallots and garlic – will last for months if harvested and stored with care, while the stem vegetables – tender spring onions and robust, hardy leeks – are staples of summer salads and winter stews.

BEAT THAT!

● **The 2005 world record for the heaviest onion** was smashed in 2011 by British grower, Peter Glazebrook. His colossal exhibit weighed in at just over 8kg (17lb 15.5oz) – equivalent to some 54 regular supermarket onions.

▼ **Grow onions in clumps** of four or five if you are short of space. As the bulbs fatten up, the stems grow out from the centre at an angle, giving the bulbs enough room to expand.

Onions, shallots and garlic

Start from trouble-free 'sets' While spring onions are always grown from seed, it's quickest and easiest to grow the main bulb-forming members of this family – onions and shallots – not from seed but from sets. These are miniature bulbs that have already been commercially grown from seed and are guaranteed to be disease-free. Garlic is grown from whole cloves, best taken from specially prepared bulbs from growers, rather than those bought for the kitchen.

● **DISCOURAGE BIRDS FROM UPROOTING SETS** Birds tend to pull out newly planted sets and garlic cloves – just for fun, it seems, since they don't eat them. Stretching lengths of garden twine or strong black cotton thread in a crosswise pattern over the bed, just a few inches above the surface of the soil, should deter them. If you find any uprooted sets, simply dig new holes, replant them and cover them with soil, taking care not to damage the roots.

● **GROW FROM SEED FOR SMALL SPACES** Onions need much less room than you think and can be grown tightly packed together, in clusters, rather than in formal rows. Sow four or five seeds together in small pots or in each cell of a module tray. Once the seedlings are established, transplant them in groups without attempting to divide them. The onions will grow on in neat clumps.

Extend your spring onion crop Sow a short row of seed every couple of weeks from early spring and you'll have enough spring onions to last the summer. For spring salads, sow seeds of a hardy variety in early autumn. These will overwinter and crop the following spring.

● **GET TWO CROPS FROM A SINGLE ROW** If your spring onions are growing too closely together, thin them to leave about 2.5cm (1in) between each plant and use this first crop in salads and stir-fries. The remaining plants can be left in place for cropping in another two weeks' time.

Grow plump, firm bulbs If your soil is heavy and damp, grow onions and shallots on a slight ridge or in raised beds. Mixing in sharp sand or organic matter will ensure the soil drains freely enough to grow garlic.

● **WATER SPARINGLY FOR FIRM BULBS** Onions, shallots and garlic are likely to soften and rot if the soil is waterlogged. Take care to water them early in the growing period but after that don't overdo it. Once established, they shouldn't need additional watering and will form fat, tasty bulbs.

● **REMOVE FLOWER HEADS** from all members of the onion family as soon as they appear. They are a sign that the plant is bolting and trying to produce seed, possibly because the soil is either too cold and wet, or not wet enough. Allowing the flowers to develop will result in smaller crops with poorer keeping qualities.

● **HARVEST SUPER-EARLY ONIONS** by growing Japanese-bred onion varieties that have been developed to survive all but the coldest winters without rotting. Plant sets in the autumn and they will be ready to harvest the following year from early summer onwards. Look for varieties such as 'Keepwell', 'Radar' and 'Senshyu'.

● **GROW BUMPER GARLIC** For the biggest, fattest bulbs, choose 'virus-free' stock and plant cloves in the autumn for a crop the following year. Garlic is not harmed by overwintering and in fact benefits from a cold spell and from the extra time in the ground. Cloves not sown until early spring will grow well but may not be as large.

● **ENJOY EARLY GARLIC** by harvesting some in spring or early summer before the bulbs fatten and the leaves turn yellow. This 'green' garlic has a milder flavour than mature cloves but needs to be used straight away, as it won't keep.

Harvest at the right time
When the leaves of onions, shallots and garlic turn yellow and die down, it means that the plants have stopped growing and the bulbs have matured. This is the signal that the crop is ready for harvesting.

● **MAKE YOUR CROPS LAST** After lifting, allow bulbs that you intend to store to dry naturally in the sun for a few days, or spread them out on wire racks indoors. Bulbs for storage must be completely dry or they will rot. Keep them in a cool, dry place: nylon tights make great hanging storage bags for use in a garage or utility room.

HOW TO GROW PERFECT LEEKS

Leeks don't fatten up into bulbs and are grown rather differently. The edible part is the long stem, from which light is excluded during growth – a process known as blanching. To produce leeks that are as long, straight and white as possible, plant deeply. Young leeks that are ready for planting are offered for sale in late spring.

1 Make deep, narrow holes with a heavy iron bar or special 'dibber'. Space the holes at least 15cm (6in) apart – farther if you want larger leeks. Drop a young leek into each hole. There's no need to trim the roots or leaves before planting.

2 Carefully fill the hole with water and top it up over the next few days if the weather is very dry. As the water soaks in, the soil will collapse loosely around the leek excluding the light but allowing the shaft to expand into the space as it grows.

3 To further assist blanching of the stems, slide cardboard tubes over the leeks to exclude the light. Cut down the tubes if necessary so that a tuft of leaves protrudes above the top.

Beans and peas

ONCE YOU'VE GROWN YOUR OWN young, tender broad beans, sweet juicy peas and crisp green beans you'll realise how quickly these crops lose their freshness and flavour on the supermarket shelves. They are all hungry plants, so for plentiful harvests add plenty of well-rotted compost or manure to the soil before planting.

French and runner beans

▶ **Climbing runner beans** are one of the most decorative of crops, especially when grown on attractive wigwams. Standard varieties have scarlet flowers, but there are white, peach and even pretty red-and-white bicolored variants.

Develop strong roots for bigger crops
French and runner beans have deep roots so if sowing under cover, use deep pots, special root trainers or long, biodegradable paper 'tube pots'. These allow the plants to develop strong, straight, well-structured root systems before being hardened off and planted out.

● **GIVE ROOTS A FOOD RESERVOIR** by making a bean trench. In late winter, dig a trench about 60cm (24in) wide and deep, add a layer of compost or well-rotted manure and gradually fill it with kitchen waste that would normally go on the compost heap [see p.236]. When it's nearly full, fill in with soil and the waste will start to rot down and generate warmth and nutrients, ready for your bean roots to delve into when planted in late spring.

Time your sowings
For early french and runner beans, sow seeds under cover then plant out the seedlings only once all danger of frost is past. Seeds sown outdoors won't germinate if it is too cold. Wait until late spring to sow outside in cold regions, even if you've covered the ground to warm it.

Use the right supports
Runner beans and many french beans are vigorous climbers and when fully laden can be very heavy. A sturdy structure is essential to prevent them from blowing over or collapsing. Use strong bamboo canes or hazel poles set about 30cm (12in) apart in double rows or wigwams.

● **HELP BEANS TO CLIMB** by sowing or planting on the inside of the supporting structure.

● **PINCH OUT THE GROWING TIPS** once beans reach the tops of the supports, or they will become tangled and top-heavy.

EXPERT KNOW HOW

RUNNER BEANS FROM SEED

Get ahead by sowing runner beans in pots in mid-spring. Keep the pots in a frost-free greenhouse or indoors on a sunny windowsill where they will get plenty of light.

1 In a deep pot, sow two seeds to a 13cm (5in) pot and grow on until late spring (or early summer if the weather is still cold).

2 Plant both young plants at the base of a cane or pole. Loosely tie the young shoots to the support to encourage them to climb.

STAR PERFORMERS...

COLOURFUL BEANS

Beans don't have to be green – try unusual colours that look great and are so much easier to see when you are picking.

- 'Blauhilde' and 'Cosse Violette' (purple climbing french beans)
- Borlotti 'Firetongue' (mottled red, purple and white; good for drying)
- 'Golddukat' and 'Rocquencourt' (yellow dwarf french beans)
- ◀ 'Purple Queen' (left) and 'Purple Teepee' (purple dwarf french beans; they turn green on cooking)

Get perfect pods every time Runner beans are notorious for failing to 'set', or produce pods. The answer is to water generously when the flower buds first appear and then every 3–4 days while in full flower. The traditional misting or spraying of the flowers just isn't enough. Attracting pollinating insects such as bees into your garden (see pp.272–3) will also help pods form.

● **PICK TO KEEP THE CROP COMING** Harvest your beans regularly, and new pods will continue to form. You'll get fewer new pods if you let old pods grow large.

Fresh garden peas

Grow the best-tasting peas
Pick your peas when they are not too large. Once picked, they quickly lose their sweetness so it's best to harvest just before you want to eat them. Once plants are growing well you can also harvest some of the shoot tips – delicious in salads or lightly stir-fried. Ready-grown pea shoots are expensive to buy in shops and won't be as fresh and tasty as those you've grown yourself.

● **ENJOY THE EARLIEST CROP** If you live in a mild area, look out for hardy, overwintering varieties such as 'Meteor' and 'Douce Provence', and sow them outdoors in a sheltered spot in late autumn. Protect them with cloches in the coldest spells, and you should be picking your first peas in late spring.

● **HELP SEEDLINGS CLIMB OUT OF DANGER** by providing plenty of small twigs or sticks pushed into the soil to encourage them get off the ground fast. The quicker they grow, the less likely they are to be eaten by slugs and snails.

EXPERT KNOW HOW

SOWING PEAS IN GUTTERING

A standard length of rain guttering makes an ideal seedbed for starting off peas. Within just a few weeks you'll have a row of seedlings ready to slide out and plant in a pre-prepared trench in the garden.

1 Cut a manageable length of guttering and half-fill it with potting compost. Sow pea seeds closely, about 2.5cm (1in) apart, and cover with another 2.5–4cm (1–1½in) of soil. Keep in a coldframe or under cover.

2 Once the weather is warm enough and the seedlings have developed, plant them out. Dig a shallow trench in the soil and slide the entire contents of the guttering – seedlings, compost and all – into place.

- **GROW DOUBLE ROWS ON A PEA FENCE** As soon as peas start to grow, construct a 'fence' made from plastic or wire netting strung between canes or stakes. Most peas are natural climbers, and they have tendrils that will cling to anything that comes within reach. You can have a double row of peas; one on either side of the fence. If you prefer natural materials, a row of twiggy peasticks offers excellent support and can also look very attractive.
- **GROW VARIETIES THAT DON'T NEED SUPPORTS** New semi-leafless peas, such as 'Markana' and 'Canoe', have been bred to have more tendrils than leaves – so many that they intertwine and if grown in blocks will support themselves.
- **WATCH OUT FOR HUNGRY BIRDS** Netting is the only guaranteed way of preventing birds, especially pigeons, from eating your crop, though wire frames or a tangled thicket of twigs may deter them.

Broad beans

Be the first with your crop For super-early broad beans, sow a hardy variety such as 'Aquadulce Claudia' in the autumn. In all but the coldest areas, the young plants should be tough enough to overwinter, and because they will be more advanced they will crop up to a month earlier than spring-sown plants.
- **KEEP THE HARVEST GOING** Sow a second batch of broad bean seeds outdoors in late winter or early spring, as soon the soil becomes workable, and a third batch a month later in mid-spring. That way you can enjoy fresh, tender beans from late spring through to late summer.
- **GIVE BROAD BEANS SUPPORT** by stretching lengths of string between stakes or canes at knee and waist-height and you'll get strong, healthy plants. Do this while the plants are still young so you don't damage the stems.

Harvest at the right time It's important to pick broad beans while they are still young and tender, before their skins toughen and become bitter. Check that the membrane by which the beans are attached to the inside of the pod is still white or green; if it has turned brown you've left it too late.
- **SAMPLE THE PODS** If you pick the pods very young, when they are still only the size of your little finger, you can cook and eat them whole, getting all the flavour without the bother of shelling.
- **PRESERVE EXCESS CROPS** Broad beans freeze very well so any excess crop won't go to waste. Once you've shelled the beans, blanch quickly in boiling water, drain and allow to cool. When they are completely dry, put them in labelled bags or containers.

▲ **Pinch out the growing tip** at the top of each broad bean stem as soon as the first tiny pods start to form lower down. This will not only encourage the plants to produce more pods but also deter blackfly (broad bean aphids), which prefer to feed on soft shoot tips.

HOW DOES IT WORK?
NUTRITIOUS ROOTS

Roots

Nodules

Nitrogen is an essential nutrient that all plants need, and peas and beans have a unique ability to 'fix' and store it in the soil. Bacteria convert nitrogen from the air and concentrate it in nutrient-rich nodules that grow on the plants' root systems. So after harvesting, cut your peas and beans down but don't pull up the roots. Next year plant brassicas there; they will thrive on the nitrogen in the soil.

Brassicas and leafy vegetables

THE VEGETABLES IN THE CABBAGE FAMILY, known as brassicas, are ornamental as well as highly nutritious. They're also slow-growing and will occupy their places on your plot for several months. You can use the space between them to plant other, faster-growing leafy crops, such as chard, spinach and oriental leaves.

A BED OF VARIED, FRESH GREENS CAN LOOK AS ATTRACTIVE AS A FLOWER BORDER

Beautiful brassicas

Keep your crops on the move
Don't put brassicas where you grew them last year. Instead, plant them where peas or beans were growing and they will utilise and thrive on the nitrogen left behind in the soil [see p.193].

● **SOW LITTLE AND OFTEN TO KEEP CROPS COMING** using varieties that mature at different times. About ten cabbages and ten cauliflowers for winter and spring, and the same number for summer and autumn should feed the average family.

● **BE FIRM WHEN PLANTING** Brassicas need to have their roots securely anchored in firm soil – so you can break the rule of not treading on your vegetable beds. Do the tug test: pull gently on a leaf at the bottom of the stem to check that the plant is planted deeply and firmly. Earth up the stems as the plants develop.

Grow brassicas for all seasons
Plan ahead and and you could be eating fresh green (or white, red or purple) leaves and heads for most of the year. It's just a matter of choosing the right varieties and sowing at the right time.

● **TRY SWEET-TASTING SWEETHEARTS** 'Duncan', 'Hispi' and 'Advantage' are 'sweetheart' cabbages with firm, pointed heads and a much longer season than traditional varieties. Sow in spring for a summer crop, in early summer for harvesting in autumn, and in late summer for harvesting the following year in spring, as soon as they have produced a solid head.

● **SOW WINTER GREENS IN SUMMER** Kale can withstand the coldest spells and is almost indestructible. Sow seeds in summer for a winter crop. 'Savoy' is a tried-and-tested winter cabbage that is ideal for cold, exposed sites and 'Spring Hero', a spring cabbage with dark green leaves, will also survive most winters.

● **ENJOY TWO KINDS OF BROCCOLI** Calabrese, often sold as broccoli, has a single dense, green head and can take just four or five months from seed to harvest. Sow seeds in mid-spring and summer for summer and autumn crops. Sprouting broccoli, which has many small white or purple florets, is slower-growing and hardy. 'Early Purple' and 'Claret' crop early, from late winter onwards.

◀ **This well-designed potager** packed with leafy green vegetables, from cabbages and calabrese to lettuces, is sited close to the house, where birds may be deterred from raiding it. Harvesting is more convenient, too.

STAR PERFORMERS...

EASY-TO-GROW BRASSICAS

If you're new to growing vegetables, try these and you'll enjoy a wide range of brassicas – all of them healthy choices.

● Brussels sprouts 'Crispus', 'Cronus' and 'Maximus' (resistant to clubroot)
◀ Kale 'Redbor' (purple-red, curly); also try 'Black Tuscan' (tall, dark-green)
● Perennial broccoli 'Nine Star' (creamy white; crops for up to three years)
● Savoy cabbages (the hardiest)
● Summer-sprouting 'Wok Broccoli' (harvest from June to December)
● Sweetheart cabbages (pointed heads, all year round)

▲ **Place collars** around cabbage seedlings as soon as you transplant them into the ground. For maximum protection, try not to let the collars get covered with soil.

BEAT THAT!

● **The tallest recorded brussels sprout** plant at 2.8m (9ft 3in) high, was grown in California by Patrice and Steve Allison. If you want to try something similar, look out for seeds of Jersey kale – this amazing 'tree cabbage' can grow up to 5.5m (18ft), with a head of leaves resembling a small palm tree. The sturdy stems make great plant supports.

● **GET A BONUS CROP OF CABBAGES** and calabrese by using a sharp knife to score a couple of cross-slits in the stump after you've cut off the main head. New shoots should soon grow to give you a small second harvest. Cut calabrese heads promptly, while they are still tight and before the tiny florets start to open, but leave the rest of the plant in place; new heads should grow from the cut stalk. And harvest tender young brussels sprout tops just as you would spring greens.

● **GROW MORE COLOURFUL CAULIFLOWERS** Children are often more tempted to try rainbow-hued modern cultivars such as the amazing purple 'Graffiti' (harvest in summer), orange-yellow 'Cheddar' (harvest in autumn), and vivid lime green 'Romanesco' (harvest from summer to early autumn).

Keep brassicas healthy All the vegetables in this family can be targeted by a range of troublesome pests and diseases. Practise good garden hygiene and ensure you take preventative action – at the right time – and you should be able to minimise damage to your crops.

● **MAKE PROTECTIVE COLLARS TO THWART CABBAGE ROOT FLY** from thick cardboard, vinyl flooring or roofing felt. These are much cheaper than commercial, ready-made versions. Slip a collar round the stem of each cabbage seedling so the flies lay their eggs on the collar – where they will dry out or be eaten by birds – rather than in the soil, where they hatch into grubs that eat the roots.

● **PIGEON-PROOF YOUR CROPS** by growing cabbages, cauliflowers and broccoli under nets. Bird scarers may work for a while, especially those crafted to look like hawks and other birds of prey, but in the end the pigeons get wise to the trick. Nets are the only reliable defence.

● **BANISH CATERPILLARS FROM YOUR BRASSICAS** by looking out, from early summer, for the tiny yellow eggs and green caterpillars of cabbage white butterflies on the undersides of brassica leaves. Pick them off by hand or spray with a garden insecticide if the infestation is serious. Fleece or fine-mesh netting is the only guaranteed way to keep butterflies out.

● **GUARD AGAINST CLUBROOT** This fungal disease, which destroys crops and is impossible to cure, is the most serious problem for brassicas. Rotating your crops and growing resistant varieties is a good start; you can also add lime to your soil, especially if it is fairly acid, before planting. Growing seedlings on until they develop healthy rootballs will also give young plants some resistance to infection.

Oriental leaves

Treat your taste buds Chinese cabbage and pak choi are now well known but there are plenty of less familiar leaf mustards, spinaches and other oriental brassicas available to grow from seed. Why not try mizuna, mibuna, choy sum or even chop suey greens? They are all easy to grow, taste wonderful and will add lots of variety to your dishes.

- **DOUBLE YOUR HARVEST** by growing oriental leaves as cut-and-come-again crops. Pick young baby leaves for salads, then let the plants re-grow and mature fully before harvesting them a second time for steaming or stir-frying.
- **ENJOY TASTY MIDWINTER SALAD LEAVES** Mizuna and mibuna are both hardy. Sow them in autumn under cloches, in coldframes, or in an unheated greenhouse and harvest for fresh, peppery salad leaves right through the winter.
- **RAISE CROPS IN POTS** Unlike larger brassicas, oriental leaves generally develop relatively shallow root systems, and are perfect for growing in containers.
- **KEEP PESTS OUT** Oriental leaves are fast-growing so they are less susceptible to the pests and diseases that affect other brassicas. Flea beetles, on the other hand, are attracted to them and will nibble a lacework pattern of tiny holes in the leaves. To keep the beetles out, cover seedlings with fleece, particularly in spring and again in early autumn when attacks are most likely.

Other leafy vegetables

Grow green superfoods Spinach, swiss chard and spinach beet are nutritious as well as easy to grow. Harvest baby leaves for salads bursting with goodness. Or steam or stir-fry larger leaves – don't boil – to preserve the nutrients.

- **SOW THINLY FOR SUCCESS** Leaf vegetables are fast-growing and hungry plants. If you overcrowd them, they will compete with one another for nutrients and water in the soil.
- **PLANT SPINACH IN A SHADY SPOT** While most crops need warmth and sunshine, spinach thrives in a cool, damp, slightly shady position. Sow early in spring, as soon as the soil is warm enough but before daytime temperatures rise.
- **ENSURE SPINACH IS SUCCULENT** For tender, sweet-tasting leaves, keep spinach well watered. Don't let it dry out in hot sunshine or the leaves will quickly turn tough and bitter.
- **HARVEST CHARD IN WINTER** Swiss chard is fairly hardy and if you sow it in midsummer you could be harvesting fresh leaves in winter. Chard will withstand moderate frosts but will need covering with fleece or cloches in harsh winters.
- **ADD COLOUR TO YOUR PLOT** The vividly coloured stems of chard varieties such as 'Bright Lights', with its vibrant red, yellow, orange or even pink stems, will not only brighten up your vegetable beds but also attract admiring glances.

EXPERT KNOW HOW

STOP YOUR GREENS FROM BOLTING

Most leafy vegetables have a natural inclination to bolt in hot, dry weather. When summer day-length increases and temperatures rise, or when plants are under stress, they rush to flower (or 'bolt') in an attempt to produce seeds. These preventative measures should stop this happening.

- Check packets for 'bolt-resistant' varieties.
- Keep plants cool and water them once – or even twice – a day in warm spells.
- ◀ Sow in spring and harvest young leaves (here spinach) before the heat of late summer.
- Sow from July onwards when days are getting shorter so that crops mature in the cool of late summer and autumn.

▲ **Bush cherry tomatoes** are a good choice for hanging baskets. Crops can be plentiful so make sure the supporting bracket and hook are sturdy enough to take the weight.

Summer-fruiting vegetables

LEARN HOW TO GROW sun-loving crops for the tastes of summer – juicy tomatoes and crisp cucumbers for salads; courgettes, aubergines and peppers for Mediterranean flavours, and the plumpest, fresh corn on the cob. All need a long, warm growing season, so start them off under cover to ensure a good crop.

Tomatoes

Choose the right tomato for best results Bush and cordon (vine) are the two main types of tomato. The bush varieties are compact, quicker to ripen and more suited to outdoor cultivation than cordon types. Grow them in sunny sheltered beds, in growing bags against a south-facing wall or in containers on a warm patio – all places where the ripening fruits can soak up maximum heat and light. Cordon tomatoes bear their fruits on a single, vertical stem, and must be staked and trained (see facing page) to get the best results.

● **SELECT COOL-CLIMATE VARIETIES** for growing outdoors in temperate regions. These specially bred varieties, which include cherry tomatoes such as 'Gardeners' Delight' and 'Sungold' and early bush varieties such as 'Red Alert', have a shorter growing season than larger-fruited cordon tomatoes and will be ready for harvesting earlier.

● **SOW EARLY TO GET AHEAD** by starting seeds in pots indoors or in a heated greenhouse (or a propagator if necessary). By the time early summer arrives, when days are lengthening and night-time temperatures are rising, you'll have healthy, good-sized seedlings that are ready to plant out.

● **TURN TOMATO-GROWING ON ITS HEAD** with a special 'Topsy Turvy' planter, a container designed to be hung upside-down wherever you would put a hanging basket. Plant seedlings in the bottom and water them from the top. The theory is the crops are improved because the plant's roots are in the sun and nutrients from the soil are drawn down into the fruits by gravity. Bush cherry tomatoes such as 'Tumbling Tom' and 'Tumbler' are good choices for growing upside-down.

● **PLANT SEEDLINGS DEEPLY FOR STRONG GROWTH** – as much as 5cm (2in) deeper than the level at which they were in their pots. This will encourage feeding roots to develop from the stems, which help the plants grow strongly and anchor them firmly in the soil or compost.

TRAINING CORDON TOMATOES

Cordon (vine) tomatoes need careful training and pruning to restrict the amount of leafy growth they make, and encourage fruiting instead. A bushy tomato may look healthy, but a plant that is putting too much energy into growing lush green foliage will never achieve its maximum cropping potential.

1 Tie in the main stem to a stake or strong cane so that it grows vertically and is strongly supported by the time the fruits begin to develop.

2 Pinch out any sideshoots you find growing between the main stem and the leaf stems on a regular basis. They are a waste of the plant's energy.

3 Remove the growing tip of the plant once around 4–5 flower trusses have developed (if grown outdoors) or 7–8 (if grown under cover).

4 To speed up ripening once the fruits have developed, cut away any large leaves that are shading them and reducing airflow, which can lead to fungal disease.

● **BUY MODERN GRAFTED PLANTS** Grafted tomatoes are relatively new to amateur vegetable growers and offer the best of both worlds: vigorous, disease-resistant rootstocks combined with the tastiest, heaviest-cropping varieties.

Feed plants for bumper crops Tomatoes can be fairly demanding plants and both bush and cordon types need rich, fertile soil and supplementary feeding. Make sure you water regularly, rather than when you see plants wilting: the fruits of plants watered irregularly develop tough, fibrous patches. Don't overfeed or overwater, or you risk getting tough-skinned, tasteless fruits.

● **START FEEDING WHEN FLOWERS APPEAR** Feed once a week with a high-potash liquid fertiliser, especially when growing tomatoes under cover or in containers.

● **GET THE BEST FROM GROWING BAGS** by pushing large pots, from which you have removed the bases, into the bags and topping up with additional compost to increase the soil depth before planting your young tomatoes. Alternatively, pile two growing bags on top of one another, cutting a hole in the bottom of one and in the top of the other so that the roots grow right through the double layer.

EXCITING TOMATOES

Not all tomatoes are red and round: they may be pear-shaped or even look more like peppers. Here are some that come in unusual colours and shapes, combining good looks with a great flavour.

- 'Andine Cornue' (long, pepper-like fruits)
- ◀ 'Chocolate Cherry' (left), 'Purple Russian' and 'Black Krim' (dark purple or black skins)
- 'Federle' (red, chilli-shaped)
- 'Tigerella' and 'Red Zebra' (red with green and yellow streaks)
- 'Tomatoberry' (small strawberry-shaped red fruits)
- 'White Beauty' (pale, white skin and flesh)
- 'Yellow Pear' (yellow, pear-shaped baby tomatoes)

▼ **Peppers are perfect** for patio pots. Pick them unripe for that distinctive green-pepper taste and crunch, or leave them on the plant to develop sweet, ripe flavours.

- **PARTNER WITH BASIL TO DETER PESTS** Tomatoes and basil enjoy the same growing conditions – if you grow one successfully you'll be able to grow the other. Basil also attracts whitefly and will draw these insect pests away from your tomato crop.
- **FIGHT BLIGHT BY MINIMISING HOT, HUMID CONDITIONS** in which this fungal disease thrives. Water carefully, at the base of your plants, taking care not to wet the foliage, ensuring there is good air circulation around them. Try blight-resistant varieties, such as 'Ferline', 'Legend', 'Fantasio' and 'Koralik'.

Promote ripening to prolong your harvest

Tomatoes taste best if they are left on the plant to ripen, even if the season is drawing to a close. In late summer cut off the lowest leaves; they are of no further use to the plant, and removing them speeds up the ripening of the last fruits by exposing them to light. It also reduces the risk of disease by improving the circulation of air. If your tomatoes are growing outside, cover them with fleece or cloches at night.

- **RIPEN GREEN FRUITS** left at the very end of the season by picking and bringing them indoors to ripen in a warm place. Avoid sunny window sills: the fruits will simply dry out. Alternatively, pull up whole plants and hang them upside down under cover.

Chillies, peppers and aubergines

Get the best results by growing under cover

A greenhouse or a polytunnel gives chillies, peppers and aubergines the hot, humid conditions they need so they will grow faster and produce bigger harvests than outdoor crops. If you're growing them outside, choose cool-climate varieties such as 'Hungarian Hot Wax' chillies, 'Marconi Rosso' sweet peppers and 'Moneymaker' aubergines.

- **BOOST THE CHANCES OF POLLINATION** by giving flowering peppers and chillies a very gentle shake so that pollen is scattered from one flower to another. The best time to do this is in the middle of the day. Take care: the branches can be brittle.

- **MAXIMISE AUBERGINE YIELDS** by pinching out the growing tip of each plant once five leaves have formed. This encourages the plant to produce sideshoots on which more flowers will appear. Each of these flowers should, once fertilised, produce a fruit.
- **CONTROL WHITEFLY BY GROWING COMPANION PLANTS** such as basil, French and Mexican marigolds, or the so-called shoo-fly plant (*Nicandra physalodes*), which will attract beneficial pest predators. In the greenhouse, yellow sticky strips capture adult flies and give an early indication of when you might need to spray; or you could try a biological control, such as the parasitic wasp *Encarsia formosa*.
- **RESERVE THE SUNNIEST CORNER** of your patio or garden for growing chillies, peppers and aubergines outdoors in containers. In a warm, sheltered site with generous supplies of food and water, pot-grown plants will produce good crops. The plants are attractive in flower as well as when bearing fruit.

Crisp, cool cucumbers

Grow delicious outdoor varieties Traditional outdoor ('ridge') cucumbers tend to be shorter than greenhouse varieties and have thicker, rougher skins. They are hardy enough to grow outside and taste just as good as those grown under glass. However, many modern smooth-skinned varieties have been bred for both indoor and outdoor growing, combining the best of both types.
- **GO FOR ALL-FEMALE VARIETIES FOR THE TASTIEST CROPS** 'Zeina' or 'Passandra' are good choices but don't grow them near varieties that produce male flowers. Female flowers pollinated from male flowers produce bitter-tasting fruits.

EXPERT KNOW HOW

EXTRA-SWEET SWEETCORN

The secret of perfectly sweet sweetcorn is to eat the cobs as soon as possible after harvesting. Once picked, their sugar starts to turn to starch and they begin to lose their sweetness – so remember, the clock will be ticking!

- Plant in blocks instead of in rows for good crops. Sweetcorn is pollinated by wind rather than by insects, and pollen is more likely to be transferred from the male flowers at the top to the female flowers lower down if the plants are closely grouped together in squares or rectangles.

- Water plants regularly in dry spells and especially when cobs are beginning to fatten up.

- Protect ripening cobs from attack by birds or mice by enclosing them in pest-proof sleeves made by cutting the bottoms off empty, clear-plastic drinks bottles and slipping the open end down over each cob.

◀ When the cobs have formed their silky tassels they are approaching ripeness. Use the fingernail test to check when sweetcorn is ripe enough to eat. Pull back the outer covering and pierce one of the kernels. The cob is ripe and ready for picking when the juice is milky.

► **Grow different courgette varieties** to make salads and cooked dishes more interesting. Yellow courgettes have thinner skins, which often makes them popular with children. Round ones can be stuffed and baked.

● **GROW 'NO-PEEL' MINI-CUCUMBERS** such as 'Cucino' and 'Mini Munch' in containers or growing bags on a patio or sunny balcony. They are thin-skinned so don't need to be peeled before eating. They are ideal for picnics, and also make a healthy addition to children's lunch boxes.

● **PROVIDE STRONG SUPPORTS** The majority of cucumbers are climbing plants and can crop heavily. In a greenhouse, train the main stem up vertical wires or canes and pinch out the growing tip when it reaches the top. When growing outdoor varieties, construct sturdy trellises or wigwams and tie in plants securely so that they don't collapse when laden with fruits.

● **BEAT GREENHOUSE PESTS** such as red spider mite by watering regularly and spraying to keep the air humidity high.

Courgettes and summer squash

Be generous with food and water These extremely quick-growing plants need rich soil and copious amounts of water to produce bumper crops. Always add plenty of compost or manure to enrich the soil before you plant out courgettes and summer squash, and mulch after planting to keep moisture in.

EXPERT KNOW HOW

POLLINATING COURGETTES

In cool summers or when plants are grown under cover, insects cannot be relied on to pollinate flowers so that fruits form, but you can increase your crop potential by doing it yourself. For this you need both a male and a female flower, not necessarily from the same plant. Male flowers have a thin, often prickly stalk, while the stalk of female flowers – which is an embryonic fruit – is smooth and often swollen or tapered.

Remove an open male flower and carefully pull off the petals to expose the pollen-carrying stamens. Gently brush them into the centre of a female flower so the pollen is transferred.

● **GET TWO COURGETTE HARVESTS** by sowing in two batches: the first in pots in April for planting out in late May, and the second direct in the ground in June. Courgettes produce heavy crops but over only a short period.

● **USE COMPACT VARIETIES IN SMALL SPACES**, such as 'Peter Pan' squash. Sold as bush or climbing squashes, these take up a lot less room than vigorous varieties that trail and sprawl over the ground. Harvest when the fruits are golfball-sized.

● **KEEP PLANTS CROPPING WELL** by removing and composting any over-large fruits. If you leave them to keep growing, the plant's energy will not go into producing new fruits. If you can't keep up with your courgette crop, remember to plant fewer plants the next year: just four, plus one or two squash plants, should be enough to feed an average family.

● **EAT THE FLOWERS** When you harvest baby courgettes, save the flowers and try them either deep-fried in crispy batter or stuffed with a soft cheese.

STAR PERFORMERS...

UNUSUAL COURGETTES

Regular green courgettes are widely available in summer. Why not grow varieties in different colours and shapes that are hard to find in shops?

- 'Bambino' (small, dark green, good for harvesting flowers)
- 'Eight Ball' (round, glossy, dark green)
- 'Goldrush', 'Soleil' and 'Jemmer' (bright yellow)
- 'Romanesco Latino' (ribbed) and 'Striato' (striped)
- 'Tondo di Nizza' or 'De Nice à Fruit Rond' (round, pale green)
- 'Trieste White Cousa' (short, bulbous, greeny-white)
- ◀ 'Tromboncino' (long, curved fruits with a gourd-like ball at one end)

Pumpkins and winter squash

THESE STURDY, VIGOROUS VEGETABLES will inject a welcome boost of late-summer colour into your plot. Harvest their fruits for Halloween and to store over winter – properly ripened, they should keep for up to six months.

Decorative and delicious crops

Allow plenty of growing space Always sow pumpkins and squash at least 1–1.5m (3–4ft) apart to give them plenty of room to spread. In case a seed fails to germinate, sow two together, then thin out to leave the strongest seedling.

● **TRY VERTICAL GROWING IN SMALL SPACES** A typical pumpkin or squash vine can grow as much as 10m (30ft), with fruits along its full length. If you don't have the ground space to allow them to trail, you can encourage smaller varieties to scramble up a frame, over a fence, or even up on to your shed roof. The plants produce strong, twining tendrils all along their stems so they shouldn't need tying in, but the fruits may need support. To make 'hammocks' for them, cut off the legs from nylon tights and slip them round the fruits, tying the ends to a frame or fence. The nylon will expand to accommodate the fruits' increasing size.

EXPERT KNOW HOW

RIPENING FOR STORAGE

To make sure that pumpkins develop a rich colour and the tough skin required for them to store well, always leave the fruits to ripen for as long as possible in the sun.

● Remove a few leaves around the ripening fruits to allow the sun to get to the skins.

◀ In a wet summer, fruits are prone to rotting on the ground so gently slide a flat stone or tile below each one to raise it off the damp earth. The stone also acts as a radiator, storing warmth from the sun during the day and releasing it at night.

● Harvest pumpkins before the first frosts and continue to ripen them in a sunny sheltered spot on a bed of straw or in a greenhouse, turning them to expose all parts of the skin.

● When harvesting, cut the vine on either side of the fruit stalk, leaving the stalk intact. This will prevent rot getting into the fruit.

- **PRODUCE THE BIGGEST HALLOWEEN PUMPKIN** For a truly monstrous fruit, first choose a mammouth variety: 'Atlantic Giant' and 'Big Max' will fit the bill. Feed weekly and, unless it's very wet, water twice-weekly – some champion growers even swear by a daily dose of beer.
- **CURB OVER-RAMPANT PLANTS** Both pumpkins and winter squashes produce two stems, which generally grow in opposite directions. Sideshoots grow off these at intervals along their full length and can be trimmed off to stop the plant spreading and engulfing its neighbours. Wear gloves and long sleeves – the stems are prickly.
- **GUARANTEE SUPERSIZE SQUASH** by limiting the number of fruits on a plant to just four. Not all fruits will develop to maturity anyway, so wait until they are about the size of a grapefruit before thinning out.
- **FOLLOW AMERICAN INDIAN TRADITION AND 'MULTI-CROP'** by interplanting squash, sweetcorn and climbing beans. The shallow-rooted squashes occupy space at the foot of the corn, their leaves acting as a mulch and keeping down the weeds, while the beans climb up the corn stalks and boost the levels of nitrogen in the soil. These three companion crops are known as 'the three sisters'.
- **CARRY CORRECTLY TO KEEP STALKS INTACT** Never carry a pumpkin by its stalk – it is not strong enough and the stalk may detach, which means that the fruit will not store well. Support the fruit by lifting it carefully from below or carry small fruits in a basket.

▼ **Squashes and small-fruited pumpkins** may be supported on a garden or allotment fence. This protects them from snails and makes for easy picking.

STAR PERFORMERS…

PINT-SIZE PUMPKINS AND SQUASH

Growing small varieties, rather than pumpkins the size of Cinderella's coach, makes much more sense for couples and small families. Even if you don't sow modest-sized pumpkins and squashes until late in the summer, they will still be ready for mid-autumn. These are varieties to look out for:

- ▼ **'Baby Bear' (below), 'Jack Be Little' and 'Munchkin'** (mini-pumpkins)
- **'Buttercup'** (green, orange or grey-blue squash, tasting of chestnut)
- **'Little Gem'** (tennis-ball-sized squash, good as a climber)
- **'Red Kuri' or 'Uchiki Kuri'** (orange-red, onion-shaped squash)
- **'Sweet Dumpling'** (squash with green and cream stripes, no need to peel)
- **'Sweet Lightning'** (ridged, yellow and orange squash, very sweet)

Perennial vegetables

ARTICHOKES, ASPARAGUS AND RHUBARB are not like other, single-season crops: **they are perennial plants,** and although they die down in winter they will reappear in spring and crop year after year. Think carefully about where you site them – once established, they'll be there for some time.

Globe artichokes

Plan for growth These are big plants, reaching a height and spread of 1m (3ft) or more, so grow artichokes only if you have plenty of space. They are worth it: the beautiful green or purple heads, picked when they are plump but before they grow too large, have a far superior taste to those sold at high prices in the supermarket.

● **GROW FROM 'OFFSETS'** These are sideshoots cut from the base of the plant with two or three leaves and a short root. A friend or neighbour will often be willing to let you take offsets from an existing plant. New plants will grow much more quickly from offsets than from seed.

● **WRAP UP PLANTS IN WINTER** Globe artichokes are not entirely hardy and severe frosts can kill them. Earth up and mulch around their stems and either wrap the foliage in hessian or cover the plant with straw or dried bracken.

▼ **Globe artichokes** are the perfect grow-your-own crop. To harvest them, use a sharp knife and start with the topmost globe (the 'king' bud), leaving a short section of stalk. Move down to the sidebuds as they develop.

Jerusalem artichokes

Save tubers and save money Once you've harvested home-grown Jerusalem artichokes, put some tubers aside and plant them in spring. If you're a first-time grower, buy tubers from specialist suppliers; don't try to grow them from seed.

● **USE AS A WINDBREAK** Jerusalem artichokes can grow to a height of 3m (10ft) so plant a row at the edge of your vegetable plot to filter the wind. Cut them down to about 1.5m (5ft) and snip off the yellow flowers in late summer so that the plant's energy is directed into the tubers, which will fatten up. In autumn, prune the yellowing foliage down to the ground.

● **MAKE KITCHEN PREPARATION EASY** by growing varieties such as 'Fuseau', which is not at all knobbly and much easier to clean and peel for cooking. Compact 'Dwarf Sunray' has such a thin skin that it doesn't require peeling at all.

● **LEAVE ARTICHOKES IN THE GROUND UNTIL NEEDED** They are a wonderful self-storing winter crop as the tubers don't need lifting until you are ready to use them.

PLANTING ASPARAGUS

Asparagus crowns bought via mail order will arrive sealed in plastic to keep them moist. To prevent them from drying out, don't unwrap them until you have prepared the site, dug a trench and are ready to plant them out.

1 Dig a trench 30cm (12in) wide and 45cm (18in) deep. Spread a thick layer of well-rotted compost or manure over the bottom and mix it into the soil. Draw up a shallow ridge about 10cm (4in) high all the way along the centre of the trench.

2 Carefully spread out the roots of each asparagus crown so that they straddle the ridge. Plant them so that they are 10–15cm (4–6in) deep and 30cm (12 in) apart. Cover with soil, water thoroughly, then add a further layer of compost or manure as a mulch.

Asparagus

Plant generously You won't get many spears from each crown so grow as many plants as you have space for. Once you've tasted your own freshly picked asparagus, shop-bought spears will lose their appeal.

● **GROW FROM CROWNS NOT SEED** Seeds may be cheaper but plants grown from them are slower to establish. One-year-old, bare-root asparagus 'crowns' (see above) are available by mail order from specialist suppliers. Buy male, not female, crowns as they crop more heavily, and choose both an early variety such as 'Gijnlim' and a later one such as 'Guelph Millennium' to extend the harvesting season.

● **BE PATIENT WITH NEW PLANTS** Don't be tempted to pick any spears at all in the first year, and be very sparing in the second. That way you'll give the plants a chance to develop strong root systems and establish themselves properly.

● **PROTECT FUTURE CROPS** Stop harvesting after 6–8 weeks and let the plants grow and build up strength for next year. In early autumn, when the feathery, fern-like stalks have dried out and turned yellow, cut them all down to the ground.

Rhubarb

Relish low maintenance Rhubarb needs little more than a sunny spot and a twice-yearly mulch of well-rotted compost or manure. Harvest stalks from late winter to early summer then stop picking to allow the plant to regenerate.

● **GET NEW PLANTS FROM OLD** Start plants off from sections, known as 'sets', taken from vigorous, mature plants. Dig up the main rootstock (crown) in winter and use a sharp spade to slice it into large pieces. Replant, making sure each section has at least one bud. This also helps to reinvigorate the parent plant.

● **DON'T LET YOUR RHUBARB FLOWER** or you'll divert the plant's energy away from the stalks, which will become spindly. Cut off and compost any flower heads before they have the opportunity to set seed.

▼ **Force rhubarb** into producing early stems by covering the crown with an upturned dustbin or large tub in winter. Always wait until the plant has been exposed to a couple of hard frosts to break its dormancy.

Salad leaves

LETTUCES AND OTHER SALAD LEAVES make perfect gap-fillers in a **vegetable plot.** Most are quick from seed to harvest and are a productive way to use the space between slower-growing crops. Ready-prepared salads are expensive to buy and don't keep well so it pays to grow your own supply of healthy, fresh leaves.

Lettuces

Sow some self-renewing salads In addition to traditional hearting lettuces such as butterheads and cos, sow some loose-leaf varieties. The big advantage of these is that you can pick just a handful of young leaves and leave the plant to grow more, instead of cutting the whole head. As long as you keep watering, the plants will produce plenty of new leaves over several weeks.

EXPERT KNOW HOW

BLANCH TO REDUCE BITTERNESS

The leaves of radicchio, chicory and endive all have a bitterness that's pleasing in moderation but unpleasant if too strong. Blanching the leaves by excluding light produces paler leaves with a mellower flavour.

1 Make sure the leaves of the plant (here a frilly endive) are dry, then gather them together and tie in a loose bundle.

2 Place a pot over the entire plant, blocking any drainage holes if necessary. Leave in place for about 10 days.

● **CHILL SEEDS IN THE FRIDGE** for a week or so before sowing. The low temperature will trick them into breaking their dormancy and encourage them to germinate.

● **FAST-TRACK SUMMER LETTUCES** by selecting quick-growing loose-leaf varieties, such as semi-cos, and by sowing indoors or under cover from late winter. Plant out in mid-spring, under cloches or fleece if necessary. Lettuces should be ready to pick 10–12 weeks after sowing.

● **AVOID A LETTUCE GLUT** by sowing little and often. When you see new seedlings appear from the previous batch, it's time to sow more. In summer, sow in the soil rather than in seed trays or modules: young lettuces will wilt and fail to establish if transplanted into hot, dry soil.

● **SOW WHEN THE SKY IS GREY** Lettuce seeds will not germinate if it's too cold or too hot. For summer sowings, choose a cool, damp overcast day, and water the soil first to cool it down. Then wait until late afternoon or early evening, when temperatures are starting to fall, before you sow.

● **SEARCH OUT A SHADY SPOT** if you're growing lettuces for summer salads. In full sun the growing lettuces dry out and are quick to bolt [see p.197] which makes the leaves bitter and

BEST BABY-LEAF SALADS

Create flavoursome mixed salads by adding a variety of unusual edible leaves, all picked young when they are still small and tender.

- Amaranth (Indian spinach)
- Beetroot and radish tops
- Corn salad and land cress
- Mizuna, mibuna, pak choi, leaf mustards and other oriental leaves
◀ Red-veined sorrel
- Spinach, swiss chard and kale
- Summer and winter purslane

inedible. A good place to site them is in the shade cast by climbing beans, sweetcorn, or vine tomatoes. Loose-leaf lettuces such as 'Salad Bowl' and 'Lollo Rossa' are the most resistant to bolting.

- **WATER THE SOIL, NOT YOUR PLANTS** Tempting as it is to give lettuces a thorough soaking, it's better not to drench them. Instead, water carefully around the base and you'll help prevent hearting varieties, such as cos, butterheads and crispheads, from rotting.

- **CHOOSE HARDY, YEAR-ROUND VARIETIES** such as 'Valdor' or 'Winter Density' to extend your lettuce-cropping season. Sow them in late summer or early autumn in a coldframe or cool greenhouse [see p.257]. The plants will be protected during cold weather and you could be eating fresh, home-grown salad in midwinter.

Other salad crops

Look beyond lettuces Pep up your salads with unusual salad leaves. Curly endive, radicchio, chicory, rocket, and many oriental leaves [see pp.196–7] are all hardier than most varieties of lettuce, and are a good source of fresh salads in autumn, winter and early spring.

- **WELCOME WINTER SALADS** Corn salad (also known as lamb's lettuce), land cress and winter purslane are all sufficiently hardy to sow in late summer for harvesting throughout the winter, although in very cold weather they'll appreciate the protection of cloches or a coldframe. Land cress makes a good substitute for watercress.

- **GROW ROBUST WILD ROCKET** instead of the larger, fleshier-leaved salad rocket. You will often see the seeds of both sold side by side. Flea beetles, which make tiny holes in the leaves, are less likely to attack the wild variety.

▼ **Mixed salad leaves** are perfect for growing in window boxes. You can buy two or three varieties and create your own mix, or buy ready-mixed seeds such as 'Saladini'.

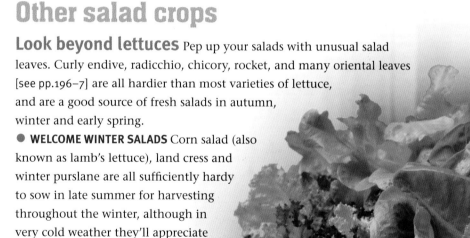

Growing herbs

FEW CROPS ARE AS EASY and rewarding to grow as herbs. Whether growing together in a dedicated herb garden, spilling out of pots and containers on your patio, or sitting close to hand on a kitchen windowsill, they look attractive, smell intoxicating and bring a world of wonderful flavours to everything you cook.

Leafy herbs for freshness

Maximise your supplies Most leafy herb plants last for only one season, and need growing afresh each year. Sow little and often, especially with herbs such as coriander and fennel that are quick to go to seed, and you'll be able to use liberal quantities in your cooking. Mint and parsley are also best sown in succession so you can pick and eat the leaves when they are young and fresh.

● **JUMP-START PARSLEY SEEDS** by soaking them in warm water overnight. It softens the hard outer coating and will help to speed up germination. If you're sowing in trays or modules, keep seedlings under cover until late spring. Don't be tempted to sow outdoors before then: the soil is still likely to be too cold.

● **GROW CORIANDER IN PARTIAL SHADE** since it is likely to bolt (run to flower) in a hot and dry position. Sow seeds in a light, sheltered spot, shaded from the midday sun, and you'll get a good supply of fresh leaves. If coriander does flower, you can always allow it to set seed and then collect the seeds for drying. Other herbs that grow well in light shade include parsley, chervil and sweet cicely.

▼ **All herbs thrive** in containers. Wiry Mediterranean herbs such as thymes and oregano can tolerate the hottest spots in the garden, while leafy herbs such as parsley prefer a part-shaded position.

Grow herbs near the kitchen

Plant up a window box or other large container with a mixture of the culinary herbs that you use most frequently (perhaps parsley, chives, basil and thyme) and site it as close to the kitchen as possible. Who wants a walk to the bottom of the garden every time you need to pick a few leaves?

● **PLANT HERBS IN STRAWBERRY POTS** to create a handy mixed-herb garden for a patio or courtyard. With a large planting area in relation to their volume, these pots enable you to grow a different type of herb in each of the large side openings as well as the top. For the best results, add broken flowerpot pieces at the bottom for better drainage and keep the plants well watered.

CONSTRUCTING A MULTI-STOREY HERB GARDEN

You will need three matching containers, one large, one medium and one small; two inexpensive terracotta pots of the same height as the large and medium containers to act as inner supports; multipurpose compost and about 12 young herb plants.

1 Place the largest container in the desired position, and set the large terracotta pot within it, upside down. This will take the weight of the pots above, stopping the arrangement from slumping, and also create good drainage.

2 Fill the container with multipurpose compost to within 2.5–5cm (1–2in) of the rim, to leave room for the rootballs of the herbs. Press the compost well under the rim if your pots taper in towards the top. Set the medium-sized pot in place.

3 Plant up the lower container, alternating bushy and trailing herbs. If you choose to plant mint, remember that it is very invasive: picking the stems and leaves frequently will help keep it in check.

4 Repeat the process with the medium-sized container and inner pot, then add the topmost container, fill it with compost and plant a taller herb, such as a sage or dwarf rosemary (try 'Pinkie', with pink flowers). Finally, water all the plants well.

● **BE ADVENTUROUS WITH BASIL** The most commonly used form, 'Sweet Genovese', is widely available in supermarkets, so why not search out and grow more unusual varieties to be more creative with your cooking? Greek basil, which makes a bushy plant with far smaller leaves, has a much more pungent flavour, while lemon and Thai basil have a subtle citrus scent and a mild, spicy flavour respectively. Cinnamon basil adds a hint of spice and is an attractive plant with purple-red stems, as is 'Dark Opal', which has deep-purple leaves and pink flowers. 'Green Ruffles' is another pretty basil with large, frilly, serrated leaves.

● **KEEP MINT UNDER CONTROL** by growing it in containers, otherwise it will quickly spread, take root from its stems and bully other plants. Sink the pots into the ground if you like – but replant the mint with fresh soil every year or two. Experiment with different-flavoured mint varieties: there are many to choose from, such as apple, lemon, ginger and pineapple mints.

● **GROW PARSLEY IN HANGING BASKETS** to keep the leaves clean. It grows perfectly well in the ground, but because the plants have a natural tendency to sprawl they can suffer from mud-splash in wet weather.

UNUSUAL HERBS TO GROW

Ring the changes with herbs that are less often seen in the shops. All are easy to grow, although in a cool summer lemongrass may do better in the warmth of a greenhouse.

◀ Chervil (subtle aniseed flavour)
- Lemon balm (for scented teas or infusions)
- Lemongrass (citrus flavour; use in Oriental dishes)
- Lovage (looks like parsley, tastes like celery)
- Par-cel (a cross between parsley and celery)
- Sorrel (adds a lemon tang)
- Sweet cicely (slightly aniseed in flavour, grows very tall)
- Winter and summer savory (similar to thyme)

Enjoy the taste of herb flowers Attractive and subtle in flavour, the flowers of a fairly wide range of herbs are edible and can transform a plain green salad into a colourful and interesting dish. Add pink chive flowers for a mild onion taste, bright-orange pot marigold petals for a slightly spicy flavour and blue borage flowers for a hint of cucumber. Herb flowers frozen within ice cubes make pretty additions to jugs of cool summer drinks.

- **GROW 'EVERLASTING' CHIVES** Ensure an almost continuous supply of fresh leaves by uprooting and dividing established clumps every three years, in either spring or autumn. Replant the smaller clumps in their new positions – you can even pot up a couple and bring them indoors over winter.

- **GROW DILL AND FENNEL FOR BEAUTY AND USE** Both of these herbs grow into wonderfully tall, attractive plants with light, feathery foliage and flat-topped flowerheads that attract masses of beneficial garden insects such as hoverflies. Harvest sprigs of foliage throughout summer for cooking, then let the seeds develop and become fully dry. You can use them freshly ground in cooking.

Shrubby herbs to use year-round

Add a Mediterranean touch Most woody-stemmed herbs, such as rosemary, thyme, sage, lavender and marjoram, are native to Mediterranean regions. Plant them in full sun in a sheltered site and enjoy their evocative, scented foliage on a warm, still day. Although sun-lovers, they are hardy enough to survive all but the coldest winters.

- **USE SHAPED BAY TREES FOR STYLE AND STRUCTURE** Bay can be pruned into decorative columns, cones or pyramids that add structure to a formally laid out herb garden. Or train a plant as a standard in a large container to make an elegant focal point. Bay keeps its foliage through the year, providing a steady supply of fresh leaves to add to winter soups and stews.

- **EDGE BEDS AND BORDERS WITH HERBS** Rosemary and lavender, both evergreen, can be clipped to create an attractive low hedge around flower beds or to separate different spaces in the garden. Pick lavender flowers in summer to make scented sachets and rosemary sprigs throughout winter to add to roasts and casseroles.

● **GROW THYME IN CRACKS** between the paving slabs of a path or patio, or in the gaps between the stones or bricks of an old garden wall. Thyme thrives in dry, sunny spots and will even tolerate being trampled on.

● **PICK HERBS FOR STORAGE WHEN IT'S DRY** The best time is early on a dry day after the morning dew has disappeared but before the sun is at its hottest, so the essential oils in the leaves won't have had time to evaporate. Hang sprigs or bunches upside down under cover in a warm, dark place, then store them in airtight containers or jars (dark glass is best) out of direct light.

● **REIN IN STRAGGLY GROWTH** Woody herbs such as rosemary, sage and marjoram have a tendency to sprawl and become 'leggy' as they grow older. Get them back into shape by pruning in late spring, once the frosts are over. Cut back main stems quite hard, by up to half their length, then give the plants another trim in summer to keep them bushy. Never prune in the autumn, or you may kill the plants.

● **PROPAGATE WOODY HERBS** and insure against plant losses by taking cuttings [see pp.268–9] Take semi-ripe or heel cuttings in late spring from thymes and late summer from rosemary. You can make more sage plants by taking softwood cuttings in spring or early summer. Always put softwood cuttings in plastic bags as soon as you gather them, to stop them from drying out.

EXPERT KNOW HOW

MAKE MORE OF SUPERMARKET-BOUGHT HERBS

Look carefully and you'll see that ready-planted pots of basil, parsley and coriander are actually made up of clumps of smaller plants. It's easy to divide them and pot them up, giving you enough separate plants to last for months.

1 Water the potted herb thoroughly an hour or so before you plan to divide it, then up-end the pot and ease out the plant (basil is shown here).

2 Holding the plant at its base, gently prise apart the rootball, separating it into single plants or small clumps of three or four main shoots.

3 Replant each one in a pot filled with multipurpose potting compost. Water in and, if necessary, harden off the plants before moving them outdoors.

Growing fruit

YOU DON'T NEED AN ORCHARD or years of expertise to grow your own fruit. Fruit trees and bushes can be grown in almost any garden, and some, such as blueberries and autumn raspberries, need even less attention than many ornamental plants. Give it a go – and enjoy the super-fresh, perfectly ripe results.

Fruit in your garden

Make the most of different varieties

Tried-and-tested local varieties that originate in your part of the country are virtually guaranteed to succeed, because they are suited to your climate and growing conditions, but look at modern varieties, too. Many of these are more compact in size and bred for cool, temperate regions, increasing the range of fruit you can grow. They establish quickly, so you may be harvesting a crop just a year after planting.

● **GROW WHAT YOU CAN'T BUY**
Certain fruits are rarely seen for sale in supermarkets, either because they have a short season (such as gooseberries or greengages) or because they are difficult to transport and have a limited shelf life (redcurrants and tayberries). Don't miss out; grow them yourself.

● **REDISCOVER FORGOTTEN FRUITS**
There's nothing wrong with modern, easy-to-grow cultivars bred to be heavy cropping and disease resistant, but sometimes traditional heirloom varieties have a flavour that's hard to beat. Try searching out old-fashioned varieties such as 'Court Pendu Plat' apples (they date back to at least 1613), French 'Catillac' pears or 'Denniston's Superb' greengages.

◄ **Growing fruit** on vertical garden structures is a great way to make the most of available space. Here, cordon apples trained on supports against a sunny fence are ripening well, while plump blackberries growing up a stout post are ready for picking.

Space-saving ideas

Try compact fruit trees Those grown on dwarfing rootstocks are ideal [see p.217] and allow you to choose a fruit tree that won't outgrow its space. The smallest apple trees crop well in fertile soils and grow to just 1.2m (4ft).

● **USE CORDONS TO SAVE SPACE** These narrow, single-stemmed apples and pears can be grown in closely spaced rows, either against a wall or fence or tied in to horizontal wires. Oblique cordons are grown diagonally, at a 45° angle; they have a slightly longer main stem and produce more fruit than vertical cordons.

● **RIPEN FRUIT ON SUNNY WALLS** Figs, peaches and nectarines grown as fans, or espaliers, on a sheltered, south-facing wall will welcome the protection they get against frost. The extra sun and warmth will also help the fruits to ripen fully. If pruning and training your fruit doesn't appeal, ready-trained trees are available to buy from growers and garden centres.

● **HARVEST DIFFERENT VARIETIES FROM THE SAME TREE** A 'family tree' is made up of two, or even three, different varieties of apple or pear that have been expertly grafted on to a single main stem (see right). Usually, the varieties of fruit on family trees are carefully chosen to flower at the same time so insects pollinate all the fruits. Varieties are also specially chosen to crop over an extended period.

● **SELECT SPECIAL PATIO VARIETIES FOR CONTAINER-GROWING** such as slow-growing 'Adam's Pearmain' or 'Sunset' apples, a 'Stella' cherry, or a 'Terrace Ruby' nectarine. Plant young, one- or two-year-old trees in 45cm (18in) containers slightly larger than their rootball. Pot them on every two years into bigger containers but stop when they reach the ideal size and remember to top-dress – renew the surface layer of compost – each spring.

● **GET THE SOIL MIX RIGHT FOR CONTAINERS** by making up your own potting compost. Start with a bag of all-purpose, loam-based compost and add sand or gravel to aid drainage and prevent waterlogging. Feed plants with a high-potash fertiliser each spring to give them a boost.

● **GROW CITRUS FRUIT IN CONTAINERS** and you can move your plants indoors to a cool position (not a heated conservatory) during the winter months. In summer, relocate them to the sunniest spot on your patio or terrace.

▲ **This family apple tree** planted in a lawn has had two different varieties, 'Katy' (dark red) and 'James Grieve', grafted onto one rootstock. Compact family trees for patio containers are also available.

Combine soft fruit with salad crops If you grow gooseberries and redcurrants as standards rather than as traditional bushes [see p.222], the area beneath the plants will not be shaded out by their foliage so you'll be able to grow salad leaves or even flowering plants around the base. The other advantage of growing standards is that the fruit grows at waist or shoulder height, which makes it much more convenient for picking.

● **MAKE A GARDEN FEATURE OF BLACKBERRIES** and hybrid berries such as tayberries or loganberries by growing them up and over garden pergolas or arches. Search out modern varieties of blackberry, such as 'Navaho', that are upright rather than spreading. These produce big berries and are almost thornless.

● **PLANT UP HANGING STRAWBERRY BASKETS** to save on valuable space at ground level. Kept well-watered, the fruit will ripen successfully and your high-rise crop will be safe from attack by slugs and snails.

Tree fruits

GROW FRUIT TREES FOR THEIR BEAUTY and especially for the wealth of wonderful, flavoursome varieties, both old and new, that growing your own opens up to you. Modern grafting and training techniques mean you can choose the varieties you want in just the right size or easy-to-prune shape for a place in your garden.

▲ **A sheltered, sunny** fence is the perfect spot to grow pears, especially varieties that need a long ripening period. Trained forms, such as this space-saving espalier, look really attractive.

Apples and pears

Plant new trees in autumn At this time of year, trees are dormant but the soil is still warm enough for their roots to settle in. If you've left it too late, wait until early the following spring. Don't plant trees in midwinter, when the ground is cold and wet.

● **TRY LATE-BLOSSOMING VARIETIES IN COLD REGIONS** Apple and pear flowers are easily damaged by frost, resulting in poor harvests, so choose varieties that blossom late. With luck, by the time the trees are in flower, the worst of the cold weather will be over.

● **GROW PEAR TREES IN PAIRS** Like most fruiting trees, a single specimen needs a second tree close by to ensure the blossom is pollinated and produces fruit. If you only have room for one tree, check your neighbours' gardens to see whether there are any possible pollinators nearby. If in doubt, choose a self-fertile variety of pear such as 'Conference' or 'Concorde': the flowers can pollinate themselves or the other flowers on the tree.

● **TRAIN PEARS AGAINST WALLS TO AID RIPENING** Pears need a sunnier, warmer spot than apples and a sheltered position that will protect blossom against spring frosts and strong winds. Training pears as espaliers (see left) and fans will give you a heavier crop if space is tight.

Maximise your harvest For the best range, grow a selection of different varieties for different uses, such as cooking and eating apples and those that have different ripening times. Keep fruit supplies topped up by growing varieties that can be eaten soon after picking alongside others that keep well.

● **ADD NUTRIENTS WITH A SPRING FEED AND MULCH** Your trees will benefit from a boost just as new growth is starting. Choose a general compound fertiliser and follow this with an organic mulch, such as well-rotted farmyard manure, garden compost, leaf mould or bark chips.

● **THIN TO GET GOOD-SIZED FRUITS** In early summer, both apple and pear trees naturally shed very small fruitlets to prevent the branches from being overloaded. At this time, a second thinning by hand of the remaining fruits is also necessary to ensure those remaining reach the optimum size. Check clusters and remove fruits that are small or misshapen, aiming to leave about 10–15cm (4–6in) between each to give it enough space to grow to full size.

● **'FESTOON' FOR MORE FRUIT** Bending down side branches so that they are as horizontal as possible is known as festooning. It slows down leaf growth and encourages apple trees to form more flowers – and therefore more fruit. Tie the branches in place with twine.

HOW DOES IT WORK?
ROOTSTOCKS

Almost all fruit trees are grown by grafting a shoot (or 'scion') from one variety on to the roots of another. The named variety gives the fruit its characteristics, while the rootstock determines the eventual size of the tree – the smallest are grown on 'dwarfing' rootstocks and the biggest, which are suitable only for large gardens, on vigorous rootstocks. Check labels for information about rootstocks before you buy, so you get the right tree for your plot.

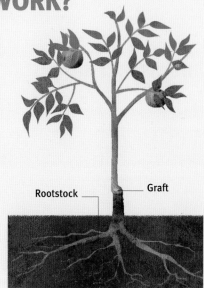

Rootstock

Graft

● **WINTER-PRUNE FOR HEALTHY GROWTH** When apples and pears are dormant, between late autumn and late winter, begin pruning with 'the three Ds', cutting out dead, damaged or diseased wood. Secondly, tackle any overcrowded areas to allow in more light and air. Wire-trained trees such as cordons, fans and espaliers need pruning to trim unwanted growth in summer, too.

● **REJUVENATE AN OLD APPLE OR PEAR TREE** so that it continues to bear fruit. Unless it's diseased, it has probably been pruned either too little or too much. Don't hurry the job; it will take two years or more to renovate. In the first winter, cut out all dead or diseased branches and start to thin out congested areas, but don't remove more than 25 per cent of the tree. The following winter, prune any overlong branches, open up the centre of the tree and thin overcrowded spurs.

STAR PERFORMERS...

BEST-TASTING EATING APPLES

The taste of dessert apples can vary from super-sweet to sharp, but the very best are finely balanced, wonderfully aromatic and have their own distinct flavour.

● 'Blenheim Orange'
● 'Cox's Orange Pippin'
● 'Discovery'
● 'Egremont Russet'
● 'Falstaff'
● 'Greensleeves'
◀ 'Jonagold'
● 'Laxton's Fortune'
● 'Pixie'
● 'Worcester Pearmain'

STAR PERFORMERS...

SELF-FERTILE PLUMS AND CHERRIES

If you are planting only a single tree, choose one of these self-fertile varieties: they don't need a pollinating partner. Otherwise, plant two or three compatible trees together that blossom at the same time.

PLUMS

- 'Czar' (early season crop)
- 'Jubilee' (mid-season)
- 'Marjorie's Seedling' (late season)
- 'Merryweather Damson' (for cooking, late season)
- 'Opal' (early season)
- 'Victoria' (mid-season)

CHERRIES

- 'Celeste' (sweet)
- 'Lapins' (sweet)
- 'Nabella' (acid)
- 'Stella' (sweet)
- 'Summer Sun' (sweet)
- 'Sunburst' (sweet)
- 'Sweetheart' (sweet)

Plums and cherries

Protect from cold winds for more fruit

Cherries, plums and greengages all grow best in a warm, sheltered position out of the wind. Although they won't thrive in waterlogged soil, they do need moisture at the roots so always provide good drainage.

- **REDISCOVER THE PLUM'S RELATIVES** Damsons, gages and mirabelles are old-fashioned members of the plum family. You'll be lucky to find these fruits in the shops, so the best way to find out how good they taste may well be to grow them yourself.

- **CHOOSE COMPACT PLUMS FOR SMALL SPACES** Thanks to modern breeding, small, ready-pruned plum trees, sold as 'minarettes' or 'ballerinas', can be grown where space is tight. Permanently staked and kept well fed and watered, they are suitable for large patio pots.

- **TRY AN ACID CHERRY** if you are unable to provide the sheltered, sunny site that sweet cherries need. Acid cherries may be too sour to eat straight from the tree but their flavour is better for cooking.

- **SHELTER CHERRIES FROM THE RAIN** to prevent their skins from splitting. This may be impossible with a large tree perhaps, but it's not out of the question to throw a sheet of plastic over a small container-grown tree or a wall-trained fan if you're expecting a downpour. It may keep the birds off, too.

- **NEVER PRUNE IN WINTER** Summer, when the trees are actively growing and their sap is flowing, is the time to prune cherries and plums. This minimises the risk that infection from the diseases canker and silver leaf will enter via pruning cuts. Free-standing cherries and plums shouldn't need a lot of attention, so prune them rarely and as lightly as possible.

Apricots, peaches and nectarines

Ripen outdoor fruit A sheltered, south-facing wall makes an ideal sun-trap for peaches and nectarines and is the only reliable place in which to grow them without a greenhouse. These, like cherries and plums, are stone fruits, so prune them in summer, not in winter.

- **SELECT THE BEST APRICOTS FOR COOL REGIONS** 'Flavorcot' and 'Tomcot' flower later than other varieties and produce more blossom, so the flowers have a good chance of surviving frosts.
- **PLANT MINIATURE VARIETIES IN CONTAINERS** 'Bonanza' and 'Garden Lady' peaches and 'Nectarella' nectarines are specially bred dwarf varieties that should not get taller than 1.5m (5ft) if grown in large pots or planters.
- **PROTECT YOUR CROPS** Peach leaf curl is a fungal disease that distorts and blisters the leaves and weakens trees, affecting peaches and nectarines grown outdoors. Spray the trees with copper fungicide in winter, then put a temporary plastic sheet over the tree until late spring to stop rain spreading the spores.
- **THIN FRUITS FOR A BETTER HARVEST** Abundant crops don't necessarily mean a bumper harvest – if you leave all the young fruits on your tree it may be so overburdened that none of them will fatten up into full-sized fruits. Thin them out in late spring and early summer so that peaches and nectarines are 15cm (6in) apart and apricots 10cm (4in) apart.

EXPERT KNOW HOW

POLLINATING PEACHES AND APRICOTS

All trees that flower early in the year run the risk that it will be too cold for insects to be active when blossom is ready to be pollinated. Hand pollination may be the only answer – although these days it can be done with a soft paintbrush instead of the traditional rabbit's tail!

Gently brush the centre of each open flower, transferring pollen from one to another (here, a dwarf peach, 'Terrace Amber'). The best time is between late morning and early afternoon on a sunny day, when blossom is fully open. Repeat as new flowers continue to appear.

Figs

Give figs a place in the sun If your fig is growing in a cold, exposed position, it is unlikely to crop well and the fruits won't ripen. Increase your chances of enjoying plump, delicious fruits in late summer or autumn by growing figs in a sheltered site in full sun or in pots on a sunny patio.

- **CHOOSE COOL-CLIMATE VARIETIES** such as 'Brown Turkey', 'Brunswick' or the Bavarian 'Violetta' for planting outdoors in temperate regions.
- **BE CRUEL TO BE KIND** Fig trees are much more productive if their roots are restricted. Plant them in a hole lined with concrete paving slabs or grow them in containers, and you should get a generous crop of fruit rather than just foliage.
- **REMOVE UNRIPE FRUITS** Fruits that are still green in late autumn will not ripen and should be picked off. Tiny, pea-sized embryo figs on the branches should be left; they will survive the winter and develop into next year's crop.

◀ **Harvest plums** before the skins start to split and attract wasps (the variety shown here is 'Opal'). They will last longer if you cut them from the branch with their stalks still attached.

Soft fruit

THERE IS A WORLD OF DIFFERENCE BETWEEN home-grown and shop-bought soft fruit. Commercially grown crops are harvested before they are ripe so that they can be packed, transported and put on display before they spoil. Grow your own, on the other hand, and you can pick and eat the fruit at exactly the right moment.

TURN JUICY LOGANBERRIES INTO DELICIOUS PRESERVES AND ENJOY THEM OVER WINTER

Strawberries

Prolong the strawberry season Grow both traditional, summer-fruiting varieties that you can harvest from early to late summer and so-called perpetual strawberries. The latter will keep cropping until early autumn – or longer if you protect them with cloches.

- **POT UP PLANTS FOR SUPER-EARLY CROPS** and bring them into the greenhouse for the winter. If they are kept warm they should produce a crop in mid-spring.
- **RAISE FRUIT OFF THE GROUND** to protect it from mud-splash, slugs and infection by grey mould. The most effective method is to use hanging baskets, high-rise strawberry planters or special table-top frames. Ready-made strawberry mats or a straw mulch around the fruit also work well.
- **CLEAN UP IN THE AUTUMN** by removing any mulching material and cutting back old foliage. Remember to leave the crowns untouched so they will fruit next year.
- **RENEW PLANTS AFTER TWO OR THREE YEARS** as even the healthiest strawberries don't last forever. Either buy new plants or propagate your own from runners (see right), which you peg down to make new plants (it takes about a month). Then sever the runner on either side, lift out the new plants in their pots and replant.
- **SAVOUR WILD STRAWBERRIES** Also called alpine strawberries, these berries may be tiny but each packs a punch of intense flavour. Once established, plants come back year after year, have a long cropping season and will even grow in shade.

▲ **New strawberry plantlets** are naturally produced along the length of long, creeping stems (runners). Carefully lift one, sink a small pot filled with compost beneath it and peg it down with a U-shaped wire clip. Once rooted in the pot, it can be cut from the parent plant.

Raspberries and blackberries

Support your crops Raspberries grow tall and are heavy when laden with fruit, while most blackberries throw out new growth at an alarming rate. Provide strong supports and spend a little time on pruning to keep plants productive.

- **TAKE THE EASY-GROW OPTION** Choose autumn-fruiting, rather than summer-fruiting raspberries. They are shorter and sturdier and pruning them couldn't be more straightforward: you simply cut all their stems (canes) right down to the

◀ **Support berries** that grow on canes and crop in summer, such as raspberries or these plump loganberries, in the traditional way on long galvanised wires held taut between sturdy wooden posts.

STAR PERFORMERS...

BEST-TASTING STRAWBERRIES

Ensure the longest season of delicious strawberries by growing a mix of these summer-fruiting and perpetual varieties.

SUMMER-FRUITING
- 'Elegance' (hardy and disease-resistant)
- 'Gariguette' (heirloom French variety, super-sweet)
- 'Honeoye' (early, crops heavily)
◀ 'Sonata' (mid-season, good yields)

PERPETUAL
- 'Aromel' (the original perpetual strawberry)
- 'Flamenco' (large berries, high yields)
- 'Mara des Bois' (aromatic fruits with wild-strawberry flavour)

ground each winter. Summer-fruiting raspberries are trickier: as soon they have finished cropping, you must remove only the canes that have just fruited but leave in place the new ones. These strong, new canes must be tied in to wires for the winter so that they are ready to bear fruit the following year.

● **DISCOVER THE BENEFITS OF YELLOW AND PURPLE RASPBERRIES** Yellow raspberries, such as autumn-fruiting 'Allgold', do not seem to attract as many birds as the regular red varieties so you may not need to net the fruit. The purple berries of 'Glencoe' are higher in antioxidants (substances that may have health benefits) than many other varieties and the canes have no prickly spines.

● **CHOOSE 'NAMED' BLACKBERRIES FOR BIGGER BERRIES** Wild brambles produce perfectly edible fruit, but you'll get a larger crop with a sweeter flavour from tried-and-tested cultivated varieties. Buy canes from established suppliers and you'll also be able to mix early- and late-harvesting types, as well as trying modern compact, thornless cultivars such as 'Waldo' or 'Loch Ness'.

● **TRY NEW BERRY FLAVOURS** Loganberries, tayberries, boysenberries and tummelberries are all cross-breeds between raspberries and blackberries and offer an interesting variety of flavours. Mouthwatering tayberries are delicious raw or cooked, loganberries are particularly good for making jam and boysenberries freeze well. Yet hybrid berries are rarely grown commercially so the fruit is almost impossible to buy in the shops. Why not give them a try?

▼ **A standard redcurrant** takes up less space at ground level than a bush, leaving plenty of room at the foot of its main stem for growing other crops – such as these chives and the raised beds full of courgette plants and small 'Tom Thumb' lettuces.

Currants and gooseberries
Choose reliable and hardy currants

Red- and whitecurrants, blackcurrants and gooseberries are all fairly easy to grow and are tough, long-lasting plants. Although blackcurrants and gooseberries require richer soil than red- and whitecurrants, all these fruits prefer cool, moist conditions, making them perfect for northerly regions where growing sun-loving fruits, such as peaches, can be a challenge.

● **PLANT SUPER-SWEET BLACKCURRANTS** If you grow only one blackcurrant, make it 'Ebony', a modern variety that produces large berries bursting with vitamin C and so sweet that they can be eaten uncooked. Whitecurrants, such as 'White Versailles' although less commonly grown than redcurrants, are also naturally sweeter than many red varieties.

● **GROW ROBUST, THORNLESS GOOSEBERRIES** Some modern varieties such as 'Invicta', 'Pax' and 'Captivator' have two very big advantages. Their lack of sharp thorns makes harvesting pain-free, while their resistance to attack by American gooseberry mildew – the most common and damaging gooseberry disease – minimises the chances of your crop being spoiled.

- **TRY A DUAL-PURPOSE GOOSEBERRY** Dessert gooseberries such as 'Leveller' and 'Whinham's Industry' can be used for both cooking and eating raw without sweetening. Pick your first crop in late spring when the berries are still unripe: the tart flavour makes them ideal for cooking and jam-making. Leave the rest of your crop to ripen fully and the fruits should be sweet enough to eat straight from the bush.
- **GROW CORDONS TO SAVE SPACE** Unlike blackcurrants, which fruit only when grown as bushes, gooseberries and red- and whitecurrants crop well when grown as vertical cordons. Cordons are single stems that produce fruit on short shoots, or spurs, all the way from bottom to top. Set young plants just 38–45cm (15–18in) apart and train on a fence or tie into wires. Prune the cordons twice a year: in winter, cut all side shoots growing from the main stem back to just one or two buds (and trim the top shoot back once it reaches the top of the support); in summer, prune the newly grown side shoots to leave five leaves on each.
- **HOLD ON TO YOUR FRUIT** Garden birds are very partial to currants and gooseberries and have a tendency to strip fruit bushes. Bird scarers may work temporarily, but if you don't plan to share your harvest, nets or a fruit cage are the only sure-fire answers to keeping birds off your crops.
- **PRUNE BUSHES IN WINTER FOR BETTER CROPS** Currant and gooseberry bushes should be pruned while the plants are dormant, between late winter and early spring. Cut out congested growth from the centre to let in light and air, then remove up to a quarter of the oldest stems. At the same time, trim overlong shoots on gooseberries and red- and whitecurrants, and prune back all sideshoots. Blackcurrants are treated rather differently: once plants are mature and getting crowded, remove an entire old main stem or two at the base using loppers, then leave the rest of the plant alone or you won't get any fruit the following year.

Blueberries

Get bumper crops with the right soil Blueberries are easy to grow, don't need complicated pruning and are immune to most pests and diseases. Provided you give them acid soil, they should produce good crops year after year. Like rhododendrons, blueberries require very acid conditions – soil with a pH of 4–5.5 [see p.233] – and good drainage. If your soil is too alkaline, grow them in raised beds or containers filled with special ericaceous compost mixed with grit.
- **ENSURE A GOOD HARVEST** For the best chance of pollination and fruit set, plant blueberries in pairs, choosing varieties that flower at the same time.

EXPERT KNOW HOW

TAKING BLACKCURRANT CUTTINGS

Blackcurrants are easy to propagate from hardwood cuttings, provided you take them at the right time of year. From late autumn to midwinter, select long, straight stems from healthy plants, cutting them off near the base.

1 Using secateurs, trim the lower part of the stem below a leaf node to leave the cuttings about 25cm (10in) long.

2 Plant the cuttings in a slit trench with added grit or sand, pushing them in about 10cm (4in) deep and firming the soil.

▼ **Blueberries crop** well in raised beds filled with lime-free compost. Keep them moist by using rainwater, which is less alkaline than tap water. These bushes are irrigated by a soaker hose that draws water from a rain butt.

5
GREEN-FINGERED TECHNIQUES

Build on your gardening skills with expert tips and your plants will reward you by giving of their best. Whether it's planting, pruning, making compost, sowing seeds or thwarting pests and diseases, there are all sorts of clever ways to make the job easier, save time and money, and ensure success.

Choosing garden tools

GOOD TOOLS CAN LAST A LIFETIME if you choose them carefully and look after them well. Find out about classic designs that have proved their worth as well as clever new tools that make gardening easier, or choose from an ever-increasing range of powered tools that can make short work of lengthy tasks.

Top of the list hand tools

Equip yourself with the essentials To plant, weed and dig your garden you will need a trowel, a hand fork and/or a hoe, and a spade or fork. A rigid garden rake is essential for preparing seedbeds, and useful for gathering up debris; spring-tined rakes are used on lawns. Your plants will need pruning, too. A pair of secateurs is the single most useful cutting tool to buy; for larger pruning tasks you may need more powerful tools such as loppers [see also Pruning, p.251]. Don't forget carrying equipment: watering cans are essential, and if your garden is too small for a wheelbarrow, a plastic tub with handles is a great alternative. You can even buy a wheeled trolley to mount it on.

▼ **A clean and organised shed** with all the tools you need at hand will positively invite you to get on with the gardening. Make the most of space in the shed by hanging small tools on the back of the door.

● **HANDLE TOOLS BEFORE YOU BUY** Handle size, shape and texture, shaft length, blade size, material, weight and angle all make a huge difference as to how a tool feels in your hands. Go through the motions of working with a tool to check that the feel and balance suit you.

Invest in quality for best results While a high price does not guarantee that any tool will be a pleasure to use, cheap tools may not be the bargain they at first appear. They may be poorly made, heavy, rough-edged and short-lived. Stainless steel tools will repay your investment; they are durable, easy to clean, and easier to use in heavy soils.

● **CONSIDER TOOLS THAT MAY HAVE EXTRA BENEFITS** Copper alloy tools are expensive, but many gardeners are convinced that they have unusual advantages, said to include antimicrobial activity – keeping plants healthy – as well as deterring slugs and snails. These garden pests are repelled by copper, and it is thought that the tiny amount of copper these tools leave in the ground protects plants from attack.

● **PICK UP GOOD SECOND-HAND AND 'VINTAGE' TOOLS** at car boot sales and auction rooms – they have already proved that they last! Check that wooden handles are sound, particularly where they join the head. Adverts in local papers and shop windows are often fruitful, too. If you choose to look for bargains on auction sites online, remember that you are 'buying blind' – check carefully that the tools being offered are those pictured, and be wary of big sellers to avoid buying stolen items.

Make gardening easy on yourself

Your back, joints and hands are your most valuable gardening assets and need protection when you garden. Combine tools that are comfortable and not too heavy with protective accessories such as gloves and kneelers. You'll find you'll be able to garden for longer and get more done – and that's great news for your plants.

● **THINK ABOUT THE WEIGHT OF TOOLS WHEN IN USE** A spade may be light when lifted in a garden centre but very heavy when loaded with soil. If a small (border) spade or fork is more comfortable for you to use, then choose that. The same applies to wheelbarrows and especially to watering cans, which can be very heavy when full.

● **TAKE CARE OF YOUR HANDS** with good-quality gloves and barrier cream. For tough jobs, choose thick gloves with cuffs to avoid scratches to your wrists and to protect the joints on cold days. You will need thin gloves as well for hand-weeding and other light tasks – choose ones that have elasticated cuffs, as these will prevent irritating soil and grit creeping inside the gloves.

Specialist tools that are worth using

Consider traditional tools for specialised tasks Look out for old-style, specialised tools such as digging hoes, which were used to break up compacted soil long before modern powered rotavators came on the scene. These classic hand tools are growing in popularity once again: they are quiet, and by doing the job of power tools, they cut energy costs.

● **TRY A LONG-HANDLED SPADE** The hand position and the action – as if using a hay fork – suit gardeners with good upper body strength but a tendency to lower back problems. The pointed blade is also excellent for digging stony soil.

TOP TEN GARDENING TOOLS

Equip yourself for all the basic cultivation and pruning jobs needed in the garden with these hand tools.

- ● Digging fork
- ● Digging spade
- ● Folding garden knife
- ● Garden rake
- ● Hand fork
- ● Hoe
- ● Loppers
- ● Secateurs
- ● Shears
- ◀ Trowel

TOP CARRYING EQUIPMENT

The size of your garden will dictate the size and scale of the equipment you need to carry your tools and collect debris.

- ● A bucket (some come with tool-tidy pockets)
- ● Plastic sheeting, for catching hedge trimmings
- ● Plastic tub with handles, or wooden trug
- ● Stout plastic sacks for fallen leaves
- ● Watering can(s)
- ◀ Wheelbarrow

TOP GARDENING ACCESSORIES

Head for the accessories aisles to find all the bits of kit that make gardening more comfortable and less frustrating.

- ◀ Gloves, thick and thin
- ● Kneeler or kneepads
- ● Rubber overshoes or clogs for quick garden trips
- ● Solar-powered light for the garden shed
- ● Strong garden twine in a tin or dispenser
- ● Trigger spray bottles for targeting plant pests

▲ Reduce a pile of prunings to a bucket of shredded material ready for the compost heap. Small shredders are reasonably priced, but check that they will be adequate for the thickness of your general garden prunings, or you risk damaging the machine.

● **PERFECT YOUR VEGETABLE ROWS WITH A RIDGER** This long-handled tool with a V-shaped blade is useful for drawing soil up to cover the bases of celery, leeks and potatoes.

● **CUT WEEDS AND ROUGH GRASS DOWN TO SIZE** with a grass hook (see facing page). It must be used with care, but it is much safer for garden wildlife than using a line trimmer. When you work slowly with hand tools you give small creatures more warning and time to make themselves scarce. If you have a meadow planting, this is the ideal tool.

Make your life easier with new tool designs

There are innovative new tools that have been designed with efficiency in mind, sometimes combining two tools in one. Hybrid tools that do two jobs include the 'spork' – like a fork, but with a cutting blade at the base. It is particularly good for digging heavy soils because soil cannot stick to the blade. A 'sprake' – a rake with a cutting edge – both cuts through and rakes up weeds and makes levelling soil easy.

● **LOOK AT TOOLS WITH CHANGEABLE HEADS** if you have a small garden – they save on both money and storage space. The snap-on heads of these 'multichange' tools allow you to adapt your tools with a choice of handle lengths, so you are able to convert, for example, your hand fork into a long-handled weeding tool. Decide which range of tools you prefer first, because different brands may not be interchangeable.

The most useful power tools

Work out which tools you really need The size and layout of your

garden will largely determine what power tools you may consider buying – a mower for lawns, a line trimmer for wild areas, a hedge trimmer or a leaf blower and shredder if you have lots of trees and woody shrubs. One tool that can really make a difference to any garden, however small, is a pressure washer – it literally

STAR PERFORMERS...

HELPFUL TOOLS

Tools specially designed to make gardening tasks easier can be a real boon. Look out for tools that are ergonomically designed, often sold for less physically able gardeners and often in bright colours so they are easy to spot in your bucket of weeds.

● **Long-handled weeding forks** are not just for gardeners who cannot bend – their increased reach saves you moving so much when on your knees.

● **Swivel-handled secateurs** take some getting used to, but make for lighter work if you do a lot of pruning.

● **Telescopic handles,** on hoes, rakes and some cutting tools, are easily adjusted for length by twisting the shaft.

● **A stirrup spade** allows you to position your foot centrally over the blade, rather than to one side of the shaft.

▶ **Tools and grips** in new shapes, as on this weeding tool – a modified hand fork – ease the strain on wrist joints. Handles in new materials such as foam are comfortable and reduce impact, especially on loppers.

saves hours when cleaning patios and garden furniture, and keeps paths algae-free and non-slip.

- **SAVE MONEY BY HIRING POWER TOOLS** you may only use once or twice a year. You will also save yourself the worry of maintaining and storing them.
- **BULK UP YOUR COMPOST HEAP** by recycling all your woody prunings through a garden shredder. To keep the neighbours happy, opt for a 'silent' shredder, which uses a grinding rather than a chopping action.

Choose the right mower for your garden
This is probably the most expensive piece of garden equipment you will buy, so do some research and choose your model carefully. First consider whether you really do need a power mower. For a small lawn, a hand-powered push-mower is quiet, with zero energy consumption, and keeps you fit – and if you keep the cylinder of blades well-sharpened, it will give a superb finish to your lawn.

- **THINK ABOUT POWER SUPPLY** Petrol-powered mowers are noisy but fully mobile, giving you freedom to mow anywhere, and are the best choice for large gardens. Electric mowers are light and easy to use, but you are restricted by your power source. Take a look at rechargeable battery mowers – combining freedom of movement and quietness, these are ideal for small and medium-sized gardens, and as battery technology improves, they are getting better every year.
- **CONSIDER WHAT DIFFERENT CUTTING ACTIONS DO** A rotary mower is the best choice if you don't enjoy maintaining tools and have a less than perfect lawn – although if you choose one with rollers, you can give your lawn classic stripes. Cylinder mowers cut the grass very cleanly, like scissors, but need more care in use: the blades can be damaged by stones or other debris lying on the lawn.
- **RECYCLE YOUR MOWINGS INSTANTLY** with a mulching mower – these chop the grass cuttings very finely, and distribute them over the lawn as you go along. The layer of clippings acts as a valuable mulch, conserving moisture, adding nutrients to the soil and actually making your lawn healthier.

Caring for your tools

Keep them safe If your tools are stored in a shed or garage, make sure it can be locked so the risk of theft is reduced. Padlocks with alarms and lockable cables that can be threaded through tools all reduce the likelihood of thefts.

- **HANG THEM HIGH** A wall-mounted tool rack not only saves space but helps you keep a check on where your tools are, and also stops sharp hoe and spade blades being blunted by coming into contact with concrete floors.

EXPERT KNOW HOW

USING A GRASS HOOK

This tool, ideal for long grass and tall weeds, is easy and efficient to use once the technique is mastered, but take great care when using it.

For safety when using this sharp blade, wear stout boots and trousers, and your thickest gloves. Hold the plants back at their tops, and swing the hook sideways, cutting cleanly across the base of the stems; don't pull the hook towards your legs. Another safe option is to use a long stick to hold back and push away the vegetation, keeping your free hand well clear of the blade.

BEAT THAT!

- **The oldest known working power mower** is a ride-on model manufactured by Ransomes of Ipswich in 1902, weighing in at a mighty one-and-a-half tonnes. This classic machine is held at a secret location by the Old Lawnmower Club, a UK society founded in 1990 that is dedicated to preserving vintage mowers.

► **Make short work** of shearing lavender and other twiggy shrubs with a well-maintained pair of shears with comfortable grips, an easy action and clean, sharp blades that don't rasp together as you cut.

● **MAKE SMALL TOOLS VISIBLE** Most secateurs have bright handles, which helps prevent them getting lost in vegetation. Do the same with other tools by painting wooden handles or wrapping bright insulating tape around plastic handles.

● **AVOID CLUTTER** Keep hand tools in a trug or tool organiser, or use a hanging fabric or plastic shoe rack for your hand tools, string and labels.

Keep tools well-maintained
Cleaning tools after use may seem a chore when you are putting away the tools but you will be pleased that you did so when you next come to use them. Clean, sharp tools are easier to use, will be better for your plants and make every job quicker and more pleasurable.

● **HAVE TOOLS THAT CLEAN THEMSELVES** Fill a bucket with sand and add some old (or new) engine oil. Push hoes and spades into the mix having wiped off the worst of the dirt: the sand will clean off the rest while the oil will prevent rust. The tools can be left standing safely in the bucket until you next need them.

● **TAKE CARE OF WOODEN HANDLES** to keep them comfortable to use. Sand them to remove splinters and then treat with linseed oil to help preserve them.

● **SHARPEN CUTTING TOOLS REGULARLY TO MAKE PRUNING EASIER** and more efficient, and lubricate the moving parts so they open and close without sticking. Do not use your cutting tools to cut wire or other hard materials.

● **AVOID THE SERVICING RUSH FOR POWER TOOLS** Don't leave it until spring when everyone will need the work done. Book them in for servicing in the autumn.

EXPERT KNOW HOW

CLEANING AND SHARPENING SECATEURS

It's easy to keep your secateurs in tip-top condition. Blunt secateurs crush plant stems and if they are dirty they can also spread diseases. Top quality secateurs are designed to be sharpened and some even come with basic tools for maintenance. Manufacturers of high-priced secateurs may offer free repairs.

1 Start with some wire wool and oil and rub with a circular motion to remove surface dirt, sticky sap and any rust, taking care not to blunt the blades.

2 Use a sharpening tool to hone the blades. An ordinary carborundum stone or kitchen steel does the job, or you can buy small secateur sharpeners.

3 After sharpening, use an oily cloth to wipe over the blades to remove dirt and prevent rust in storage. Always keep your secateurs closed when not in use.

KEEP YOUR TOOLS WELL-MAINTAINED TO MAKE GARDEN TASKS MORE SATISFYING

Working with your soil

THE SOIL IS WHERE your garden begins: it anchors the roots of your plants and provides them with water and vital nutrients. Improving and nourishing your soil, especially with home-made garden compost, is a fast track to floriferous plants and heavy crops – and need not involve as much digging as you think.

Get to know your soil

Good groundwork pays dividends Identifying your soil type and understanding its attributes will help you choose the right plants for your garden and grow them well. The simplest way to assess your soil is to get down, look at it and handle it. You can discover a great deal just by pressing and rolling it in your hands (see below). Always take a number of soil samples from different parts of the garden, in case builders have left rubble or imported untypical topsoil in some areas.

WHAT'S YOUR SOIL TYPE?

Take a close look at your soil and handle it when both moist and dry. Its look and texture will tell you which of the four soil types below it most closely resembles. A pH test (see facing page) will complete the information you need to manage your soil well and choose plants that will thrive in your garden.

☐ **SANDY SOILS**	☐ **CHALKY SOILS**	☐ **CLAY SOILS**	☐ **PEATY SOILS**
Sandy soils feel gritty between the fingers and may include gravel too. Typically they are light, low in nutrients and organic matter, and dry in summer. When moistened they are difficult to roll into a ball.	Chalky soils are often shallow, with a thin layer of soil overlaying chalk bedrock. They are often very pale in colour and usually low in organic matter. They can get dry in summer and have a high pH (alkaline).	High in nutrients but heavy and difficult to dig, clay soils can be wet and sticky in winter and bake hard in summer. When moistened, they can be rolled into a ball easily. The pH may be high or low (acid or alkaline).	Often dark in colour, usually acid (low pH) and high in organic matter, these are easy to dig and potentially rich in nutrients, but can dry out in summer. They can be rolled into a ball but it will crumble when pressed.

Improve your soil structure All
soil types can be made easier to work with and more hospitable for plants. Spend time improving the soil in a new bed before planting up and you will reap the rewards.

● **ENRICH SANDY SOILS**, which are dry and lack nutrients. Adding organic matter (see overleaf) solves both problems; either dig it in, or apply in a thick layer as a mulch [see p.247], which will help retain water in summer.

● **LIGHTEN CLAY SOILS**, which can be heavy and airless, by working in organic matter. Water will drain more easily in winter and the soil will not bake as hard in summer. Lightening the soil texture will also make it easier for plant roots to grow deep. Keep off clay soils in winter, when walking on them can damage their structure. Dig in autumn, before the soil is wet and cold and in time to allow frost to break down clods.

● **DIG OVER NEW GARDENS** or land that has not been cultivated, adding plenty of organic matter as you do so, as they often have thin topsoil (dark, fertile soil). Making trenches and filling them with organic matter will also help, in time, to increase the depth of fertile soil.

● **DON'T BE RESTRICTED BY YOUR SOIL** There is a wealth of plant choice for every soil type [see p.20]. For a broad idea of what is suitable, look at what your neighbours grow, then investigate the varieties of those plants so that you can choose something a little different. If your soil is not suitable for certain plants that you really want to grow, simply grow them in pots.

EXPERT KNOW HOW

UNDERSTAND THE CHEMISTRY OF YOUR SOIL

A simple, inexpensive pH testing kit will help you to discover if your soil is acid or alkaline. These kits are readily available and, once you know your soil pH, you can save both growing time and money by avoiding plants with specialist needs that may not really thrive in your soil.

1 Take several soil samples from at least six parts of a border to eliminate any localised discrepancies. Take the sample 5cm (2in) below the soil surface. Remove any large stones and allow the soil to dry naturally before doing the pH test. Do not take soil from near walls, by compost heaps or where animals frequent.

2 Depending on the test kit, add the test solution, or water and the test powders, to the soil sample. Agitate the mixture and allow the solution to settle. When it has cleared the colour of the solution can be compared to a chart. Values between 5.5 and 7.7 suit most plants: lower numbers mean an increasingly acid soil, and high numbers an alkaline one.

Work with the chemistry of your soil It is difficult, time-
consuming and can be expensive to change your soil pH, whether it is acid or alkaline. Fortunately, most soils will sustain a wide range of plants. Some plants are certainly fussy: rhododendrons, most heathers, camellias and pieris will not tolerate alkaline (high pH) soils. But most plants recommended for alkaline soils will grow in neutral (pH7) and acid soils, too. Success growing plants is much more closely dependent on good planting and early care.

Soil chemistry can be modified, but the process is slow and will be ongoing. Adding lime will increase the pH; it can be spread on soil in autumn. It is most often used on vegetable beds to help prevent clubroot, a disease of cabbages. Adding organic matter and/or sulphur powder or chips can decrease soil pH but must be applied every year. Also, some inorganic fertilisers are naturally acidic.

TOP GREEN MANURES

Growing a green manure is a great way to improve your soil. Simply scatter the seed over a bed and wait for the plants to grow; then, before any flowers set seed, chop the plants down and dig them into the soil to boost its fertility.

● **Mustard** grows fast and covers the soil. It can also reduce wireworm, which eat root crops, in new gardens. Sow early spring – early autumn.

● **Winter tares** are tall and bulky, but not so easy to dig in. They add nitrogen to soil. Sow early spring–early autumn.

● **Phacelia** is pretty, with blue flowers that attract bees. Sow early spring– early autumn.

● **Crimson clover** grows densely, with flowers that bees love, and adds nitrogen to your soil, boosting its fertility. Sow mid spring–late summer.

▼ **Grazing rye** adds bulk to your soil and helps prevent nutrients being washed out in winter. Sow late summer–mid autumn.

Boost the fertility of your soil

Put back what plants take out Plants take nutrients from the soil and for good performance year after year, you must replenish them. Add organic soil improvers when you make new beds, and as you cultivate them through the seasons. These organic materials not only add nutrients but also, more importantly, they help the soil to retain nutrients, so what you put back works harder.

You can add any composted plant material; garden compost is one of the most valuable soil improvers, but it is not always possible to make enough of your own. Buy in bagged compost from your local recycling centre or garden centre; spent mushroom compost is another option. Fallen leaves can be composted [see p.142] if you have enough to gather. Manures, once rotted, are valuable too, though not usually as rich in nutrients as people think. Any mixed-in bedding material (straw, shavings or sawdust) also reduces their nutritional value.

● **DIG IN THE GOOD STUFF** The quickest way to add organic matter to your soil is to dig it in when you prepare your beds or when you dig planting holes. Work organic matter in with the soil with a spade or fork, then leave the worms to carry on with the mixing. Adding organic matter also encourages earthworms – an indicator of healthy, fertile soil.

● **ADD A LAYER OF NOURISHMENT** Mulching is the natural way to add organic matter, mimicking the way plant material falls to the ground and rots, to be taken into the soil by worms. Add organic matter thickly in spring to retain soil moisture and to keep down annual weeds. It is especially useful around new shrubs to give them a good start.

PREPARING A NETTLE PLANT TONIC

This is a very simple way to make a totally organic, nutritious – if somewhat smelly – plant tonic. If you don't have access to nettles, grow a patch of comfrey. Nettles and comfrey also make great additions to the compost heap.

1 Wear thick gloves to cut or pick the nettles; they can be used fresh or dried. Put them into a large bucket or barrel and use garden shears to snip them up. An alternative is to stuff them into a hessian sack or a net bag, such as an onion net.

2 Fill with water to cover all the plant material and cover with a lid. Leave for a month and then use the liquid as a feed for plants in containers or in the open garden, either watered in or sprayed on to foliage. Be warned – it really does smell foul!

● **NOURISH SOIL WITH A LIVING MANURE** Compost and manures are bulky and most effective when applied in large amounts. Avoid the bother of moving and applying them by growing a green manure (see facing page). These plants have several advantages: they are cheap and easy to sow, they add lots of bulky organic material, retain soil nutrients, especially in winter, and also suppress weeds. Some varieties, such as clover, will contribute nutrients to the soil.

● **USE A SUPERFOOD FROM THE SEA TO ENRICH SOIL** Seaweed is not high in the main plant nutrients but contains an invigorating cocktail of other minerals that may be lacking in over-cropped soils. Fresh seaweed can be added to the compost heap or used as a mulch; seaweed fertiliser products are also available.

Boost soil with plant feeds and fertilisers Perennial plants and shrubs will thrive without extra feeding if the soil is kept fertile, but some plants – bedding, crops and plants in containers – benefit from nutrient supplements. To boost the growth of these plants, use a general fertiliser containing balanced amounts of the three main plant nutrients: nitrogen (N), needed for leaf and stem growth; phosphorus (P) for root growth; and potassium (K) for flowering and fruiting. For more flowers and fruits, many gardeners choose a fertiliser that is high in potash (K) – tomato feed is the most familiar. There are organic alternatives to chemical formulas: both pelleted chicken manure and fish, blood and bone meal provide a wider range of nutrients and last longer. For container plants, use liquid fertilisers which act more quickly and are more controllable.

● **USE A FOLIAR FEED** on plants that are not thriving; these dilute liquid fertilisers are sprayed directly on to a plant's leaves. Seaweed-based products are popular.

● **MAKE YOUR OWN 'PLANT TEAS'** Keep plants healthy with a home-made tonic (see above). Nutrient-rich nettles and comfrey are the best choices: if planting comfrey, use the variety 'Bocking 14'; it does not set seed and so will not spread.

HOW DOES IT WORK?

NUTRIENT UPTAKE

Plants make carbohydrates in their leaves to give them the energy to grow. But they also need a complex cocktail of other nutrients – nitrogen and minerals such as calcium, for example – from the soil. Plants do not 'eat', they 'drink'; they are able to absorb these nutrients with their roots when they are dissolved in water, but can struggle when the soil is dry.

Make your own super-compost

Set up a compost powerhouse If you don't have a compost bin already, you're losing the nutritional value of everything you take out of your garden – weeds, spent bedding and crop plants – and impoverishing your soil. Buy or build a compost bin – not a thing of beauty, you can site it out of the way but make sure you can still access it easily to encourage you to use it. Traditionally bins are placed on soil but this is not necessary; putting it on concrete or slabs can help deter rats. A healthy, efficient compost heap gets hot in the centre, and large bins are better than small ones because they get warmer, speeding up the process. Aim for a well-sized bin, 1m (40in) cubed.

● **DOUBLE YOUR COMPOSTING CAPACITY** With two bins, you can fill one, then turn its contents into the second bin and leave it while you start filling the first one again. This turning mixes the compost so it will rot down well – by the time the first bin is full again, the compost in the second bin should be ready to empty out and use.

▲ **Made to around** the dimensions of a wooden pallet, the traditional slatted wooden compost bin remains one of the most useful designs – big enough to generate heat in the centre yet allowing good air circulation around the edges.

Nurture your compost for quick results Compost doesn't just make itself: it will need some help from you. As well as getting the ingredients right (see below), try these tips to get rich, sweet compost in double-quick time.

● **GET THE COMPOST ENGINE RUNNING** by adding activators – substances that add nitrogen to feed beneficial bacteria. They include raw manures, comfrey and nettle stems and leaves and proprietary activators. Be sure to water them in well.

● **FUEL THE COMPOSTING PROCESS WITH MOISTURE** A dry heap will not warm up and will be colonised by ants. If your compost is not rotting and there are ants, add water. It may be that there is too much 'brown' material that is slow to compost. Mix in fast-composting 'green' material together with water to get things going.

WHAT TO COMPOST

Slow-to-compost 'brown' material will form the bulk of your compost. This includes woody prunings (ideally shredded), dry leaves and cardboard. You also need wet, 'green' material that will feed the bacteria in the heap: young green weeds, fresh leaves and vegetable and fruit waste from the kitchen. Mix it all up well.

☐ GREEN: QUICK TO COMPOST

These are all soft, green materials: annual weeds, soft hedge prunings, grass clippings, vegetable peelings and old bedding plants. On their own they compost rapidly but as they rot they exclude air and encourage action by bacteria that produces nasty smells.

☐ BROWN: SLOW TO COMPOST

These are dry, woody materials: autumn and winter prunings, paper, cardboard, straw, dry leaves and dead weeds. On their own they do not contain moisture or nutrients to feed the beneficial bacteria; a mostly brown compost heap will not change much over months.

☐ DO NOT COMPOST

Avoid any animal remains, dairy or cooked food. These will all encourage vermin. You can add manures, including horse, rabbit and guinea pig but do not use cat or dog wastes. Ideally do not add roots of pernicious weeds, seeding weeds or diseased plants.

SETTING UP A WORM COMPOSTER

Although a wormery won't produce barrow-loads of compost, it is convenient and, as it doesn't smell, can be kept in a garage. It needs careful management but produces compost that's ideal for patio pots and a nutritious liquid feed too.

1 A wormery kit will provide you with the basic setup, the worms, and full instructions. This bin is in sectioned layers, and is raised off the ground, with a tap that allows you to drain off liquid that is full of plant nutrients.

2 At the bottom of the bin, add a layer of damp straw or newspaper, then a 5cm (2in) layer of garden compost or manure. Then add the worms. These brandling or tiger worms are more productive than earthworms.

3 Layer in kitchen waste up to a depth of 15cm (6in), then leave the worms to get to work before adding more. Build up the bin in layers as you fill it. When the bin is full, empty it and sieve out the worms before starting again.

● **MIX MATERIALS TO ACCELERATE THE COMPOSTING PROCESS** Do not make discrete layers. Turn your compost regularly, too: either use a fork or compost turner or, even better, turn the materials into a second bin. Add water and activator too and you will halve the composting time.

● **SHRED BULKY MATERIALS FOR FASTER COMPOSTING** Micro-organisms in the heap digest what they need from the surface of materials. If you increase the surface area, composting is faster. Tear up paper, and snip or shred woody prunings.

● **PUT A LID ON IT** In winter, rain will cool the heap and slow the composting process. Cover the heap with old carpet or bubble plastic to keep in the heat.

Composting options for small spaces

You do not need a large area to make compost and there are options for even the smallest garden. But once you start you will want to make more, so be prepared to be hooked!

● **TRY A TUMBLER** Supported on frames, these rotating bins are easy to fill and empty, although turning them gets harder as the bin fills. When it comes to speed and quality of compost these are among the best. A fun new design is the compost 'ball' or orb, which you simply roll around the garden.

● **BUILD A WORMERY** (see above) if your garden is tiny and your main compost ingredient is going to be kitchen waste. They're also great for family gardens.

● **BUY AN ATTRACTIVE BIN** If you do not have room to hide a heap, then make a feature of it by opting for a pretty beehive compost bin. They are small but attractive, and practical too, being made of wood and allowing for good airflow.

The dos and don'ts of digging

Dig to improve soil structure Even the simplest task, such as digging, can give your garden an added boost if you perform it correctly. When you dig, lift and turn a full spade's width and depth at a time to work the soil systematically, rather than tickling the top layer with a lighter touch; this will improve aeration and reduce soil compaction, making it easier for plants to spread their roots and take in oxygen and water – all helping them to grow bigger and better. Adding organic matter as you dig is always beneficial.

● **PICK THE BEST TIME TO DIG** Heavy soils, high in clay content, are best dug in autumn, when the soil is still warm and not too wet and sticky. Winter frosts will break the clods down further, making it easier to plant and sow in spring. Wait until spring to dig light, sandy soils; they are poor in nutrients and are best left intact over winter so that rains do not penetrate and wash what nutrients there are away.

EXPERT KNOW HOW

HOW TO DIG

To dig, simply push the spade into the soil, lever it back and turn the soil. Bend at the hips and knees to protect your back. To incorporate more organic matter, spread it over the soil first so it gets dug in. Annual weeds, before they have set seeds, can be dug in and will rot down, adding more organic matter.

1 Dig a trench across one end of the bed, putting the soil into a barrow. Do not dig too deep and only remove the fertile, dark topsoil. Take the soil to the other end of the bed and tip it on to a plastic sheet, returning for more until the first trench is dug.

2 Fork in compost or other organic matter at the base of the trench. Because it will be buried it need not be fully decomposed. If you have heavy soil or are planting shrubs and roses, use the fork to break up the soil at the bottom of the trench.

3 Dig a second trench parallel to the first, turning the earth into the first trench, and add organic matter to the base. Repeat the process, digging trenches and adding organic matter, until you reach the end of the bed or area to be dug.

4 When you have dug the last trench, add your compost or manure, then tip or shovel in the very first load of soil you removed. You can then rake the bed over for a perfect finish.

- **KNOW WHEN NOT TO DIG** Do not dig if it's too wet – you will do more harm than good, compacting the soil and creating a mud bath. Never try to dig if the soil is frozen. Don't dig beyond your own physical limits. Digging is hard work, so do not attempt it at all if you are under the weather or tired, and always pace yourself, doing a little at a time. Use a smaller spade if you find it hard going. If you have stony or clay soils you may find that a fork is easier to use than a spade.
- **AVOID PROPAGATING WEEDS** Some pernicious weeds, including couch grass, bindweed, ground elder and creeping thistle, will grow from tiny pieces left in the soil and digging can worsen the situation. Ideally, spray these weeds with a systemic weedkiller (such as glyphosate) in summer or autumn [see p.248].

▲ **Raised beds** concentrate your efforts on a small space and their deep soil encourages vigorous root growth and productive plants. Once prepared they do not need digging. You do not need to edge them, but edging gives a neat finish and contains the organic matter that is regularly spread on the surface to nourish the soil.

Dispense with yearly digging
The no-dig method is a way of cultivating raised beds that, once the initial preparation is done, never need digging again. After digging once and removing all perennial weeds, you just add a thick layer of organic matter every year to keep in moisture, feed the soil and encourage worms.

YOU ONLY NEED DIG YOUR BEDS ONCE – THEN LET THE WORMS DO THE HARD WORK FOR YOU

- **DIVIDE YOUR PLOT INTO SMALL BEDS** Because you will not be digging your soil to let in air and relieve compaction, create beds that are small enough to enable you to cultivate your plants without walking on the soil and compressing it. Ideally, beds should be no more than 1.2m (4ft) across each way.
- **EDGE YOUR BEDS THE EASY WAY** Ready-made raised bed edging kits are about 15cm (6in) high, enough to increase the depth of soil for the no-dig method. If beds are higher they may dry out in summer and watering may become a chore.

Planting out

WITH GARDEN CENTRES WELL-STOCKED all year round it is tempting to buy plants for your borders whenever they catch your eye – but as with so many garden jobs, there are good and bad times for planting. Pick the right time and prepare the ground well to get the greatest rewards from your new acquisitions.

Give your plants the best start

Pick your season Spring and autumn are the traditional – and best – times to plant. In spring the soil is warming yet plants have time to establish before the heat of summer. This is a great time to set out young plants, slightly tender plants and evergreens. Summer planting means more work: while it is easy to be tempted by plants in flower, you will need to water almost daily for weeks until the roots spread into the surrounding soil. Add a few irresistible plants this way, but delay large-scale plantings of hardy perennials, trees and shrubs until autumn, which allows them months to establish before the heat and dryness of summer.

▼ **Remove plants** from small pots and cell trays by gently squeezing the sides of the pot; do not pull the plants out, or you will damage the roots. The rootballs will come out more easily if soaked first.

Don't be fooled by an early spring Most hardy plants can withstand a spring chill but bedding and slightly tender plants cannot. Garden centres should sell plants at the right time for planting – but you will always find tender plants for sale while late spring frosts are still possible. Be cautious. Keep plants in a greenhouse or a cold frame until all danger of frost is past, then get them used to the great outdoors gently, leaving them in a sheltered place for a week or so before planting [see also p.267].

Pamper young plants for best growth Any damage to the fragile root systems of young plants will set them back, so handle them gently and they will reward you with fast growth. Even if you have lots to plant, take time to scoop out a generous hole for each one and firm it in carefully.

● **POT UP PLUG PLANTS** into small pots or larger cell trays until they are established: they are too small to be planted out in outdoor conditions when you buy them. Grow them on in a greenhouse, coldframe or sheltered spot outside and if necessary, protect them from cold nights with a blanket of horticultural fleece.

- **SOAK BEFORE PLANTING** Water is essential to help your plants get established. It is very difficult to re-wet a dried-out rootball once the plant is in the ground, so soak the plants in their containers before planting. After planting, water plants in well so that the roots are in contact with the surrounding soil.
- **PLANT ON DULL DAYS** Don't plant bedding on a hot, sunny day: the plants will dry out and exposed roots may suffer. Pick a cool, overcast day if possible.

Planting for perfect perennials If you can bear the wait, perennials are much better planted young, in spring, to allow them to establish before they bloom. Garden centres increasingly sell perennials only in full flower, in mid-summer, and if you have to buy plants like this then be prepared to water regularly – daily in dry spells. It is, after all, a quick way to add instant colour to your borders and they will repeat the performance year after year.

- **BUY WITH CARE** Check the label to be sure your plants are perennial. Many large plants for sale may be annuals, especially in late summer. Annuals, such as pots of cosmos, give an instant splash of colour but will only last for a few months.
- **CHECK THE SIZE** Some plants are artificially dwarfed and are sold as compact plants. They may grow much larger in the second year. This applies especially to asters and chrysanthemums.

BEAT THAT!
- **The world record for planting out** the most bedding plants in the shortest time is held by Steve Thorpe, who in 2006 planted 2,021 plants in just one hour in Haworth Central Park, Bradford, Yorkshire. Don't try to emulate him – take time to plant out your bedding with care.

EXPERT KNOW HOW

PLANTING A CONTAINER-GROWN PERENNIAL

When planting out pot-grown plants the aim is to encourage the roots to grow out from the rootball into the soil. Mixing the surrounding soil with some potting or garden compost will help the plants to make the transition. The top of the plant rootball should end up flush with the surface of the surrounding soil.

1 Make sure the roots are well soaked. To ensure all the compost is wet, plunge the plant in a bucket of water for a few minutes until the bubbles stop rising.

2 Dig a generous planting hole, mix in some compost and soak the hole before planting. Add or remove soil until the plant is at the right height.

3 Position the plant in the centre of the hole and fill in with soil. Firm gently with your hands, adding more soil until level. Then give it another good soak.

● **SUPPORT YOUR BLOOMS** Tall, well-grown perennials such as delphiniums, lupins, heleniums and monarda will have packed their pots with roots, and if these are to grow into the surrounding soil the plants must be supported. Push a cane through the rootball and into the soil beneath to keep the plant steady.

Successful tree and shrub planting
Trees and shrubs will enhance your garden for many years, so you need to position them carefully and prepare the site well. You can plant woody plants all year round, but autumn is best. Keeping new woody plants well watered through summer can be a struggle: if you plant in autumn, the soil should be naturally moist for the next six months.

MAKE PLANTING HOLES AT LEAST TWICE AS BIG AS THE ROOTBALL OF THE TREE OR SHRUB

● **CHOOSE THE BEST PLANTS** Look at the rootball before buying shrubs and trees in pots. If you can barely see the compost for a mass of tightly packed roots, then select another specimen – such 'potbound' plants will not establish well.

● **ALLOW ROOTS ROOM TO SPREAD** Prepare a large planting hole, at least twice the width of the pot – do not squeeze the rootball into the soil. The latest thinking is that square holes are best, preventing the roots circling in the hole.

● **GET WATER TO THE ROOTS** To get water deep into the soil where tree roots need it most, set a pipe or a bottomless plastic bottle in the soil when planting.

● **AVOID PLANTING IN NEAT COMPOST** It is tempting to fill planting holes with organic matter and plant into that, imagining that this will give your new shrub or tree a treat. But resist the temptation. The roots will stay in this 'comfort zone' instead of venturing out into the soil, and the plant will become unstable and more vulnerable to drought. Mix the organic matter and soil together well.

HOW DOES IT WORK?

MYCORRHIZAL FUNGI PRODUCTS

These new products exploit a relationship between plant roots and a group of soil fungi that extract extra nutrients from the soil and 'share' them with the plants. They are especially important on poor, sandy soils where they help conifers to flourish. The fungi can be bought in packet form and added to the soil when planting. Many growers swear by their effectiveness in helping new plants establish faster.

Provide some support
The aim of staking trees and large shrubs is not to keep the stems upright but to prevent the roots moving in the soil. If the plant is rocked by wind, any delicate new roots that have formed will break, and although the plant may survive and flower, it will never get the chance to make much new growth.

● **KEEP STAKES SHORT** – you do not need to stake a tree right up to its neck. A short stake that keeps the base of the tree secure is best. Short stakes allow the trunk of a tree to flex and that makes it thicker and stronger, so your tree will be able to look after itself in a few years' time.

PLANTING A CONTAINER-GROWN TREE

This method can be used to plant young trees, standard roses and fruit bushes and any shrub, although only the largest shrubs will need staking. Before planting, stand the plant, in its pot, in water for a couple of hours, or ideally overnight, so that the compost is fully moistened.

1 Dig a generous hole and mix garden compost or other organic matter into the soil at the bottom and into the excavated soil. Sit the tree in the hole and use a cane to check that the tree will be planted at the same depth as it is in its pot, adding or removing soil below the pot as needed.

2 Remove the tree from its pot, set it in the hole and hold it steady. Pull the excavated soil and organic matter into the hole, firming it evenly with your knuckles or heel all around the tree so that the trunk stays vertical. Create a dish-shaped depression around the trunk to retain water where the tree needs it.

3 Use a short stake and knock it in at an angle so that you do not have to drive it through the rootball of your tree. Once it is firmly in position, secure the stake to the trunk with a purpose-made buckle-and-spacer tree tie which will allow the trunk to expand. Give the tree a good soak of water.

▶ **Check tree ties** regularly and loosen them if necessary to accommodate the trunk's expanding girth. After three or four years, the tie and stake can be removed.

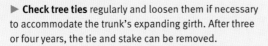

Watering

ALL PLANTS NEED WATER but not all need as much as we might think. Target your water efficiently to minimise waste, collect rainwater and reuse household water to cut down on your bills. Install easy-to-use, affordable irrigation systems for your garden and patio and watering need never again be a chore.

DELIVER WATER TO THE ROOTS, NOT OVER THE LEAVES, FOR MAXIMUM BENEFIT

Make your water go further

Use water wisely Plants take up water through their roots so sprinklers, which spray water all over the plants, are inefficient and waste water. It is always better to use a hose to direct water at the base of the plant where it is needed.

● **TARGET KEY PLANTS** Not all your plants need watering. The most vulnerable are those that are newly planted, plants in pots, and any plants that are positioned by walls, in beds under trees or by conifer hedges. Do not worry if established plants wilt in the heat. In most cases, as long as the plants are healthy, they will pull through, though growth and flowering may be affected.

● **WATER DEEP, WATER WELL** Frequent light watering encourages plants to form roots near the surface, just as far as the water penetrates. When this water evaporates, the roots are left high and dry. Give more water less often and it will penetrate deeper into the soil, and the roots of your plants will follow it.

● **WATER WHEN IT IS COOLEST**, in the evening or early in the morning. Plants will have time to absorb the water before it evaporates.

● **PUT THE WATER WHERE IT COUNTS** Direct water at the base of plants and avoid spraying it over the leaves. Make saucer-shaped depressions in the soil around plants so that water gets to the roots and does not run away over the surface.

Make the most of the rain Gallons of rainwater flow away down household drains that could be saved to water plants when the weather becomes dry. Water butts are easy to install and don't have to be ugly. Fit guttering on sheds and greenhouses, too, and harvest that free water.

● **WATER WHEN IT RAINS** It seems crazy – but watering in showery weather makes sense. The air will be humid, so evaporation will be reduced and your water will do more good than if applied in bright sunshine.

● **REMEMBER PLANTS THAT THE RAIN CANNOT REACH** Beds and borders near walls and buildings will not get the rain that the rest of the garden receives. Give plants in these beds special watering attention, especially with new plantings.

Get smart with automation

Watering can take up a lot of time, especially if you have lots of pots and hanging baskets. Run a porous soaker hose around your borders, on or under the soil. The water seeps out gently and slowly just where it is needed. Lay it along rows of vegetable plants and you will save yourself a lot of time watering. Drip irrigation systems are easy to set up and take water directly to your patio plants via spurs fitted to a central supply hose; simply turn on the tap, and your plants will receive a gentle, even watering. Attach a battery-powered water computer to your

◄ **A soaker or seep hose** is made from a porous material that allows water to leak very slowly into the soil all along its length. Simply turn on the water – or fit an automatic timer to your tap and your young or precious plants will receive a gentle watering at a set time every day.

HOW DOES IT WORK?
HOW PLANTS CAN 'DROWN'

Plants can suffer from overwatering as well as drought, so don't overdo it. Plant roots need to breathe air, just like the rest of the plant, so if the roots are under water for long periods, they will suffocate and die. This is more of a problem with potted plants but if your borders are poorly drained, it may explain why plants die.

Foliage wilts as if plants are dry

Standing water encourages rot at stem bases

Water displaces air around roots

TOP TIPS FOR SURVIVING DROUGHT

Most people look forward to long, hot summers, but they can be a nightmare for gardeners. But there are plenty of clever ways to help your garden plants survive the perfect summer.

◀ In a sunny, dry position, choose plants that prefer these conditions. A passion flower, for example, is a better choice for a south-facing wall than a clematis or honeysuckle. Silver and grey-leaved plants such as lavenders, stachys (lamb's ears) and santolina are naturally adapted to drought conditions [see also p.102]. They may even struggle in moist soils.

● Avoid the need for continual watering of new plants by planting in autumn, when evaporation is minimal and the soil should naturally receive lots of moisture for months.

● Mulch to reduce soil water evaporation (see facing page). There is a range of materials to choose from, from purely decorative mulches to organic ones that also improve the soil.

● Hoeing is not just a way of controlling weeds. Regular light hoeing, close to the surface, creates a dust-dry 'mulch' of loose soil that reduces evaporation.

● Group container plants together to reduce the area that the sun strikes and create a larger canopy of growth to shade the compost surface.

outside tap and your watering will be completely automated; you simply programme in your 'start' and 'stop' times and the device does the rest. The most basic timers cost little more than a garden hose.

Recycle household water Plants don't need clean water from the tap to grow and survive. It makes sense to re-use water used for bathing or washing vegetables to irrigate plants, making the water you have to pay for do double duty. In the kitchen, for example, use a washing-up bowl to wash and prepare fruit and vegetables, rather than putting them straight in the sink. It makes it that bit easier to take the water out to your plants – and then put any peelings on the compost.

PLANTS DO NOT NEED CLEAN DRINKING WATER – YOUR BATHWATER WILL SUIT THEM JUST FINE

● **CATCH WATER BEFORE IT DRAINS AWAY** The detergents used in washing machines and dishwashers are too harsh for plants, but bathwater suits most plants. Avoid using it long-term for container plants or plants sensitive to soil pH, such as camellias. If your bathroom is conveniently sited, you can use plastic tubing to siphon the water out of the window directly on to the garden (wait for it to cool down first) or collect into a butt for later use. Alternatively, fit a diverter on the downpipe from the bath or shower to fill containers to water your garden.
● **AVOID UNPLEASANT SMELLS** Household water – known as grey water – can be stored but it may start to smell, so make sure storage containers can be sealed. If the water in a water butt begins to smell, there are mild, non-toxic sterilising products on the market that will keep it sweet.

Using mulches

Lock in the moisture A mulch is a layer of anything, from compost to old carpet, that creates a physical barrier between the soil and the air, reducing evaporation. Mulches are most effective around new or widely spaced plants. Always apply a mulch after rain, or a good soak with water.

- **MAKE THE MOST OF MULTIPURPOSE MULCHES** Mulches do not just retain moisture. They also prevent annual weeds growing, and if thick enough, they can help the soil warm up in spring and insulate it from cold in winter. Use organic mulching materials such as garden compost, manure, bark chippings and cocoa shells that will eventually mingle with and improve the soil – and encourage helpful earthworms, too.
- **CHOOSE GEOTEXTILES FOR TOTAL COVERAGE** These weed-suppressing fabrics keep weeds under control and they also retain moisture. On a new bed, first remove any perennial weeds, then lay the fabric and peg it down. Cut holes to plant through and then disguise the fabric with a layer of bark, gravel or pebbles.

Get mulching materials for free You can use materials from the house and garden that you would otherwise throw away to mulch your plants. Not only do they cost nothing; they can save trips to the recycling centre. With a shredder, you can reuse woody prunings as a free mulch. Fresh wood chips and shavings are said to rob the soil of nitrogen as they decompose, so to be on the safe side, either compost them first or add extra nitrogen in the form of powdered hoof and horn, a slow-release fertiliser. In the vegetable garden, cardboard and newpaper makes a good mulch, either along rows or around large plants like squashes. Cover with grass clippings, which can also be a problem to dispose of, and the entire mulch will be rotted down by autumn and feed the soil.

▲ **Use a circle** of geotextile and bark to mulch new trees. Do not let the grass grow right up to the trunk – it will compete with the tree for water and food and you may damage the trunk when you trim the grass.

▼ **As well as being useful,** mulches can look good. An even covering of composted bark, cocoa shells or gravel will set off your plants to perfection, and helps moisture-loving plants, such as these hostas, survive dry spells.

Weeding

GARDENERS FACE A CONSTANT BATTLE against weeds. Nature hates bare soil and if you dig it, clear it or make a new bed, weeds are sure to grow unless you plant something else and keep them down. Get to know the tools and techniques that can reduce the impact of weeds, and cut down your weeding workload.

Show weeds who's boss

Don't give ground to weeds
If you plant densely so that the ground is covered, or mulch deeply between your plants, weeds won't have space or light to grow and weed seeds will not germinate. Use fast-growing, spreading perennials [see p.83] or plant bedding thickly. You may need to weed at first but once the plants begin to interlock the weeds won't stand a chance.

Nip weeds in the bud
The key to controlling weeds is to tackle them early, before they spread or set seed. Take the upper hand and don't give them a chance to swamp your plants. It's also important to know what weeds you are dealing with. Annual weeds live less than one year, but grow fast. They propagate themselves from seeds that may blow in from neighbouring ground. Hoe them off or spray them before they flower; do not let them set seed and reproduce.

Perennial weeds such as bindweed and couch grass survive year after year, spreading by means of underground or creeping stems. Chopping off the tops merely slows these plants down. They must be dug out, ensuring every small piece of root is removed, or killed with weedkiller. Do not add the remains to your compost heap.

● **HOE IN DRY WEATHER** Hoeing is most effective when the weather is hot and dry. In wet weather there is a chance that weeds could root again (especially groundsel and chickweed); if you have to hoe when the ground is moist, rake up the weeds, let them dry out and add them to the compost.

● **SMOTHER WEED GROWTH** Prevent weed growth when creating low-maintenance shrub plantings by planting the shrubs through holes made in geotextile fabric pegged over the soil [see p.150]. The fabric can be covered with an attractive mulch to disguise it.

CHOOSING THE RIGHT WEEDKILLER

Weedkillers work in different ways: to get the best results and avoid wasting money, match the right weedkiller to your weeds. Most weedkillers (apart from lawn weedkillers) are not selective and will kill any plant that gets sprayed, so use them on dry, still days so that the spray does not drift onto your garden plants.

☐ **CONTACT WEEDKILLERS**

Often working within hours, many of these products are based on natural substances and strip the waxy coating of the leaf. The weeds quickly wither (in hot weather) and die. These products are only effective on annual weeds.

☐ **SYSTEMIC WEEDKILLERS**

When sprayed onto a weed these are absorbed by the plant and interfere with its growth in such a way that the plant dies. They may take a week or more to show any effect. They are effective against perennial weeds.

USING WEEDKILLERS AROUND THE GARDEN

When weeds grow among plants or on hard surfaces, digging them out can be difficult or impossible, and chemical products may be needed. Always choose a still day to avoid spray drift onto garden plants, and wear gloves.

PROTECT OTHER PLANTS

Hold a sheet of thick card between your plant and the weed. Spray, wait a few moments and move on. Always offer up the same side of the card to the weeds.

KEEP EQUIPMENT SEPARATE

Concentrated products require dilution and are applied with a watering can or sprayer: never use the can or sprayer for anything other than weedkilling.

SPRAY PATHS AND GRAVEL

A systemic product will kill leafy weeds on hard surfaces; mosses and algae require specialist products, some of which are suitable for decking.

Vanquish problem weeds Although many gardeners shun weedkillers, they are safe to use and should not pose any harm to wildlife. Use them on tough weed problems such as infestations of perennial weeds and you can spend more time on more enjoyable garden tasks. It is essential to remember that weedkillers do not distinguish between garden plants and garden weeds. Keep weedkiller off your plants by putting a plastic cone or funnel over the spray nozzle, using a sheet of stout cardboard to shield plants (see above), or placing plastic carrier bags or bin bags over plants to protect them until the weedkiller is dry.

● **REMOVE PLANTS TO SAFETY** Sometimes it is easier to rescue perennials and bulbs from beds infested with perennial weeds than to try to weed around them. Dig the plants up in autumn or early spring, rinse the roots thoroughly and tease out every scrap of weed root. Pot the plants up, clear the ground of weeds and then replant.

● **CLEAR NEW BEDS FOR PLANTING** When there are no valuable plants in a border it is easy to spray weeds thoroughly. Systemic weedkillers are most effective when the weeds are growing vigorously, so spray when the soil is moist in spring or summer. These products are absorbed by plant leaves, so do not spray tiny, emerging shoots, but wait until the weeds have plenty of leafy growth. Some perennial weeds, such as ground elder, are very persistent, and may need repeated applications of weedkiller. An organic alternative to spraying is to smother these weeds with a light-excluding covering of geotextile fabric, black plastic or old carpet, but be prepared to wait for several months for the weeds to succumb.

● **CLEAR PATHS AND PATIOS** with a path weedkiller, which usually contains a combination of chemicals that will kill existing weeds and prevent any weed seeds from germinating. Do not use these products on beds and borders.

▼ **Annual weeds** can produce thousands of seeds, so hoe them off when young. If you choose a dry day, the weeds can be left on the soil surface to die and, eventually, rot down into your soil.

Pruning made easy

WE PRUNE THE WOODY PLANTS in our gardens to keep them
healthy but we can also influence and improve their growth with judicious pruning
at the right time of year. Find out how, with just a few simple techniques, you can
encourage your trees and shrubs to develop attractive forms and flower as never before.

Essential pruning know-how

Prune to keep plants healthy Trees and shrubs naturally shed
dead and dying twigs and branches in harsh, windy weather, but by the time
this happens, disease may have spread into the rest of the plant, eventually
killing it. When you see diseased or dead stems on garden shrubs and small trees,
you can minimise the risk of further damage to the plant by pruning them out
immediately, cutting well back into wood that is perfectly sound.

● **LET AIR INTO DENSE GROWTH** As plants grow older their branches become
congested. These conditions encourage fungal diseases, so thin out crowded
branches to improve air circulation and keep plants healthy.

● **KEEP PLANTS TRUE TO TYPE** Variegated shrubs (those with attractive leaf
markings or splashes) often produce shoots with plain green leaves that, if left,
can overwhelm the shrub. Cut them out as soon as you see them. Plants grafted
onto rootstocks such as roses and fruit trees [see p.217] often produce shoots from
below the graft union. They may spring up from ground level, as in the case of
rose suckers, or grow from the trunk of a top-grafted plant such as a standard rose
or a weeping Kilmarnock willow. These shoots also need to be removed.

HOW DOES IT WORK?

CUTTING TO A BUD

Plant growth is regulated by hormones within the plant.
There is a particular concentration of hormones in the
shoot tips that encourages the tip to lengthen while
also suppressing growth in the buds below. When the
shoot tip is removed, the plant redirects its energies
and buds lower down develop into shoots. If you want
a stem to grow in a particular direction, find a bud that
is pointing that way and make an angled pruning cut
just above it **(1)**, and a new shoot should grow. With
plants that have pairs of buds opposite each other,
make a straight cut above a pair **(2)**.

STAR PERFORMERS...

RIGHT TOOL FOR THE JOB

Choosing the right tools for your pruning will make the task easier and also prevent damage to your shrubs and trees.

1 Secateurs Used for light pruning and deadheading almost all year round, these are suitable for cutting through stems up to a pencil-thickness.

2 Loppers Like giant secateurs with a more powerful bite, and used for pruning stems up to 2cm (¾in) thick.

3 Pruning saw Narrow-bladed for tight gaps, these cut on the backward stroke.

4 Bow saw For thick branches, and tidying up rough pruning-saw cuts.

Make clean cuts Always use sharp, clean tools so that cuts are neat, with minimal damage to the stem tissue. Rough wounds encourage disease to enter and this may spread into the rest of the plant. 'Wound paint' is available for sealing big cuts made with a saw, although not all experts agree on its usefulness.

● **CUT TO A BUD** Always cut just above a bud, or pair of buds, where these are visible, or just above the junction of a sideshoot or stem. If you leave stubs, they tend to die back and this dieback can spread down into the healthy stem. This is especially true of roses: when pruning these in winter, look for a 'dot with an eyebrow' on the stem – which is a dormant bud.

● **AVOID SPREADING DISEASE** Keep your secateurs clean by wiping with disinfectant on a cloth or a disinfectant wipe after each task, and you will avoid transferring the micro-organisms that cause disease from one plant to another.

Maintain shapely plants When selecting shrubs, always check their eventual height and spread to avoid buying plants that will become too big for the site you have in mind. Unless you are planting a hedge, for example, where regular light pruning is used to keep plants within bounds, pruning to make a big shrub smaller can spoil its natural shape and affect flowering – and it is an unnecessary chore. Most species of shrub include varieties of different sizes, so research the options and choose the one that will fit your space without intervention. An exception to this rule is a small number of plants that are naturally very big but in gardens are commonly hard-pruned to remain small in size with much bigger leaves – these include cotinus, eucalyptus and catalpa [see also p.149].

THE FOUR BASIC PRUNING METHODS

Different shrubs call for different pruning methods, according to how they grow and the role they play in your plantings. These four basic methods apply to most of the plants in your garden. Another method used on some fruit trees, climbers and wall shrubs is spur-pruning [see p.148].

THE SPRING CHOP

Hard pruning in spring encourages vigorous new shoots. Use this method on plants that are grown for the colour of their new stems (cornus), that flower on new growth in summer (buddleias) or that are grown for their foliage (catalpa). Use secateurs or loppers.

THE LIGHT TRIM

This can be done at any time and is necessary in spring on evergreens grown for neat, small foliage or in midsummer on shrubs that flower early, such as santolina and lavender. Most of these plants have small leaves and you can trim them with shears.

THE SHAPE

Large shrubs and evergreens can have branches removed or shortened to create a better shape, or to clear low branches away. It should not be necessary to do this every year. Use loppers or a pruning saw, and cut well within the plant to hide the cut.

THE THIN

The branches of some shrubs get old and lose vigour and are replaced by new shoots from the base. Thinning out old stems, cutting them out at the base, keeps plants healthy, allows room for new growth and will not prevent flowering. Use loppers.

● **KEEP EVERGREENS SHAPELY** Evergreen shrubs can develop middle-aged spread as they mature and may obstruct paths or views of other plants. Splayed-out branches may also be vulnerable to breakage in areas that experience heavy snowfall. Prune conifers, bay, laurel and other evergreens where necessary to improve their shape from late summer, after they have stopped growing, to winter.

● **MAINTAIN A FORM** Plants selected for the attractive way that their stems grow, for example *Viburnum plicatum* 'Mariesii', can produce wayward shoots that spoil the shape. Cut these back to where they arise from a main stem.

Improve flowering performance Pruning can enhance flowering on most deciduous shrubs (those that lose their leaves in winter) by removing less productive older wood, but timing is critical – prune at the wrong time and you could cut off potential flowers. Shrubs that flower in spring to midsummer should never be hard-pruned if you want them to flower next year. Thin them instead by removing some old stems at the base, leaving the younger stems intact to produce next year's flowering shoots. Shrubs that bloom in late summer produce their flowers at the end of long shoots that start growing in spring. Hard pruning – cutting right back – in spring encourages new, vigorous shoots that will bear larger flower heads.

Make cuts at the right time Don't expose your plants to danger by pruning at the wrong time. Summer-flowering shrubs that are slightly tender – such as cistus, choisya, lavatera – should be pruned in late spring, after frosts have passed, to avoid exposing delicate buds to the cold.

● **FOR HEALTHY FLOWERING CHERRIES** prune only in summer, when they are in leaf. Never prune in winter when the spores of a disease called silver leaf are in the air and can infect cut surfaces. Flowering cherries and fruiting cherry and plum trees are very susceptible to this disease.

▲ **A philadelphus** pruned in the right way will reward you with a mass of fragrant blooms. Thin it after flowering, removing old branches by cutting low down – never give this shrub a 'haircut'.

Pinch-prune for showier plants You can influence not only flowering but the number and size of flowers on some perennials with a type of pruning called pinch-pruning. Using just your fingertips, remove the small sideshoots and buds on a stem, for example on dahlias and chrysanthemums, to leave one, or a few, flowers: if there are fewer flowers on a stem to support, they will grow bigger than usual. If, however, you want a bushier dahlia or tender fuchsia with lots of flowers, pinch out the growing tips of all the shoots in spring before flowerbuds form; the stems will branch to result in more flowers overall.

THE RIGHT TIME FOR PRUNING

Knowing which time of year is best for pruning is actually quite simple once you understand that most plants flower on either the current season's growth, or on stems that grew the previous year. Think about when your plants come into bloom or fruit and follow these guidelines for timely and effective pruning.

☐ EARLY SPRING

● Hard-prune summer-flowering shrubs that flower on that season's growth, such as *Buddleja davidii*, bush roses, caryopteris and perovskia, and late-flowering (viticella) clematis.
● Most trees are best pruned in spring, at the beginning of their growing season, as the rising sap will help to heal the wounds.

☐ MID–LATE SPRING

● Prune early-flowering shrubs and climbers such as such as forsythia and *Clematis montana* once they have finished flowering.
● Pinch-prune the shoot tips of dahlias, chrysanthemums and fuchsias for bushier plants. A very light trim of lavender with shears will also have the same effect.

☐ LATE SUMMER

● Prune plants that flower in midsummer, on stems that grew the previous year – for example, weigela – after flowering.
● Prune trees that naturally have a high circulation of sap now so they won't "bleed" too heavily; these include birches, cherries, maples and walnuts.
● Prune broad-leaved evergreens only if needed for health and shape.

☐ AUTUMN & WINTER

● Prune summer-flowering shrubs that flower on shoots developed earlier in the same year. Frosts can damage cut stems, so if weather is poor, leave pruning until spring.
● Trim lavender to remove the faded flower stems.
● Prune conifers in autumn or early winter if necessary, but avoid frosty spells.

Overwintering plants

MANY OF THE LOVELIEST PLANTS in our gardens come from regions with climates warmer than ours, and not all are hardy enough to survive cold winters. With a little preparation and a few simple techniques you can ensure that your tender plants survive to give you pleasure year after year.

Prepare for the inevitable

Don't leave it too late We know winter is coming so don't bury your head in the sand – prepare for the cold and your plants will be safe.
- **LIFT AND STORE** the tubers of dahlias, cannas, begonias and gladioli, which cannot be relied on to survive outside [see also Bulbs, pp.126–7].
- **TAKE PLANTS INDOORS** Make sure large frost-tender plants survive by growing them in pots and moving them into a frost-free greenhouse in autumn.
- **GROW REPLACEMENT PLANTS** from cuttings of vulnerable plants that you might lose to cold, such as fuchsias, pelargoniums and penstemons. Take the cuttings in late summer and you will have new plants to set out in spring.

Protect plants from winter wet Cold, wet soil can be far more damaging to some plants than cold dry soil. Grow plants that hate 'wet feet', such as those from Mediterranean regions, in well-drained soil or compost that will stay relatively dry in winter. (Bone-dry soil can kill plants, especially evergreens in pots, so aim for soil or compost that is barely moist.) Add grit and sharp sand before planting to improve drainage. Do not add organic matter, which will increase soil moisture.
- **PLANT BY A WALL** Walls prevent rain reaching the soil and can help vulnerable plants survive. A south-facing wall will catch every ray of winter sun, too.

STAR PERFORMERS...

WINTER-HARDY CROPS

While crops may not grow appreciably in winter, there are a number of hardy vegetables that will stand well in the ground through the cold months. They even include a salad leaf – peppery land cress.

- Brussels sprouts
◀ Kales (curly kale and black-leaved Nero di Toscana, also known as cavolo nero)
- Land cress
- Leeks
- Parsnips (said to taste best after frost)
- Savoy cabbage
- Shrubby herbs (bay, rosemary and sage)

HELPING PLANTS SURVIVE IN THE WINTER GARDEN

Not all plants that are vulnerable to cold can be moved under cover to protect them in winter. There are easy, cheap and simple ways to help your plants survive outside in the garden provided that you take action in good time.

◀ Wrap tall plants in loosely tied fleece from late autumn until spring. To protect the crowns of tree ferns, where the fronds spring from, first wrap the trunks, then fill a fleece bag with leaves or straw and tie it over the top. Alternatively, make a cage with chicken wire and canes and pack it with straw.

◀ Cover plants that have died back low to the ground, such as agapanthus, alstroemeria and crinums, with straw, dry leaves or bracken, held in place with wire netting. Keep the mulch loose and never use plastic, which encourages rot. You may find that wildlife appreciates these winter shelters, too.

● **RAISE YOUR POTS** Keep containers off the ground by setting them on special 'pot feet', bricks or other supports so that water can pass through the drainage holes, preventing waterlogging of the compost.

● **KEEP THE RAIN OFF** Protect plants with an open-ended plastic or glass cloche [see p.261] to keep off rain while still allowing air to circulate.

Safeguard patio and container plants Move plants that may fall victim to the cold into a greenhouse or other light, frost-free place wherever possible. Deciduous plants such as fuchsias and some agapanthus (the ones that die down in winter) can be kept in a garage, but check on them occasionally as they need a little watering. Large pots can be hard to handle, but there are wheeled pot movers that make the job easier.

● **CHOOSE THE RIGHT POT** Plastic and metal pots offer no insulation from cold (or heat in summer). Terracotta pots protect roots from cold but unless fully frostproof (not 'frost-resistant') they may crack in winter. Wood, rigid foam and double-skinned plastic pots give the most protection.

● **WRAP YOUR POTS** Layers of bubble plastic will protect valuable pots and the roots of the plants within them. Do not take the wrapping up around the stems or cover foliage in plastic, or rots will develop and kill your plants.

● **USE LOST HEAT** Move pots of vulnerable plants beside the house where lost heat from the wall, plus shelter from the rain, will aid their survival.

HOW DOES IT WORK?
WHY IS FROST SO DAMAGING?

When plant cells freeze they rupture and their fluid content is lost, which is why frost-damaged growth appears desiccated and scorched. Soft, young growth is especially vulnerable. Plants that have evolved in climates with cold winters have developed a natural 'antifreeze' to prevent cell damage but when tender plants freeze, their tissue is damaged irreparably.

Greenhouses

A GREENHOUSE ADDS a new dimension to gardening, allowing **you** to grow a wider range of plants over a longer growing season. Discover how it can provide a cosy environment in which to raise seedlings, nurture delicate flowering plants and produce bumper crops – and offer a refuge in inclement weather.

YOUR GREENHOUSE CAN BE THE ENGINE ROOM FOR GROWING THE EARLIEST CROPS

A garden within a garden

Add a new dimension The shelter provided by a greenhouse will allow you to garden whatever the weather. You can use it to start the growing season early, garden in the rain, raise warmth-loving crops and protect tender plants in winter. It's also perfect for cultivating gorgeous flowering plants such as fuchsias and pelargoniums whose blooms will be unspoilt by cold and rain. But if a greenhouse is beyond your budget, consider a polytunnel – an unheated plastic, tent-like structure that is ideal for raising and growing fruit and vegetable plants.

● **CAN A CONSERVATORY DO THE SAME JOB?** 'Garden rooms' with soft furnishings are not practical for raising plants, but there is a middle way between a greenhouse and a conservatory that could meet your needs: a lean-to greenhouse, supported by a house wall, is practical for growing plants while providing a snug and convenient sanctuary from adverse weather conditions.

To heat or not to heat? Even though heating costs may continue to increase, most gardeners still choose to heat their greenhouses to increase the range of plants that can be grown. A 'cool' greenhouse heated just enough to keep out frost – to about 5°C (40°F) – allows you to keep valuable tender plants over winter, raise new plants from seeds and grow many hobby plants. To grow absolutely everything a 'warm' greenhouse is required – heated to a minimum of 10°C (50°F). It will cost more to run, and is really only an option for gardeners who want to keep very specialised plants, such as orchids.

● **CHOOSE THE BEST HEATING OPTION FOR YOU** Bottled gas is reliable, controllable and clean but produces water vapour that can cause problems with moulds in winter. Electric fan heaters are inexpensive as long as you already have a power supply in the greenhouse. They give you good control over the temperature, and the circulating air spreads the heat and helps prevent fungal diseases. Paraffin heaters provide a steady heat, but it may not be adequate on cold nights. These heaters need constant maintenance to prevent the production of damaging fumes.

● **HAVE THE BEST OF BOTH WORLDS** by dividing your greenhouse with bubble plastic sheeting and only heating half for the plants that really need it. Use the unheated half for plants that just need shelter from winter wet and severe frosts.

◀ **With the protection** of even a modest greenhouse you can sow your seeds early and buy young vegetable plants as soon as they appear in garden centres, giving you the best choice of plants and varieties.

STAR PERFORMERS...

FOR A COOL GREENHOUSE

With just a few degrees of heat to protect plants from frost, especially at night, you can grow lots of special plants.

● Cacti
● Camellias (for perfect flowers protected from frosts)
● A fig tree
● Freesias
● Non-hardy fuchsias
● Grapevines
● A peach or nectarine tree, fan-trained or in a pot
● Regal and angel pelargoniums
◀ Schizanthus

The healthy greenhouse

Manage the microclimate
Your greenhouse plants rely on you for their growing needs. Cool them and water them well in hot weather, protect them from scorching sun, and keep them warm and give them light in winter to ensure that it is the plants, and not pests and diseases, that thrive.

● **KEEP IT CLEAN** Fungal diseases spread quickly from dead plants to living ones in winter so pick up and pick off dead flowers and leaves before problems start.

● **MAXIMISE LIGHT AND VENTILATION** Keep greenhouse glass clean, both inside and out. Open the vents whenever possible to keep the air cool in summer and help prevent fungal diseases such as mildew taking hold in autumn, winter and spring.

Keep pests in check
The protected environment of a greenhouse perfectly suits some warmth-loving pests as well as your plants. Look over plants weekly, or whenever you water, for insect pests; be sure to check the undersides of leaves.

● **CATCH WINGED PESTS WITH TRAPS** Chemical-free sticky traps will catch flying insects. Always place them just above the plants, not in the roof eaves. Brush the plants to disturb any pests so that they fly up on to the traps.

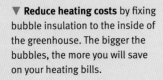

▲ **Control sap-sucking** whitefly on your tomatoes and fuchsias with chemical-free sticky traps. Different pests are attracted to different colours, so you can customise your traps to match your pests.

GOOD GREENHOUSE HYGIENE AND VENTILATION KEEPS PLANTS HEALTHY AND PEST NUMBERS LOW

● **USE PEST PREDATORS** Red spider mite, whitefly and mealy bug can be controlled with other, tiny insects that prey on them. These biological controls [see pp.275–6] are available to buy from garden centres or by mail order. Do not use them in tandem with insecticides, which will kill the helpful predators as well as the pests.

● **GET TO THE ROOTS** Use systemic insecticides that are poured on to the soil and taken up by the plants to kill sap-sucking pests like mealy bug and scale.

● **MAKE LIFE TOUGH FOR RED SPIDER MITE** by wetting the greenhouse floor in hot weather. This increases the humidity, which these troublesome mites hate.

● **SUCK UP PESTS** A hand-held rechargeable mini-vacuum cleaner is a fantastic tool in the greenhouse; you can literally make pests disappear.

▼ **Reduce heating costs** by fixing bubble insulation to the inside of the greenhouse. The bigger the bubbles, the more you will save on your heating bills.

Buffer extremes of temperature
in the greenhouse to keep your plants happy in summer and reduce your bills in winter.

● **PROTECT PLANTS FROM THE SUN** with shading to keep temperatures down in high summer. Paint-on shading is inexpensive and easy to apply (and remove in autumn), and does not interfere with vent-opening. Or, fix fleece to the inside with glazing clips, or roll netting over the outside and thread canes through to secure it to the gutters.

● **INSULATE IN WINTER** Heated air is expensive to produce. Reduce heat loss by installing bubble plastic insulation in the autumn, taking it down in the spring. Insulation reduces light levels in the greenhouse, so before putting it in place, move plants outside and wash and scrub the glass so your plants get as much of the weak winter sunlight as possible.

THE HIGH-PERFORMANCE GREENHOUSE

Everyone uses their greenhouse in the summer, even if only to grow tomato plants, but there is no excuse to use it just to store your barbecue in winter. Plan, be adventurous and find ways to use your greenhouse all year round.

SPRING

- Sow bedding plants; you get a much wider choice of varieties by starting from seed.

◀ Make up your hanging baskets early so they are well established when you hang them out in late spring.

- Sow peppers and tomatoes. Growing from seed gives you a greater choice of varieties.

- Sow your cabbages and other brassicas throughout spring for planting out in late spring and summer.

- Start regular watering and potting on of tender plants that have overwintered in the greenhouse.

- Check stored summer bulbs such as cannas for soft rots and plant out only the healthy specimens.

SUMMER

- Grow your own pesto. Basil loves the warmth and sun of a greenhouse and is traditionally grown under tomatoes. Greenhouse warmth brings out its flavour.

- Enjoy early fruit by growing strawberries in pots. Keep them outside until spring then bring into the greenhouse so that they flower earlier and crop before those grown outside.

- Feed and water your ripening tomatoes regularly to swell the crop.

▶ Sow spring bedding such as primulas and forget-me-nots for garden colour next year.

- Deadhead flowering plants, which should be at their beautiful best.

- Take cuttings from hardy shrubs, including evergreens.

AUTUMN

- Enjoy tender crops such as aubergines, peppers and chillies; a greenhouse extends the ripening season for these heat-loving plants.

◀ Plant up pots of bulbs for outside display and prepared hyacinths for spring scent in the home.

- Sow pots of leafy herbs for winter, especially parsley.

- Sow seeds of salad crops and oriental leaves for supplies throughout the autumn and into winter.

- Protect tender container plants by bringing them in. Pull off any dead leaves and check for pests beforehand.

- Take cuttings of tender plants such as fuchsias and pelargoniums so you have lots for your pots next year.

WINTER

- Store dahlias for next year by lifting them from the garden, drying and cleaning them and storing under the bench, covered in paper or fleece.

- Cut blooms from perpetual carnations and late chrysanthemums growing in pots.

- Pot up lily bulbs for early flowers on the patio next year.

- Keep plants safe by watering them as needed and checking heaters periodically.

▶ Enjoy fresh salads such as lambs lettuce, winter lettuce and land cress sown in autumn.

- From midwinter, start sowing half-hardy annuals and early vegetables in a propagator to get ahead next year.

Coldframes and cloches

THESE SMALL GLASS OR PLASTIC STRUCTURES can be used to give your plants a flying start. Their low cost, versatility and ease of use make them real winners in the garden. Best of all, cloches and even some coldframes can be moved around to wherever plants need protection from the worst of the cold.

Mini-greenhouses for big results

Beat the chill with a coldframe These low structures, which have a transparent lid and either solid or see-through sides, can stand on soil or on hard surfaces – or be moved around to to give seasonal protection to vegetables. Coldframes made from wood and double-skinned polycarbonate give plants more protection from cold in winter but plastic and glass give plants more light.

● **RAISE YOUR OWN PLANTS** A coldframe is the ideal place to sow seeds in late spring and in autumn, to grow plants from cuttings throughout summer and to grow on young plants before you put them in the garden.

SOWING IN POTS FOR A COLDFRAME

A coldframe will protect spring-sown seeds and encourage them to germinate, but other seeds need cold conditions in winter before they will grow in spring (see Star Performers, facing page). The protected environment of a coldframe is perfect for these seeds, but be prepared to wait for growth to appear.

1 Fill pots with a multipurpose compost, firm it down and then water thoroughly. Sow a pinch or two of seed evenly over the surface.

2 Seeds that are to stand in the frame over winter should be covered with fine grit (above). Otherwise, cover with a thin layer of compost.

3 Once the seedlings appear and develop true leaves, transplant them carefully into individual pots, or the cells of a module tray [see p.267].

STAR PERFORMERS...

SEEDS TO SOW IN A COLDFRAME

Many seeds that you can collect from plants in your garden will benefit from the protection of a coldframe. Try sowing a pot or two this year.

- Aquilegias (sow in spring)
- Delphiniums (sow in spring)
- Eryngiums (sow in autumn)
- Forget-me-nots (sow in summer)
- Foxgloves (sow in summer)
- Hellebores (sow in autumn)
- Parsley (sow in spring or autumn)
- Primulas (sow in summer)
- Sweet williams (sow in summer)
- Wallflowers (sow in spring)

- **GROW SUMMER-FRUITING CROPS** Use your coldframe to grow bush tomatoes, planted in a growing bag in late spring. The protection from cold and wet will allow them to grow away well. In summer, you can close the lid in the evenings and on cool summer days to give the fruits the heat they need to ripen perfectly.
- **ENJOY WINTER SALADS** Sow salads in a coldframe, in the soil or in pots, in late summer and you will be picking fresh leaves through autumn and winter.
- **PROTECT YOUR PLANTS** Keep young plants safe from extremes of cold in winter. For extra protection in very cold spells, cover the frame with old carpet at night.

Be prepared with bell cloches
Pop bell cloches over plants you need to protect in a hurry. Whether plastic or glass, they will keep frost and rain off spring flowers and young vegetable plants, and stop birds attacking them.
- **MAKE YOUR OWN MINI-BELL CLOCHES** from see-through plastic bottles, cutting away and discarding the base. Put them over young seedlings or to provide extra warmth and frost protection for outdoor-sown seeds of beans and sweetcorn. Leave the cap on at first for warmth, then remove it to allow some ventilation.

Protect rows with tunnel cloches
Whether glass or polythene, tunnel cloches provide an inexpensive way to protect rows of plants against the elements. You can also use them to create favourable sowing conditions. Place them over the soil for a couple of weeks prior to sowing to warm and dry the soil: it will be easier to sow into and your seeds will grow and not just rot.
- **THWART BIRDS AND OTHER PESTS** by creating a barrier with plastic or fleece cloches over vulnerable plants. Put them over young brassicas, and on sowings of carrots to keep off carrot fly.
- **MOVE CLOCHES AROUND TO MAXIMISE THEIR USEFULNESS** through the year. Use them to protect seedlings in spring and keep caterpillars off cabbages in summer, then put them over bush tomatoes to help them ripen, or onions to help them dry. Then place them over late sowings of salads, or over celeriac and leeks to keep them in perfect condition.

▼ **Tunnel cloches** may be constructed from plates of glass supported by a wire frame, or bought ready-made with wire hoops fixed in polythene. They are perfect for protecting young peas and early salads from inclement weather and hungry pigeons.

Raising your own plants

HOWEVER MUCH YOU ENJOY BUYING PLANTS, nothing beats the satisfaction of growing your own. Raising healthy young plants is easy, and costs a fraction of garden centre prices. You don't need lots of equipment: many seeds can be sown straight in the ground, and cuttings will grow on a windowsill.

STAR PERFORMERS...

TOP PLANTS FOR COLLECTING SEEDS

Most of these plants hold their seed in pods or capsules so it is easy to collect. All grow well from home-collected seeds.

- Aquilegias
- Foxgloves
- Hollyhocks
- Lupins
- Marigolds
- ◄ Poppies
- Sweet peas
- Wallflowers

Collecting your own seeds

Grow more of your garden plants
Almost every plant in your garden will set enough seed to fill an entire border, but not all seeds are easy to collect or clean, or practical to grow. Trees and shrubs can be grown from seed, but will take many years to mature. Berries are fiddly to prepare, and fluffy seeds or those that are dispersed suddenly when the seed capsules pop open can be tricky to collect. If you are new to seed-raising, start with some annuals and easily grown perennials (see Star Performers, facing page). You can never be sure that all the seedlings you grow will be the same as their parents – that is part of the fun. But the highly bred F1 hybrids [see p.178] never breed true to type; you need to buy them fresh every year to guarantee you will have the same plants blooming as you did last season.

Harvest seed at the right time
Collect your seeds when they are ripe for the best results. Wait until pods and capsules turn from green to brown or straw-coloured, but before they split. Pick them on a still, dry day and put the pods in a paper bag or on a sheet of paper in a tray so the seeds can dry naturally. With marigolds and dahlias, cut off old flower heads when they are starting to expand and release the seeds, and dry them to allow the seeds to drop out. Never use plastic when collecting or drying – it encourages moulds that may kill the seeds.

Store seed safely
Sow seeds of hellebores, peonies, cyclamen, meconopsis (Himalayan poppies) and primulas as soon as you collect them; they should then germinate well. Other seeds need to be kept cool and dry until spring sowing time. You will need to clean the seeds before storage. Once they are dry, separate the seed from the seedhead debris, or chaff, which is usually lighter – try blowing very gently while shaking the paper or envelope. Put the seeds in paper envelopes, then in airtight plastic boxes in the fridge or another cool place (not the freezer). Label them so that you know what you are sowing the next year.

BEAT THAT!
● **The oldest seed** ever to be successfully germinated was a 2,000-year-old date palm seed, nicknamed 'Methuselah', found on the edge of the Dead Sea in the 1960s. That's 700 years older than the previous record-holder – a 1,300 year old lotus seed from China.

◄ **Provide extra warmth** to encourage seeds to germinate by putting transparent covers over pots and trays. These miniature bell cloches are attractive, but the same effect could be achieved with a clear plastic bag secured around the pot with an elastic band.

HOW DOES IT WORK?

HOW A SEED GROWS

When soil reaches a certain temperature and a seed is wet for prolonged periods, water penetrates the protective seed coat and the seed begins to swell. Enzymes in the seed tissue absorb ogygen and convert fats and starches to sugars, which fuel rapid growth. A root emerges first, to hold the seedling in the soil, and then a shoot pushes through into the light, holding, in most cases, two seed leaves or cotyledons. This is a critical stage: the shoot cannot produce shoots below these cotyledons. Adult, 'true' leaves grow from the centre of the cotyledons. From between these leaves the shoot tip grows on and develops, forming more leaves.

SOWING IN ROWS

Choose a dry day for sowing outdoors, but do not sow during prolonged dry periods. Check seed packets for spacing distances between rows; if you are sowing two rows of different seeds, add the distances together and divide by two.

1 Dig over the soil and remove any weeds, especially any roots of perennial weeds. Level the ground roughly by breaking up large clods of earth with a fork or the back of a rake, then rake over the soil surface until it is fine and even.

2 Make your seed drills (shallow trenches) with a trowel, the corner of a hoe blade or a dibber (shown here). Use a line pegged at each end to keep your rows straight. It is easier to hoe between rows if they are straight and evenly spaced.

3 Water along the row before you sow – it helps light seeds stick to the soil so they do not blow away before you cover them. Water after sowing and you risk washing the seed out of the drill.

4 Some seeds, such as beetroot and peas, are large enough to be planted one at a time at the recommended final spacings for the plants. With fine seed such as carrot, sow as thinly and evenly as you can, then thin the seedlings (see picture, facing page).

Sowing directly into the soil

Choose the best time to sow Most seeds need the soil to have reached a certain temperature before they will germinate successfully. Seed packets and sowing guides will give a broad window of sowing times for any plant, but if you are aiming to sow at the earliest possible time in spring, it is better to watch the weather than the calendar and consider what sort of spring it is before you sow. If the weather is cold and wet, and your soil is heavy, seeds are more likely to rot than grow if you sow too early. Plants usually catch up if you sow later than you planned, but when conditions are better for growth.

● **ASK THE LOCAL EXPERTS** Quiz gardening neighbours and friends about what grows well in your area's soil and when they sow and plant out. Local knowledge about climate and weather patterns is invaluable.

● **WARM THE SOIL** For your earliest sowings, put black plastic, geotextile fabric (mulching sheeting) or a cloche or portable coldframe over the soil a few weeks before you sow to warm the soil and assist germination.

Knock out the competition

Prepare your seedbeds a month before you sow, then cover with clear plastic or fleece so surface weed seeds germinate. Then hoe the weed seedlings off or spray with weedkiller before you sow your seeds. This removes a whole generation of weeds that would otherwise compete with your young plants. If you have sown small seeds, your own seedlings will also need thinning so they do not compete with each other. Do it once when the second set of leaves (the 'true' leaves) appear, then again when plants touch each other until you achieve the recommended spacing for that plant or crop.

● **PROTECT YOUR SEEDLINGS** Birds, slugs and snails will all be waiting for your seedlings to emerge, so set up a defence system. Thread crisscrossed over the bed just above the surface will deter birds. Slugs and snails are repelled by scatterings of bran or sand – or draw them away with traps [see also p.275].

Keep track of your seedlings

Some seeds are broadcast-sown, or scattered randomly over the soil. These include grass seed for lawns, and the seeds of green manures [see p.235]. For all other seeds, whether flowers or vegetables, it is best to sow in rows, so that you will be able to tell, once the seeds germinate, which seedlings are your plants and which are weeds. Even if the effect you are aiming for is drifts of plants, sowing in rows, or concentric circles, is still a good idea [see Planting for Rapid Results, p.84]. Once the plants start to grow together they won't look regimented at all.

Get to grips with fiddly seeds

Some seeds, such as flax and carrot, are tiny and hard to handle. Pour them into the groove of your partly cupped palm and tap your hand to make the seeds fall while controlling the flow. Alternatively, mix fine seed with sand, or dry used coffee grounds, to make sowing easier.

● **TRY EASY SOWING AIDS** Many vegetables and some flowers are available in seed tapes, with seeds pre-spaced at the right distance. You can also buy seed dispensers, often called pro-seeders, that release a seed every time you squeeze or click.

● **MAKE A SEED DISPENSER FOR FREE** Wash out an old artificial sweetener dispenser and you have a seed dispenser that costs you nothing.

▲ **Thin out your seedlings** for vigorous young plants. Hold down the soil on each side of the seedling you want to keep, so that its roots will not be disturbed when you remove its unwanted neighbours.

STAR PERFORMERS...

EASIEST FROM SEED

Hardy annuals (HA on the packets) are the easiest seeds to grow and the plants will flower where you sow them. They are ideal for children and new gardeners, flowering in as little as two months after sowing.

● **Amaranthus**
● **California poppies** (*Eschscholzia*)
● **Candytuft** (*Iberis*)
● **Cornflowers** (*Centaurea cyanus*)
● **English marigolds** (*Calendula*)
◀ **Nigella, or love-in-a-mist**
● **Nasturtiums**
● **Sunflowers**
● **Sweet alyssum** (*Lobularia*)

Raising seedlings under cover

Find a place for propagation
Seeds and seedlings need warmth, moisture, air and plenty of light to grow. The main reason to sow under cover is to give the seeds more warmth than outdoor conditions can provide, either to get ahead of the growing season or to give tender crops such as tomatoes as long a growing season as possible to produce crops that will ripen. If you don't have a heated greenhouse, you can raise your seeds on an indoor windowsill, or in a propagator – or even both. A propagator is an enclosed case that maintains some heat and humidity, giving seeds favourable conditions for germination. The simplest propagator is a clear plastic bag held over a pot with an elastic band, but you can buy unheated or heated propagators comprising clear-lidded trays in various shapes and sizes. Look for useful features such as vents, heated bases and thermostats – a little heat will allow you to raise seeds in an unheated room.
- **SEEDLINGS ON A BUDGET** Many items of food packaging can be used to raise seeds. Yoghurt pots can be given 'lids' of cut-down drinks bottles, and the clear containers used for fruit and vegetables make great propagators or seed tray lids.

Use the best compost
Don't scrimp on compost or use old bags that have been open over winter. Fungal spores in the air will have infected the compost and may kill your delicate seedlings. Use fresh compost recommended for seed-sowing, or sieved multipurpose compost – a fine-gauge gardening sieve is ideal, but an old kitchen sieve works just as well.
- **DO NOT PRESS THE COMPOST DOWN** in your seed trays or pots; if the compost is compacted, the seedling roots will lack the air they need to grow. Fill the tray or pot and then tap it down sharply on a hard surface a couple of times to settle the compost, or tamp it down very gently with the bottom of another pot or tray.

Raise super-strong seedlings
The key to success is to grow your new plants in stages: sow in small to medium-sized pots or trays, and then transplant the seedlings into individual small pots or the cells of a module tray. Once they are making good growth, move them into bigger pots.
- **COVER SEEDS LIGHTLY** with just a sprinkling of compost so that the seedlings can easily push up to the surface. Do not sieve the compost you use to cover them; if it is too fine, it may form a cap that hampers germination and is lifted by the seedlings as they grow.
- **SOME SEEDS NEED LIGHT** to germinate, including busy lizzies, poppies and foxgloves. Check seed packets for this detail, and cover these seeds with vermiculite or perlite instead of compost: these light, granular mineral-based materials are available from garden centres.
- **KEEP SOME SEEDS IN RESERVE** Tempting though it is, don't sow all your seeds, especially in a small pot. When seedlings are crowded they grow spindly and weak, and quickly succumb if diseases strikes. Keep some seeds in reserve and you can try again if your seedlings fail, or save them for a later sowing or another year.
- **ENSURE STRAIGHT SEEDLINGS** Seedlings growing on a windowsill always lean towards the light. Either turn the pots or trays daily, or make a reflector in which

▲ **Sow fine seed** lightly over the compost in small pots or trays. Large seeds such as those of beans or nasturtiums can be sown one or two per small pot or individual cell of a module tray.

▼ **Choose a propagator** with vents on the top of the lid; on warm days, when you see the lid start to mist up a little, open the vents to allow for ventilation and air movement around the seedlings.

TRANSPLANTING SEEDLINGS

Seedlings grown one per cell of a module tray can be transplanted into their own pot or larger module cell complete with their own plug of compost, but those grown together in pots and trays will need lifting and replanting individually.

● Transplant on a cool day, when the compost is damp, to reduce the shock to the seedlings. They will recover better if kept in the shade.

● Water the compost in the new pots or modules first, to minimise disturbance once the seedlings are transplanted.

● Never pull seedlings out of the compost. If they are growing in pots, gently squeeze the pot to loosen the compost and tip the potful out on its side. You can then easily separate the seedlings. If in trays, push a dibber under the seedlings and lever out a clump of compost so the roots are easy to tease out.

● Make a hole in the new compost with a pencil or dibber and use the tool to hold the hole open as you lower the root in. Firm them in very gently.

◀ Never hold seedlings by their stems. If you crush them they will die. Hold them by the cotyledon leaves; if you damage these the seedling will still grow.

to sit them: take a shallow cardboard box, cut it away on the window side and line it with kitchen foil to bounce the light in evenly around your seedlings.

● **TRANSPLANT AT THE RIGHT TIME** Once your seedlings have grown you will need to transplant them into pots or cell trays to grow them on until they are ready to plant outside. Do not leave this too late or the seedling roots will become entangled and hard to separate, and damage will be inevitable. The right time to transplant is when the first pair of leaves (the cotyledons) are fully expanded and the second or 'true' leaves are just starting to grow in the centre [see How a Seed Grows, p.263]. At this stage the main root has only just started to branch, so the seedlings can easily be separated.

Prepare young plants for the great outdoors

Seedlings nurtured in a greenhouse or on your windowsill will have been protected from strong sunlight and wind. If planted out directly they will get scorched and their growth will suffer. Put your seedlings in a mini-greenhouse or coldframe, ideally in a sheltered, shady place, to acclimatise them to outside conditions (this is called 'hardening off'). Watch the weather forecast and cover the frame or cloche with a blanket or fleece on cold nights to keep in the heat. If you don't have a coldframe, move your pots or trays of young plants outside on mild, cloudy days and bring them in at night for a couple of weeks, then (if there is no danger of night frost) leave them out permanently for a week, then plant out in the open garden.

▼ **Acclimatise young plants** gradually to outdoor conditions by placing them in a coldframe in a sheltered spot for about two weeks, closing the lid at night until the last few days.

Growing plants from cuttings

Multiply your favourite plants It's so easy to grow plants from cuttings that once you've started, you'll wonder why it took you so long to try. Unlike plants grown from garden-collected seed, cuttings produce plants identical to their parent, so if you have a favourite delphinium or dahlia you can grow lots more.

● **PLANTS FOR FREE** Some planting plans and ideas require quantities of the same plant – hedging, for example, or ground-cover schemes. While they will take longer to mature, growing these plants from cuttings is very economical.

● **KEEP PLANTS SAFE** Insure against losses in a hard winter by taking cuttings in summer of plants that are not completely hardy and growing them on in a greenhouse or coldframe. Or, if you have a plant that was a present or took some finding, take cuttings and give one to a friend. That way, if you lose your plant you can always get a piece of it back. The best way to keep a plant is to give it away!

● **REPLACE TIRED OLD PLANTS** Some plants do not live long. Dianthus (pinks), penstemons and erysimums all perform best in their second year and then deteriorate. Keep your borders looking good by taking cuttings to renew them.

Use the perfect compost Cuttings compost should be light and airy. Never firm it down. Equal parts of multipurpose compost and perlite, vermiculite or coarse sand is just right. (Use horticultural sand from a garden centre, not builder's sand.) Never sieve the compost – it should be coarse and drain freely.

EXPERT KNOW HOW

TAKING STEM-TIP CUTTINGS

Use a sharp knife to make clean cuts, and make holes in the compost with a pencil so you do not bruise the cuttings. Hormone rooting compounds are an optional aid to rooting. Place the pots of cuttings in a light but shaded place. Once roots have formed, move the cuttings into individual pots and grow them on.

1 Cut a firm, healthy shoot from the plant and trim it just below a leaf, or pair of leaves; this area of the stem is where roots are most likely to form.

2 Trim off the lower leaves so that there will be none on the portion of stem you insert into the compost. Trim off any flowers and flower buds.

3 To help roots form, dab the base of the cutting into hormone rooting powder, then insert to a quarter of its depth into the compost, and water in.

SELECTING THE BEST CUTTINGS MATERIAL

Most cuttings are ideally 5–8cm (2–3in) long. Select shoots without flowers if you can. Nip off flower buds if necessary. When taking semi-ripe cuttings, you can use sideshoots of the correct length; pull them from the main stem so that there is some bark attached, then trim the ragged base of the cuttings neatly.

☐ SOFT TIP CUTTINGS

Take cuttings in spring and summer from soft shoot tips of tender bedding plants such as diascias, penstemons and fuchsias. They root speedily but also wilt quickly, so can be tricky; use a propagator, or cover with a clear plastic bag secured over the pot with an elastic band, to reduce evaporation.

☐ SEMI-RIPE CUTTINGS

Ideal for pelargoniums (pictured opposite), lavender and rosemary; if you are new to taking cuttings, this method is the one to start with. Take the cuttings in summer and early autumn, when the shoots have started to become firm; they do not wilt as quickly as soft-tip cuttings but take slightly longer to root.

☐ BASAL SHOOT CUTTINGS

Use this method for lupins, dahlias and delphiniums. As they start to grow in spring, cut or pull off a shoot with a piece of the woody rootstock attached at the base. Do not trim. Root them in a jam jar with 1cm (½in) of damp sand or perlite in the base; keep moist until you see roots, then pot them up.

Help cuttings to grow Cuttings need some shade and high humidity to reduce evaporation from the foliage until the cutting has roots of its own. Keep the compost moist but not wet and keep the air moist. A propagator [see p.266] can be used for cuttings after the spring sowing rush has passed.

● **GET THE DEPTH RIGHT** Only push cuttings in deep enough to hold them upright. The bases of the cuttings must have air. If pushed deep into compost they may rot.

● **TRY ROOTING AIDS** Hormone rooting compounds are not essential but they can help. Most have an added fungicide to prevent rots. Dip the base of the cutting in the rooting powder or rooting gel. Do not dip the cuttings in water first to make more powder stick. Buy fresh compound every year – it 'goes off' fast.

● **ALLOW TIME FOR ROOTS TO FORM** Never pull up cuttings to check whether they are rooted. You may damage tiny roots that are forming and kill your cuttings. You can tell when roots are forming, because the cuttings will stop wilting and look healthy. When new shoot growth starts you can be sure there are roots.

Special types of cuttings Not all plants are grown from soft stem tips. There are other parts of some plants that can produce new plants. To propagate your favourite shrubs – and fruit bushes – take hardwood cuttings [see p.223].

● **TRY ROOT CUTTINGS** for primulas, acanthus, Japanese anemones and oriental poppies. In winter, dig up a plant, cut the thickest roots into sections about 5cm (2in) long and set these horizontally in a tray of compost. Cover with grit, place in a coldframe [see p.260] and keep moist. New plants will appear in spring and these can be potted up, grown on and planted out later.

● **GROW MORE CLEMATIS** from leaf-bud cuttings taken from new shoots. Prepare them by cutting a stem into sections in midsummer. Cut just above a pair of leaves, then about 8cm (3in) below the leaves. Insert the cuttings so the stem is buried and the base of the leaves is just below the compost. After a few months new shoots will appear from the top of the cutting.

▼ **Basal shoot cuttings** are taken as perennials start to grow in spring. Once the emerging growth is 8–10cm (3–4in) tall, scrape away a little soil from the base of the plant and cut or pull away a strong shoot right at its base (see box, above).

Keeping plants healthy

NO GARDENER WANTS TO SEE PLANTS succumb to pests and **diseases,** but there's no need to reach automatically for chemical sprays. Keep your plants growing strongly, enlist beneficial garden wildlife to help you deal with pests, and learn the very best techniques, both old and new, to ward off problems.

PROTECT YOUR CROPS WHEN THEY ARE YOUNG, AND AT THEIR MOST VULNERABLE

Preventing problems

Work with your garden
Choose plants that are suitable for your climate, soil and position and you will have fewer problems. Start by checking your soil pH [see p.233] to avoid nutritional problems that are difficult to correct. Gooseberries and currants, for example, are better suited to alkaline (limey) soil than raspberries. In addition, there are many plants that have been bred to be resistant to diseases and even some pests. Look for these when making your selections and gardening will be easier and more rewarding.

● **BOOST PLANTS' NATURAL RESISTANCE** Healthy plants are less likely to attract pests and fall prey to disease. Maintaining soil fertility will keep them growing strongly, and avoid nutrient deficiencies – the signs of which often resemble those of disease. Make sure plants are not stressed, either by drought or by the wrong growing conditions, and keep them well fed. Avoid high levels of nitrogen-rich fertilisers, which encourage soft, sappy growth that is especially attractive to aphids and caterpillars. There is some evidence that using only organic fertilisers and feeding the soil, not the plants, encourages natural, strong growth and helps plants to fight off problems.

● **GET ON TOP OF WEEDS** Weeds compete with your plants for light and moisture and they also crowd them, which will encourage fungal diseases (see box, below). Many weeds also harbour pests that may spread on to your plants.

● **LET NATURE HELP** In many cases, nature will solve your problems for you, if you are prepared to wait. When aphids multiply, for example, they are often followed by armies of ladybirds and hoverflies whose larvae will devour them.

● **ACCEPT COSMETIC DAMAGE** Unless you are growing for a flower show, you do not need to worry about a little damage. Some may be caused by pests that do not really do much harm. Round sections cut from rose leaves, for example, are made by leafcutter bees that are only removing what they need to make egg cells in their nests. These harmless creatures remain active just for a short time.

▲ **Although it** resembles signs of disease, the yellowing on this raspberry leaf indicates that the soil is either lacking in the nutrients iron and magnesium, or too alkaline for raspberries to thrive. Raspberries grow best in a neutral or slightly acid soil.

◀ **Erecting barriers** of garden netting over and around your crop plants protects not only against birds, but also certain vegetable pests such as carrot fly and cabbage white butterfly.

Maintain good hygiene under cover
Cleanliness is the first step to preventing diseases in artificial, enclosed environments such as greenhouses and coldframes. Remove dead flowers and leaves, cut away diseased stems and dispose of badly affected plants.

● **SPRING CLEAN THE GREENHOUSE**, clearing out dead plants before you start sowing seeds, and clean thoroughly again in autumn before you bring in tender plants. In winter, check stored bulbs and tubers regularly and remove any that show signs of rot so that any disease does not spread.

● **DON'T IMPORT PROBLEMS** Look carefully over any new plants before you buy, especially for the greenhouse where pests multiply rapidly. Twisted leaves and shoots are a sign of aphids; sticky leaves and black deposits often indicate that scale insect is present.

HOW DOES IT WORK?
HOW CROWDING ENCOURAGES FUNGAL DISEASES

Fungal diseases such as mildew, rust and black spot are spread by spores that are always in the air. When they land on a leaf they need moisture to germinate and invade the leaf. Crowded plants, with poor air circulation, are more likely to remain wet after rain and dew and this encourages fungal diseases to take hold and spread. Giving plants space lets air flow freely and combats disease.

The gardener's friends

Let wildlife protect your plants A delicate balance exists in your garden between your plants and good and bad insects. Some pests introduced from foreign countries will have no natural predators, but in most cases there are beneficial insects or animals that will help you defend your plants from attack. The greater the diversity of wildlife you can encourage in your garden – bugs and beetles, bees and butterflies, amphibians and small mammals – the more allies you will gain to keep pest populations down. Birds can be a nuisance when they attack fruits or flowers but on balance they are helpful: thrushes eat slugs and snails, and starlings will march across your lawn pecking up leatherjackets, grubs that eat grass roots.

● **KNOW YOUR APHID ALLIES** Three of the most useful aphid predators are rarely recognised for the work they do in controlling these sap-sucking pests. Ladybirds, both the colourful adults and their long, black crocodile-like larvae (young), are voracious feeders on greenfly and blackfly. Hoverflies are bright, wasp-like but harmless insects, often seen landing on bright flowers to feed on pollen. Their maggot-like crawling grubs eat hundreds of aphids before becoming adults. Lacewings are delicate-looking green insects with transparent wings that fly weakly by day and night; their larvae are also fearsome aphid predators.

EXPERT KNOW HOW

CREATE A COSY HOME FOR WILDLIFE

A simple fruit crate can be used to make a wildlife shelter that will allow small creatures to feel secure and free from disturbance, and give them protection and a hibernation area in winter. Site it in a quiet, shady spot, among undergrowth so that the creatures can approach and leave the shelter in safety.

1 Cut the crate down to size, if necessary, so that it sits about 15cm (6in) above the ground, and then cut away an entrance. Put it in place.

2 Pile straw or rough, dry garden debris over and around the box, finishing with a few branches to hold this insulation in place.

3 Roll bundles of grass stems in waterproof polythene and lodge them at the sides of the crate; ladybirds and lacewings will overwinter in them.

● **ENCOURAGE AMPHIBIANS** As well as bringing life and entertainment to your garden, frogs and toads will feed greedily on pests such as slugs and woodlice. If you don't have a pond, at least leave some wild areas and a few large stones or logs for cover. A few half-buried clay pots in quiet places make perfect residences for toads. Decking, often considered sterile to wildlife, also gives amphibians cover from the sun.

Create wildlife-friendly areas
The simplest way to attract wildlife into your garden is to leave a few native plants to grow in an out-of-the-way place. A rough patch of grass will feed the caterpillars of butterflies, and provide cover for slug-eating beetles and a quiet place for bees to nest. A patch of nettles will feed caterpillars and encourage ladybirds – and the cut nettles make a fantastic addition to a compost heap.

● **ATTRACT BIRDS TO HELP YOU** Birds feed on insects as well as fruit and seeds. Put out food in trees and they may also eat pests on the branches. Grow climbers up walls and fences where insects can thrive and survive, until nesting wrens and other insect-eating birds find them. Don't forget to provide clean water year-round. Put up bird boxes and roosting pockets for a range of species to provide shelter in bad weather. Dig over soil to expose grubs that birds can feed on, and use loose organic mulches that they can rummage in.

● **PROVIDE SHELTERING AND HIBERNATION AREAS** A purpose-built shelter (see facing page) or a pile of logs will become home to a variety of species. Specially made 'insect hotels' can be mounted on shady walls for lacewings and ladybirds.

● **MAKE A POND** Even if it is small, a pond will attract an amazing array of wildlife and bring your garden to life. Avoid adding fish if you want to encourage wildlife.

● **ADD EARLY AND LATE-FLOWERING PLANTS** Bumblebees start to fly and feed on the first warm days of spring. Help them out by planting early sources of nectar: bulbs, lamiums, celandines, primroses and forget-me-nots. At the end of the season, few plants are as helpful to insects as ivy. The late flowers are one of the last sources of nectar.

TOP PLANTS FOR BEES AND HOVERFLIES

Bees reach into tubular flowers with their long tongues to feed on nectar; hoverflies prefer flat, readily accessible flowers.

- ● Achillea
- ● Asters
- ● Coreopsis
- ● Echium
- ● Foxgloves
- ● Lavender
- ● Marigolds
- ● Sedums
- ◀ Verbenas

TOP PLANTS FOR BUTTERFLIES

Like bees, butterflies use their long tongues to sip nectar from tubular flowers. They are attracted to pink and purple flowers.

- ◀ *Buddleja davidii*
- ● Candytuft *(Iberis)*
- ● Centranthus
- ● Heliotrope (cherry pie)
- ● Phlox
- ● Scabious
- ● Solidago
- ● Sweet rocket *(Hesperis)*
- ● Sweet williams
- ● Wallflowers

TOP PLANTS FOR BIRDS

Red-berried varieties of fruiting trees and shrubs are birds' favourites. Small birds such as finches enjoy seedheads.

- ● Echinops
- ● Cotoneaster
- ● Crab apples *(Malus)*
- ● Hawthorn *(Crataegus)*
- ◀ Hollies
- ● Ivies
- ● Mountain ash *(Sorbus)*
- ● Pyracantha
- ● Sunflowers
- ● Teasels

'RABBIT-PROOF' PLANTS

Hungry rabbits will eat anything they can find, but you can try to minimise their depredations by growing plants they will eat only as a last resort – or using them to edge garden boundaries or beds and borders. These are said to rank among their least-liked foods.

▲ **Aconites**
- **Alliums**
- **Astilbes**
- **Bergenia**
- *Cornus sanguinea*
- **Eschscholzia**
- **Euphorbia**
- **Hemerocallis**
- **Nepeta**
- **Pulmonaria**
- **Silybum**
- **Stachys**

Combating pests and diseases

Keep pests off your plants
Even when plants are grown well and your garden bustles with beneficial wildlife there are times when intervention is needed to protect your plants. You don't always need sprays and chemicals to fight off problems. Physical barriers, traps and repellents can prevent many pests from landing on your plants.

● **PICK THEM OFF** Pest-patrolling can be an effective way of preventing pest numbers building up to harmful levels. Inspect your plants and pick off and squash pests between your fingers. Enlist helpers to join in snail hunts at dusk – perhaps with prizes for the biggest 'bag'. The snails can be released on to waste ground or drowned in salt water.

● **SCARE THEM OFF** Shiny CDs hung among your plants will alarm cats and birds – and put unwanted discs to good use. Ultrasonic devices can be effective against cats, birds and also moles, but work best if they are regularly moved around.

● **COVER VULNERABLE PLANTS WITH NETTING AND FLEECE** to keep off pests. Protect your vegetable plot from rabbits with a fence of chicken wire that is not only at least 45cm (18in) tall, but also buried to at least 15cm (6in) under the soil, and use garden netting to protect ripening strawberries and soft fruit against birds.

● **LOOK OUT FOR LILY BEETLES** These distinctive scarlet beetles and their larvae, which strip lilies of their leaves and flowers, have no natural predators in most temperate regions, so must be picked off by hand.

● **USE COLOUR-CODED STICKY TRAPS** to target particular pests. Yellow traps in the greenhouse [see also p.258] attract greenfly and whitefly, while thrips (thunderflies) are drawn to blue. Outdoors, proprietary white sticky traps can keep down populations of raspberry beetle.

▼ **Rabbits find** ornamental alliums unappetising, and along with other members of the onion family, to which alliums belong, they are said to repel a number of insect pests, too.

WAGE WAR ON SNAILS AND SLUGS

Snails and slugs eat a wide range of plants and are especially destructive to newly planted bedding and vegetable plants. There are many effective alternatives to slug pellets, which are unsafe for pets and in family gardens.

◀ Snails will be reluctant to cross barriers of dry or coarse, sharp materials such as fine grit, pine needles, wood ash or crushed eggshells encircling vulnerable plants.

● The metal copper repels both creatures; try using copper tools [see p.226] or surround vulnerable container plants with copper tape [see p.137].

◀ Make beer or milk traps to attract and drown both slugs and snails. Sink a plastic cup into the ground and fill it with beer or milk. Leave the rim of the cup 1cm (½in) proud of the soil surface; the slugs and snails will be able to clamber over, but unwary ground beetles (which are beneficial insects) will not fall in.

● Slugs and snails will also be drawn to congregate under hollowed-out citrus skins; they will remain alive but can be easily collected and disposed of.

● There are nematodes, in the form of a biological control (see below), that can be applied to the soil to attack slugs that live below the ground.

Try companion planting There is little conclusive evidence that plants such as African marigolds actually repel pests, but it is certainly true that growing a mixture of plants will prevent pests reaching epidemic proportions. Growing a few bright flowers among your crops and especially in a greenhouse will attract beneficial insects such as hoverflies: the adults will pollinate flowers and their larvae will devour pests.

● **REPEL PESTS WITH SCENT** Pungent-smelling plants such as tansy, sage, artemisia and members of the onion family are said to repel pests. It is possible that the strong aromas from these plants confuse pests that seek out their favoured plants by scent. Try pink-flowering chives or purple sage for a traditional, attractive, useful and possibly beneficial edging for your vegetable beds.

● **PLANT A SACRIFICIAL CROP OF NASTURTIUMS** or even lettuce in vegetable beds. Aphids and other pests such as caterpillars may be drawn to these in preference to crop plants such as beans and courgettes.

Enlist the help of tiny pest predators

'Biological control' is the practice of using natural pest predators – some very small – to target particular pests. Bred under controlled conditions, they are sold by mail order and may also be available in larger garden centres. They work best when released into confined areas – into

BEAT THAT!

● **In 2010 amateur observer** Ruth Brooks astonished scientists by proving what gardeners have always maintained – that snails have a 'homing instinct'. She did this by collecting snails by hand, marking their shells with nail polish, then transporting them increasing distances from her garden, discovering that even when left 30m (100ft) away, they managed to find their way back. She is continuing her experiments over longer distances. Meanwhile, gardeners accustomed to tossing their snails over the fence will have to make a longer journey.

HOW DOES IT WORK?

BIOLOGICAL CONTROLS

Biological controls exploit the fact that most pests have natural predators. Although these may be present in your garden or greenhouse, in small numbers they do not make an impact

on a serious pest problem. Adding large populations of these predators, if kept in suitable conditions and applied correctly, can control many pests including whitefly, mealy bugs and red spider mite (under glass) and slugs, caterpillars and vine weevil outside. Some are applied directly on to the plants; others are watered into the soil.

a greenhouse or on container plants, for example – although there are also products for dealing with lawn pests and the small soil-dwelling slugs that ruin potatoes. Many of the firms that produce biological controls also supply lacewing and ladybird larvae, to be released into the garden. This is an ideal way to introduce more of these helpful 'mini-beasts' into your plot.

Choosing and using garden sprays

Get the right product
Efficient application of pesticides and fungicides will save time and money. Identify the problem, then check product descriptions to select one that is going to work. Remember when choosing formulations that no control is going to be effective if it remains in the bottle. Mixing up sprays can be tedious; if this is going to deter you from dealing with a problem as soon as you see it, buy ready-to-use sprays that can be applied in seconds.

● **CHOOSE ORGANIC SPRAYS** based on naturally occurring substances such as soaps, plant extracts, sulphur and even sunflower oil if you want to limit your use of synthetic chemicals in the garden (see also facing page). Most organic pest controls are contact insecticides: they need to come into direct contact with the pest itself to be effective, so you must spray plants thoroughly all over, and repeat applications may be needed.

EVEN ORGANIC PESTICIDES CAN BE HARMFUL TO BEES – SPRAY IN THE EVENING TO KEEP THEM SAFE

● **CHOOSE SYNTHETIC FORMULAS** to deal with pernicious pests and diseases such as vine weevil and apple scab. Some formulas must come into contact with the pest, but the benefit of others is that they are systemic: they enter the plant and kill the pest when it eats the leaves or sucks the sap. This makes them useful for dealing with pests that have a thick protective coating, such as scale insects. Systemic insecticides usually remain active in the plant for weeks, so you do not need to spray so frequently. They must be used with care on edible crops: always observe any recommended waiting time between spraying and harvesting.

Use sprays safely
Garden chemicals are extensively tested for both efficacy and safety and should pose minimal risk to wildlife, the user and the environment. Even so, it makes sense to take basic precautions to minimise

NATURAL OPTIONS FOR PEST CONTROL

If you garden organically there are chemical-free options for combating some pests and fungal diseases. These products are safe to use on crops and around pets and children, provided that you follow the manufacturer's instructions, but are toxic to fish and amphibians and should not be used around ponds.

☐ INSECTICIDAL SOAPS AND FATTY ACIDS

A spray with soapy water was for many years the traditional weapon against small insect pests such as aphids and whitefly, and insecticidal soaps and fatty acids are today used to make some effective pest control sprays for use against aphids, whitefly, thrips, mealy bugs, scale insects, leafhoppers and red spider mite. Ready-to-use sprays are widely available; concentrated soap-based products are more effective if they are diluted with soft rather than hard water.

☐ PLANT OILS AND EXTRACTS

Products based on plant oils such as rapeseed and sunflower block the breathing pores of small insects and mites, such as aphids, whitefly, thrips, scale insects and red spider mite, but leave bees and ladybirds unharmed. Plant oil washes can also be used against overwintering aphid eggs on fruit trees and bushes. Pyrethrin, derived from pyrethrum flowers (*Tanacetum cinerariifolium*), controls many pests including whitefly, small caterpillars, aphids, thrips, leafhoppers, capsid bugs, ants and some beetles.

☐ DUSTS AND POWDERS

Sulphur dust was once widely used for its effectiveness in controlling powdery mildew and leaf spots on fruit, flowers and vegetables. It is available to gardeners in the copper sulphate formulation Bordeaux mixture. Another copper compound, copper oxychloride, is also sold in wettable powder form for the control of vegetable and fruit diseases including peach leaf curl and potato and tomato blight. Pyrethrum powder (see left) in a puffer pack is useful for applying to ant nests and runs.

any risk. Wear gloves and wash hands thoroughly afterwards; follow the manufacturer's instructions carefully, and observe any precautions listed. Remember that although natural and usually of low persistence, organic pest controls are usually just as harmful to beneficial insects as to the pests.

● **CATCH PROBLEMS EARLY** and reduce your use of sprays and chemicals. Watch your plants carefully so you spot the first signs of pests and diseases. That way you will only have to spray a few plants. Fungicides in particular will never remove existing disease – they only work preventatively. So although you can spray fungicides on your plants to prevent a disease problem getting worse, there will still be signs of the problem. Ideally, you should spray plants before the problem occurs to offer better protection.

● **PROTECT BEES** To avoid doing any harm to bees, spray only in the evening when bees are less likely to be active. The cool of the evening also helps prevent sprays evaporating before their active ingredients are absorbed. Never spray any chemical on a windy day when drift can affect other plants, and never spray open flowers.

▼ **Sunflower oil** and rapeseed oil are two of the most recent ingredients found to have uses in the control of garden pests.

Index

Page numbers in *italics* refer to illustrations.

nitrogen 235, 247
  stored in the soil 193, 195
North American plants 112
nutrient uptake 235

O

Olearia macrodonta 104
onion 180, 186, 188–9, *188,*
  261, 27
    Japanese 182, 189
    spring 182, 188
    world's heaviest 188
    'Keepwell' 189
    'Radar' 189
    'Senshyu' 189
oregano *210*
organic matter 155, 170, *180,*
  192, 233, 234, 238, *238,* 239,
  239, 243
    adding to decrease pH 233
organic sprays 276
oriental leaves and salads 178,
  179, 182, 196–7, 209, 259
    combating pests 197
osteospermum 102, 131
overwintering
    containers 255
    hardy crops for 254
    plants 254–5, *255,* 259
    see also frost

P

palm tree *39*
pampas grass *(Cortaderia*
  selloana) 112
panicum 111
pansy 97, 131, 137
parking areas 40–1
Papaver see poppy
parsley 210, *210,* 259
    grown vertically 12
    in containers 211, 213
    sowing seed 210
parsnip *180,* 182, 185, 186
parthenocissus 76
    Boston ivy 164
    Virginia creeper 164
passion flower *(Passiflora)* 170,
  246
paths 24, *24,* 46–49, *46–9,* 249
    cleaning 87
    in meadow planting *35*
    in small gardens 32
    making practical 40
    materials for 46, 48

patios *31,* 52–7, 249
    avoiding damp in house
      walls 53
    change of level 52–3
    foundation 54
    materials for 52, 53, *53,* 54,
      54, 55
    shading 54
    sheltering 53
    see also decking, paving
Paulownia see foxglove tree
paving 53, 54, 55, *55*
    in kit form *55*
    plants for 55
peach 219
    fans 215
    pollinating 219, *219*
    'Bonanza' 219
    'Garden Lady' 219
    'Terrace Amber' *219*
pear *(Pyrus)* 154–5, 216–7
    cordon 215
    espalier *216*
    wire-trained 217
    'Catillac' *214*
    'Concorde' 216
    'Conference' 216
peas *180,* 192–3, 195, 264
    sown in guttering 192, *192*
    'Canoe' 193
    'Douce Provence' 192
    'Markana' 193
    'Meteor' 192
peat 135
pelargonium *83,* 129, 131, 254,
  259
    cuttings 269
pennisetum 111
penstemon 97, *128,* 254, 268, 269
    insulating 110, 255
peony *(Paeonia)* 94, 263
peppers 182, 200–1, *200,* 259
    combating pests 201
perennials 73, 76, 81, 106–15,
  238, 241, *241,* 242, 253, 263
    annual versions of 84
    border *16*
    caring for 113
    climbers, quick-growing 165
    cutting back 94, 114
    deadheading 12, 94
    different shapes 108, *108*
    dividing 88–9, 115, *115*
    fast-growing 83
    filling gaps between 128
    for big leaves 107
    for containers 133, 135

perennials (continued)
    for foliage 109–10
      top foliage perennials 109
    for height 107, *107*
    for impact 106, 107
    for revitalising schemes 87
    for screening 27
    ground-hugging 114
    long-flowering 94
    mildew 114
    plant supports 10, 87, 113, *113*
    planting for impact 6
    planting out 241, *241*
    prairie planting style 112, *112*
    second flush 114, *114*
    self-seeders 58, 114, 115
    watering 114
    with bulbs 124, 125
    with grasses 110
periwinkle *(Vinca)* 133
perovskia 83, 253
    'Little Spire' 83
pests 258, 271, 272, 274–7, *277*
    and container plants 137,
      275, 276
    netting crops against 13, 274
    plants attracting pest
      predators *107,* 273
    predators 10, 121, 201, 272,
      273
    see also biological controls,
      birds, blackfly, greenfly,
      rabbit-proof plants, slugs,
      snails, whitefly, individual
      plant entries
petunia 129
    'Black Velvet' 80
pH testing 233, *233,* 271
phacelia 234
phalaris 111
philadelphus *253*
Phlomis russeliana 41
phlox 107, *128*
    'David' 114
    'Miss Pepper' 114
    P. paniculata 97
    P. paniculata 'Nora Leigh'
      109
phormium 75, *142*
phosphorus 235
phygelius 102
Phyllostachys nigra 'Boryana' 111
pieris 233
pine *(Pinus)* 163
pineapple lily *see* eucomis
Pittosporum tobira 104
plant health 270–3

plant supports 10, 113, *113,*
  168–9
plant tonic, nettle 235, *235*
planting out 240–3
    see also perennials, trees
planting plans 90–105
    brightening shade *101*
    late summer interest *96*
    hot, dry border *103*
    late winter *98*
    long-flowering summer *95*
    making 73, *73*
    year-round interest *92*
planting, symmetrical 40, *40,*
  50
plum 218, *219,* 252
    self-fertile kinds 218
Polemonium caeruleum 'Brise
  d'Anjou' 109
polianthes (tuberose) 130
pollarding 156
pollution, plants to withstand
  104, 105
polyanthus 131
Polystichum aculeatum 110
polytunnel 257
ponds 62–7, *65,* 273
    attracting wildlife 66
    black, mirror-like surface 63
    children, safety 64
    maintenance 67
    making 65–7
    planting near 66, 107, 111
    plants for 66–7
    stepping stones *65*
    see also water features
poplar *(Populus)* 153, 156
    P. tremula 'Pendula' 93
poppy *(Papaver)* 9, 38, *84,* 97
    oriental 84, 88, 269
      'Medallion' 9, *9,* 94
      'Snow White' 94
    P. somniferum 84
potager *195*
potassium 235
potatoes 38, 178, *180,* 181, 182,
  228, 276
    blight-resistant 184
    chitting *184*
    growing 184–5
    in containers 182
potentilla 107, 119, 147
pressure washer 228–9
primula (primrose) 80, 100, 131,
  137, 259, 263, 269, 273
propagators 128, 266, *266*
privet *(Ligustrum)* 76, 159, 163

Acknowledgments

Cobalt id would like to thank the following for their help with this book: Richard Bloom, Peter Anderson and Mark Winwood for photography; Blooms of Bressingham, Bressingham Gardens and East Ruston Old Vicarage for use of props and locations; Daphne Ledward for the planting plans; John Ledward-Hands for additional photography; Scott Jessop for his great artworks; Clare Elsom and Joe Najman at NB Illustration; Liz Eddison at The Garden Collection; Burgon & Ball.

Reader's Digest would like to thank the following for permission to use images featured in **Gorgeous Garden Boosters**.

The following abbreviations indicate the position of the image on the page:
a –above; b – below/bottom; c– centre; l – left; r – right; t - top

The following abbreviations indicate picture agency names:
GAP – GAP Photos; GET – Getty Images; GWI – Garden World Images; RD – Reader's Digest; TGC – The Garden Collection

Front Cover: tl TGC: Andrew Lawson; **tr** TGC: Derek Harris; **bl** Reader's Digest / Mark Winwood; **br** GAP: Christa Brand. **2c** GAP: Christa Brand; **4tl** GET: Peter Anderson; **4cl** TGC: Liz Eddison/Phillip Osman; **4bl** GAP: Elke Borkowski; **5tl** GET: Garden Picture Library/Franois De Heel; **5cl** TGC: Derek Harris; **5bl** Richard Bloom; **6-7c** GAP: Elke Borkowski; **8t** TGC: Liz Eddison; **8cr** TGC: Liz Eddison/Bob Purnell; **9tr** GAP: Elke Borkowski; **9b** Honda; **10tr** GET: Mary C. Legg; **10cl** GET: Peter Anderson; **11tr** GAP: J S Sira; **11bl** GAP: Clive Nichols/Clare Matthews; **12t** GAP: Elke Borkowski/Jack Dunckley; **12cr** TGC: Emma Peios; **13tc** Marek Walisiewicz; **13bl** TGC: Neil Sutherland; **14-15c** TGC: Liz Eddison; **16b** TGC: Steven Wooster/Laara Copley-Smith; **17b** GAP: Nicola Browne/Steve Martino; **18tl** GAP: Jonathan Buckley/Katherine Crouch; **19b** GAP: Frederic Didillon; **20tl** GAP: Christa Brand; **20tr** GAP: Ron Evans; **20bl** GAP: Jan Smith; **20br** GAP: Manuela Goehner; **22bl** TGC: Nicola Stocken Tomkins; **23c** GAP: Marcus Harpur/Lucy Redman; **24bl** TGC: Nicola Stocken Tomkins; **26bl** TGC: Emma Peios; **27tr** TGC: Nicola Stocken Tomkins; **27bc** TGC: Andrew Lawson; **28bl** GAP: Clive Nichols/Chris Maton; **29c** TGC: Nicola Stocken Tomkins; **31tr** GAP: Friedrich Strauss; **32tl** GAP: J S Sira; **32br** GAP: J S Sira; **33tr** GAP: Ron Evans; **33b** TGC: Derek Harris/Adam Frost ; **34c** GAP: Carole Drake; **35br** GAP: Rob Whitworth/Piet Oudolf; **36tl** GAP: Marcus Harpur/Judith Sharpe; **36bl** GAP: Maayke de Ridder/Darren Saines; **38bl** TGC: Nicola Stocken Tomkins/Hergest Croft; **39t** GAP: Lynn Keddie; **40bl** GAP: Clive Nichols; **41t** GAP: Martin Staffler; **42b** TGC: Steven Wooster/Louise del Balzo; **43tr** GAP: Maddie Thornhill; **44tl** TGC: Liz Eddison/ Lesley Faux; **45tr** TGC: Nicola Stocken Tomkins; **45bc** Peter Anderson; **46c** TGC: Liz Eddison/Louise Ward/ Daphne Jones ; **47br** TGC: Nicola Stocken Tomkins; **48tl** GAP; **48b** GAP: Elke Borkowski; **49tr** GAP: Elke Borkowski/Bill Butterworth; **49br** GAP: Elke Borkowski; **50bl** GAP: Mark Bolton; **51tl** RD; **51tc** RD;

51tr RD; **51br** TGC: Derek Harris; **52bl** TGC: Derek Harris; **53tr** GAP: Clive Nichols/Charlotte Rowe; **53b** GAP: Clive Nichols/Chris Maton; **54b** TGC: Torie Chugg/Anny Konig; **55tc** TGC: Derek Harris; **55br** TGC: Liz Eddison/Sue Beesley; **56tl** GAP: Rob Whitworth/Angus Thompson/Jane Brockbank; **57c** TGC: Steven Wooster/Anthony Paul; **58tl** GAP: Martin Staffler; **58-59br** TGC: Andrew Lawson; **60bl** TGC: Andrew Lawson/Ivan Hicks; **61t** GAP: Clive Nichols/Erik Borja; **61br** GAP: Elke Borkowski; **62c** Jonathan Buckley: Tom Stuart-Smith; **63br** TGC: Torie Chugg/Andrew Harper; **64bl** GAP: Flora Press; **64bc** GAP: Flora Press; **64br** GAP: Flora Press; **65t** GAP: Rob Whitworth/Roger Platts; **65br** GAP: Jerry Harpur/ Thomas Hoblyn; **66b** TGC: Gary Rogers/Rendel & Dr James Barton; **67tr** TGC: Modeste Herwig; **67cr** Alamy: David Boag; **67br** TGC: Derek Harris; **68bl** TGC: Liz Eddison/Christopher Bradley-Hole; **69br** GAP: Michael Howes; **70-71c** GAP: Elke Borkowski; **72bl** GAP: Ron Evans; **74tl** TGC: Nicola Stocken Tomkins; **74b** GAP: Nicola Browne; **75tr** TGC: Derek Harris/Tomoko Osonoe/Kei Iwata; **76bl** TGC: Derek St Romaine; **76bc** TGC: Derek St Romaine; **77ca** GAP: Fiona Lea; **77cb** GAP: John Glover; **78cb** TGC: Derek Harris; **78br** GAP: Leigh Clapp; **79c** GET: Garden Picture Library/Howard Rice; **80tc** GET: Garden Picture Library/Howard Rice; **80bl** TGC: Nicola Stocken Tomkins; **81bl** GAP: Richard Bloom; **81bc** TGC: Derek St Romaine; **81br** GWI: Flowerphotos/ Gillian Plummer; **82c** TGC: Christopher Lloyd; **83crb** GET: Garden Picture Library/Brian Carter; **83br** GAP: Dave Zubraski; **84bl** RD; **84bc** RD; **84br** GAP: BBC Magazines Ltd/Bob Purnell; **85t** GET: Garden Picture Library/Anne Green-Armytage; **86bl** GET: Britain on View/David Sellman; **86-87br** Richard Bloom; **87crb** Richard Bloom; **88tc** GWI: Darren Warner; **88bl** Garden Picture Library: Allan Pollok-Morris; **89bl** RD; **89bc** RD; **89br** RD; **90c** Richard Bloom; **91bc** GAP: Clive Nichols/Sheila Stedman; **93b** GAP: Christa Brand; **94clb** GAP: Pernilla Bergdahl; **94bl** GAP: Jonathan Need; **97bc** GWI: Len Thomassen; **99c** Garden Picture Library: Richard Bloom; **100b** GWI: Andrea Jones; **102cl** GAP: Carole Drake; **104bl** GAP: Clive Nichols/Mark Laurence; **105tl** GAP: Fiona McLeod; **105tr** GAP: Jonathan Buckley/John Massey ; **105bl** GAP: Jonathan Buckley; **105br** GWI: Martin Hughes-Jones; **106c** TGC: Derek Harris; **106bc** GET: Garden Picture Library/Pernilla Bergdahl; **107br** GWI: Liz Every; **108tl** GWI: N+R Colborn; **108tc** TGC: Torie Chugg; **108tr** GWI: Trevor Sims; **109b** Bios: Claude Thouvenin; **110tl** GAP: Howard Rice; **111tc** GET: Garden Picture Library/John Glover; **111br** GAP: Clive Nichols/Amir Schlezinger/My Landscapes; **112t** GAP: John Glover/Piet Oudolf; **113bl** GAP: Maddie Thornhill; **113bc** GAP: Mark Bolton; **113br** TGC: Andrew Lawson; **114tl** GAP: Elke Borkowski; **114bc** GWI: Martin Hughes-Jones; **115tl** GAP: Jonathan Buckley; **115tc** GET: Garden Picture Library/ Buckland/Rice; **115tr** GAP: Elke Borkowski; **116bl** Mark Winwood; **116bc** Mark Winwood; **117tr** TGC: Derek Harris; **117b** TGC: Neil Sutherland; **118c** GET: Garden Picture Library/Ron Evans; **118bc** GAP: Visions; **119tr1** TGC: RHS Hyde Hall; **119tr2** TGC: Andrew Lawson; **120tc** GAP: Anne Green-Armytage; **121bc** Marek Walisiewicz; **121br** GAP: Visions; **122c** GET: Garden Picture Library/Ron Evans; **122bc** GAP:

Heather Edwards; **123bl** Richard Bloom; **123bc** Richard Bloom; **123br** Richard Bloom; **124bl** TGC: Jonathan Buckley; **125tr** GAP: Jerry Harpur; **125b** GET: Garden Picture Library/Howard Rice; **126bl** GET: Garden Picture Library/Maggie Rowe; **127tr** GAP; **127br** GAP: BBC Magazines Ltd; **128bl** GWI: John Swithinbank; **128-129br** TGC: Derek Harris; **129tr** GET: Garden Picture Library/Mark Turner; **130tl** TGC: Torie Chugg; **131tr** GAP: Fiona McLeod; **131bc** GAP: FhF Greenmedia; **132c** TGC: Liz Eddison; **133tr** GAP: Jerry Harpur/Luciano Giubbilei; **133bc** GAP: BBC Magazines Ltd; **134bl** GAP: J S Sira/Sharon Hoconhull; **135tl** GAP: Mark Winwood; **135tc** GAP: Mark Winwood; **135tr** GAP: Mark Winwood; **136tl** TGC: Nicola Stocken Tomkins; **136bc** TGC: Nicola Stocken Tomkins; **137tl** TGC: Torie Chugg; **138-139c** GET: Garden Picture Library/Franois De Heel; **140cl** TGC: RHS Garden Rosemoor; **140-141br** GAP: Christa Brand; **142tl** GAP: Matt Anker; **142bc** GAP: Tim Gainey; **143c** GET: Garden Picture Library/Ron Evans; **143bc** TGC: Andrew Lawson; **144-145b** GAP: Christa Brand; **145tr** GAP: Neil Holmes; **146bl** GAP: Geoff Kidd; **148tl** GAP: J S Sira; **148b** GAP: Michael King; **149tc** Richard Bloom; **149br** GAP: Christa Brand; **150tl** GAP: Mark Winwood; **150bl** TGC: Tom Stuart-Smith; **151bl** RD; **151br** RD; **152c** GAP: Matt Anke/Robert Myers; **153bc** GAP: Richard Bloom; **154b** GAP: Dave Zubraski; **155br1** RD; **155br2** RD; **156tl** GAP: Friedrich Strauss; **158c** GET: Garden Picture Library/J Paul Moore; **159bl** RD; **159bc** RD; **159br** RD; **160cla** GAP: J S Sira; **160b** TGC: Andrew Lawson; **161br** GAP: Mark Winwood; **162bl** Marek Walisiewicz; **162bc** Marek Walisiewicz; **162br** Marek Walisiewicz; **163tr** GWI: Andrea Jones; **164bl** TGC: Louise del Balzo; **165tl** GAP: S & O; **165tr** TGC: Derek St Romaine; **165bl** GAP: Juliette Wade; **165br** TGC: Andrew Lawson; **166c** GAP: Elke Borkowski; **167b1** Marek Walisiewicz; **167b2** Marek Walisiewicz; **167b3** Marek Walisiewicz; **167b4** Marek Walisiewicz; **168tl** RD; **168tr** RD; **169br** GAP: Christa Brand; **170cla** RD; **170cl** RD; **171cr** GAP: FhF Greenmedia; **171crb** GAP: Dave Zubraski; **171br** GWI: MAP/Nathalie Pasquel; **172b** TGC: Louise del Balzo; **173tl** GET: Juliette Wade; **175tl** RD; **175bc** TGC: Torie Chugg; **175br** GAP: Victoria Firmston; **176-177c** TGC: Derek Harris; **178bl** GAP: Maxine Adcock; **178-179br** GAP: Howard Rice; **179cra** GAP: FhF Greenmedia; **181cl** RD; **181c** RD; **181cr** RD; **181bl** RD; **181bc** RD; **181br** RD; **182tl** GAP: Charles Hawes; **183c** TGC: Emma Peios; **183bc** GWI: Gary Smith; **184cla** TGC: Derek St Romaine; **184bc** Garden Picture Library: James Guilliam; **186tl** GWI: Dave Bevan; **187cra** GAP: Paul Debois; **187b** GET: Garden Picture Library/Lynn Keddle; **188bl** GAP: Nicola Browne; **189tr** GAP: FhF Greenmedia; **189cr** GAP: FhF Greenmedia; **189br** GAP: Maxine Adcock; **190bl1** Alan Buckingham; **190bl2** Alan Buckingham; **191c** GET: Garden Picture Library/Mark Bolton; **191bc** Garden Picture Library: Maxine Adcock; **192bl** TGC: Neil Sutherland; **192bc** TGC: Neil Sutherland; **193tr** GAP: Maxine Adcock; **193br** Science Photo Library: Nigel Cattlin; **194c** TGC: Nicola Stocken Tomkins; **195bc** GAP: J S Sira; **196tl** TGC: Derek St Romaine; **197br** Arco Images GmbH; **198l** TGC: Jon Wheatley/ Mary Payne/Terry Porter; **199tl** Alan Buckingham; **199tr** Alan Buckingham; **199cl** Alan Buckingham; **199cr** TGC: Nicola Stocken Tomkins; **200tc** GAP:

Clive Nichols; **200bl** GAP: FhF Greenmedia/Michael Balston/Marie Louise Agius ; **201bl** Alan Buckingham; **202bl** GAP: Leigh Clapp; **203tc** GAP: Jonathan Buckley; **203c** GAP: Elke Borkowski; **204bl** GAP: BIOS; **204-205br** TGC: Andrew Lawson; **206bl** GAP: BBC Magazines Ltd; **207tl1** RD; **207tl2** RD; **207br** GAP: Lynn Keddie; **208bl1** TGC: Derek St Romaine; **208bl2** TGC: Derek St Romaine; **209tc** TGC: Neil Sutherland; **209br** Marek Walisiewicz; **210bl** Garden Picture Library: Linda Burgess; **211tl** Richard Bloom; **211tr** Richard Bloom; **211cl** Richard Bloom; **211cr** Richard Bloom; **212tc** GAP: Jonathan Buckley; **213bl** Alan Buckingham; **213bc** Alan Buckingham; **213br** Alan Buckingham; **214bl** TGC: Torie Chugg; **215tr** GAP: Graham Strong; **216cl** GWI: John Martin; **217bc** GET: Garden Picture Library/ Claire Higgins; **218b** GET: Garden Picture Library/ Mike Powles; **219cra** GAP: Mark Winwood; **220c** GET: Garden Picture Library/Georgia Glynn-Smith; **221tr** GET: Garden Picture Library/François De Heel; **221bc** Garden Picture Library: Andrea Jones; **222bl** GAP: Elke Borkowski; **223tr1** RD; **223tr2** RD; **223br** TGC: Neil Sutherland; **224-225c** Richard Bloom; **226bl** RD; **227tr** Mark Winwood; **227cr** TGC: Locus Flevum; **227br** Burgon & Ball; **228tl** GAP: BBC Magazines Ltd; **228br** Radius Garden; **229tc** Mark Winwood; **230bl** Mark Winwood; **230bc** Mark Winwood; **230br** Mark Winwood; **231c** Garden

Picture Library: Eric van Lokven; **232b1** Marek Walisiewicz; **232b2** Marek Walisiewicz; **232b3** Marek Walisiewicz; **232b4** Marek Walisiewicz; **233ca** RD; **233cb** RD; **234b** TGC: Mr & Mrs St Romaine; **235tl** Mark Winwood; **235tc** Mark Winwood; **236tl** TGC: Michelle Garrett; **237tl** GWI: Leonie Lambert; **237tc** GWI: A Graham; **237tr** GWI: A Graham; **238clb** RD; **238crb** RD; **238bl** RD; **238br** RD; **239t** Garden Picture Library: A S Milton; **240bl** TGC: Marie O'Hara; **241bl** Mark Winwood; **241bc** Mark Winwood; **241br** Mark Winwood; **242cb** Science Photo Library: Dr Jeremy Burgess; **243tl** Mark Winwood; **243cl** Mark Winwood; **243bl** Mark Winwood; **243r** Mark Winwood; **244c** Mark Winwood; **246tl** GWI: Flowerphotos/Ines Roberts; **247tr** GWI: A Graham; **247b** GAP: Fiona Lea; **249tl** Mark Winwood; **249tc** Mark Winwood; **249tr** GWI: Jacqui Dracup; **249br** Mark Winwood; **250bc** RD; **250br** RD; **251tc** GWI: MAP/Nathalie Pasquel; **251tr** GET: Garden Picture Library/Sarl Akene; **251ca** GAP: Jonathan Buckley; **251cra** GAP: Jason Smalley; **252tl** GWI: N+R Colborn; **252tc** GWI: A Graham; **252cla** GAP: BBC Magazines Ltd; **252ca** RD; **253tr** GET: Garden Picture Library/ Jerry Pavia; **254cb** GET: Garden Picture Library/ Joshua McCullough; **255tl** GWI: Trevor Sims; **255tc** GWI: Trevor Sims; **256c** Garden Picture Library: Leroy Alfonse; **257bc** GWI: Jenny Lilly; **258tl** GWI: Rowan Isaac; **258bl** Practical Pictures: Peter Anderson;

259tl TGC: Modeste Herwig; **259cra** GAP: Marcus Harpur; **259clb** GAP: Mark Bolton; **259br** GAP: Martin Hughes-Jones; **260bl** RD; **260bc** RD; **260br** RD; **261tc** TGC: Liz Eddison; **261br** GAP: Elke Borkowski; **262c** Garden Picture Library: Eric van Lokven; **262bl** GAP: Victoria Firmston; **263br** Corbis : AgStock Images; **264tl** Mark Winwood; **264tc** Mark Winwood; **264cla** Mark Winwood; **264ca** Mark Winwood; **265tr** RD; **265bc** GET: Garden Picture Library/Carole Drake; **266tl** RD; **266bl** Garden Picture Library: Eric van Lokven; **267tl** GAP: Jonathan Buckley; **267br** Garden Picture Library: Andrea Jones; **268bl** RD; **268bc** RD; **268br** RD; **269br** RD; **270c** Mark Winwood; **271tr** GET: Garden Picture Library/Claire Higgins; **272bl** GAP: Mark Winwood; **272bc** GAP: Mark Winwood; **272br** GAP: Mark Winwood; **273tr** GAP: Dave Zubraski; **273cr** GAP: Dave Zubraski; **273br** GET: Garden Picture Library/ Neil Holmes; **274cla** GAP: Richard Bloom; **274b** GET: Garden Picture Library/Dan Rosenholm; **275tl** RD; **275ca** RD; **276tl** GWI: John Swithinbank; **277br** Garden Picture Library: Hemant Jariwala.

All other images are © Reader's Digest. Every effort has been made to find and credit the copyright holders of images in this book. We will be pleased to rectify any errors or omissions in future editions. Email us at **gbeditorial@readersdigest.co.uk**

Gorgeous Garden Boosters published in 2012 in the United Kingdom by Vivat Direct Limited (t/a Reader's Digest), 157 Edgware Road, London W2 2HR using the services of Cobalt id

First published in 2012 under the title **1001 Gardening Boosters**

Gorgeous Garden Boosters is owned and under licence from The Reader's Digest Association, Inc. All rights reserved.

Copyright © 2012 The Reader's Digest Association, Inc.
Copyright © 2012 Reader's Digest Association Far East Limited
Philippines Copyright © 2012 Reader's Digest Association Far East Limited
Copyright © 2012 Reader's Digest (Australia) Pty Limited
Copyright © 2012 Reader's Digest India Pvt Limited
Copyright © 2012 Reader's Digest Asia Pvt Limited

Reader's Digest is a trademark owned and under licence from The Reader's Digest Association, Inc. and is registered with the United States Patent and Trademark Office and in other countries throughout the world. All rights reserved.

All rights reserved. No part of this book may be reproduced, stored in a retrieval system, or transmitted in any form or by any means, electronic, electrostatic, magnetic tape, mechanical, photocopying, recording or otherwise, without permission in writing from the publishers.

We are committed both to the quality of our products and the service we provide to our customers. We value your comments, so please do contact us on **0871 351 1000** or via our website at **www.readersdigest.co.uk**

If you have any comments or suggestions about the content of our books, email us at **gbeditorial@readersdigest.co.uk**

Book Code 400-604 UP0000-1
ISBN 978-1-78020-132-0

FOR COBALT ID

Art Director
Paul Reid

Editorial Director
Marek Walisiewicz

Managing Designer
Lloyd Tilbury

Managing Editor
Louise Abbott

Designers
Darren Bland, Rebecca Johns

Editors
Anna Kruger, Richard Gilbert

www.cobaltid.uk

Writers and Consultants
Alan Buckingham
Julia Cady
Ian Hodgson
Daphne Ledward
Richard Rosenfeld
Geoff Stebbings

Photography
Peter Anderson
Richard Bloom
Mark Winwood

Artworks
Scott Jessop

FOR VIVAT DIRECT

Senior Art Editor
Julie Bennett

Editor
Deirdre Headon

Editorial Director
Julian Browne

Art Director
Anne-Marie Bulat

Managing Editor
Nina Hathway

Trade Books Editor
Penny Craig

Picture Resource Manager
Sarah Stewart-Richardson

Pre-press Technical Manager
Dean Russell

Product Production Manager
Claudette Bramble

Production Controller
Jan Bucil

Origination FMG

Printed in China